'THE SPY WHO HAD NO FAITH IN THE WORLD'

*A Semi-documentary account
of the exploits 1900-1904 of
Sidney Reilly AKA "The Ace of Spies"
and Ian Fleming's role model for James Bond.*

*Sidney's Reilly's role is, "One of the unsolved riddles about The Russo-Japanese War"
Professor Ian Nish. L.S.E. author of "The Causes of the Russo-Japanese War"*

Written by Ronald Fairfax

MUTINY PRESS

J. B.

Other Works

'Defiance' - Hull and the English Civil War in the North

'Corky's War' - The Diary of a Stretch Bearer 1915-1919

Copyright © 2011 Ronald Fairfax
First published in 2011 by Mutiny Press
All rights reserved. No part of this work may be reproduced or stored in any information retrieval system (other than short extracts for the purposes of review) without the express permission of the Publishers given in writing.
Ronald Fairfax has asserted his right under the Copyright, Design and Patents Act 1988 to be the identified as the author of this work.
Printed and bound by Fisk Printers, Hull.
Cover design by Andy Gill

ISBN 978-0-9559705-2-8

CONTENTS

Introduction	5	Chapter Twenty One	114
Acknowledgements	10	Chapter Twenty Two	118
References	10	Chapter Twenty Three	123
Chapter One	11	Chapter Twenty Four	133
Chapter Two	17	Chapter Twenty Five	138
Chapter Three	21	Chapter Twenty Six	144
Chapter Four	25	Chapter Twenty Seven	151
Chapter Five	30	Chapter Twenty Eight	158
Chapter Six	37	Chapter Twenty Nine	165
Chapter Seven	41	Chapter Thirty	174
Chapter Eight	44	Chapter Thirty One	184
Chapter Nine	49	Chapter Thirty Two	190
Chapter Ten	51	Chapter Thirty Three	198
Chapter Eleven	56	Chapter Thirty Four	204
Chapter Twelve	67	Chapter Thirty Five	212
Chapter Thirteen	70	Chapter Thirty Six	222
Chapter Fourteen	79	Chapter Thirty Seven	231
Chapter Fifteen	84	Chapter Thirty Eight	244
Chapter Sixteen	88	Chapter Thirty Nine	250
Chapter Seventeen	95	Chapter Forty	256
Chapter Eighteen	100	Chapter Forty One	264
Chapter Nineteen	104	Chapter Forty Two	271
Chapter Twenty	109	Epilogue	283

Ron Fairfax left school in 1956 and went into a number of dead-end jobs. In 1964 he trained as a teacher and left that to go to Hull University as a mature student. On graduating he went as a lecturer to what became Hull College. In 1989 he was made redundant and started a new career writing and presenting a series of TV/Video documentaries on Cities in the North of England, Hull at War, The Sheffield Story, Yorkshire at War to name just a few. Until he retired in 2005 he was a supply teacher in schools in Hull and The East Riding. He has two daughters, Jane a graduate of the universities of Hull and York, and Sally a Leeds University graduate. They are both products of Hull's primary, secondary and tertiary state education system. Ron lives in Hull with his wife Janet who for some years managed student services at Hull College.

To properly understand the story-line of this semi-documentary account please read this introduction.

The Dogger Bank Incident

At around one o' clock in the morning on October 21st. to 22nd 1904 a group of around one hundred Hull and Grimsby Trawlers known as "The Gamecock Fleet" was fishing off The Dogger Bank. The "Dogger Bank" is an area of relatively shallow water renowned as fishing grounds off the East Coast of England in the middle of The North Sea. On that same date, heading South out of The Baltic on a voyage to reach the Far East to engage the Japanese Navy In The Russo-Japanese war, was a fleet of Russian warships, The 2nd Russian Pacific Fleet. It sailed east of The Dogger Bank and the Russian warships steamed into the area where the trawlers of "The Gamecock Fleet" were fishing and mistaking the trawlers for Japanese torpedo boats, they opened fire with machine-guns and artillery. Three fishermen were killed and a number wounded. One trawler sank and others were badly damaged.

The 'incident' was also described in the press as 'The Russian Outrage' for it was blamed on the supposedly, incompetent, trigger happy even drunken Russian sailors manning the Imperial Czarist Naval fleet.

There is a memorial to the men killed and injured. It is In the form of a booted and souwestered fisherman holding up in his hand a codfish, It stands at the junction of Hessle Road and Boulevard in Kingston Upon Hull, East Yorkshire.

In 1917 young sixteen year old Billy McGee of Porter Street Hull lied about his age and volunteered for The Royal Navy. That same year saw him as a rating on The Battleship HMS Glory in Archangel and Murmansk Harbours, Arctic Russia in the middle of The Russian Revolution.

I met Billy in the 1970's and as he knew of my interest in Russia and the period of the Revolution, he passed on to me a note book in which he had kept a diary of his time in The Royal Navy in Arctic Russia. The story of how he got the note-book is worth telling. He took it from the dead body of a young Russian mid-shipman who had been killed when the United States Ship Olympia sailed into Murmansk Harbour and opened fire with light and heavy machine guns on the crew of the Russian Navy ship Askold anchored there. The sailors on board the Askold had mutinied. Scores were killed and wounded. Billy was in a boarding party sent to the Askold from HMS Glory to take charge of it.

However once on board the party did not do their duty. Instead they looted the ship. They were looking for the heavy woollen sweaters that Russian sailors used. They were waterproof and weather proof.(Smokers and ex-smokers will recognize the Askold as that ship behind the head of the bearded sailor on the twenty packet of Players cigarettes. The British Navy commandeered her. She was known however in the service as "The packet of Woodbines" because she had five funnels.) Billy didn't get a sweater but found a leather covered note-book on one of the bodies. The first few pages had entries in Russian as it had been used as a diary by the young dead Russian sailor Billy took it from. Billy kept it and filled it in afterwards with his personal entries from October the 5th. 1917.

I went through Billy's entries with him. They were brief, daily, one or two line references to navy activities such as the arrival of mail or other navy ships coming into port and notes on activities on shore in Murmansk where there had been strikes and demonstrations.

One entry stood out from the ordinary ;"June 4th (1918). Russian aboard, suspected of spying." I asked Billy about this entry and Billy said that the man had been on board for some time when he, Billy was given the responsibility of taking meals down to him as he was imprisoned in Glory's "Brig". Billy said that on one occasion while delivering his dinner the man had asked him where he was from. When Billy said Hull, the prisoner's reply was that he knew Hull and had stayed there.

Some years later I learned that the man Billy as a young naval rating had delivered meals to was not a Russian Spy but a British Agent working for the British Secret Intelligence Service. He had been arrested by mistake. He was put on board HMS Glory and into custody and then he was released when his identity was checked and the British S.I.S. confirmed that he was one of their agents and that he had been working for them for nearly twenty years.

The man arrested and imprisoned in "The Brig" of HMS Glory although not a Russian spy was a Russian however. He was born as Sigmund Georgievich Rosenblum, sometimes known as Solomon Rosenblum but later under an alias and new identity provided for him by the British Special Branch, notorious as Sidney George Reilly he was the the man who later came to be known as "The Ace of Spies". A super spy and role model for Ian Fleming's famous James Bond, 007.That was the man Billy McGee had taken his meals to and that same man had visited Kingston Upon Hull.

The questions were, if Sigmund Georgievich Rosenblum AKA Sidney George Reilly, Master Spy, the original James Bond and agent for The Secret Intelligence Services of Great Britain had been to Hull, when did he visit the city and what were the reasons for him being there?

There are so many stories about Reilly that it is difficult to separate fact from fiction but facts relating to Reilly's connection with Hull did emerge.

In terms of Reilly's associations with Kingston Upon Hull, a number of names came to light. They were, Sir Arthur Kaye Rollit M.P. and Charles Henry Wilson M.P. In association with Sir Henry Hozier of Lloyds of London (Hozier had established a Lloyds of London Wireless Listening Station in Hull) and others they formed 'The Oleum Syndicate'. In 1899 and after, with the sanction of William Melville of Special Branch his employer, they enlisted Sigmund Georgievich Rosenblum AKA Sidney George Reilly in a scheme of enterprises. These included a frame work of industrial espionage that involved Reilly in collecting information on Russian and Persian crude oil resources. For this Reilly was dispatched, by 'The Oleum Syndicate' to Baku in Azerbaijan. At the same time he was to spy on Russian Military Installations that the British Foreign office and the War Department thought were being deployed for an invasion of India through Afghanistan. (Then Rosenblum was working for The British Special Branch, The British Secret Intelligence Services had not yet been established).

Sir Arthur Kaye Rollit M.P. for Islington was more associated with Kingston Upon Hull than Islington. He was from Hull. He was an influential and successful solicitor in Hull and an ex-Lord Mayor of the city with a reputation for philanthropy especially related to education. He was also a well known Japanophile and in 1905 he was awarded, for services to the Japanese State, with The Order of The Rising Sun including a stipend of £2.500, worth 30 to 50 times that in today's values. Charles Henry Wilson M.P. for Hull West was born and educated in the city. He was Sheriff of Hull and one of the members of Hull's Shipping family, Arthur Wilson and Sons. The net of associations Reilly had with Hull widened until it included The Prince of Wales, later King Edward V11.

Sigmund Georgievich Rosenblum alias Sidney George Reilly "Ace of Spies", knew Hull well and he also knew some very important people from, and associated with the city.

Sigmund Georgievich Rosenblum was born in the late 1870's in Odessa the son of a lower middle-class Jewish family. Details of his early life are sketchy but he seems to have been well educated enough to go to University and there to qualify as a chemist. Whether he got into trouble or simply decided to spread his wings abroad, is not clear but shortly after graduation he left Russia and most authorities say he went to France. Certainly at the time Tsarist Russia had a negative attitude to its Jewish community and it is known that Rosenblum resented this. He may well also have been associated with the anarchist movement in Russia that was then causing the authorities much concern. There was also the question of avoiding compulsory military service.

Rosenblum did become associated with the Russian Anarchist movement in Paris but it was as an agent provocateur working for the Deuxieme Bureau,The French Secret Service ,informing on Russian émigrés. In fact it was later alleged that he had murdered the treasurer of the Paris Anarchists and his assistant and then stolen the funds. With these funds he fled to England and there became associated with The Ozone Preparations Company selling patent medicines.

It was through this company, it is supposed that he met perhaps, around 1896/7 the 68 year old Reverend Hugh Thomas and his 24 year old wife Margaret Callaghan Thomas. The Reverend Thomas was a sick man and Rosenblum prescribed a patent medicine for him. It did not cure him and he died shortly afterwards. Then a brief time after that Rosenblum married the widow of the Rev. Thomas who had been left a substantial sum of money and property in her late husband's will. By this time and through the latter years of the 90's Rosenblum was already working for The Special Branch using his linguistic skills (He Spoke English ,French and German as well as Russian) in the exposing and entrapment of Russian and Polish Anarchists in England, but especially In London.

In 1900 Special Branch provided Rosenblum with a new identity. He was from then on known as Sidney George Reilly. With his new pass port and papers Reilly set off from England accompanied by his wife. His mission was to spy on the Russian Oil industry and Russian Military Installations. After completing that task he left for Port Arthur in the Far East. He stayed there posing as a businessman until 1904. There is strong evidence that Reilly continued his espionage work there and that it was his clandestine interference that led to the Japanese being able to carry out a surprise attack on the Russians at Port Arthur using torpedo boats. That successful attack precipitated the Russo- Japanese war in February 1904. At that time Reilly could have been described as a 'double agent' working for both the British and the Japanese.

By December 1903 William Melville, Reilly's original employer, had resigned from The Special Branch and he had taken up a confidential appointment to head a secret organization that was a loose alliance of British Military and Royal Naval Intelligence. When Reilly returned from the Far East to Europe and France in the July of 1904 he was enlisted into that organization by William Melville. Melville and Reilly then spent time in the south of France persuading the Australian plutocrat Knox D'Arcy to sell his Persian Oil concession to British and Admiralty interests.

In 1909 the organization that Melville had founded was to develop into The British Secret Intelligence Services, sometimes described by the press as MI5 and MI6. Reilly stayed with S.I.S. until at least 1925.

When Reilly met Melville again in London in what was left of the summer of 1904, Melville was then working under the alias of William Morgan an ordinary business man with an office in Victoria Street, He described himself as a 'General Agent'. This alias covered his new Secret Intelligence responsibilities.

Then in September 1904 , a student under the name of Stanilaus George Reilly was enrolled to study electrical engineering at The Kensington School of Mines. It wasn't Sidney George Reilly but someone, and here is the extraordinary 'coincidence', with almost the same name as him.

Let us just say that if anyone, for one nefarious purpose or another wanted to tour the North East of England, incognito, carrying a set of fake documents that were qualifications and identification relating to coal mining and electrical engineering, he could not have a better cover story.

Through October and November of 1904 Sidney George Reilly is not heard of until he surfaces again at Christmas . What was he doing during those two months; especially during October? That was the month of "The Dogger Bank Incident" and the Hull and Grimsby Fishing Fleet "The Gamecock" being fired upon by Russian warships in mistake for Japanese torpedo boats as the Russian fleet sailed off to engage the Japanese in the Russo-Japanese War.

Was the "Mystery Man" that the fishing community talked about at the time as going round Hull asking questions about the "Gamecock " fleet and wanting details about hiring a fishing boat no less a person than Sidney George Reilly? Was he the same mysterious personality who wanted steel tubes welding to the deck of a trawler? The question as to the identity of this man was raised by witnesses after a Declaration in St Petersburg and following that at The International Inquiry into "The Dogger Bank Incident" in Paris 1905.

Was " The Dogger Bank Incident" then (or "The Russian Outrage", call it what you will) not an accident caused by drunken, inexperienced, incompetent Russian sailors hysterical with fear about Japanese torpedo boats . But more the direct result of the conspiratorial activities of the man who became the template for the most famous fictional spy of all time , James Bond… Sidney George Reilly…"The Ace of Spies"……. and his first major operation in Britain is from Hull?

But that is the end of the story. Before Reilly came to Hull he was busy establishing his career with the Special Branch and it was a career touching activities that still strike a modern chord. He was involved in terrorism in Britain, Spain, France and Russia. He engaged in espionage activities during the Boer War. He conspired with others to establish British interests in the oil producing regions of Russia, Persia and Mesopotamia (Modern Iraq) . He worked for the SB on Afghanistan, in Egypt and The Far East (Japan and Russia) . Added to all this he was an assassin, a multiple bigamist and an inveterate womanizer and gambler. And that was what he did during the 1890's to 1904. His career went on for many years after.

Acknowledgements

There are people that I need to say thank you to.

Robert Addy for his advice on fishing and fishing boats. Charles Lewis for his invaluable comments on the Royal Navy, Jorgen Kraag for his knowledge of the Danische Compagnie Est-Asiatique, Dr Jan Hammerson for her knowledge of Japan 's History. Billy Mcgee for his diary, Rollit's Solicitors Hull, the Staff of the History Centre Hull. Dr Robb Robinson for information on "The Gamecock Fleet".Dr. Alec Gill for similar information. The Royal Hotel Hull. The Beverley Arms Hotel .The Central Library Hull. "Rayners" Hessle Road. The City Council of Hull and its Archives and Hull Maritime Museum. I want to mention especially , Ian Herbert, Marion Irvine, Judith Allsop and Charles lewis for giving their valuable time to read the manuscript. I don't think I took all the advice they offered and I hope that they will pardon me. What it means is that any errors or lapses in style and presentation are my own. I would like to thank Andy Gill at Fisk Printers for all his help and encouragement.

References

"The North Sea Incident" Arthur Credland.

"Sidney Reilly" The True Story. Michael Kettle.

"The Day the Russian Fleet fired on The Hull Trawler men" Brian Lewis,

"Trust No One" The Secret World of Sidney Reilly. Richard B. Spence,

"The Ace of Spies" The True Story of Sidney Reilly. Andrew Cook,

"Russia Against Japan 1904/5" John N. Westwood,

"The Fleet That Had to Die" Richard Hough,

"The Causes of The Russo-Japanese War." Professor Ian Nish. L.S.E.

"The Dogger Bank Incident and the Development of International Arbitration."

Thesis offered by Karen Katzman Jackson at Texas Technical University.USA

The Spy who had no Faith in The World By Ronald T.C. Fairfax

A Semi-documentary account of the exploits 1900-1904 of Sidney Reilly AKA "The Ace of Spies" and Ian Fleming's role model for James Bond.

Chapter One

They had been in such a hurry to get into bed that he had forgotten to close the shutters and the curtains, so the pale yellow light of an early summer dawn over London had wakened him earlier than he had wanted. The day before he had promised himself that he would 'lie abed' until time to dress for his lunchtime appointment at 'the office' but then he thought he would be at home. He wasn't at home. He had stayed the night in"his rooms". He wasn't alone and he wasn't with his wife. He didn't even know the first name of the woman he had woken up next to.

His yawn as he stretched screwed up his face, and again he forgot to put his hand over his mouth. He would one day acquire the English manners that now seemed so important in the society he was these days moving in."The bloody Victorian bloody English bloody middle-classes, they had such impeccable manners. Of course they always said 'please' and 'thank you' and 'excuse me' especially when they were lording it over you. And what good manners they had when purloining, in the name of the bloody British Empire, somebody else's country or shooting down Fuzzie Wuzzies armed only with spears at Omdurman. Well, the Bloody Boers weren't bowing and scraping that's for sure."

He didn't hold his knife like a pen anymore and he made a little pile of salt at the side of his plate instead of sprinkling it all over his food…what else was there …? Should he lose his foreign accent? No, they seemed to like that, especially the women. It gave him a mysterious air, made him seem of romantic character and just a little dangerous. That was of course just the impression he wished to cultivate. It was worth money that and if nothing else this was an age of money.

These days you were no one and nowhere without money. It bought you everything and most importantly, in the England he found himself in, it bought you 'class'; all that about 'breeding' was just 'tosh'. Money was what mattered. Money bought you not just material things of the finest quality, which he yearned for and cherished but position and social standing. With money you were a 'toff'. Without it you were a tramp. Even the English aristocracy could not appear superior if they were skint, and many of them were. He had already met a few.

He had done things to get the money he had; bad things. He didn't mind thinking about what he had done. He would do all he had done again, for money. There were few realities in this life and as far as he was concerned money was one of them. The pleasure of women was another.

He brought himself up with a start and as he passed out of the reverie his mind had slipped into he slid out of bed, being considerately careful enough not to wake the young woman he had lately slept alongside of and made love with. She still lay asleep. He vaguely remembered having brought her to 'his rooms' in the only Hansom cab in sight. They had drunk rather a lot as guests at the Japanese Embassy. Then they drank more before they tumbled into bed.

He curled his toes and his feet searched for his monogrammed slippers. They were navy blue and embroidered in gold thread with the capital letters S.R. and made for him by his shoemaker Peal & Co. His scratching toes found them and he walked naked, but for his slippers over the yet uncarpeted floorboards of the bedroom of"His rooms off Baker street." A bit of a squeeze," He said to the chaps at the Imperial Club, Cursitor Street near his home address,"But they'll do for what I want them for and who knows I might meet Sherlock Holmes and Dr. Watson."

The night jar he wanted to relieve himself in was behind the 'scrap-book' decorated screen in the cupboard below the marble -topped wash-stand he had bought at auction along with all the other furniture, bed. tall-boy, desk, cheval mirror, chaise longue, dining chairs and drop-leaf table etc. All that now equipped the once empty, dusty space. Only the mattress was new, as were the covers, sheets and pillows You didn't buy those second-hand…bed bugs, fleas..Ugh.

He shuffled the few steps to the wash-stand and in the basic privacy of the screen he found out a 'pot' and held the decorated blue china pot below his groin, he took himself in his left-hand and peed onto the glaring blue 'eye' that was fused into the glaze at the bottom. The odour of his urine and that already deposited in the pot blended with the smell of lamp oil from wicks that had been left to burn out and the human smell of bedroom.

When he had finished and returned the pot to its cupboard, he washed his hands with Wrights Coal Tar Soap and then splashed himself with cologne from a bottle of Agua de Pravia he kept on the white marble top next to a large jug and bowl whose colour and design matched the chamber pot.

He poured a little water from the jug into the bowl and with the same sort of self-conscious appreciation of quality he took the lid off a tin of Eucril dentifrice and dipping his toothbrush into the pink powder it contained, he brushed his teeth and freshened his breath. He rinsed his mouth and spat into the pot in the cupboard. As he got out of bed he had already observed that his breath 'smelt like a peasant's crotch' as his paternal grand -father used to say in those far off days in Odessa. He had not been back there for so many years. He knew he wasn't welcome anymore.

He brought himself out of his nostalgia by thinking to wash his own member and crotch with a cloth that he soaped with the same soap then dipped into the water."God, I don't want Syphilis." It was a plague in France, killing young men by the score. He washed himself again, holding his member with his finger and thumb and perusing it for blemishes.

How careless he was becoming. He thought of the woman still sleeping in bed behind him. Who was she? How clean was she? He had thought she was a very well-dressed and quite a prepossessing young woman when he had met her at The Embassy of The Empire of Nippon. The Japanese were known to procure women from dubious sources for their parties."One never knows quite where they have been old boy." A Foreign Office aide from the Commercial Section had confided to him over drinks before dinner when the ambassador's secretary had introduced them. Anyway the fellow from the F.O. had seemed to be more interested in the diminutive Korean waiters than in the women. Sidney was at the Embassy as,"A representative of the London and British/ Far East Association of Chambers of Commerce".Sidney knew that it was his boss at Special Branch who had arranged the invitation through a contact and his brief was as always in his function as informer,"Keep your ear close to the ground and your eyes open and see what you can pick up. There is something brewing between the Japanese and the Russians. If there is we want to know about it first."

"Please for you to meet these English ladies," the lugubrious and obsequious bespectacled Japanese attache in his white tie and black tails said, with a sing-song accent bowing low. It was noticeable that the kimono draped white-faced and red – lipped 'geishas' did not make an appearance after the formalities of introduction." Too good for us barbarians" was the continuing skepticism of the F.O. type.

In the gathering of invited western guests Sidney's eye had lighted straightway upon a woman he thought was very attractive. She was wearing
a green silk dress that showed off her full breasts. It had only the suggestion of a bustle. She had chestnut hair piled up and curled on her head. Her eyes were green and she had smiled at him as soon as he approached. That for him was the first sign of attraction. He had paid her attention all the evening to the exclusion of everyone else. A technique that came as naturally to him as the charisma of his personality charmed the women he met.

In the end all that, combined with the heady effects of the wine she drank perhaps persuaded her to consent to coming back to"his rooms" with him. She was at least five years older than him maybe more. But then he loved older women. They had taught him all he knew. If she was a whore, she was 'high born'. And anyway he did not have any prejudices. His view was that in the end," we are all whores and it was only a question of negotiating the price." He wasn't a liberal. He was what he had decided to be a long time ago, a cynic. A bit young to be one but a cynic nonetheless and an utterly ruthless one at that.

He turned from his basic toilette and sloped back to bed. As he did so he caught a glimpse of himself in the long cheval mirror he had initially placed tactically at the bed-end the better to see the reflected nakedness of himself and his partner as they made love.He shifted it and he saw his own image and narcissus that he was, admired his just above average height at five nine or ten, slim but muscular figure. His thick black hair was tousled with sleep and his Jewish dark featured, but quite handsome face
already needed a shave."Not a bad specimen of manhood for the new century and at twenty six years old the world and women are my oyster." As he said this to himself he turned from full-frontal to a side view of his flat belly and pushed his hands down his flanks to the tops of his legs. He loved women and he loved himself.

Threading his way through the jumble of her clothes, he saw her green silk dress, that he noticed she had been so careful of when taking it off. He looked at her corset. When he had helped her off with it he had quoted lines from a poet whose name he had forgotten,"Off with your wiry corset, and show, The hairy diadems which on you grow."

Then he saw his trousers draped over the same chair and he had taken them off with the similar care. The trousers and corset were folded together and so enveloping each other had the air of the symbolic; the male and female principal almost. Certainly as he saw it the practical, expedient even executive nature of the trousers was compared with the frivolous eroticism of the corset. Not an image he thought, that would appeal to some modern women in this age of 'Votes for Women'. The cords of the corset were serpentine, curling round the trousers. The pale pink, whale-bone ribbed undergarment seemed almost arachnid with its multi-stringed web over the chair. Was it the black-widow spider that they said ate the male after mating?" The female is more deadly than the male."

He continued his steps back to bed through the line of his cream silk underwear and polished shoes and her lacy drawers and petticoats that made a 'paper-chase' path leading to the bed. They had been urgently stripped off and thrown down with an energy fuelled by drink and passion. Two empty champagne bottles stood on the small folding gate-legged table with one glass next to a half-full bottle of Russian vodka. The red Double Headed Imperial Eagle on its label contrasting with what colourless spirit was left in the bottle. A pale blue tin of Beluga caviar had a spoon still in it and its lid was opened and jagged where he had stabbed at it with a letter-knife in lieu of an opener. It rested on a plate of half-eaten blinis"That's not French Champagne",she had half complained.

"No", he had said,"It's Russian, it's as good if not better, Imperial Russian Champagne, it says so in Russian on the etiquette, Champagne Prince Leo Galitzine, Novyi Svet 1894," and he added,"A good year to drink it, its five years old."

She had looked over the edge of her champagne cup first to the Cyrillic letters on the label then to him and asked quizzically and tipsily with her very pretty head leaning to one side She had taken her long thick chestnut hair down so now its tresses flowed in corrugated curling curves over her bare shoulders."Can you read Russian?"

"Read Russian!! Me read Russian!" He had blurted this out impulsively and more forcefully than he intended. Then standing, he lifted his glass and in the light of the lamp he toasted the ceiling"Nastdarovia," He downed his drink in a gulp and threw the glass so that it shattered in the small unlit fireplace."I am Russian." He had then recited lines from Pushkin in the original.

"I say to myself the years are fleeting,

And however many there seem to be,

We must all go under the eternal vault,

And Someone's hour is at hand."

He sat down on his chair with a bump, immediately regretting his drunken boastfulness. Why had he gone to so much trouble over these last few years to conceal his original identity just to blurt it out to a near stranger over a drunken assignation? There was still so much of the immature boy in him. He would have to watch that. He insisted to himself," I am Sidney Reilly, I am no longer Sigmund Georgievich Rosenblum, Sigmund Georgievich Rosenblum is already dead and buried."

But something positive and interesting did come out of his reference to his Russian origins. As he was reflecting on what he saw as an indiscretion the woman said that she had another"friend" who was in The Russian Navy. He was from Vladivostok originally and he worked as an attaché at the Russian Embassy. She said that he had taught her how to say"please","thank you" and"excuse me" in Russian.

Sidney pricked up his ears and began to gently interrogate her."Where was he from? What did he do?" Sidney masked his real intentions by saying that he was interested in the commercial opportunities that he might exploit in Russia's Far-East. She, seemingly unsuspecting, seeing his questions as quite practical asked naively,"Is Port Arthur in the Far East?"

"Yes", Sidney said," It's a harbour and the Russian Navy is there."

"That's where he was serving after a transfer from Vladivostok and before he was sent to London. His wife and family are still there. He says that he would like them to join him in this posting. He's worried about them."

"Why would he be worried about them?" Sidney had queried.

"Oh just something about the Japanese Navy and suspicions about an invasion. Oh I don't know. I suppose I got a bit tired of him talking about his wife and family." She said.

But it had been enough for Sidney. He now had something to take tomorrow to his lunchtime meeting at the 'office'.

His interest in what she had said had not however escaped her notice.

The recollection of the conversation was dismissed from his mind as he reached the bed and saw that she was on her side away from him. She had in her sleep pushed the sheets off of her. Now in the light from the window of a brightening sky he saw the curve of her back, her waist and the delightful roundness of her hips and her buttocks. He wanted her again and what did the Spanish say?"Al amannecer que cuando su major."At dawn that's when its best"

He kicked off his slippers and as he lay beside her he embraced her and she came drowsily to wakefulness muttering,"What time is it. I must go soon.""Her maquillage was still on her face. Under her awakening green eyes, heavy lashed, were black smudges of kohl and the rouge on her lips had gone beyond her mouth with the force of their kisses so that it looked almost like the painted smile of a clown. She still had a lace camisole on, its strings twined round her freckled breasts and black stockings to the white skin of her mid-thighs tied with shiny scarlet satin ribbons. The sight of her brought to mind a phrase he had come across in his reading of English texts,"Where stockings end and love begins."

She sleepily opened herself to him and he glimpsed the thick chestnut coloured bushiness of the triangle of hair covering her sex as he went down to kiss her there.

When he got home he would tell his young wife of only one year that the meeting at the Japanese Embassy had gone on so long that he had decided to sleep at his club. She didn't know about 'his rooms' nor did she know about leaving her stockings on or the other erotic and carnal mysteries this woman and he had explored in the night they had just passed together.

Sidney Riley as he called himself now, Sigmund Rosenblum as he had once been known as before he faked his death in Odessa harbor. Then he had stowed away on a British ship bound for France. Sidney Reilly believed in being alive to every waking moment of his life and he was true to this principle as he turned his lover over. He parted the luxuriant waves of her chestnut hair and from behind her beautiful head whispered in French in her pink delicately shaped ear "Les plaisirs et les fruits Interdit" "Forbidden Pleasures and Forbidden Fruits".

What a flair for languages, and for women, he thought he had.

Chapter Two

The sun of that same dawn on that same day shone in through the windows of the offices of Superintendant William Melville Head of Scotland Yard's Special Branch and found that William Melville was already at a desk covered with official papers and detailed maps describing the borders of Imperial Czarist Russia. William Melville was conscientious and an early riser. He was usually at his desk by six in the morning and he did not leave it until late in the evening.

He lifted one map up from the layers covering the desk top. It had marks and crosses, dotted lines and shadings and English names and descriptions written and drawn over the Russian lettering of the original. In the margin in red ink there was the addition, 'Strictly Confidential to Secret, Foreign Office copy.' Across the top as a title it said in black, underlined,"The Caucasus Prospected 1888---Deposits of Mineral Oil."

Melville gathered all the other maps together leaving the Caucasus map flat on the desk top. He drew open a wide map drawer underneath the desk above his knees. He stowed the maps there and taking a bunch of keys out of his pocket, on the end of a long chain chose one key and locked the drawer. He then shuffled the papers together and after securing them on the spring of a box file he wrote"Last consulted May 1st 1899" on a document attached to the lid of the file. He then got up from the desk and put the file onto one of the shelves of an already opened safe set against the wall. Choosing another but larger brass key from the bunch he closed the door of the safe and locked it.

Outside the frosted half-glass of his office door he heard the outer door being opened. He had locked it behind him when he had come in. His professional reflexes were such that although he intuitively knew that it would be his secretary arriving to take up her work, still he clasped the butt of the loaded service Issue Webley 45 revolver he kept held on a simple clip screwed to the side of his desk. If there had ever been a suggestion in his own mind that he was being melodramatic he did not tolerate it for long.

He called out,"Miss Lukerson is that you?"Yes, Mr. Melville." was the reply.

Miss Lukerson was a spinster lady in her late forties. She always came to her work in the same outfit, a hobble skirt and white broderie anglaise shirt tucked into its waist band under a short bolero jacket. Her simple hat over her pile of long brown hair now with one or two threads of grey, was secured with a long pin and she wore high boots that she had to get on with a shoe-horn and a button hook. She was just a little myopic but corrected this with low strength spectacles. She lived alone with her cat in a rented room in Camberwell. She had been pretty once and betrothed to a sergeant in the Metropolitan Police but he had been killed in an anarchist bomb outrage. She never found anyone else to be betrothed to. She still had some of her looks but she now dedicated herself to her work as one of the few female stenographers in Scotland Yard. And she typed letters and documents for Superintendant Melville and she made the tea and she kept a record of visitors to Superintendant Melville's office.

She knew there was more to it than that but she was the soul of discretion and because of this was relied on completely by Superintendant Melville As far as she was concerned the men who came and went from the office were ordinary policemen whose job it was to further the interests of The Metropolitan Police Force and William Melville in particular.

She knew her place as a woman within the scheme of things. She would have no truck with those suffragettes. They were,these days causing as much trouble as the Irish Fenians and the Russian and Polish anarchists. And as for those devils, they should stay in their own countries if they wanted to make trouble.

Before taking this morning's tea into the 'super's' office she went into her bag again and brought out two buttered scones which she put into the saucer.

"I have taken the liberty of bringing you these for I know you will not yet have had any breakfast. They are 'home-made." She said as she went through into Superintendant Melville's office, placing the cup and saucer with its contents on Melville's desk.

"Miss Lukerson, you are a treasure. I do not know what I would do without you." Said Melville. When you have had your tea would you bring me the Reilly file? Miss Lukerson knew that what he meant was"bring it right away". She had her own bunch of keys and her own locked cupboard and she went back into her office and unlocked the tall cupboard that contained the files of all the people who came and went to and from the office of William Melville. The file of Reilly Sidney was on the top shelf. It was thicker than most and on the label on the front of the box that held all the papers on him was written his name and in brackets 'Shlomo Rosenblum first employed 1896'. She took it into Mr. Melville and returned to her desk and typewriter closing the door quietly behind her as she left.

Melville opened the box and looked at the table of contents on the first page of Reilly's file. It was a list that began with a date of birth, 1873. As he did this William Melville thought about his own file and he wondered if anyone was consulting that as he was consulting this. His file was in The Office of the Commissioner of Police and his file would have had his name and title on it 'William Melville', Superintendant, Head of Scotland Yard's Special Branch. He sat back and drank his tea and ate one of Miss Lukerson's home-made scones and when he had finished he brushed the crumbs off his mouth and from his waistcoat His curriculum vitae was just as interesting as Reilly's but more formally detailed.

William Melville was an imposing six-feet, well-built Irishman, born in County Kerry who like so many of his country men and women left their Irish home to seek their fortunes in London's streets that were said to be paved with gold. He was, although prematurely balding a handsome man with a fashionably thick moustache over a strong mouth and he had a firm chin He had green eyes whose unblinking stare made the subjects of his gaze think he was looking into the depths of their souls. Actually he was just a little short sighted and cultivated his 'look' for effect. He almost invariably wore a high starched collar and rejecting the fashionable necktie in favour of a cravat, held it place with an expensive gold jeweled pin. Winter or Summer he wore the same sort of heavy velvet corduroy suit and waistcoat with a gold chain linked to a large gold watch in a waist coat pocket. He had a trick when taking it out of giving a small swing to land it back in the pocket. Before joining the Metropolitan Police in the 1870's he had, like his father before him been a baker. After working in the Criminal Investigation Department he was selected because of his origins and because he was not an Irish Nationalist, to be one of the founding members of the Special Irish Branch. His job was to organize the infiltration by informers and spies into the secret ranks of the Fenians and Anarchists.

Britain did not control the entry of any foreigners through its borders so it attracted the malcontents and political activists not just of Europe but the world. It was a hot-bed of clandestine political and National Liberation activities. As these activities, particularly those of the Anarchists affected neighbouring and continental countries The Special Irish Branch found itself, through the pressure of Foreign Office Diplomats, not to say Government Ministers, with responsibilities in France and Czarist Russia. It was to placate the F.O. and its master that Melville had once found himself posted to Le Havre in France. From there he was instructed to keep an eye on whoever came from England to France and more significantly those who went from France to England. He worked hard and was successful in recording information on groups who set up their organizations in France and individuals whose intention it was to form 'cells' generally in England or, more likely London.

In December 1888 returning to London Melville was assigned to duties he had no real interest in but he did not at the time realize where they would lead to. His duties were to protect visiting dignitaries and later the Royal Family. One of his first jobs was to organize the protection of the Shah of Persia during a state visit. More important than it seemed on the surface for The British Empire had its eyes on the reserves there of the new 'super' fuel, Oil. Edward The Prince of Wale put his oar into that one when he snubbed the Shah as he would have done some upstart interloper. William Melville had to go to a lot of trouble later placating the insulted Shah.

One of his great coups was the foiling of the plot by Irish Nationalists to assassinate Queen Victoria on the occasion of her Jubilee in 1887. From then on and into the following years he played an important part in an exercise to purge London of anarchist influence by the systematic raiding of anarchist clubs and the smashing of their networks of propaganda printing and distribution.

He was also credited with the exposure of the complex anarchist bombing campaign, known as 'The Walsall Plot', although there were some who stated, unkindly that there was evidence that he had planted agents provocateurs and 'set the whole operation up just to knock it down'. Whatever the judgment Superintendent William Melville came out of the affair with, in 1893, the appointment he held now in Special Branch. With this job in his pocket he organized the S.B. over the next few years into a force that put the boot on the other foot and terrorized the Anarchist Movement in London. He saw to it that there was plenty of press interest in these 'anti-subversion 'activities. Because of this attitude he did not object to the fact of his going to arrest the bomber Theodule Meunier at Victoria Station, being described in the press as having been 'stage-managed'. The event, that he personally supervised got a great deal of attention both from the broadsheets and the new tabloids.

It was through the investigations of Russian émigré groups in 1896 and a need arising for Russian speakers as agents that Superintendent Melville first recruited in 1896 the young man whose file he was about to open, Shlomo Rosenblum.

Chapter Three

Sidney Reilly, also known as, Shlomo Rosenblum and Sigmund Georgeivich Rosenblum now fully awake turned in his bed from his new lover and consulted the time by the full hunter Omega gold watch that was hung by its gold chain around the brass knob of the bed. It was 8.30 in the morning. He shook the still sleeping woman gently by her naked shoulder and as she opened her eyes he said. 'We must get up and get dressed, I have to leave very soon and I think, so do you.'

As she got out of bed, although completely distracted by the loveliness of her almost complete nakedness with her red hair to her shoulders, he directed her to the washstand behind the screen and told her that there was water, albeit cold, in the jug and soap and clean towels on the stand. She only needed to wrinkle her nose and incline her head to one side for him to understand the unspoken enquiry. 'In the cupboard below', he said.

He did what he had become unaccustomed to doing, dressing without washing or shaving and putting on underwear and a shirt that he had worn the day before. He would change when he got home. He didn't wait for his guest to finish but went behind the screen and made to clean his teeth again standing next to her as she sponged and toweled herself. But first he took the towel from her and dried her breasts and kissed the mouth she had washed the lipstick from. Her face, clean and freckled as it was now, was like a girls. As he stood there desiring her again. She asked for the small case that she had brought with her. "It's in the bag over there." He hadn't noticed that she had placed her bag on the top of the desk as she came in the night before. He took the small leather case she had asked for from the bag and passed it to her and opening it she took out its contents, a long tube with a rubber bulb attached to the end. It was a douche.

As he brushed his teeth to a foam, quite un self consciously, ignoring his presence, she filled the bulb with mildly soapy water from the bowl and inserted the tube into herself and squeezed the bulb. She winced a little at the cold water and puckered her mouth into half cringe and half smile. The water came out of her and ran down her legs onto the towel she was standing on. This lady had been in this situation before, he thought.

He dried his mouth and went to his waistcoat which he picked up from the floor and undid the button on an inside pocket. In it were ten gold sovereigns. He took three and put them in a little pile on the marble top of the washstand. Having put on her drawers, corset and skirts before stepping into her dress she asked him to tie her corset strings. She saw what he had done and she smiled, turned her head to him over her left shoulder and as she breathed in while he pulled in her waist she held on to the brass bed knob and she said, "You are generous". He then looked at her over the back of her lovely neck from behind with her auburn hair still down and her breasts full in the fastened camisole and said. "You are beautiful."

He then apologized for there being no breakfast but the stale blinis and caviar. 'There is not even a glass of flat champagne.' He said turning one of the two bottles upside down. 'There is the vodka' he said with a laugh. She made a choking sound and put out her tongue.'There's a caretaker's wife downstairs. I could send out for something....' He looked at his watch and she took the hint and very quickly put up her hair saying as she did. 'No I'm late too. I'll get coffee later.'

Within the next few minutes he had put on his coat, locked the door of his 'rooms' and they went together down stairs. He motioned her to go on as he knocked on a door at the bottom of the stairs. A middle-aged woman answered it. She was wiping her hands on her pin a -fore.

'G'mornin' sir, was there something?' She had lost a number of her teeth. She recognized Sidney as a 'Gentleman Tenant'. Sidney passed a sixpenny piece to her and said. 'Give my rooms a bit of a dust round would you. The usual things, a couple of empty bottles etc.' She knew what the etc. was.' Yes sir thank you sir, always ready to oblige sir.' As Sidney followed his friend into the sunshine of busy Baker Street, the caretaker's wife looked at the sixpence in the palm of her hand and said to herself, 'If 'e don't start upping 'is tip he can start emptyin' 'is own bleedin' piss-pot.'.

He was still in evening dress and she was obviously not dressed for out of doors. No one noticed as he hailed a cab. One soon trotted up to them as they stood on the pavement. As she stepped up into it, he took his summer overcoat that he had put over her shoulders. He asked her if she had a cigarette. She took a packet from her bag and handed them to him. He accepted them and saw that they had a red 'collar' at the end." Think of me when you smoke them, the red end is to hide the marks of lipstick." She laughed.

He kissed her hand and gave her his business card 'Ozone Preparations Company,Consultant Chemists, Imperial Chambers, 3 Cursitor Street, Holborn.' It was the legitimate business he had established shortly after arriving in England. He said sotto voce out of the hearing of the cabbie, 'Should you want to contact me drop me a card here. Please don't make a visit. You do appreciate of course, that I am married.'

'Don't worry Sidney, I will be discrete. My name by the way' she said with a wry smile, ' Is Caroline'. With that she climbed into the cab, pulled the small folding safety doors shut and she sat down and smiled at him.'

He put his hand in his trouser pocket and pulling out half a crown he passed it up to the cabbie and said,

'Take this lady where she wants to go.'

'Right you are governor' said the cabbie touching the brim of his hat and slapping the reins over his patient horse he pulled the cab out into the morning traffic. Sidney watched it become anonymous amongst the many other cabs and felt a memory in his lower abdomen of the night they had spent together. He did not expect that he would ever see her again.

For her part after giving the cabbie her address Caroline settled back on the leather upholstered seat and turned in her fingers the white business card Reilly had given her….'Hm', she reflected, 'a respectable business man is he?.'

Unlike most consultant chemists, (Sidney Reilly was a university qualified chemist)'Ozone Preparations' peddled patent medicines, panaceas for the gullible and the desperate, and desperately ill.

One sufferer had been The Reverend Hugh Thomas. The power of prayer and modern medicine having failed him he turned to Ozone Preparations for a treatment for his kidney disease. The cure was worse than the disease and the Reverend Hugh Thomas died. That was in March 1898. Six weeks later Margaret his 25 year old widow, as the only beneficiary in his will, inherited £9.000. About five months later in August 1898 the grieving Margaret Callaghan Thomas walked up the aisle with the 'Chemist' who had prescribed The Rev Thomas his medicament, Sidney George Reilly of 'Ozone Preparations'.

No eyebrows were raised in the corridors of New Scotland Yard and no questions were asked. There were not even any enquiries about the nurse that had attended Hugh Thomas on his death-bed. The fact that she had been involved in an arsenic poisoning case during a previous employment in Japan escaped notice as did the credentials of the 'Mysterious Dr T. W. Andrews ' whom she assisted with the case and it was he who signed the Death Certificate certifying 'Natural Causes'. Dr.T.W. Andrews was described as a young man, slim, of just above average height with dark, one might say Mediterranean features and colouring. There was no inquest ordered.

The two witnesses to Margaret and Sidney's wedding vows 'in the presence of God and this congregation' were later found to be relatives of a professional associate of William Melville, chief of Scotland Yard's Special Branch.

As Caroline's cab departed Sidney put on his light summer overcoat over his evening dress, tailored like all his clothes by Henry Poole of Savile Row and stood at the curb looking for a cab. One soon came and he stepped up into it saying curtly to the cabbie as he did so '6 Upper Westbourne Terrace Hyde Park.'

'Isn't that address nearer to Paddington Sir?.' Questioned the cabbie, who's only intention was to see that his client got home to the right place. It did however irritate Sidney. Hyde Park sounded more prestigious, a point that was important to him. 'Just get me there,' he had grunted. The cabby took no exception. He was used to 'toffs' and their superior ways. He just slapped the reins over the back of his black horse and they were off. He did mutter under his breath however," Sometimes I gets more manners from me bleedin' 'orse."

Sidney and his new wife had moved to Westbourne Terrace only a short time before, 'A row of recently built substantial terraced villas, near to town with spacious accommodation and separate rooms for live-in staff'. Sidney had returned from a trip to Spain to find that his wife had organized the move from her late husband's country home in Kingsbury to their new home in Paddington. In fact on instruction from Melville,

Reilly had departed for Spain just after their wedding on 'business'. The business being more in the interests of The State than Ozone Preparations.

Since his recruitment by 'The Special Branch' in 1896 as a paid informer and undercover agent his special talents being fluency in English, Russian, German and French, Sidney had become Melville's right hand man when it came to investigating Russian émigré Anarchists wherever they were in Europe. Melville had specific instructions generating from the government to provide a stronger link of police co-operation between Britain and Spain after that country had become a major terrorist centre and because of this had witnessed a series of spectacular outrages including bombs in Barcelona that killed 12 people and the assassination just a year before of Spain's Prime Minister Canovas del Castillo by the notorious anarchist Angiolillo.

It had been Sidney's brief to report on the extent to which there were connections between Russian and Spanish Anarchist organizations. The report he submitted stated that Spanish Anarchism was largely home-grown and it detailed that the centres of most activity were in the Basque and Catalan regions with anarchist bombers learning their skills with dynamite through their work in the coal mines of the Asturias in northern Spain. His report then observed that there were more connections with anarchism is South West France than with the Russian émigré groups in Paris.

Melville had grown to trust Sidney and the accuracy of his reports and the information he was able to pass on even though he knew everything about his history and background. Shortly after his recruitment Sidney Reilly had more than proved himself when he had supplied information that had led to the arrest and later prosecution on incitement to murder of the Russian revolutionary émigré Vladimir Burtsev. Burtsev had advocated the assassination of Czar Nicholas II. Melville took the credit but not before placing a few feathers in Sidney's cap and what interested Sidney more, a large sum of tax-payer's money into his pockets.

Chapter Four

It was not far from Baker Street to Number six Upper Westbourne Terrace in Paddington but the morning traffic had built up so it was nearly 10.00 when Sidney Reilly stepped out of his cab. Before turning to his front door he handed the cabbie a florin and waited for the change; no tip for this impertinent type. He pulled his silver key chain from his evening dress trousers and walking up the steps to the imposing door of number six, and unlocked the door. As he opened it he lost his grumpy mood when he saw that Joanne the eighteen year old maid, dressed in her conventional black satin lace trimmed dress with its small white pinafore and her white lace hat had walked down the hall having seen him arrive through the front window.' Madam is still in her room.' She said. Judging by her smile when she saw him she was just as pleased to see him

She put his coat, hat and gloves on the oak hall stand as he looked in its mirror. Joanne stood next to him, very close and looked in the mirror alongside him. He turned his head and whispered in her ear, 'How is my pretty maid, are, as you say in your English nursery rhyme, her cockle shells all in a row?' Mis-quoting the line he managed to make it sound salacious He put his chin on her cheek and rubbed it. She grimaced. ' I haven't shaved this morning', he said in the same whisper.

'Where were you last night?' He ignored her question thinking as he did that she asked more questions as to his whereabouts than his wife did.

He didn't have a valet yet, that would soon be remedied. Until then the maid could provide some of a valet's functions."Now be a good girl, run along and lay out my white linen suit, a blue shirt and fresh underwear and tell cook that when I am dressed I would like a late breakfast of eggs, bacon, toast, marmalade fresh orange juice and coffee and if cook has my favourite sausages…"As Joanne turned to go he patted her gently on the bottom. She gave a little skip as he did so and over her shoulder gave him a brief but inviting smile.

He loved the English breakfast. Sometimes he went to Simpsons in the Strand to sample their English breakfasts. On sideboards spirit burners with little blue flames heated lidded silver chafing dishes of Kedgeree made with salmon. There were Hull and Grimsby Kippers, smoked haddocks, rings of Cumberland sausages, medaillons of black blood pudding, devilled kidneys, shavings of crisp, curly bacon and fresh eggs, poached, soft boiled, coddled or fried followed by hot toast or muffins and scones with butter and marmalade then Earl Grey breakfast tea. In France he had once met a Chef de Cuisine who had given him the advice that," Si vous voulez bien manger en Angleterre, commander petit dejeuner trios fois par jour"If you want to eat well in England, order breakfast three times a day." Sidney shouted after the maid."Tell cook that I will eat it on a tray in the library."

Joanne did just the suggestion of a courtesy and said coquettishly, but very quietly and emphasizing the first word. 'Whatever my master commands. Would sir like poached or fried eggs.?'

'Poached.' Was his only reply. He then climbed the stairs to his bedroom, undressed, dropped his clothes on the floor and walked into his bathroom and turned on the shower he had arranged to have plumbed in when they first took possession of the house. He rejected the English custom of the bath believing it unhygienic to sit in water that has just been dirtied. As the deluge of the shower warmed up he sat on the WC pedestal. How he loved the world of comparisons he now lived in; a water closet indoors. In most of the environments he had lived in the WC had been outside or just outside with no WC at all. He sat, he thought like Rodin's 'Penseur'. He had seen the sculpture in a Paris art gallery. He put his chin on his fist and his elbow on his knee to complete the picture. He cleaned himself with his left hand using water from a small jug and bowl at the side; another continental custom he preferred. He then pulled the chain.

He then stepped into the shower. The hot water cascaded down on his head and over his shoulders. He soaped himself and washed away the previous night's smells and sweat. He stepped out of the shower and still dripping, stood in front of his shaving mirror naked and took an open razor, made by Brookes and Crookes of Sheffield from off the wash basin and honed it on a leather strop hanging by the mirror. He filled his shaving mug with hot water from the tap and put shaving soap on the badger hair shaving brush that he used. He then lathered his face and carefully but skillfully, with a steady hand gave himself a close shave without nicking himself once.

Inevitably for him, he could not shave with an open razor without thinking about the man whose throat he had cut with one in Paris in the winter of 1895. He fled to England that year to escape the French police and the anarchist comrades of the man he had murdered. The anarchists still wanted him for that but also for the very substantial amount of money he had stolen from his victim, who had happened to be the treasurer of the Paris unit. The fact that the Paris Anarchists might still be looking for him did not bother him much. Nor did his thoughts dwell on how the young man had died, taking minutes, choking on his own blood. What had fascinated Reilly was how the blood had spurted from the man's neck and then pulsed out in little fountains. It was his first kill and his only surprise was how little it had seemed to bother him. His motive wasn't politics and it wasn't ambition. It was, as it continued to be, money.

The cash he stole had been enough to set him up in London and to establish 'Ozone Preparations'. He then supplemented his income as a result of responding to a suggestion by a very perceptive journalist at his club. He was also as it happened a Special Branch operative and talent spotter. He told Sidney that he should contact a certain Superintendent William Melville of Scotland Yard and to state his talents as a linguist. He was wary at first of contacting a policeman but his doubts were dismissed when he was promised a £150 per month retainer if he consented to be a 'free lance' agent for Special Branch.

As Sidney Reilly was at his ablutions on the morning of that fine May summers day in London in 1899, across the continent in Vienna, one of the capitals of the Austro-Hungarian Empire, a young Doctor was making a name for himself defining, clinically the kind of personality disorder our young Sidney and people like him suffered from. Which was it to be? Sociopath; Self-absorbed individual with no conscience or feeling for others and for whom rules have no meaning, or Psychopath; anti-social and aggressive, prone to criminal behavior without empathy or remorse. In Sidney Reilly's case not much to chose between the two really.

He washed the shaving soap from his face then he dried himself on the large white bath-towel that the maid, who had come into his room to lay out his clothes said through the bathroom door was on a chair by his bed. He sprinkled talcum powder on himself and splashed his face with the same cologne he had used at his rooms earlier, Agua Pravia. He dressed, opening a chest of drawers and choosing to put on first a fresh set of the same cream silk underwear. Then he put on the trousers of a cream coloured linen suit, by Henry Poole of Savile row, a pale blue Egyptian cotton shirt, hand made by Hilditch and Key with attached collar and under it, a dark blue polka dot spotted Chavet neck-tie. He selected a pair of black calf-length fine woollen socks, smoothed them on and stepped into light brown doe-skin boots with elasticated sides made by the shoe-makers who had him in their 'foot-book': Peal and Co.

Sidney Reilly liked to reel off the names associated with the things he had and the clothes and shoes he wore. He reveled in the material things the wealth his new wife brought with her. For him, La style c'est l'homme and contrast was its essence. He pulled his jacket straight as he put it on and left the bottom button of his waist-coat undone, as he did this he saw through his mirror his wife Margaret walk into the room still in her night dress covered by a dressing-gown patterned with the prints of large yellow sun-flowers. She was petite and slim with a shock of blonde curls surrounding a pretty girlish face that looked younger than it was. She wore no make-up and her pale blue eyes were just a little blood shot.

"I missed you last night," She said, with a yawn." I waited up until midnight. Where were you.?" Her tone wasn't complaining just dozily querulous.

He turned to her and drew her very close to him so that his stomach was against hers. His chest was against her young breasts and his hands inside her dressing gown, one on each cheek of her bottom. He felt it naked under her silky night dress. He pulled her even closer to him and then he looked her straight in the eye and said,"The damn meeting went on so long with its interminable speeches that I didn't finish until around two, I then had to offer a client a measure of hospitality at the club so I decided in the end to stay there to save disturbing you." He smelt the whisky on her breath and gently, without a trace of recrimination, he said,"You have been drinking again." Touching her nose with his finger as he did so, as if he was correcting a naughty child. She blushed and said,"I just had a night –cap. It helps me sleep. I get so lonely when you are not here."

In fact Margaret Callahgan Reilly lately Margaret Callaghan Thomas was becoming more and more dependent on her 'night-caps'. She had discovered the favourite tipple of Queen Victoria, malt whisky mixed with claret in equal measures. Her 'night-caps' not only helped her sleep they kept away the demons that had begun to visit her more frequently, especially in the wee small hours. Sidney did not betray the concerns he increasingly had regarding her drinking. It was a problem he would have to solve someday, one way or another.

"Look", he said," I've got another meeting at mid-day and I haven't breakfasted yet and I'm famished. Come downstairs and sit and have some coffee with me and I promise I'll make it up to you this evening. How about I take you somewhere swell and buy you a posh dinner?" Ignoring her whisky breath he then kissed her full on the lips while tracing the fingers of his left hand down the cleft in her buttocks and moving his right hand across the nipples of her breasts. She took in a breath, as she always did whenever he touched her. With his arm around her waist he walked her down the wide staircase into the library just as the maid was carrying in his breakfast tray."Bring another cup Joanne, for madam." Joanne had anticipated this request and had placed two cups on the tray.

"I had thought that madam would like a cup so I have taken the liberty of bringing two cups sir."

Even in such small things his faithful maid wanted to please him.

That young doctor over in Austria Hungary went back to his desk picked up his pen and began another paragraph in his case-book under the heading, Socio/ Psychopath."Subjects found to be glib and pathological liars, allied sometimes to superior intelligence. Tend also to employ superficial charm and charisma, especially with women and to manipulate them, use sex and sexual intercourse. May fit well into the board rooms of some high level business enterprises or social institutions such as, the police force or military."

Sidney made short work of his breakfast with an appetite that had been built up by the activities of the night before. He munched the last crust of toast with its spread of Frank Cooper's Oxford Marmalade, drank his black Douwe Egbert's coffee, wiped his mouth with a white damask napkin and said,"I am sorry my love but I must go. I will be back, I promise as soon as I can."

She got up and walked with him to the door where Joanne the maid was waiting holding his light summer overcoat, a dove-grey homburg hat, pale yellow pigskin gloves and a black ebony walking cane topped with a silver knob. Sidney kissed Margaret on the cheek and Joanne smiled at him, privately wishing he would kiss her too.

She wished for even more than that now as she lay naked with her hands between her legs each night before going to sleep on her little bed upstairs in her attic room. She wished it more and more often since Sidney had begun to visit her there occasionally when his wife was in one of her inebriated sleeps.

Sidney ran down the steps of the house front like a dancer and raising his walking cane hailed a cab. He had no time to take the underground and anyway he had prejudices against it; too many of the great unwashed used it and Sherlock Holmes never did. Within a minute a black Hansom cab stopped at the kerb before him. He climbed in tapped the roof of the cab with his cane and said," New Scotland Yard as quick as you can." How he loved giving that instruction.

The cabbie knew how to avoid the traffic of Central London. He got Sidney to the Norman Building on the embankment and the offices of New Scotland Yard just as Big Ben was striking the quarter past twelve. Sidney's appointment was at 12.30 and Melville liked punctuality. Sidney felt clean and refreshed after his toilette and the satisfying breakfast had put him into a very good temper plus he knew that his chief would be pleased with the information he had to give him. All that meant that he was in a generous mood too. He took off his glove and feeling into his waistcoat pocket took out a half crown and handed it up to the cabbie and told him to keep the change.

Chapter Five

Pulling on his glove Reilly walked to the side entrance of 'The Yard'. A policeman on duty there asked him what his business was. Reilly told him he was from' The Electric Ozone Company ' and that he had an appointment with Superintendent Melville at 12.30. Prudently non-police 'employees' of Special Branch did not carry any pass or document that might identify their function. They were to all intents and purposes ordinary citizens going about their ordinary business. The duty police-man buzzed a button on the wall and said into a mouthpiece,"A Mr. Reilly for the Super" A sound crackled from the instrument which presumably said something like"send him up". For the guardian policeman stepped aside and indicated the stairs."Third floor, there's a notice at the top of the stairs." Sidney knew where it was. He had been before.

Sidney climbed the stairs and through another door saw the notice on the wall with an arrow that directed the way to Superintendent William Melville's Office. He walked straight in to Miss Lukerstone's ante-room and she looked up from her work and smiled when she saw who it was."I am sorry Miss Lukerstone I was in such a hurry I did not get time to buy you your orchids." I promise next time….." He never had bought her orchids. It was a standing joke and one that Miss Lukerstone cheerfully replied to by saying,"That will be the day. Go straight in Superintendent Melville is expecting you."

As Sidney opened the door and stepped into the office Melville looked up and stepped out from behind his desk and welcomed Sidney warmly." How good to see you, pull up a chair. We have a lot to talk about." He returned to his desk and opened Sidney's file" We are very pleased with you". Sidney felt his self esteem rising. He loved praise and approbation but hated criticism, no matter how constructive. Melville went on."The report you delivered from Spain was first class and it cleared up a number of misinterpretations and it has put the Spaniards onto the right track."

He turned more pages in the file"I won't go over the Burtsev affair again. I hope you think we settled up with you adequately. And while we are on that put your expenses and charges for Spain into the system with Miss Lukerstone". When on a mission agents were expected to fund their own costs and then to indent for them on return and completion. The 'office' was not ungenerous and it seemed that they didn't check into submissions too deeply. That's what most agents thought anyway. Actually the accuracy of expense accounts was very strictly checked and any ' overcharges' were kept on file and used against them if necessary.

Settling into his chair Melville called out,"Miss Lukerstone bring some tea will you please. You'll join me won't you?" Sidney thought it politic to say yes but really he didn't like the tea Miss Lukerstone usually served. It was either the cheap tea she used or the water in New Scotland Yard, or both. The tea came in and Melville lit his pipe."Do feel free to smoke Sidney". Sidney felt in the pocket of his overcoat which he still had on and found the packet of cigarettes that he had omitted to return to Caroline and opened it to take one out. He began to remove his coat."May I….?

Melville gestured to him to take it off."Of course, hang it on the stand."

Sidney put his gloves in a pocket and with the hat hung his coat on the hooks of a hat stand. He poked his cane through the support on the base. He put a cigarette in his mouth and leaned over Melville's desk for a light.

Melville saw the red end and said," They're very colourful are they foreign?"

"Er no sir." Sidney said, as if found out in a misdemeanor by a school-master. They are a new brand."

Not much escaped Melville's notice. He knew exactly what the cigarettes were for and he also knew of Sidney's reputation with women. There was little he didn't know about Reilly..

"Well." Said Melville let's get down to business, how did the party at the Japanese Embassy go?"

Sidney sucked on his cigarette and held it stylishly he blew the smoke out of his mouth as if whistling and picked a thread of tobacco off his lip."I have not had time yet to put it into writing but briefly, a Naval attaché at the Russian embassy seems to be expressing, albeit unofficially, significant misgivings regarding Japanese intentions in the regions of Vladivostok and Port Arthur." Sidney added Port Arthur to give his meager report more substance.

"What misgivings?" Queried Melville, sitting back in his chair and holding the bowl of it his pipe.

Sidney put a note of authority into his voice and said,"There seems to be a generally held view on the Russian side that Japan has designs on Port Arthur and the worry amongst service personnel is that it may go as far as a preemptive invasion and if it does they will be unprepared." Sidney was using his not insubstantial intuitions now. It was obvious to him. If service personnel lacked confidence it was because they were in the best position to judge any negative or positive state of preparedness.

Melville had become interested and he said."Can you enlarge upon that?"

It did not disappoint him when Sidney said that was all he could report. ' That's alright, good, good, you did well. Get it into writing before you go. Miss Lukerstone will take your dictation. And now I have another assignment for you, what do you know about the Oil industry ?'

Sidney pricked up his ears. Very shortly after his arrival in England Sidney had established his business, Ozone Preparations and become a Fellow of the Chemical Society. For Sidney that had been for him a passé partout into the British Establishment. Only a little time elapsed before he was permitted to progress to membership of the prestigious Institute of Chemistry and that membership had opened a number of doors and provided the opportunity for him to meet important contacts. It was around this same time that he was recommended for, then initiated into, 'The Brotherhood'. He could now count among his associations Sir Thomas Boverton Redwood an expert in the new technologies associated with petroleum and through The Institute's Foreign Fellowships and his knowledge of Russian he had been introduced to no less a person than the renowned Russian chemist Dmitrii Ivanovitch Mendeleev, a pioneer in the Russian Oil Industry.(Mendeleev was also the compiler of The Periodic table of Elements.)

In the hallowed corridors of The Institute, chemistry and oil were being talked about in the same breath. Sidney could boast a little knowledge of this innovatory industry and if he didn't have the knowledge he knew somebody who did.

Sidney didn't betray too much interest but merely said," I have some knowledge but it is generally academic in character. As you know I am a Member of the Institute of Chemistry and I understand that a number of its Fellows are involved in research related to prospecting and refining."

Melville became untypically sententious. He leaned over his desk and his face took on a very serious air. He pointed his pipe and then jabbed it towards Sidney as he said,

" Reilly we are at a turning point in history and it's not just because we are reaching the beginning of a new century. It is because we are coming to the end of the supremacy of coal. The thousands of workers involved in coal will begin to diminish as a political and social force. We are at the gate of the age of Oil. Oil will be the new super fuel. It will change everything, politics, society, industry, manufacture, armies, navies, nations and the world. The nations that have it and control it will rule the world."

"Have you had lunch?" Sidney shook his head at what seemed a non sequitur. He did not mention his late breakfast." I supposed not." Said Melville." I want you to come with me, we have an invitation to lunch and there are two or three people who want to meet you". Melville called to Miss Lukerstone to arrange a plain police vehicle to take them to the Army and Navy Club in Pall Mall.

They arrived at the club and waited at reception while a club servant checked their invitation and then the same servant led them into the dining room. As they walked in two men stood up at their dining table and the older of the two welcomed Melville warmly. Smiling he held out his hand. He was a slim but well built man wearing a formal black suit. He had a fresh boyish looking face topped by fair hair with a moustache of the same colour. His name was Sir Henry Montague Hozier. The other man a deal younger but dressed in the same garb was Sir Albert Kaye Rollit M.P.

Melville, Introduced Sidney.

Sidney said," I am pleased to make your acquaintance, Sir Henry, Sir Albert." Sidney gave the handshake that he had been taught on his induction into"The Brotherhood" and its form was returned precisely by each of his new acquaintants.

Sir Henry called to the waiter who had been hovering, waiting for an order and then turned to his guests," I recommend the confit de canard and if you don't mind I'll choose the wine. What do you say that we start with a couple of dozen oysters?" The other three nodded. But Sidney added that he would like a light salad for his main course."Good, Good" Sir Henry said. And he turned and looked up to the waiter standing discretely by his right shoulder." Bring us an extra cover. We are expecting another member of our party, he will order when he arrives. Three confit de canard and a salad, a couple of bottles of Cote de Duras '95 with a Bergerac dry white to go with the oysters, Unless of course you want the cod in Mornay sauce, Albert,"Sir Henry said with a laugh," Sir Albert's from Hull the home of fishing and I know he likes to support home industries."

"I'll have the oysters if you don't mind Henry," Sir Albert said with good humour, 'You'll be inviting me to a fish and chip supper out of a newspaper next you old joker."

"If I ever do, Albert it won't be any old newspaper" and here he touched his friend's arm and again laughing said,"I'll make sure it's 'The Times'. The four men laughed together.

The informal, if not casual atmosphere of that luncheon in the hallowed precincts of The Army and Navy club disguised the significance of the political and social roles that the four diners played in the milieu they each circulated in. William Melville was Head of the Special Branch, which to all intents and purposes was Britain's Political Police and of course Sidney Reilly was one of his agents.

Sir Henry Montague Hozier had been part of a group of army officers selected for The War Office's new Intelligence Branch. On his demobilisation he had joined Lloyds of London as Managing Secretary. He was ostensibly concerned with the business of shipping insurance but his real function was to oversee the practices of Lloyd's Maritime Intelligence Service. LMIS was a global system of inter-related agents and signal stations that communicated, information on The Merchant Marine and Naval activities of every ship that sailed the oceans of the world. Lloyds had formal relationships with The Royal Naval Intelligence Division of the British Admiralty and The War office intelligence Division. It involved sharing any relevant intelligence. He was to have further claim to fame in that Winston Churchill, later in time to become First Lord of the Admiralty, was to fall in love with his daughter Clementine and then to marry her.

Sir Albert Kaye Rollit M.P. was a very successful solicitor and as such he was made president of the Law Society. He was also the Director of The London and British Chambers of Commerce (It was he who had arranged the invitation for Sidney to The Japanese Embassy). His professional relationship with Sir Henry Hozier and William Melville was through his responsibility on the British Board of Trade's Commercial Intelligence Committee. It was a committee that cooperated with Lloyds Maritime Intelligence Service and shared Intelligence material with Melville's Special Branch and The War Office Intelligence Division. Sir Albert Kaye Rollit was also a Member of Parliament for Islington whereby he had become a knight and he had been a well known philanthropic Lord Mayor of Kingston upon Hull.

This connection was not to be underestimated in terms of Lloyds for Sir Albert had strong associations through his own shipping and oil interests and his legal consultancy, with the biggest shipping line in the world, Arthur Wilson and Sons and that was based in Sir Albert's home town, the northern shipping and fishing port of Kingston Upon Hull. He also had an association with his fellow Member of Parliament and High Sheriff of Kingston Upon Hull, Charles Henry Wilson M.P. representing the Parliamentary ward of West Hull. He was a director and joint owner of the Wilson Shipping line. He was the other member of the lunch party but his arrival had been delayed by business"In the House." His company, Wilsons was to become a member of the Oil interest Syndicate that Sir Albert and his colleagues were setting up, that being the purpose of the meeting with Melville and Sidney.

Arthur Wilson and Sons was so big, the company paid The Admiralty for a brand new Royal Navy Destroyer to help with the task of looking after the shipping lanes their one hundred merchant ships sailed in and although Charles H. Wilson M.P. opposed the Boer war his company had loaned their most modern ship"The Ariosto" to The British Government for help in the war effort.

The offices of Arthur Wilson and Sons in Kingston Upon Hull, using the new technological development of Wireless Telegraphy were also home to one of the most comprehensive of the Lloyds Maritime Intelligence Service listening stations. Its brief was to survey the whole of the North Sea, The waters of the Low Countries, Germany, Belgium, Scandinavia and all the sea going traffic coming out of the Baltic and then to telegraph all relevant information back to Lloyds. Lloyds had ships equipped with Wireless Telegraphy equipment onboard that were on permanent station in those waters to do just this.

The sea-port of Kingston Upon Hull as the home port of Wilsons Shipping line was the epi-centre of the British Empire's Merchant Marine. Placed as it was on The Humber Estuary with its neighbour Grimsby, Hull was also the base of the World's largest fishing fleet.

When the four had finished their luncheon, each having tasted a lemon sorbet for dessert, they were now drinking an Armagnac digestive ordered with black coffee and they were choosing a cigar from a box proffered by the waiter. Sir Albert turned to Sidney and said,"You and I have an acquaintance in common." Sidney gave Sir Albert a quizzical look. Sir Albert went on to clarify his remark," He is Sir Thomas Boverton Redwood of The Chemical Society. He has told me a lot about you. Sir Thomas,as you no doubt know is very interested in any development, anywhere in the world that is to do with the oil industry. With his and our support a group of like- minded people have got together and we have formed a syndicate. One of the, shall we say 'sleeping members' of the syndicate is someone else that you know as a fellow of The Institute of Chemistry albeit a foreign member, Dimitri Ivanovitch Mendeleev." Sidney could not hide the surprise on his face when the name of Mendeleev was mentioned, Sidney had spoken with Mendeleev a number of times with particular reference to the progress of oil exploration and refining in The Caucasus.

Sir Albert went on,"We have called the our organization 'The Oleum Synidicate' but I want to point out and if I didn't, if he was here Sir Thomas would most decidedly want to point out, our main intentions in forming this syndicate are to ensure that The British Empire, that we all owe allegiance to, is not cut off from access to the kind of very substantial oil reserves it is going to need commercially and militarily in the future. We have selected you Mr. Reilly because you are a Russian speaker, a chemist and you work for Mr. Melville. As far as we are concerned you are just the man for the job we have in mind for you. I should also give you the assurance that we have the complete support of H.M.G. and without putting too fine a point on it a very influential representative at the palace."

Sidney did not need to ask who that was. Edward Prince of Wales was a good friend of Sir Thomas Boverton Redwood and it had already been hinted at by Boverton Redwood that the Prince, through substitutes wanted financial interests in oil.

Prince Edward also knew Hull, Sir Albert Kaye Rollit and the Wilson Family very well. He had often visited Arthur Wilson at his family home there, Tranby Croft. His visits had become less regular after what became a national scandal. It involved a one time friend of Edward Prince of Wales, Baronet and soldier Sir William Gordon Cumming. A game of baccarat, illegal in England, went sour during a Tranby Croft house party at which Prince Edward was a guest. Because of an accusation of cheating on the part of Gordon Cumming, Edward was exposed to the public gaze of a court appearance.

There were other attractions of Hull and Tranby Croft for Edward Prince of Wales, notorious womanizer and heir to the throne of the British Empire, apart from games of baccarat. These were Muriel Thetis Wilson and Susannah West Wilson… They were Arthur Wilsons's beautiful and intelligent daughters. Rumour and gossip had it that he had been in sexual relationships with both of them.

Sir Albert looked at Sidney and said,"We want you to go to Russia, to the Caucasus, to Baku in Azerbaijan, more precisely to investigate the Russian oil industry there and to bring back a survey of production and facilities, refining systems, transportation systems and ownership patterns etc. etc. We will set it down chapter and verse, fine print and all that sort of thing so that you know exactly what you have to do."

Sidney lowered his voice and said as carefully as could, only in the hearing of those at the table."There might be problems for me in going back to Russia." Sidney addressed his remarks particularly to Superintendent Melville." I left illegally. I would be arrested almost immediately and the charge would be at least avoiding military service. And there is the work I did in France. I had to convince the Anarchists I was bono fide so I was involved not just in Anti-Tsarist propaganda, I procured arms and explosives…."

Melville stopped him but was equally discrete. He would rather that Reilly had brought this matter up in the confidentiality of his office."That can be sorted out." Said Melville."We can give you just what you have been striving for since you came to England in'95, a completely new identity and a genuine British one at that. You will be Sidney Reilly born and bred in England. We can make you a British citizen with a birth certificate, family tree and a British pass-port. You'll be a successful English business man with international interests. The Russians won't know you from Adam." As Melville addressed Sidney, Hozier and Rollit talked to each other as if there was no one else at their table.

At this point Melville finished his coffee and drained his brandy glass of Armagnac and still puffing on his cigar he said,"I wonder if you two gentleman would excuse us so that we can get back to my office, where I can complete the arrangements with Mr Reilly. We would both like to thank you for an excellent lunch and of course I will be in touch." Melville shook Sir Henry and Sir Albert by the hand and Sidney followed suit.

Sidney and Melville left The Army and Navy Club and went back to New Scotland yard in the plain police vehicle that had waited for them.

As they left Sir Henry said to Sir Albert," I think we have chosen just the right man for the job."

Sir Albert said,"So do I Henry, so do I, but there is one thing that is certain, if we haven't and he gets it wrong with the Russians and the Secret Police get their hands on him we will never hear from him again. He will simply be, as far as our people are concerned another Jewish anarchist sympathizer travelling on a stolen passport with a false identity. Now how about another drop of that excellent Armagnac, I am beginning to get a taste for it."

As Sir Henry reached for the decanter their late guest arrived at his elbow. Sir Albert exclaimed,"Ah Charles, you got here. Too late to meet the chaps I was telling you about, but I can assure you, you haven't missed anything. Henry and I can fill you in on the details. The project I told you it was very important to be in on has been set in motion and you are part of it, right Henry?"

Sir Henry said,"Like a Swiss watch Charlie, now we are on the digestive, what can I order you for lunch? I am in the corner."

The newcomer said." Hello Albert, Henry, good to see you both. No thanks Henry, we were served a snack lunch in The House during the committee meeting I have just attended" As he took his place at the table he said,"I will have a glass of that however." The person late for the luncheon was Sir Charles Henry Wilson, joint owner of the largest shipping line in the world, The Wilson line, and Liberal Member of Parliament for West Hull.

Chapter Six

When Melville and Sidney got back to the office Sidney thought he had better finish off his reports before returning to the question of The Oleum Syndicate.

"There is something I have not reported yet, I have been biding my time until I got more information. I have had it confirmed that a group of South African Boers have made contact with Dutch Anarchists who have offered to help them obtain light artillery, small arms and explosives from a Dutch sympathiser in Amsterdam via an arms dealer in Hamburg, Germany who is certainly involved. I have made contact as a supporter of the Boer cause and directed them towards an arms dealer who is in our pay so that we can keep an eye on them. There is also information that the same organization is recruiting Irish Nationalists to fight on the side of the Boers. Would you want me to go to Holland and confirm that before this other business?"

'That's good yes good, but let me have the details you have because we already have somebody working on that. I want you to concentrate on the Russian trip to the exclusion of all else"

Sidney didn't usually introduce personal notes and he was aware of this as he said to Melville,"My only concern is my wife's reaction. She was getting the impression I was settling down. But I must also say that I am a bit uneasy about travelling across France. I am absolutely sure I can handle the Russian end……but"

Melville interrupted,"Oh yes Mrs. Reilly," and then he said pointedly. How is your young wife?. Oh yes Reilly we know about her and you have said before that you had a few problems but you will have to resolve them off your own bat. Don't worry, we are fully aware of the incident in Paris with the Anarchist Treasurer. But look at it like this, the Paris anarchists and The Deuxieme Bureau will find it even more difficult to get their hands on you with the new identity we will give you."

Melville paused and screwed up his mouth, furrowed his brow and looked at Sidney."There is something else that might be of interest to you." He took a letter out of a foolscap sized green leather wallet on his desk and unfolded it. It had Russian Cyrillic writing on as a heading. He passed it Sidney to read. The Cyrillic print had been translated and the text written over it in English. It was from The State Prosecutor's Office in St. Petersburg. it referred to a diplomatic request for assistance in the matter of apprehending the members of a criminal forging consortium based in London who were counterfeiting Russian ruble bank notes, arranging for their delivery to Russia and having them distributed there. Sidney's saw that the letter was from the office of Petr. Rachkovsky. Rachkovsky had been a senior officer in the French section of the Ochrana when Sidney had been undercover in Paris. He had been promoted. Now he was chief of the Ochrana in France.

Sidney was marginally involved in the counterfeiting organization that Melville was referring to. He had been using the chemistry credentials of Ozone Preparations to obtain the specialist inks necessary for the plates used for printing the money and had been well paid for it. But it wasn't Melville's implication that he knew all about Sidney's involvement in the criminal counterfeiting ring that concerned him. Falling into the clutches of the the Ochrana in England was a possibility he had not bargained for. The Ochrana were The Imperial Tsarist Russian Secret Police; The Department for Protecting The Public Security and Order. He had been on the run from them effectively, since he left Paris. He did not want to come into contact with the Ochrana. They were well known as the most ruthless secret police force in the whole of Europe. And Melville did not sound as if he was prepared to protect him from them if he didn't accept this assignment. Melville wasn't. He had already decided to cut him adrift without a second thought if he didn't cooperate. He didn't like his agents sub-contracting their activities without his permission.

During his time in Paris Sidney had informed The French Deuxieme Bureau about a courier for an Anarchist cell and got a nice reward. She was a young Russian émigré girl of about eighteen. Apart from a concern he had that she suspected his motives for membership of the movement, she had not responded all that positively to his advances. When The Bureau had finished with her they passed her on to the Ochrana in Paris. He had not bargained for that and had thought at the time that the French would have dealt with her without involving the Russians. But then the French government went into an alliance with the Russians and part of the agreement was a joint campaign against the anarchists. When he had last seen her she had so aged that she looked about fifty. The Ochrana had just released her. She didn't suspect that he was her betrayer. She had no finger nails, she walked with a limp because they had broken her toes with a hammer and then used it to smash her kneecaps. Even after all that she had not talked.

It did not take much time for Sidney to think that he was the best person for the job that was on offer by The Oleum Syndicate.. After all, he could speak Russian, English, German and French. He was an accomplished forger. He was capable of assuming other identities and he had acquired the skills of lock-picking that made most safes open to him. Melville had taught him that skill and he had been taught in his turn by Houdini no less. Who else was there with his qualifications? Although he might have had minor reservations about the mission, they evaporated at the thought of falling into the hands of The Ochrana.

"Where do you think I should be making a start? Said Sidney.

Melville said," We will come to that There was another reason why I've appointed you to go, the boys from the F.O. want an assessment of the Russian Military situation in the Caucasus. For my money it's the most important factor as far as they see it. They get up in the morning and go to bed at night worrying about Russia's intentions as far as India is concerned, and certainly since The Tsar has annexed a large slice of Afghanistan. They even believe that there is a spy in the pay of the Amir of Afghanistan in the palace. So they want to know if the Russian Army is around the Caucasas in strength and not just as the guardians of a territory of The Russian Empire. They want to know if there are ammunition dumps, supply depots and arsenals that would be big enough, if It came to it, to fit out and equip an army of invasion across the Caspian. In a phrase is Tsarist Imperial Russia in a state of readiness for a war against the British Empire in India?' At that point he pushed a book over his desk to Sidney."Read that and you will see exactly what they mean.'" The title of the book was 'The Defence of India.' By Charles Metcalfe MacGregor.

Melville continued."C.M.MacGregor was Head of Indian military Intelligence. I have learned a lot from his writings and so could you. If you couldn't before, you can see why I've put your name forward. This is not just a case of industrial espionage. For that, if you are unlucky and get caught, it will be a kick in the belly and deportation. If you are caught sizing up military potential, you know and I know it's a firing squad and they'll mess you about a bit before, no doubt about it."

Sidney, his confidence returning quickly as he assessed this opportunity as a very necessary escape route, spoke up.'"At the risk of repeating myself, when do you want me to go?"

Melville replied with the casual authority that he acquired when things had gone the way he wanted."Well, really as soon as possible. Don't worry about the other business. I mean the Russians. I can keep them running round the houses for a couple more months if necessary and you will be well on your way by then. The information most urgently wanted relates to the quantity and quality of oil the Russians are refining for the use in their navy ships. Obviously The Admiralty and Rollit's, Wilson's and Hozier's ' Oleum Syndicate' would like that"toot sweet". As you have probably gathered they are the real agency we are working for and I tell you Sidney", Melville leaned across his desk. He did not often get this familiar and his voice took on a quiet conspiratorial tone as he said it, although there was no one else in the room." If this one goes according to plan you are a made man." He himself had already made a mental note that his position would improve quite significantly too if Reilly brought home the bacon." You, and I say this with confidence, will be able to write your own cheques for future assignments. Indeed the resources for this enterprise are not coming out of our budget and the usual practice of you funding yourself and then reclaiming has been set aside."

Melville went on to say,"An account will be opened in your name in the Russo-Asiatic Bank of Moscow. I can assure you an ample sum will be deposited in it. First class rail tickets will be bought for you and your wife through to Moscow and after that you will keep a record of expenses and draw on your Moscow Account. You will be given a code book and the location of Lloyds Listening Stations and their agents so that you can send confidential messages by telegraph. Oh by the way there is another name and contact you need to know of, Leslie Urquhart, he is British Vice-consul in Baku. You will no doubt be passing through Paris and so there is another contact I would like you make and that is with Colonel Akashi Motojiro. He is with the Japanese Secret Service. The FO have asked me to pass his name on to you. To arrange a meeting with him, visit the Japanese Embassy in Paris. All the details will be delivered to your house by special courier in the next few days and I expect everything to be in place for your departure around the end of June, earlier by a week or so if there are no cows on the line." As he said this he turned the pages of an appointment book in front of him on the desk.

Melville got up and proffered his hand and said in what was an untypically avuncular tone,"Well my boy I suppose you want to get back to tell your wife….Mrs. Reilly about the new arrangements. She will of course be on your passport. If you have any problems about your house, let me know. You can give your staff a generous notice. We will foot the bill. If you need to sell it leave it in our hands we'll handle that for you and if you want to rent it, have no worries on that account either, we will find a reliable tenant for you and you can be assured that we will look after the interests of your company while you are away so that you will be able to pick up where you left off on your return. We will keep it ticking over." He had already thought of everything.

"I don't suppose I will see you again for some time. Let me wish you luck and God's speed. As I said, you will get all the information you need. You will also get details of your contact at the British Embassy in Moscow. He will be ready to collate the information you send and he has chapter and verse on you and the assignment. Oh and by the way, have you got a side-arm? Miss Lukerstone will give you a chitty for one. Take it down to the armoury and they will fit you out with one and cartridges. A Webley 38 is the usual mark but pray to God you don't have to use it."Sidney didn't ask for a chitty. His gunsmiths C.V.Carter had already supplied him with a 9mm Pocket Browning. He didn't like revolvers. He preferred slim little automatics." Keep it clean and it won't jam." Mr. Carter had said as he handed it over.

Sidney was sharp enough to interpret the reference to the contact at The British Embassy in Moscow as a warning,"Put a foot wrong and the Russians will get the full story of you and your real identity." Was what Melville was really saying.

Sidney took Melville's hand and as usual was surprised that it wasn't that of a man with a grip of iron. Instead it felt like holding a cold wet fish even with 'The Brotherhood' signal. He got his coat, hat and cane and closing Melville's door behind him went into the office of Miss Lukerstone. He sat down subdued and pre-occupied and dictated to her his brief report from the night before. She saw that he wasn't in a frame of mind for their usual banter. He didn't forget however to put in his expenses which included the champagne, the caviare and the cab fares from the 'information gathering exercise' of the previous night.

As he let his light lunch digest and he collected his thoughts he found to his surprise that they were summoning up feelings he hadn't expected. He was going back to Russia and he was looking forward to it because he was homesick.

Chapter Seven

Sidney got another surprise when he arrived back at upper Westbourne Terrace, Margaret his wife, did not react to his news in the way he had expected at all. He told her the story that Melville had introduced, that he was going to Russia to investigate the commercial possibilities of the oil industry. She assumed immediately that she would be coming with him. He had decided to tell her that he would be going alone but that decision was only based on his expectation that she would object to his going and her accompanying him.

"I think I would like a change." She said." We could make it almost like a holiday. How long will we be away? What shall we do with the house; close it up or rent it? We could even sell it, although there is little time. Of course we will have to give Joanne and Mrs. Sawyer their notice." Mrs. Sawyer was the cook."That will be a pity." She said."She is very good and good cooks are difficult to find, especially these days when everybody is looking for them. What is the weather like where we are going this time of year? I shall have to have a new wardrobe of course and new luggage. Will we be there over winter? I have heard that the Russian winters are quite hard. One thing I will have to do is cancel the order I have placed at Libertys for new curtains for the drawing room.'" She chattered on almost manically and it slowly dawned on him that she wanted to get away and he knew intuitively what it was that she wanted to get away from.

'They do not love who love not at first sight.' That maxim had certainly applied to her when she first met Sidney. What he had been unprepared for was the passion with which she had expressed it. Most significantly it had been Sidney who had given Margaret her first orgasm. She had come to a sort of climax during her pubertal and adolescent fiddling with herself but it was not to be compared to the voluptuous physical sensations she experienced with Sidney. The Rev. Thomas, her husband had not felt that such sexual phenomena were appropriate to the behavior of a respectable woman in spite of them being within the acceptable boundaries of married love. Of course the questions of him getting such satisfaction as he thought she should supply as her duties on the nuptial couch were not considered. And then there was the question of a child. The Reverend Thomas had wanted a child. The one she became pregnant with had not been her husband's and Sidney didn't want it. He had given her a potion that he had made up to get rid of it when she was only a few weeks gone.

She remembered a lot of pain and a lot of blood. There was even talk of the hospital. But then, she miscarried. She had felt such a sense of loss. Sidney had talked about it being part of the natural order of things. You can always have another, he had said, just as if it was some sort of game that had been lost or as if it had been a plant in a garden that had not taken. Later on he had changed his mind and suggested that she would probably not be able to have any other children ;as if he could possibly know.

At the time she had not seen the significance of what she had done. Now it gnawed at her conscience like a rat. She had effectively aborted herself. She was a Christian and a Catholic. Was there any greater sin? And it was against the law to procure an abortion.

Then he had made a suggestion which she could not believe now that she had accepted. The horror of it, of its awfulness as she recalled it made her now feel physically sick.

Margaret was about twenty four and the Rev Hugh Thomas was sixty eight and seriously ailing. The virility of a young man of twenty five as Sidney was, could not be compared with that of a sick old man in his late sixties. May should never marry December. What Sidney was further unprepared for was the equanimity with which she agreed to the plan he hatched to dispose of her husband, the Reverend Thomas.

Margaret had even begun going to mass again. She hadn't told Sidney. Attendance at Mass and so taking communion, involved confession. It would not have made any difference had she told him that even in the face of eternal damnation she had kept her counsel. She certainly asked,"Bless me Father for I have sinned". And although she had looked through the fretwork of the confessional box at the anonymous shredded face of the priest and she had received his blessing she could still assure Sidney that she had only confessed to minor sins. There were only the penances of a few Ave Marias and a handful of Paternosters ordered for them.

"Jesus Mary and Joseph", she confided to herself hiding under the sheets of her lonely bed, pulling them around her as if they would armour her against the arrows of guilt that seemed to be piercing the walls of her belly. She was almost hysterical with remorse," Holy Mary Mother of God, what did they give for murdering a husband, and for aborting a child?" She gripped the sheets and her rosary with one hand and teeth chattering with fear, crossed herself as vigorously as a voodoo witch.

Sidney was right. Margaret wanted to get away, to get as far away as possible from the memory of the part she had played in her husband's demise and the loss of her child. Central Russia might well fit the bill. It was so far away she might be able to leave her guilt behind.

Sidney gave the impression of listening to her chattering on. He nodded and made the appropriate noises of agreement and then said,"I am sure we will have time to do all the things you suggest, we do have a few weeks to get sorted out and prepared and I am glad that you are as excited as I am about the trip we are going to take to my 'Motherland.'

Margaret then said," Perhaps we will be able to meet your family."

That was the last thing Sidney wanted." Oh no they are far too far away." It would be necessary to explain to her that in no circumstances should his Russian nationality be revealed. He was going to Russia as an English Businessman with his English Wife." Now he said what about that dinner I promised you? We can make it something of a celebration of our new venture together."

"Oh no no no", And she quickly shook her head as she said,"I shall ask cook to make dinner here as usual. I have far too much to think about and far too many things to sort out now."

However the prospect of the move did not prevent Margaret from drinking too much again that night and as she snored and twitched next to him, Sidney furtively got up out of bed and went once more into the arms of Joanne. The two of them squeezed together on her little bed. But he didn't tell Joanne then that he was going away. That would have spoiled things. He would have to chose the right moment for that, if he told her at all. He might let Margaret do that. Even as he manipulated Joanne's young,lithe,willing, supple naked body into a position comfortable enough on her narrow couch for him to enter her he said to himself,"Yes I will let Margaret break the news. She was the one who dealt with the staff."

Chapter Eight

For the next couple of days Sidney got up and left the house every morning to go to The British Museum where he spent the day until closing time in The Reading Room and The Reference Library reading and taking notes on the subjects he had tasked himself to find out about British India and the history and make- up of the Oil Industry. When not considering those factors he was reading MacGregor's book. When Sidney set his mind to work he was conscientious to the exclusion of just about everything else. He took time away from his 'studies' only for an hour or so on one afternoon and that was to transfer the lease of his rooms to a fellow member of his club. To close the transaction quickly he had reduced the lease to a bargain price and thrown in all the furniture there was.

Researching the oil industry was another question. He had never thought that the history of oil went back such a long way, at least 5000 years. He noted that The Egyptians had used it for preserving mummies. Then it had been known as 'naphtha'. Under that name there were numerous references to it in the bible. Herodotus had referred to bitumen being used along with mortar in the walls of Babylon and Roman builders had it mixed with clay to bind cement. Rivers of inflammable naphtha ran from rocks in the deserts of Mesopotamia and the oil and gas of the Apsheron peninsula on the southern side of which lies Baku, one of his destinations, were that well known in ancient times that a Zoroastrian temple with eternal flames had been built 2.500 years ago. It was at Surakhany north of Baku where there was a seepage of gas from an underground fault. Priests from the Zoroastrian cult in India were still visiting it to worship and pay homage. The extraction of oil and its transportation by camel to be used as lighting fuel had not escaped the notice of that great adventurer and traveler Marco-Polo and in that same age it was being used as an embalming fluid, a varnish and a medicament for chest problems and headaches.

All this was very interesting and enlightening, thought Reilly as he pored hour after hour over reference books and learned tracts and essays but what he needed most if he was to bring off this first time venture into the field of 'industrial espionage' successfully was one, some sort of cover story for his being in Russia and two an apprehension of the modern context of Caucasus oil exploration and production. He would work on an idea for a cover story but to be prepared before he embarked on his 'expedition' he needed the advice of someone who had been there recently. Someone who's brains he could pick so as to provide him with a short-cut. He found the source of the knowledge he wanted in the form of one Clarence Merlan a man he met on the recommendation of one of his journalist cronies at The Imperial Club.

Merlan had been to the Caucasus only a few months before and had come back and written a series of articles under the title of 'Fountains of Flames.' Which he intended gathering together into a book. For a few drinks over the bar, a couple of good dinners and the promise of gold coins Sidney Reilly got his homework done for him. He learned of the relaxing of the Russian Government monopoly that it had maintained over Caucasian Oil reserves and how an influx of European entrepreneurs had revolutionised methods of extraction, refining and transportation.

There were drilling rigs now that had replaced the laborious business of digging pits by hand and the number of wells had increased to nearly 2000 producing 11 million tons a year, Refineries had become more sophisticated and their products diversified into kerosene, petroleum, fuel oil and oil for lubrication and engines.

Transportation had developed far beyond the carts and camels that were still in operation at the beginning of the eighteenth century and it was now an efficient mix of road, rail and sea tankers with the prospect of pipelines a coming reality. As information literally poured out of Clarence Merlan, liberally eased by the best malt whisky, Reilly, always with his eye on the main chance was seriously thinking that his job was half done and he didn't have to necessarily, in the best journalistic traditions 'reveal his sources' to Melville when Merlan introduced information on The Samuels, The Rothchilds and The Nobels. They were the international capitalists who had largely bought up Russian oil concessions in the region. Sidney had heard reference before to the Samuels and the Rothchilds.

With Rothschild he had heard more about his unique butterfly collection than his interest in oil but hearing of the Nobel family was a surprise. In fact the Nobel family were well established in the Caucasus region, Albert, Robert, Ludwig and Emanuel senior. Albert was the inventor of Dynamite, Robert, who had initiated the family interest in Baku and Ludwig who was a pioneer in the Russian Petroleum Industry. The founding members of the Nobel family had passed away but the petroleum company Branobel and the engineering interests they had initiated were still working and Robert's son Emanuel was now the president of Branobel. The Nobels had been among the first to buy concessions offered by the Georgian Government.

But it was Merlan's aside in reference to engineering, that caused Sidney to doubly increase his interest in what Merlan was reporting. The Nobel company was staffed by celebrated Swedish engineers and so was of great interest to the Russians. The Russians were employing the company under great secrecy on the construction of oil-fired marine engines and the work they had been set to was not by any means finished. The designs were still being worked on.

Through his conversations with Merlan it became obvious to Sidney that most of the information he had been instructed to obtain was in the field of statistics. The significance of those would be gauged by how confidential they were and he was sure that he would be able to winkle those out of wherever they were being kept. However the blue prints of innovatory marine engines would be of a different order of things. Sidney easily deduced that if the work was secret then they would be for a military purpose, that is for war-ships. What a prize they would be. Obtaining them would be an extraordinary coup and one he would get significant plaudits for. Add to this any formulae for new refining processes for the oil these engines might use as fuel and it would not just be something included as an afterthought but it would be a package of information whose value it would be difficult to calculate.

Even from the distance he was from Baku, that is the member's bar of the Imperial Club Cursitor Street London, Reilly coolly calculated that his ambition would be to get the designs of these engines along with any associated information and present them like a tribute to Rollit's Oleum Syndicate and to the Sea Lords of the Admiralty. The thought that he might not achieve this goal did not enter his head.

It was a supremely confident but pre-occupied Sidney Reilly that alighted from the cab in front of the steps of number 6 Upper Westbourne terrace on that summer evening in late May after leaving a somewhat inebriated Clarence Merlan leaning on the members' bar of the Imperial Club holding another glass of single malt, smoking a cigar and counting the sovereigns that Sidney had dropped into his pocket. Sidney did not remember turning the key in the lock of the front door and Joanne was very disappointed that he did not greet her in any way but let her take his hat and coat and cane without a word as he walked the length of the hall to the library. She stood perplexed and rejected his coat over her arm and his hat in her hand and felt tears pricking at her eyes. It was as if he had never seen her before. It was as if she had not existed. Given the totally introverted and self-absorbed frame of mind Sidney was in at the time, that could well have been the case.

Sidney went into the library and sat down in one of the large arm chairs and began to imagine a number of scenarios wherein he stole the plans of the new marine engines that Emmanuel Nobel was working on. Sidney did not find such a mental exercise absurd. For him they were a series of cerebral auditions for focusing on the real thing. He asked himself, would the plans be in his home.? Would they be in a workshop? Would they be in a safe? Would they be in strongbox? How would they be guarded, dogs, bodyguards? As they were for the Russians would The Ochrana be involved? How would he get to the Blue-prints? The ways and means, given his over weaning confidence were to some extent irrelevant. He knew already that he would succeed. Failure was something he did not contemplate. Now all the doubts about the trip to Russia and the Caucasus had been expunged from his consciousness. He had a goal. He was going to Russia and he would come home the conquering hero. He could hardly contain his excitement at the prospect.

His almost hypnotic trance was interrupted by his wife Margaret coming into the room. She said. 'I didn't know you were home. I found Joanne weeping in the kitchen and when I asked her why she was crying she said you had just come home. What did you say to her to put her into that state.? Have you given her notice, is that what it is?'

Sidney looked up from his contemplation and said. 'I don't know what you are talking about. I have said nothing to the girl." However his steady return to reality gave him an inkling of the problem and he added. 'I'll go and see her. She probably thinks I have been rude to her. Young girls like her are very sensitive.'

'Good', said Margaret,"And tell her to pull herself together and to come into the dining room to lay the table for dinner. I am busy writing out the advertisement for the house sale.'

He went into the kitchen leaving Mary in the library.

He found a tearful Joanne at the kitchen table her head on her arms sobbing quietly. Fortunately the cook was not there, being away on an errand for supplies. As they were alone he could safely take Joanne in his arms and reassure her.

"What is the matter? I am sorry, I know it must have seemed to you that I was ignoring you but I have a lot on my mind at the moment. Dry your tears and I promise I will make it up to you. In the next few days Mary will be away in town on business and I will find a way of taking you out for the day."Or perhaps," He lowered his voice and said seductively,"You would prefer to stay in, I will find something for cook to do or give her the day off."

It did not completely cheer Joanne up for the real problem emerged when she said through her sobs and tears,"Mrs. Sawyer says you and Mrs. Reilly are going away and will not be back for some time and that you are selling the house which will mean that we will get our notice. What will become of me? You promised that you would look after me. You said that you would not stay married to Mrs. Reilly for much longer and then we would be together."

Sidney thought immediately that he had to get this situation under his control." Yes. I was going to tell you. I am going away on business but it won't be for very long. Mrs. Reilly wants to close up the house while we are away because she is coming with me so that will mean we won't need you or Mrs. Sawyer for a while. But don't you worry, I will put you in a little place until we come back and I will see to it that you have enough money to be going on with. Now dry your eyes and compose yourself otherwise you are going to give the whole game away." He then embraced her and kissed away the tears in her eyes and said, smiling."You are a silly girl, as if I would let you down. Now off you trot and lay the table for dinner before Mrs. Reilly begins to suspect that something is amiss and comes into the kitchen and catches us. That would really put the fox among the chickens."

That made Joanne give a little laugh and he knew it would. It was his habit to deliberately get his English wrong sometimes. It gave her an opportunity to gently correct him.

"It's not put the fox among the chickens silly, Its put the cat among the pigeons."She found his little linguistic errors endearing. She wanted to mother him so that he got it right next time.

Meanwhile Margaret had stayed in the library and at the desk she was composing the advertisement for the house sale;

That night Sidney could not sleep and in spite of Margaret's drunken snoring to her usual volume he did not vacate his bed to go into the arms of Joanne. His mind was concerned totally with the strategies and tactics he proposed to use when delivering the spoils of his project in Russia. The night passed into the small hours and it was just the time before dawn that Sidney had an epiphany. He had been designing in his mind a way that would enable him to acquire the plans he was sure were part of Emanuel Nobel's work. The obstruction he saw was that once the theft was discovered there would be a hunt and suspicion would inevitably fall on him(he had choreographed the 'burglary', in his imagination to the finest detail). He wouldn't steal the plans. He would photograph them, then their guardians would be unaware that anything at all was untoward. He could settle to sleep now. In the morning he would set about discovering all the possibilities and difficulties involved in photographing documents.

Sidney rose early, showered shaved and performed the rest of his ablutions and dressed in a plain inexpensive suit. It was a suit he had worn when doing business in his workshop at Ozone Preparations. He did not want to give an impression of affluence to whomsoever he might meet this day. He bid goodbye to Margaret and a much subdued Joanne and he left the house earlier than usual after a rushed breakfast saying to Margaret that he would not be back until late and not to wait dinner for him.

Chapter Nine

He once again travelled to The British Museum but all he asked to consult were trade directories. He was searching for a photographer but one out of town. London was a big place but surprisingly it was a place where sometimes everyone knew everyone else. He wanted somewhere where he was not at all known. He found what he was looking for in Brighton, H.T. Edwards Photographer, 10-11 Lewes Road Brighton. He got a cab to Victoria station and caught the 10.30 to Brighton. He hardly noticed the time passing on the train and soon he was asking a cabbie to take him to the address he had found.

The shop of H,T, Edwards was small but his studio seemed well equipped. Sidney explained that he did not want as such any photographs taken, (Edwards' business was taking photographs for visiting cards). He wanted lessons in how to take photographs as per the advertisement in the trade directory he had consulted. Mr. Edwards a portly man of moderate height with ice blue eyes, a round, rosy face with an almost completely bald head and dressed in a jacket and trousers but covered with a light brown overall coat asked Sidney what sort of photographs he wanted to take. Did he want to take portraits or perhaps and here he paused and Sidney immediately understood the reason for his pause, 'life studies?"For, I also offer a very discrete photographic developing and printing service." Mr Edwards said.

Mr. Edwards first thought was that Sidney wanted to take 'studies' of young ladies. Sidney put on his best embarrassed act and said that his intention was to make himself reasonably competent at photographing documents as a means of keeping copies. They were to be large documents of a confidential nature so he imagined that there would be a special technique. He said also that he would like advice on the purchase of a small, portable travelling camera that could be relied on to produce accurate images of the fine print of documents. He wanted too, to discuss a technique for taking photographs using artificial light.

Mr. Edwards saw straightaway the possibility of a profit both from tuition fees and the sale of a camera or cameras and he said," Come back after lunch, that is in around an hour. Usually I have an assistant working for me in the afternoon then I will be able to give you my fullest attention."

Sidney had no inclination to embark on a search for a good restaurant and anyway he had no appetite for a full lunch so he spent the hour in a local hostelry with a hot mutton pie and a pint of bitter and looked forward to learning a new skill,

After lunch Sidney went back to Lewes Street and he was shown into the studio at the back of the shop where Mr. Edwards had set up a large camera with a brown wooden varnished case and brass lens holder on a tripod. The camera had burgundy coloured leather bellows running on two brass rods at each side. Sidney allowed Mr. Edwards to demonstrate the taking of a photograph of a large print of Westminster Cathedral that he hung on a wooden easel propped against the wall opposite.

"This camera." Explained Mr. Edwards,"Takes photographs on a full glass plate measuring 6.1/2' x 8.1/2'He slid a plate out of its light proof holder and fixed it in the back of the camera.' Now I select my aperture for light intensity and adjust the timer on the lens. Because I want all the detail of the print and because we are using natural light from the studio window I have timed it at 1 50th of a sec and the aperture is a 4, the widest, I then measure the distance from the print to the lens of the camera." He then turned to Sidney and indicated that he should perform the operation.

Sidney spent the rest of the afternoon following Mr. Edwards' instruction. And then, his tuition over, Sidney said he would be back the next day and as Mr. Edwards pointed out that the afternoon was best, Sidney said that he would be willing to pay for the whole day if it could be arranged as 'time was of the essence' for him. He said to Mr. Edwards that If he needed an extra fee for employing his assistant all day it would be forth coming. Mr. Edwards agreed and said that he would have the prints of the day's work ready for him in the morning.

Chapter Ten

Sidney returned to London Victoria on the 7.35 from Brighton but he did not go home right away he went to the offices of Ozone Preparations, Imperial Chambers in Holborn and there he consulted the notes that he had taken during the day at the photographers. The session with Mr. Edwards had very much awakened his interest and he saw the potential of making photographic record. He thought that he would let Edwards give him another day of tuition with the large conventional camera and then ask him to demonstrate the technique of using a small camera in artificial light.

Sidney opened the street doors and passed through the front office of Ozone Preparations. Sidney lifted the flap on its polished brown wooden counter behind which were equally polished drawers with their brass handles and brass framed identification labels. Above the drawers there were shelves full of the different preparations the company dispensed.

Sidney then went into the back room where commodities and products were stored in bulk. Small bottles and empty jars, Phials, pill-boxes sachets, scoops and balances for measuring were arranged on tables ready to be used to reduce large wholesale quantities to the excessively profitable smaller quantities that the company sold to its trusting customers.

Seeing the paraphernalia of his company always made him think that the massive fortunes of the Medici family in medieval Italy had been made by mixing herbal compounds to roll into pills for the constipated of Florence, Siena, Pisa, Rome and the towns, villages and other great cities of the time of the Italian Renaissance. At one time he had thought that it was in patent medicines that his fortune lay. As he reflected on this it gave him the idea for his cover in Russia.

In order to keep the damp out of some of the packages he used the patent product 'Vaseline' as a seal. He knew that 'Vaseline' was simply a refined petroleum jelly recovered from the workings of oil wells. If he used his Ozone Preparations credentials he could cover his real activities by presenting himself and his company as in the business of researching the possibility of establishing a Russian version of the product. It would give him a very good excuse for travelling around seeking samples to test. But his 'new' product would need a name. He would give it some thought.

He then went to the large green painted Chubb safe that was kept with its back against the far wall of the store room. He opened it with the large brass key he kept on his key chain. Pushing back the heavy door he took from the safe two very large wads of bank notes. He divided the notes into two bundles one of English denomination and the other Russian rubles and secured them with elastic bands and stuffed them into an inner pocket of his overcoat and the other into the inside pocket of his jacket. They both made visible bulges. He then went back to the other contents of the safe.

He retrieved a substantial leather purse which contained some scores of gold sovereigns wrapped in tubes of brown paper with the white black-printed label on each one of the issuing bank stating, 'Ten Gold Sovereigns'. There were so many that he wondered how he should carry the weight of them. He decided to leave them in the purse and to put that in a canvas satchel normally used for mail. It had a strap that he could put over his shoulder.

Further in the back of the safe was a cloth bundle that had the smell of oil about it. He unwrapped it. It was a small automatic pistol in a holster with a belt along with the Japanese made open razor he had used in Paris. He put the razor in the top pocket of his jacket. The pistol was a pocket Browning automatic of 9mm calibre with a barrel of four or so inches long. It was the one he had bought at C.V. Carter's gunsmiths in Bond Street. With the pistol was a box of twenty five cartridges. He pressed the button on the cross-hatched grip of the pistol and the ammunition magazine clip slipped out to reveal a full charge of six brass cartridges. He slipped the clip back in and it gave a satisfying click and checking to see that the safety was on put it back in the holster.

He had designed the holster and the belt cum strap himself and he had enlisted the leather goods maker Henry Atkins to perform the task of making it. The holster was so made and shaped in soft leather that, held by the attached belt, it fitted against his lower abdomen and so was secreted under the front of his trousers. He had got the idea from an old villain he had met in Paris. He advised him that,"If ever you are being searched for hidden weapons, they will never feel there."

Sidney undid his trousers and placed the holster and pistol over the front of his silk underwear taking the belt round the top of his hips and fastening the buckle at the side. He felt it for comfort and then 'adjusted his dress.' He did this and checked the money in various pockets of his coat and jacket and slung the satchel and strap over his shoulder having put the box of cartridges in with the gold coin.

Suddenly he was startled to see a bright light shining in the window of the front office. He went through and he opened the door to a an officer of the metropolitan police who he recognized as the local policeman. He was holding a lamp that gave out a very bright light that shone in to Sidney's eyes. The policeman greeted him and touching the rim of his helmet said,"Evening sir, I was just doing my rounds when I thought I saw something suspicious and I now realise it was you. I hope I haven't disturbed you?".

"Not at all constable", said Sidney,"I am only too grateful for your vigilance, you never know these days who is lurking about." The policeman said," Just doing my job sir. Good night then sir and don't forget to lock up when you leave." Sidney said cheerfully,"Goodnight constable and thank you again."Ah the British Bobbie," Sidney mused,"The best in the world."

Sidney locked the safe first checking that there was nothing incriminating left in. If anyone else looked in it he didn't want to be compromised even though he would keep the key. If as Melville had said,"They would keep the business ticking over", they would also be into everything and a locked safe would not deter them.

Sidney secured the outside door, carefully, as advised and walked out in to Holborn towards The Circus. The cabs that passed him were taken so he thought he might have a better chance of catching one if he walked towards Smithfield Market and Farringdon Station. To get there quicker he walked down a little alley that led to a paved open space called Saffron Court. It was not lit quite as well as the main street and the permanent swirl of misty smoke that plagued London summer and winter diffused even more the dim yellow light of the single gas lamp that lit the entrance to the alley.

As he walked along the narrow flag-stoned passage he found the satchel's weight was beginning to be uncomfortable and he thought he would be glad to take the weight off his feet in a cab. He did not have too much time to think on that for as he passed along, two burly shapes stepped out of the shadows. In a second they had confronted him, blocking his way. The tallest of them, a man just a bit younger than Sidney, said,"Out for a late constitutional are we governor?" His partner of about the same age was more threatening as he grunted."Ooh aren't you the 'toff' me old chum."

Both of them were shabbily dressed with large flat caps pulled down over their eyes and dirty white mufflers round their necks. They were both holding short bladed knives that with black tape round the handles, looked home-made. The taller one said,"What 'ave you got in the bag me old pal? Lets 'ave a look." When he dragged the satchel off Sidney's shoulder and opened the flap, and picked out one of the brown-paper tubes, he could not believe his eyes."Jesus Christ 'arry we've won the fuckin' first prize 'ere. Its full o' fuckin' sovs. Let's 'ave a look an' see if 'es got more 'on 'im."

At this point Sidney gave one of the best performances of his life. He whimpered like a kicked dog."Please don't hurt me I've got a wife and family." And then he said" Oh dear I want to pee. Oh I am going to pee myself. Please let me make water. If I don't I will wet myself." The two ruffians stopped their searching of him and one said to the other, laughing, "Es so fuckin' scared 'es goin' to fuckin' piss 'iself." The shorter of the two said,"Lerim fuckin' piss 'iself, what do I fuckin' care?." The other said," I don't want 'im pissin' all over me when I've got me 'and in 'is fuckin' trouser pockets. Lerim 'ave a piss. There's nobody abaht. Go on," He said to Sidney, ''ave a piss if yer want one."

They stood back and Sidney unfastened the buttons on his overcoat and opened his trousers and turned from them as if to do a pee. Instead of what they expected to see, Sidney pulled out the Browning automatic pistol and slipped off the safety. With one voice they said"Fuckin' 'ell 'es gorra gun."Yes," said Sidney," And I will use it, have no doubts on that." Covering them both with a gesture of the pistol Sidney said,"Now the satchel please." The short one timidly passed it back. As he took it Sidney said,"Both of you unfasten your trousers and let them drop." They looked at each other. Sidney did not speculate on what was going through their minds. He hadn't the patience, so he said it again but this time in a tone that might have frozen the air in front of his mouth it was so full of slow cold menace."Let your trousers drop. I warn you, I will not ask you a third time."

They both responded to the murderously malevolent tone and unfastened their stained ragged trousers and let them drop to their sockless ankles and their broken, down at heel boots. Neither of them had anything else on under the long laps of their dirty shirts and their emaciated flanks were revealed. They both stank and Sidney recognized the stink, it was of poverty. He had known it himself.'"Now turn round with your hands on your heads and get on your knees."

Unbalanced they dropped down clumsily on to the cold flags, banging their bony knees painfully on the stones." Now let me now give you some advice." Said Sidney. They were facing the wall and Sidney pressed the barrel of his pistol at the back of each of their heads in turn forcing their noses to flatten against the brick work.

"You stay where you are and you don't move. I am going on my way now but if I turn round and see that you have moved in the slightest, I will shoot you and I will aim carefully for your groin, and you can take my word for it I am an excellent shot. Or perhaps I should say for your benefit I shall shoot your worthless balls off. You will stay where you are in this position until I am out of sight and then you will wait for a little longer before you move a muscle. Do you completely understand me? I can assure you I am perfectly serious. Now, drop your knives." They dropped their knives and Sidney picked them up and threw them way down the alley. They clattered on the stones of the alley in the darkness. He repeated but in a louder voice." Do you understand me and say sir?" They both one after the other said meekly,"Yes sir we understand you."

Sidney initially backed away, his trousers still unfastened. He then did something that in its sentimental generosity even surprised him when he thought of it later. For if the moon had been in the right quarter or a West wind had ruffled his hair and irritated him in the slightest he might well have put a bullet in each of their necks with no more thought than he would have had if he had pressed his thumb on an insect. He took two florins from the pocket of his waistcoat and dropped one then another in turn into the coat pockets of their threadbare jackets. From one of their pockets he lifted a crumpled packet of what he saw were the cheapest of cigarettes it was possible to buy. He took a silver vestas match box from his own pocket and one of the cigarettes from the packet and struck a match, and put the cigarette to his lips.

The taste of the smoke as he inhaled was harsh and unpleasant. Sigmund Georgievich Rosenblum, also known as Sidney George Reilly, was nothing if not a mass of contradictions. He scattered the few cigarettes left in the packet all over the flagstones. Then he turned and moved quickly down the alley and into the brighter light of Saffron Hill. He clicked on the safety catch and replaced the pistol in its holster and fastened his trousers. As he did so he thought passersby would think he had come out of the dark alley after relieving himself. He crossed the road into Farringdon Street and within seconds a cab had responded to his wave. He gave the cabbie his address and added Paddington. He did not want any argument this time. He settled back on the leather of his seat and enjoyed the adrenaline still coursing round his body and it making his heart beat faster with the excitement of the episode he had just experienced.

The two footpads were still in the same kneeling position with their trousers down when the policeman who had checked the locks on Sidney's office came upon them, lighting them up with his lamp."'Allo 'Allo what 'ave we 'ere then? What 'ave you two mucky buggers been up to? Get bloody dressed and be on your way before I run you both in for indecency and in future keep it in your trousers and you won't go far wrong.

You pair of dirty little dogs". They pulled up their trousers urgently and tucked in their shirts. Then, asking permission to pick up the scattered cigarettes both slouched away, miserable and ashamed at their humiliation. As they did they shifted the blame for the failure of the 'blague' from one to another. Then, with their bravado returning, vowed what they would do to Sidney if they ever met with him again.

When the cab he had had such a job finding did eventually drop him off at home it was past one o'clock and the house was in darkness, everyone having retired. He let himself in and walked down the hall to the library. Having put down his coat and jacket, he unfastened his trousers again and took off the belt and holster with the gun still in it. He checked that the safety was on and being careful to take his other ' treasures' out of his pockets he locked all with the satchel 'full of sovs' in a cupboard under his desk in the library. He afterwards went into the kitchen and made himself a meal of scrambled eggs on the still glowing coals of Mrs. Sawyer's stove. Then he opened a bottle of Claret and poured himself one glass before carefully replacing the cork. He felt a dynamic within himself that was wanting to move him as the wound up spring of a clock energizes its works.

He went upstairs to bed, undressed and after his ablutions and getting into bed naked he folded back the sheets and tried to wake up his wife with kisses to her neck and the fondling of her breasts. The event in the alley had aroused him as surely as a pornographic picture would have aroused a voyeur and he had to be satisfied. Margaret hardly responded, complaining only half awake that she was tired and had a deal to do the next day. But Sidney was not to be deterred. He persevered and made love to her anally although she was almost asleep so that the next morning when she awoke she thought she had dreamed it. It wasn't the first time he had taken her like that and it wasn't something she particularly disapproved of. In fact given her Roman attitudes to carnality, she saw it, in certain circumstances as,"so much less of a sin."

Chapter Eleven

The following day, again, Sidney rose early and busied himself after his shower, shave and dressing with packing a 'Gladstone Bag'. He included clean shirts, underwear and socks with his leather dressing case. He breakfasted and left quickly. He told Margaret as he left that he would probably stay in Brighton overnight as the business that he had there would keep him very late. It did not escape his notice that his alacrity in leaving left Joanne standing at the door somewhat nonplussed.

Victoria station was full of people coming in from the suburbs for their work in London and his train to Brighton was relatively empty.

Once seated he opened 'The Times' that he had bought at the station but he didn't read it properly. Instead he took out a pencil and began to list in the margin possible names for the mythical product that was going to be his excuse for touring the works and installations of the oil region of Baku.

It did not take him long to come up with a name he thought fitted the bill, 'Vodasalve'. Voda was the Russian for water and water was clear, so was petroleum jelly. Using the word 'salve' as a suffix, he thought was obvious. He felt very satisfied with that. He could relax. He had been so late going to sleep the night before and allied with rising early he felt tired. He let his copy of 'The Times' drop to his feet and drifted into a sleep that he stayed soundly in for the whole journey to Brighton.

Mr. Edwards was waiting for him at his studio with the camera and tripod set up and the prints that he had developed from the work they had done the day before. He carefully pointed to the differences that could be seen in each print and talked of shutter speeds apertures focal lengths and accuracy of focus. He then allowed Sidney to insert the photographic glass plates and showed him again how to set the timings and apertures. He spent the morning practicing these operations until lunchtime. Sidney used lunchtime not only to have a meal but also to find a small hotel off the main thoroughfare. The idea that he was being too cautious did not pass through his mind. He booked in and left his bag in the small sparsely furnished but comfortable room he was allocated. He then went round the corner where a public house, 'The George' recommended by the hotel keeper, served a simple but passable lunch.

After lunch he was back promptly at the studio and he spent the afternoon watching in wonder as the images he had photographed in the morning appeared magically on the glass plates Mr. Edwards chemically washed in the red lit darkroom of his studio. He saw that he had accurately, photographically reproduced the material Mr. Edwards had arranged. With the aid of a magnifying glass it was possible to judge the lines of the prints and the printing on the documents used as subjects in quite fine detail.

Sidney concluded the work of the afternoon by enquiring of Mr. Edwards whether he could spend the next day using a smaller portable camera and a method, if there was one of using artificial light, Mr. Edwards said that he would arrange that certainly for the next day.

Sidney walked back to his hotel and saw that the time was near to seven. The evening was fair with the warmth of an early summer day still in the air. The sea was calm and there were still quite a few people on the beach enjoying what was left of the day. He had not known that Brighton had such an imposing sea-front with its multi-floored apartment houses and hotels looking to the sea. He had heard that Queen Victoria didn't like Brighton. Quite unlike previous Royalty who liked it enough to build their personal palace here. He said good evening to the woman who had taken the place of the hotel keeper and went up to his room. He undressed and put on a light dressing gown with a Japanese motif on it and went to the bathroom with his dressing case where he washed and shaved and splashed himself with cologne. He returned to his room and dressed in a clean white shirt, put his suit back on, changed his socks and gave something of a polish to his shoes and thought he would find himself a quiet little inn or restaurant where he could have dinner.

As he left the hotel the lady at the desk said that there was a night bell for the porter if his intention was to come back late. Sidney walked along the promenade and past the grandiose and eccentric shapes of the architecture of The Prince Regent's Brighton Pavilion and went into the doors of a restaurant that had not only taken the name of the palace, but also used it as an inspiration for its decor. Within a very few minutes, for the restaurant did not seem to have many clients, a waiter came to take his order. Sidney had already decided that the best choice from what seemed a fairly restricted list was fish. He was after all near the coast and surely Brighton had fishermen. He made a simply selection of hors d'oeuvres and asked for sole and a bottle of dry sauternes.

Before the waiter turned to go Sidney asked him to make sure that it was chilled and to bring him a dry sherry as an aperitif. The sherry came and Sidney sipped it and looked around the relatively small space that was the restaurant's dining room. There were about six or eight other diners but the one who took Sidney's eye was a woman sitting a few tables away, by herself and seemingly unaware of him because she was engrossed in the pages of a fashion magazine.

She was well dressed in a fashionable midnight blue dress that came up to a discrete lace collar that almost hid the whole of her neck up to her chin He could see her face in profile and he was struck by the pile of luxuriant red tresses on her head held in by large tortoiseshell comb. She was unmistakable. It was Caroline the woman he had known from The Japanese Embassy. He wondered if she had seen him and was pretending not to have, out of embarrassment or, and here a more disconcerting thought struck him, was she following him?

He decided that what he had to do at least was introduce himself. He got up and walked the few paces to her table. He said as courteously as he could." I hate to dine and drink alone and I wonder if you would like to join me." She looked up, and with what could only be described as genuine surprise she took a sharp intake of breath and said,"Sidney, is it really you?" Sidney said,"May I?" And without waiting for her to reply, sat in the vacant seat at her table and said,"Are you dining alone because if you are I would like to invite you to dine with me?"

"Well, Sidney," She said," what a surprise to meet you. what are you doing in Brighton.""I could ask you the same thing." Said Sidney." That is an easy question for me to answer," Caroline replied." Brighton is my birthplace. What is left of my family lives here, that is to say my aunt, my mother's sister. She is not too well at the moment and I came down from town yesterday to stay with her. She lives quite close to here and she has a friend looking after her this evening so I thought I would treat myself to dinner and who should I bump into? But what about you? What brings you to Brighton. Is it our Electric Railway on stilts or perhaps the fact that we now have mixed bathing in the sea? Or is it that the Spanish have come to Brighton?"

Sidney was non-committal and dismissive, He looked at her lovely face, her beautiful hair and her red mouth smiling revealing her beautiful white teeth.Her light emerald green eyes shone in the candle light. He recalled without any effort the exquisite pleasure of her naked body and the seductive perfume she wore. She was wearing it now. Sidney smiled enigmatically."Oh just a bit of business I have to sort out before I go back to Spain." He remembered having told her that he had been to Spain the last time he had met her at the embassy. Sidney reflected on his tactic to get away from London where he wouldn't be known. There was always the unexpected and there was always coincidence.

When Caroline's order came Sidney told the waiter he would be dining at the same table as the lady and to bring his dinner there. He observed that the waiter had the temerity to raise an eyebrow. Sufficient of an insult as far as Sidney was concerned for him not to get a tip. They settled down to their respective meals and when they had finished Sidney ordered a dessert of strawberries and cream and asked the waiter to serve it with a bottle of champagne. It came in its bucket of ice and Caroline said jokingly," Ah this is real French Champagne. Are you disappointed that they don't have any Russian?" Sidney noted that she had not forgotten that. Sidney sometimes underestimated the effect he had on women. He usually entertained them so effectively they never forgot anything about their meeting with him.

They drank a coffee together and Sidney ordered brandy for both of them. Sidney insisted on paying the bill and Caroline said that when she took the decision to find somewhere for dinner she did not expect to have it bought for her. He picked up his overcoat and hat from the waiter and Caroline was handed her evening cape which Sidney took and draped over Caroline's shoulders."You see", he said, The age of chivalry is not dead."No" she said,"It is kept alive by young knights like you."

As they walked back along the promenade night had fallen and the stars were out in a black sky complimented by the lights of cab, carriage, cart and bicycle traffic passing to and fro with the murmuring sea as a background. Brighton's new Pier. lit from end to end was still thronged with people. For a night-cap they stopped by a small discrete bar that had embellished,polished wooden cubicles in it that were entered by doors that cut them off completely from other clients. Their drinks, two more brandies but this time with soda water, were brought to them by a white-shirted waiter wearing a wrap around black apron.

Caroline talked of her life in Brighton with more familiarity than Sidney remembered from their first meeting. She recounted her life as a girl in Brighton and where she went to school and of her ambitions to study but she had married fairly young to a much older man who had died and left her fairly well-provided for. But widowhood had proved too lonely for her although she did not have any intention of marrying again. She had, she said gone up to London and become involved in what she called 'The Embassy Set'. She enjoyed the company of men of culture and experience; men who had interesting jobs and who travelled. 'Like you I suppose.' She said this as a matter of fact rather than as a congratulation.

She then turned to Sidney and said frankly," You know what I am Sidney, we have met before. I suppose it would be kind to say that I am what in a previous age would have been called a courtesan."She then laughed out loud. '"And there are others who have another name for it that is less complimentary. Perhaps the notorious Mr. Wilde's plays have made my position in society more respectable."Sidney looked at her without saying anything. His expression did not betray the cruelty that lay behind his thought." I hope for your sake that is all you are Caroline because woe betide you if you are not."

Sidney said out loud,"How is your friend from the Russian Embassy. the Russian sailor?" Caroline saw that he was teasing her and said," Well you know what they say, about girls and sailors." Sidney poured the last of the soda water into their glasses and watched it fizz. He asked her for another one of her red-tipped cigarettes and lit it from a match which he took from a holder in the middle of the table and struck on its serrated edge. For a few seconds he was alone with his suspicions. Then he said,"Drink up and I will escort you home."

When they got outside again a cabbie looking for a fare trotted his horse alongside them for a while. Sidney offered to get the cab for her and to take her home but she said that it was not far and that it was easy enough to walk. He dismissed the cabbie with a wave and its red lights moved quickly away. She had taken a cab to the restaurant she said but then it didn't do for a girl to be walking the streets alone, what would people think? It was bad enough she said that she should be eating alone easy prey to be picked up by any strange predatory man. She then added after a pause,"Do you want to come home with me?"

"But what about your aunt?" Said Sidney."Won't she object?"

"My aunt," said Caroline, has taken to her bed and the house is so big I will be able to let you in without her being any the wiser. The maid and the cook don't live in and anyway tomorrow they will not be in until ten and the cleaning lady only comes in the afternoon." She then said with a mischievous laugh while looking out to sea, and signaling with her right hand."The coast is clear. I will take you up to my room and you can stay there until I have said good night to my aunt's companion and seen to it that my aunt is settled and comfortable. Then we can finish our very pleasant evening over another drink and perhaps a game of cards."

She laughed again and with both her hands, she pulled his arm close to her and looked at him and converted her laugh into a smile. She also remembered the pleasure he had so passionately given her. Sidney thought to himself that if there was another motive behind her generous and very tempting offer it was one he would be able to deal with.

They reached the house within a short time passing along a well-lit suburban street but with few people on it. Carriages and cabs trotted by, reins jingling, hooves of horses clip-clopping and red and white lights dancing.

It was quite a large house in its own shrub and tree shrouded, iron fenced garden with a drive big enough to take a carriage. The drive began through large decorated wrought iron gates in between two stone pillars that led up to an imposing front door before which there was a porch illuminated by a hanging lamp. There were lights on down stairs and one lighted window on the first floor at the front."My aunt is in bed but I think her companion is still here I am later than I said I would be." Caroline indicated that they should enter by a door at the side and Sidney said jokingly,"Oh I see I am only worthy of the tradesman's entrance."

"Be careful of the steps in the dark." Caroline said as she took a key from her purse and unlocked the door to the side of the house."The house lighting is being converted to electricity but so far only the main rooms are working".

She went in first and turned up the flame of a lamp that gradually illuminated a scullery with a great brown sink and brass water tap. There was household equipment stowed against the wall, mops and buckets and in the corner a 'copper' boiler with below, its fire door open spilling cold grey ash onto its hearth. Beside it was an empty coal-scuttle. Caroline said,' Wait a moment and I will give us some more light." She went first through a door at the end and reached up and turned up the gas light and as its mantle glowed to bright white light he could see that the door led into a very big kitchen one wall of which was taken up by an enormous black iron stove. There was just the hint of red coals from behind the grill of the fire bars. Around the other walls there were pine cupboards and a large 'welsh' dresser with blue willow pattern plates along the shelves and cups hanging from hooks. In the middle of the room was a grand kitchen table its surface devoid of anything except the impression that it had been carefully cleaned and scrubbed.

Caroline picked up a small oil lamp, struck a match from a box on the dresser, lifted the lamp's glass chimney, lit the wick and holding it by the finger ring before her, she beckoned Sidney to follow her through a door at the other end of the kitchen and up a narrow set of stairs. He stepped up the stairs behind her and in a minute they were both through a door at the top that led onto a spacious landing on one side of which there were four doors. At the far end of the landing was a fifth door in a wall at right angles to the landing. A thin band of light came out from the gap at the bottom of the door. Sidney deduced that that was aunt's bedroom. On the other side of the landing was a substantial mahogany landing banister and a wide carpeted staircase with a banister leading down to a darkened tiled entrance hall and the front door. The door had glass panels in the top of it and he could see the faint glow of the porch light outside. Caroline's lamp was just bright enough to pierce the gloom of the ground floor. As they stood together leaning against the balustrade one of the doors downstairs opened letting into the hall a trapezium of pale but bright yellow electric light. Caroline quickly pushed Sidney against the second door on the landing and unlocked as it was, it opened and let him in just out of the light from downstairs.

Sidney moved further into the unlit room and noticed the smell of Caroline's perfume. He guessed that he was in her bedroom. Outside on the landing he heard her say the name of someone but could not make it out precisely. There was an almost inaudible cry, at least to his ears, from downstairs and then he heard louder, a woman's voice say,"Oh Mrs. Belvedere is that you? You did give me a fright". It was the first time that Sidney had heard Caroline's family name. He then heard Caroline say," I am sorry to startle you Mrs. Sheppard. I came in through the scullery entrance and up the servant's stairs. I hope I have not kept you by coming in so late.'" She then said,"No Mrs. Sheppard you needn't come up, I will come down and then you can go home and I will see that aunty is settled for her night's sleep. And I will lock the doors."

Sidney found his way to the bed and sat down to wait for Caroline to come in and turn on the light. He saw that the mantle of the gaslight had been converted to an electric lamp holder with a glass ampoule in it so it only needed turning on but then he thought that Mrs. Sheppard might see it as she left the house. He lay back on the down pillows of Caroline's bed and kicked off his elastic sided boots. They clumped on the floor making a sound louder than he expected but were cushioned by the thick carpet that covered the floor. Fumes of heady perfume, a good dinner and two brandies induced in him a light doze.

He was gently wakened by Caroline shaking his shoulder and whispering,"Sidney, Sidney, wake up." He awoke to see her standing by the side of her bed. The new electric light was shining on the ceiling. She said,"You didn't want to sleep did you?" He sat up saying,"Of course not I simply closed my eyes for a few minutes, Has Mrs. Sheppard gone? Is your aunt asleep?" Caroline smiled and said,"Mrs. Sheppard went 45 minutes ago and my aunt has been snoring peacefully for the last 30 minutes,"

Sidney sleepily and sheepishly put his legs over the side of the bed and sat up. Caroline had brought a bottle of wine and two glasses on a tray. She put the tray on a small table and sat on the bed next to him. He got up and picked up the table with the tray on it and carried it away from the bed. He turned the light down low and he came back and knelt before her burying his face in her lap. As she opened her legs to accommodate him and heard him say, his voice muffled by her dress."I don't want another drink, I want you." As he lifted her skirts and dress up past her white stockinged thighs to her hips and lace trimmed knickers and put his face between her legs she lay back on the cover of the bed, pressing his head to her with both her hands. Sidney was aroused by the musky slightly acrid odour of Caroline's pudenda. He eased aside the perspiration dampened gusset of Caroline' underwear and put his tongue in the division of her sex. Caroline put her head back on her pillow, closed her eyes and opened her mouth to show her white teeth and her red lips. She moaned with the exquisite pleasure of his cunniligual kiss.

There was no urgent stripping off as had happened the last time they had been together. Instead, Sidney got up and lay beside her and they slowly undressed each other kissing and caressing as they did so. When he had undressed her to her plain white stockings and he was naked he lay with her and saw her red hair like a pool of dark water, rust red about her head. He still had his doubts, but then he thought, he suspected everyone and trusted no one so really what difference did it make that he was to go to bed with her. The only thing that niggled at the back of his mind was that he found her attractive and enjoyed being with her very much and his desire for her was very strong.

Their lovemaking combined a reserve borne out of their only recent acquaintance with measures of a tenderness inspired by their brief knowledge of each other. They enjoyed each other for a long time and were only interrupted by hearing the bell Caroline's aunt kept at her bedside that she used to call her niece. Caroline got up and put a pink chrysanthemum decorated brocade dressing gown over her nakedness and went to see what her aunt wanted.

Caroline was gone a little while but when she did come back she was carrying another tray with this time hot buttered toasts with roundels of Pate de Foie de canard on them. They ate this in bed kissing the crumbs of toast from each other's mouths and drinking the sweet white wine Caroline had brought up at first that Sidney now had a thirst for. Their jointly enjoyed snack was for them a restorative and they turned from it back to their desire. Sidney had his fingers in Caroline's sex and was pressing her clitoris with his thumb, and he was kissing and nuzzling the nipples of Caroline's breasts. Then he mumbled into the division between them,"What did your aunt want?" Caroline managed to say, pausing between breaths of orgasmic ecstasy,"Her pot de chambre."

They slept until Caroline's aunt rang her bell again. It was her usual call for her breakfast Caroline said. It was 6.30. Caroline left Sidney sleeping and went downstairs where she made tea in the kitchen and took it up to her aunt with a plateful of plain biscuits that was all her aunt ever had for breakfast. She went back down stairs and made coffee in a large spouted silver pot with an ebony handle. She made toast against a gas fire in the kitchen and boiled four eggs. She put on a large wooden silver trimmed breakfast tray, blue willow pattern cups, saucers. Egg cups and plates, a milk jug and sugar bowl and pats of butter in a dish and a pot of home- made strawberry jam. Which she brought upstairs.

She carried the tray to the side of the bed and Sidney drowsily pushed himself up to the brass bars at the top of the bed. Caroline put the tray over Sidney's middle and got back into bed beside him being careful not to upset the crowded tray. They spent the next twenty minutes buttering hot toast, munching it with spoons full of soft-boiled eggs and in Caroline's case drinking cups of sweet milky coffee. Sidney preferred his coffee black. They both ate with gusto, their appetites motivated by the night of passion they had just spent together.

After their shared breakfast, Sidney took the tray and set it down at the side of the bed and he turned to Caroline again. They embraced and gently and feelingly made love both coming to climax at the same time. Sidney stayed on Caroline and still connected to her, he rested his head on her breast and she gently stroked his hair and head. They both went back into a light sleep. It was Caroline who woke first and she woke Sidney by telling him that it was nine 0' clock. He kissed her on the lips and got out of bed without a pause.

She said jokingly,"I can offer you more than you did me in 'your rooms'. I have a bathroom."

The bathroom was in Caroline's dressing room which was off the bedroom."What I can't offer you is a razor or any clean clothes. At one time I could have. I kept my late husband's clothes and things for a long time but I threw them out some time ago. He was about your build too."

Sidney went to the top pocket of his jacket which he had hung over a chair. He took out his Japanese open razor with a flourish."I always come prepared."Goodness," Caroline said,"Do you carry a razor in your pocket?"Only for old time's sake." he said, cheekily. It was as well that she was unaware of what it had once been used for.

Sidney walked naked into Caroline's bathroom and ran a shallow bath of hot water. He bathed standing using her fragrant soaps and when he got out of the bath he stood still dripping in front of the mirror over a wash basin that had coloured spring flowers fired into the glaze. He lathered his face with the same soaps and shaved as skillfully as always. When he had finished he rinsed his face, dried himself and his hair on one of her capacious towels and lifting the mahogany seat cover,sat down on the WC. Its long pipe on the wall connected it to a wooden cistern above. The pedestal porcelain was also ornamented with painted coloured spring flowers fired into the glaze. Next to the W.C. similarly decorated was a plumbed in bidet. It raised a mild curiosity in him,"Unusual for an English bathroom." He thought.

He had not cared to lock the door and she came into her bathroom as naked as him and ran her bath. The delight that they had shared together could have carried on through the simplicity of this act of complete intimacy. Sidney did not give it a second thought and grasped the porcelain 'pull', decorated like the lavatory bowl and yanked the chain it was attached to. Water rushed from the cistern above down the pipe and swirled in a torrent around the gaily flower decked porcelain. He stood and washed his hands in front of the decorated wash-basin and through the mirror above it could see the reflection of Caroline naked standing in the bath like a painting by Alma-Tedema he had once seen in a magazine and not forgotten.

Having finished his ablutions Sidney left Caroline to complete her bathing and he went back into the bedroom to dress. Ordinarily Caroline would have spent a deal of time at her toilette but she was aware that he would have to go and that she would have to let him out of the house with a degree of discretion. He was aware of this too. It was rapidly approaching the time when the maid and cook usually arrived. She put his mind at rest on this point by saying that they rarely arrived on time. 'Neither she nor her aunt were particularly strict employers,' she said.

Caroline put on a her basic underwear and once more donned her dressing gown. He drew her to him and said,'I will kiss you here and say goodbye.' She was gratified that he had not attempted to give her 'a present'. He had the same feelings and had thought that she would have been disastrously insulted had he behaved the way he did on their first meeting. This meeting had not been a 'business' arrangement. Sidney had an acquired chivalry. He then lied to her. 'I am going to Spain in a few days so I don't expect I will see you again for a little time' In fact he did not know how long he would be in Russia. It might be weeks but it could be months even a year.

Having said this to her he lied again and said; 'I will keep in touch with you if you will in the first instance write to me at my company's address. You have my card.' She nodded. He did not know if in saying the things he did he was letting her down gently or merely covering his tracks. There was a deal of him wishing that he was able to see her again and soon. The sex with her had been superlative But the other part of him thought of what now he saw as his mission. He said, striking a thespian pose,"As the best Englishmen say when leaving their loved ones ' Duty Calls'. She said quietly, 'I quite understand but I want you to know Sidney that the short times we have spent together have so far been so memorable.'

Caroline was capable of much and part of that was a seeming sincerity. Sidney for his part, if he could be said to experience the normal range of human emotions found himself uneasy at Caroline's declaration. Apart from anything else he felt a hint of obligation, a dash of the beginning of commitment and a revival of the memory of the pleasures of the night just passed. This caused him to wonder if he would have other opportunities of the same quality. He dismissed the thoughts without any effort with an observation to himself he had often made, 'One woman is just like another.' He did not make Caroline at all aware of these reservations. As she was about to lead him down the stairs they had come up the night before he embraced her and kissed her as a lover would.

They reached the bottom of the narrow stairs in 'indian file' and passed through the daylight lit kitchen with the sun shining on the copper pans he could see now hanging from hooks and the scullery, cheerless the night before seemed ready for the industry 'Mrs. Mop' would put it to. Caroline opened the scullery door to what was, in the summer sunlight almost a park of a garden. There were flowers in borders and flowering shrubs, a vegetable garden to the back and in the middle of that stood the person she must have forgotten about, the gardener. He was an old man in something of his sixties There was no use in any more subterfuge. Caroline said, "I'm afraid our secret is out." The gardener touched his forelock and said 'G'd Mornin' Mrs Belvedere.' Caroline returned his greeting and kissed Sidney goodbye as if he was a husband departing to catch his train to the city.

Sidney walked down the drive through the dappled shadows cast by the trees that lined its edge. When he got to the pillared iron gate he opened it and turned to look up the drive towards the house.

Caroline was still at the top of the small flight of steps that led to the scullery. She was shading her eyes with one hand and waving to him with the other. Caroline stood on the steps and watched Sidney pass completely out of sight, then with a nod of her head in the direction of the gardener she indicated that he should follow Sidney. He immediately set down the hoe he had been using and went off down the drive. She then turned and went back into the house, through the scullery into the kitchen and then out into the ground floor of the house.

She walked along the hall and into the oak paneled library. She moved across to the bookcase beside a large desk that was against the window and touched the spines of three volumes of English Common Law on the middle shelf. All three spines opened on a hinge to reveal the door of a small polished wood cabinet. She took a key from a pocket in her dressing gown and opened the cabinet door. Inside on a brass hook was the mouth piece and listening piece of a telephone. On the box they and their wires were attached to, there was a winding handle. She gave this about half a dozen quick turns and the telephone rang its bell on each turn. She held the mouth piece in her right hand and put it to her mouth and held the ear piece to her left ear with her left hand. In a few seconds she heard in her ear the crackle of a voice. She spoke into the mouth piece in German, 'Sidney Reilly, British Special Branch informer and agent, alias Sigmund Georgievich Rosenblum, Nationality Russian, posing as Businessman, Ozone Preparations. Next destination believed to be Spain where he is to investigate and report on Anarchist Movement. Has been in Brighton on Business but real reason unknown. Have subject under observation. Have made contact. A low level agent not considered to be high priority. Please advise on action to be taken.'

Chapter Twelve

Sidney stepped out into Brighton's already quite crowded suburban streets. Cabs and carriages passed to and fro. House maids with baskets hurried on their errands and governesses wheeled their perambulators along the pavements. There were already young and old heading for the beach and promenade. Little boys in sailor suits holding a guardian's hand with one hand and a bucket and spade with the other, half ran along the flagstones with their little sisters who were in frilly short dresses with ribbons in their fair curls. Old gentlemen in white linen jackets, watch chains in their waistcoats were doffing their panama hats in polite greeting to the young ladies who were tapping the stones with the sounds of the leather of the soles and heels of their fashionable high button boots. They had parasols covering their frivolously hatted, piled up hair. They held their parasols over their slim lace trimmed shoulders as the polite gentle men excused themselves as they passed.

Sidney came to the promenade with its railings and the sea beyond. Momentarily he wondered whether he should turn right or left but before he could decide a cab stopped by him at the curb and the cabbie touted for a fare. Sidney chose to get a cab rather than asking the way to Mr. Edward's studio and walking. The cabbie knew the way and it was not far for within a few minutes Sidney was being set down outside the shop. Sidney paid the cabbie the few pence of the fare and entered the shop. Mr. Edwards was at the counter and he said when Sidney came in, 'I was beginning to think that you weren't coming, Mr. Parker. However now you are here we can make a start right away.'

Mr. Edwards gestured to Sidney to follow him and they both entered the studio where once again the easel was set up against the wall but this time the broad sheet pages of 'The Times' newspaper were pinned to a board on it. 'I thought that as you want to photograph documents with small print this would do very well. We will use the standard camera first we have so far used but I have obtained a portable cameras as an example of what you have requested.' Mr. Edwards pointed to a small rectangular case on a shelf behind the easel. It was about five inches by six or seven inches and around two inches thick. Its case was of dark brown polished leather. Sidney said, 'I don't want to sound impatient, but do you think we could get right on with working with the portable camera? I don't think I will be able to spare another day to come to Brighton for more tuition."

Mr. Edwards looked a little disappointed that Sidney would not be coming again for the fees he was paying were very welcome. Trade was dropping off as more and more of the holidaymakers coming to Brighton were 'snapping' themselves and their families with their own personal Kodaks. The only thing he could rely on was the money he got from developing and printing the photos 'snapped'.

'If you wish., you, as they say are paying the piper…' Mr. Edwards said. As he did this he took the portable camera out of its case, pressed a small button on its body and its bellows concertinaed open. There was a calibrated brass ring around a lens at the end of its stiff leather folds. 'This camera,' said Mr. Edwards, 'is at this moment quite a rarity in England. It is a Nydia by Newman and Guardia. It is a folding tapered pocket camera with a 240mm or 6.3 lens with a shutter speed of ½ to 1/100th of a second. If I could suggest, this will be perfect for the purpose you have for it. The Nydia does not tilt but as you can see it is small; one of your important criteria. That disadvantage can be overcome by attaching a cramp to the camera like so and not only will it tilt, it will also be kept rigid when operating, essential as you will be using a slow shutter speed and artificial light.

Sidney thought that he had understood all that. Mr. Edwards then set up the camera screwing the cramp to the table. He then measured with a tape five feet from the camera lens to the subject of the photograph, The Times newspaper on the easel. After that he placed a black painted hand lamp on the table and opened the back and with a match lit the wick of a small spirit lamp behind the convex magnifying glass set in the front of the lamp. He then closed the back of the lamp and fastened it with a hook. He blacked out the studio completely and opened the shutter of the hand lamp. A very bright light lit up the room with the main luminosity illuminating the news paper brilliantly. Mr. Edwards then said, as he touched the knurled timer and turned the brass focusing ring,' I am now going to set the camera to its slowest speed, half a second, the aperture of the lens to 4 and with the special film I have loaded it with and the fact that it is fixed rigid and unmoving, add to that the bright light, and I will be able to guarantee that you will have a perfect photographic reproduction of the subject.

The rest of the morning was spent in Sidney practicing the complete operation, the most difficult part being loading and unloading the camera using the black bag. It gave him an idea of the problems someone like Houdini might experience escaping from a locked mail-bag. At one point Sidney asked to have the special film explained to him. Mr. Edwards said that he could make up the special film which was his preparation of emulsion and chemicals that he coated the roll with and it made the film 'fast' so that the film worked at slow shutter speeds and wide apertures in artificial light. He said that he would give Sidney enough reels for the job he wanted to do so he would set about preparing them..' Of course the film would be a little expensive and because the materials were of an organic nature it would be wise to use them within a few months of their manufacture otherwise the film surface would begin to decay.' He then said that Sidney would also have to buy the hand-lamp as well.

Sidney asked if they could work through lunchtime so that film could be processed and the work of the day developed and printed. 'Of course I will pay extra', Sidney said.

Meanwhile the gardener had returned to Caroline's house and had to report that he had been unable to follow Sidney as he had taken a cab. Caroline interviewed him in the library. Again she spoke in German. She spoke with authority and vehemence. 'Get to the cab ranks. Give them a description and if anyone recognizes your description find out what address he was taken to. Don't come back until you have some positive information.'

She then went up to her aunt's room. The old lady was sitting up in bed and Caroline told her that she would be going back to London for a day or so but Mrs. Sheppard would see to her needs. Caroline kissed her on the cheek and asked her if she wanted anything then. The old lady smiled and said that Caroline was too good to her, adding"You have your own business to see to. Don't worry about me. I will be alright."

Caroline went back to her room to dress. She left the house to catch the train to London. Once there she got a cab to an address in Hackney. She climbed stairs to a first floor flat, She knocked on the door and was let in by a broad shouldered man with a scarred face. Once in she passed down a corridor to a door that had flashes of blue light coming from under the gap near the floor. She entered without knocking.

In the room there was a handsome, mature man in his forties with greying hair. He was sitting at a table. He had earphones on and was, with the two fingers and a thumb together of his right hand, as if picking up a pinch of salt tapping out a bleeping noise on a small black knobbed brass contraption. To the left of him was a strange apparatus taking up most of the space on the table top. On a rectangular wooden base were fixed, on brass stands two thick brass rods with balls on the end of each rod. They were in opposition to each other. The brass balls, each about six inches in diameter were fixed around one to two inches apart. Behind on the same plinth was a two feet by approximately eight inch cylinder with corrugations that were varnished shiny toffee brown. Each time the black knobbed device was tapped a spark of miniature electric blue lightning crackled across the gap between the two brass balls. The equipment which had dials that twitched, vibrated and oscillated was giving out a low hum. It was an electric radio telegraph transmitter and the man was sending off a signal using a morse code key.

Caroline stood to the side of him and touched him behind the ear. He said, 'Later for that mein liblich, you are distracting me. Read the message from HQ. We are to concentrate on discovering Chamberlain's secret intentions regarding the Transval and the Boers. Then we are to report direct to Von Bulow MOST URGENT. About Reilly? Well it says that it is doubtful that he is going to Spain, more likely Russia. There is also a reference to your work at the Japanese Embassy. it seems that there are more diplomatic moves a foot for some sort of alliance between Japan and Britain. You are to concentrate on finding out as much as possible on that, especially if, as is rumoured, it has a naval dimension. Your Russian contact might be useful there. More hard work for you my sweet.' He said this last as if putting the words 'Hard Work' in parenthesis.

Caroline frowned and said, 'What about Reilly? I don't think he's a risk for us do you? If he is going to Russia he won't be cutting across our work will he?

He said." No you are right it might be that what he is up to could well be useful to us. I'll get our people in St. Petersburg and Moscow to keep a watch on him when he pops up which I have no doubt he will. The important thing is that your sprat to catch a mackerel ruse worked. We have information that he reported your 'Port Arthur' observation to Special Branch so we now know definitely who he is and who he is working for"

Caroline was relieved, against her better 'professional ' judgment she had grown to quite like Sidney and she wished the situation of their association could have been different. She stroked the head of her accomplice and he shook it and tutted irritably trying to concentrate on the dots and dashes now coming through his head phones and said 'Caroline, behave yourself.'

He was Herr Karl Frederick Mueller Deputy Head of Germany's Secret Services in England.

Mr. Edwards had made up six rolls of film and he put them in a cardboard shoe box with the Nydia camera, its cramp and the hand lamp and black velvet bag. Sidney then asked Mr. Edwards how much he was owed. Edwards took a piece of scrap paper and with a pencil scribbled down a set of calculations. He stopped occasionally to lick his pencil and to add up. Eventually he said, ' With everything, tuition, camera hire, printing and developing facilities etc. film stock and sale of equipment that will be 10 guineas.' Mr. Edwards recognized that Sidney saw he was being over-charged and quickly added, 'Of course I offer a 5% discount for cash.'

Sidney passed over the money and picked up his box and as he turned to go Mr. Edwards said,"Don't forget, one fiftieth of a second at aperture four approx five feet from the subject and supplement the light of the lamp if you can."

Sidney left the studio satisfied that he had learned another skill. He went back to his hotel and collected his bag and paid his bill and made his way to the station feeling that the walk would do him good and enable him to collect his thoughts. He thought much about Caroline and if he would see her again. She did seem to turn up quite unexpectedly.

He came out of Victoria station and he could not get a cab so he did what he rarely did and got on a horse tram which took him through Sloane Square to Knightsbridge. He went up to the top deck where he lit another of Caroline's cigarettes. He was beginning to get a taste for the brand. He got off at Kensington High Street and managed to find himself a cab to Paddington and on to Westbourne Terrace. He was glad to get off the Horse tram. He did not care for public transport. It brought him too close to his fellow man; particularly his fellow working man. He never travelled on the Underground.

Chapter Thirteen

When Sidney arrived home the household of Westbourne Terrace was in something of a crisis. Margaret welcomed him at the door with the news of it. She had been in the middle of packing when suddenly Joanne said she felt sick. She was so sick that she wanted to go home. She could not be persuaded to stay at the house and go to bed. She insisted on going home to her mother who lived on the other side of the River at Camberwell. Margaret had asked Mrs. Sawyer to put Joanne on a horse tram with money for a cab if she couldn't get all the way on it but had no idea when she would be coming back. Margaret cried out almost in anguish,"What on earth am I going to do?"

Sidney had just a frisson of concern at the news. He had not taken too much care when with Joanne and it occurred to him that Joanne's 'sickness' might have a cause that could be just a little inconvenient. He then began to hatch a simple plan that would take him out of things a little earlier than originally intended. He would depart London for the journey to France first and leave Margaret to close up the house. He would meet her at Newhaven. That would be his contingency plan. For the moment his primary concern was the other matter that Margaret had referred to and that was that the courier had brought the material for the Russian venture.

After freshening himself up and drinking a cup of coffee he took the parcel of sealed papers the courier had delivered into the library and put it on the desk with his box of photographic gear. Margaret put her head around the door and asked again what she was going to do. Sidney dismissed her worries and said that he would make his own arrangements so that would ease things as for the rest he said.' We have moved before and then had to take furniture. At least we are not having to do that and only have to take our own clothes.' That seemed to placate her a little. He called after her,' I only want a snack meal so don't go to the trouble of setting the table.' He then went back to the package.

He was most interested in the documents that Melville had promised would give him a new identity. He turned out the whole contents and found what he was looking for in a folder the type of which he had seen before containing legal documents. It was wrapped round with red tape and sealed with red sealing wax. The seal on it was that used by the Foreign Office. He broke the seal and looked at the details that would make him a new person. There were certificates of birth, death certificates of fictitious parents, marriage certificates in his new name Sidney Callaghan Reilly.

He had been born he observed in Ireland and there were personal letters and all the papers that the ordinary but genuine individual collects in a lifetime. He had relatives and friends he had of course never heard of before. He then looked at the single sheet of paper that would ensure his safe passage across Russia, his passport. It was an impressive document with the Royal Coat of Arms and copperplate writing that talked of 'Her Britannic Majesty' and 'Without let or hindrance'. Margaret did not have a passport of her own but was officially included on his. There were other papers that he would have to give himself time to read, letters of introduction and headed letters that hinted at the business he was supposed to be going to Russia for.

Sidney looked through all the papers again and found an envelope with the details of their through rail tickets from Paris to Moscow and London to Paris via Newhaven. Sidney decided there and then that he would alter the itinerary that Melville's office had organized for them. First of all he would stay in Paris for a few days. He pretended to himself that it would be a short holiday for Margaret but really it was for himself to renew his acquaintance with the city. Paris was a city that you did not forget and a number of things had happened since his rather speedy exit from that city and that country it was the capital of. There had been the Paris Exhibition and The Eiffel Tower."We must see that", he said to himself. He had also to make a rendezvous at the Japanese Embassy to meet with the intelligence agent Melville had said he should.

The other alteration he would make he thought was that he would not journey initially to Moscow but go first to St. Petersburg. He was concerned that others might have got hold of the information relating to him. It just might confuse the issue enough for him to make his way to the Caucasas without anyone else being on his tracks. He had also decided that he would leave Margaret in St. Petersburg. She would be a hindrance. He wouldn't tell her that she was to stay in St. Petersburg until they got there.

Sidney sorted out the large quantity of the papers that there were and went to the back of the room and brought out a big brown leather brief case that had a brass lock on it. That would do to carry everything. The next thing to look at was the financial situation. Melville had been as good as his word and there was a green deposit book in his name stamped with the double eagle emblem in gold of The Russo-Asiatic bank in Moscow. Melville had been very generous. This job must be important. Wait until he got, in the diplomatic bag from Moscow more than he had asked for. Not just a collection of statistics but the secret blueprints of new marine engine designs.

He had also his own money brought from the office, the sovereigns, always negotiable wherever you went in the world and the ruble notes. They were of course counterfeit but their forgers had made sure that they could be presented by testing a quantity with a bank in Zurich. They had been accepted as completely genuine. The printers had done a good job. But then they would have wouldn't they? The plates had been stolen from The Imperial Russian mint. There was not enough room in his lockable cupboard for the brief case and the box he had brought from Brighton so he put the brief case in and took the box with him when he went to bed. in the meantime he locked the library and went into the kitchen for the soup and sandwich he usually had when he only wanted a snack.

Margaret was in the kitchen with the cook, Mrs. Sawyer, and he heard just the tail-end of their conversation and if he wasn't mistaken Mrs. Sawyer deliberately raised her voice when she saw him enter." The girl's not been well for a few days and I've not been able to get out of her what was wrong. I know she has been very poorly lately and being sick and all." They were obviously talking about Joanne. Sidney cut across it and said to Mrs. Sawyer,"You know that madam and myself are embarking on a business trip in a short time. We shall be leaving the house but we might be able to arrange for the next tenants to keep you and Joanne on."Mrs. Sawyer then said. 'That is very kind of you sir but when I was told of the new arrangements I decided to find myself a new position and as another household had already offered me a situation I decided to accept that. So I will be seeking a notice and if I may make so bold, references from you sir and if possible right away." Margaret interjected immediately. 'You will be staying until we leave won't you Mrs. Sawyer? You won't be leaving us in the lurch will you? Mrs. Sawyer thought but didn't say it 'Oh no like you were going to leave me.' Out loud she said, 'No Mrs. Reilly 'Mrs. Sawyer said, taking advantage of the new conditions to be sarcastic and impertinent. 'I don't have a reputation for letting my employers down when I have given my word.' She stressed the first person singular.

Sidney indicated to Margaret that he wanted to talk to her alone and they left Mrs. Sawyer to prepare the simple meal that Sidney had asked for.

When they were in the hall Sidney told Margaret that he had to leave a few days earlier and so he would meet her in Newhaven prior to getting the ferry for France. Margaret protested initially but when Sidney said that he would handle the arrangements for luggage and that the office would handle the rest, getting a tenant or even a buyer for the house including furniture, fixtures and fittings, she was more accepting of his declaration. He also reminded her that she had fixed everything up when she had disposed of the house at Kingston and that had involved the sale and the removal of all the furniture. Margaret did not raise any serious objections. Her desire to get away was still her prime motivation in all the decisions she was taking.

Sidney sat alone and ate a little of his meal.Margaret had already eaten. Mrs. Sawyer hovered around to tell him that she wouldn't be staying that night but would be back in time for breakfast. Sidney was pre-occupied and mumbled that he would see her in the morning and with that she went.

He then went back to the library for a short time and took the camera and film material out of the cardboard box and put it in the satchel that had held 'the sovs' carefully packing the space around with old newspaper. The camera and what he was to do with it had begun to obsess him. Most of that evening both he and Margaret spent packing their respective luggage.

Sidney had many suits, shirts and accessories but then there were plenty of heavy leather luggage cases with great double straps to put his effects in and anyway someone else would be carrying them. He advised Margaret not to take time deciding what she would take but just to put everything in cases and trunks. The carter that he would arrange would see that it was labeled and delivered to the station and on to the train. Mary was pleased with that. One of the benefits of their new found affluence had been that she had indulged her passion for shopping and either buying clothes or having them made. She had not wanted to leave anything behind.

Sidney left Margaret to her sorting, folding and packing and he left the bedroom with its open drawers, open cupboard doors and open wardrobes and went once more in to the library where he emptied his desk of all his papers. There wasn't much of any importance to collect together as he, as a matter of course did not keep any material from his 'office' affairs that might compromise him. He either destroyed it himself or left it at 'the office' for it to be filed or disposed of. Most of the stuff related to his business, Ozone Preparations. It consisted of all the paperwork of an average business enterprise and in the ordinary scheme of things it should have been kept for auditors and accountants not least for taxation purposes. Sidney never bothered with all that formality and he didn't call upon anyone else to do so. There was never any occasion to. His special situation at 'the office' seemed to belie any consideration of it. If he gave any thought to it at all he imagined that was the reason his business functioned in the way it did.

He gathered up all the papers in bags and sacks he got from the kitchen and in a couple of journies took it in to the garden and made a bonfire. When the pile was well alight he stood before it, his front and face demonically lit by the multi coloured flames of bookbinding glue, carbon papers and account books and watched a thick column of smoke go straight up in to the black star-spangled sky of a windless summer night.

That same night Sidney was untypically troubled by minor pangs of conscience and he peevishly lamented that it was not possible to consign everything that was surplus to requirements, inconvenient and useless, to the consuming flames of a bonfire. At the same time he cursed himself for not finding out earlier about Joanne's condition. He could have so easily mixed something up for her so that her next visit to the lavatory would have seen her problem got rid of.

Joanne had been a virgin and typically naïve before Sidney had pressed his attentions on her. She had been reluctant at first, then hesitant, then reassured by his charm. Afterwards drawn by the undeniable magnetism of his personality. This was allied with her own awakening desires. It had started with stolen kisses and after led on to profuse but tactical apologies from Sidney for his presumption but it had ended with Joanne realizing with mounting horror that there was a connection between Sidney's uncontrolled love-making, her passionate and totally uninhibited acceptance of it and participation in it and the unexpected but complete cessation of her' monthlies' She had begun to feel sick in the morning and had to vomit into her chamber pot even before getting out of bed.

Frequent visits over some few weeks from the kitchen to the outside privy to be sick plus the cheerful mood that she usually began the day with not being forthcoming caused Mrs. Sawyer to be the first to notice that Joanne was not quite herself. Mrs. Sawyer was in a good position to observe and deduce what condition Joanne was in. She was the mother of six children. It should have been eight but two had died in childhood.' I know what ails you my girl and it is something that it will take time to cure but it will in its own time, you mark my words. Now what you need to do is go back to your folks with your young man and start sorting out a wedding double quick if you don't want it born in the vestry.'

Joanne gave Sidney the benefit of an absolutely undeserved loyalty. She did not betray to Mrs. Sawyer or Mrs. Reilly for that matter, that he was the father. Things did not improve and while Sidney was in Brighton the situation had come to a head and

Joanne cried to go home. Margaret had given Mrs. Sawyer five shillings to put her on the tram and Mrs. Sawyer had said goodbye, repeating the advice she had already given.

On the tram, before it had taken her very far, Joanne was sick and some of the other passengers were uncharitable enough to accuse her of being drunk. She had to get off and she didn't quite know where she was. She walked for a long way not feeling very well at all and she was sick again, this time in the gutter. Eventually she came upon a place she recognized, Piccadilly Circus and there she got on another tram and that took her through Trafalgar Square to Charing Cross. She was able to get a train then across the river to Waterloo and to Camberwell Gate Station and from there she was able to walk the short distance to the house in Cancel Street where Joanne's family, the Gallaghers lived.

Joanne went in through the front door of her Mother's house which was straight off the street. It was one of a long terrace. It had one small room on the ground floor and one above. Behind the house was a small yard with a brick outbuilding with a sloping slated roof that was an earth closet. There was a bucket of water against the wall of the closet used for washing and the collection of drinking water fetched from the standpipe at the end of the terrace that served the whole street. The houses on the other side of the street were the same. The door was never locked.

Her mother was sitting in front of the cold ashes of the fireplace nursing the youngest of the eight children she had given birth to. The child in her arms, a little girl was about six months old. Joanne was the eldest of the four surviving children. They had lost a little two year old brother to typhoid fever only the year before. And three others had died, within a few months of their birth, of diphtheria measles and whooping cough.

The room that Joanne walked into had bare floorboards, a cheap deal table with nothing on it except a half eaten loaf of bread, the knife that had cut it, a saucer with a scrap of what looked like margarine smeared on it and a cracked tea mug with an assortment of empty jam tins and jam jars around. There was evidence of candle on the mantel piece; smudges of candle wax with black wicks in the middle and ovoid carbon marks on the wall that the smoke of their flames had left.

The only chair in the room was the one her mother was sitting on. The room was prematurely dark because the houses on the other side of the street had already cut off the setting sun. What light there was came from the one window. Joanne's mother was a woman in her late thirties but multiple child bearing under the expected physical strains plus the added strains of extreme poverty, had made her look twice that.

Joanne's mother was surprised if not shocked to see her. The first thing she said was, 'What are you doing home? Oh dear you haven't got the sack have you.' There was no disaster bigger, than having another mouth to feed. Joanne said nothing but sat down in a heap in the alcove on the other side of the fireplace and covering her face with her hands she sobbed only interrupting her sobs from time to time by saying as she rocked from side to side. 'Oh Mother what am I going to do, what am I going to do.'

Mrs. Gallagher guessed immediately what the matter was when Joanne got up abruptly and dashed into the yard. She could hear the choking sounds of Joanne vomiting in the earth closet. When Joanne came back in wiping her mouth and wiping away tears even more exaggerated by her being sick, Mrs.Gallagher said without a pause, 'You've got yourself caught 'aven't you, you silly little bugger, well, who's the father because 'e'll make an honest woman of you or I'll know the reason why."

It wasn't as simple as that. If she had been 'caught' by someone she was 'walking out' with then the first problem would have been solved. She would almost certainly have been married as a matter of course. The man courting her would have had little choice but to wed her. The child would have a father and a name. It would not be a bastard and Joanne would not be an unmarried mother. This was different, Sidney in spite of his promises was already married and he was well off and he could and no doubt would deny all responsibility. Joanne had to tell her mother who the father was. Her mother's response was.'Wait 'til your father gets home and hears of this he will sort him out. ' But even as she said it the threat began to empty itself of any significance. Mrs.Gallagher head slumped on her chest over the still sleeping child and quietly wept with the despair that for some time now had seemed to be her lot. She had thought that there had been one glimmer of light in the last few dark impoverished years and that was when, ' Our Joanne 'got a good place with a good family and might have prospects.'

The baby in the mother's arms began to fret and mewl. 'I've just fed her,' she said to no one in particular, 'She's still hungry because I've got no nourishment in my milk.' She got up saying,' I'll pop next door to Mrs. Holiday's. She's per'aps got a drop of cow's milk she can spare.'

She went out leaving Joanne sitting on the floor, staring into space, her arms by her side with both hands palm upwards as if in some sort of prayer position that the follower of an oriental religion might adopt. The mother came back shortly with the cracked mug half full of milk. She gave Joanne the baby to hold but the girl hardly noticed it in her arms it was so underweight.

The mother wrapped a dirty cloth round the handle of the kettle that was on the cold coals and lifted it so as to put a twist of paper and a few sticks on the ashes. She lit the paper with a match from a box on the mantelpiece and put the kettle on the flames. She let it rest for a few minutes and picked it up again and let a drop drip from the spout on to her finger and thumb which she rubbed together. She then poured water out into the mug of milk and mixed it together. She poured this in turn into a baby's feeding bottle but before she fixed the teat she took a little phial with a glass stopper from a pocket in the ragged dress she was wearing. It had a label stuck on decorated with a sleeping baby out of whose tiny mouth 'zeds' were streaming. The printing described it as' 'Baby's little comforter. Not Weepy but Sleepy.' That was in large black print. In smaller print at the edge of the label ' Ozone Preparations co. Coursitor street. London.' When Sidney had given it to Joanne to pass on to her mother he had not told her that it was liquid opium mixed with diluted heroin. The mother took the glass stopper out of the bottle and dripped a few drops into the milk and water.' That will make her sleep.' She said. So saying she took the baby from Joanne, cradled it in her arms and pressed the end of the half-moon shaped baby feeder to its lips. It clamped its little mouth greedily on the artificial teat and began to suck noisily on the diluted feed from the bottle.

Time passed and it began to grow dark. The mother rocked backwards and forwards while baby now meagerly fed and drugged, gently snored in her arms. The daughter still sat as before no longer sobbing, her grief having completely exhausted her.

The house was in complete darkness when the door opened and a man's voice said 'What are you doing you silly girl sitting in the dark?' It was Joanne's father. He was a casual labourer on the docks and had just come home from his work. He walked to the windowsill where he knew a candle was kept. As he did so he stumbled over the sitting form of his eldest daughter. 'Its our Joanne, she's come home.' His wife said. He found the candle and lit it with his own matches and the flame showed a face that looked like that species of monkey which has a fringe of white fur round its head. Mr. Gallagher had been unloading sacks of flour all day and the dust of it had stayed all over his face. His eyelashes and eyebrows were dusted with it and the pulverized cereal had changed the colour of his hair and beard from black to white.

Dropping wax on the table from the lit candle he stuck the stub in it. He plonked a cotton bag on the table and it gave off a cloud of dust. 'There's five pounds of flour there but it's all I could get. The tally man was checking pockets. What's our Joanne doing home?' At this Joanne got up and giving a great wail ran from the room and up the narrow steep stairs that led to the room above. Mr. Gallagher, startled looked from the door to the stairs and back to his wife and said,'What's that all about.' Mrs. Gallagher did not reply for almost a minute but before she did Mr.Gallagher already knew the answer to his question.' 'Oh God Vinny I don't know what we are going to do. She's in the family way.' Joanne had been his first child and when a little girl had been the apple of eye.' What's she been up to? Who's the father? If I get my bloody hands on 'im. Well he'll marry her double quick and that's an end to it.'

'She sez it's that man she works for, Mr. Reilly.'

As she said this the rest of the family began to traipse in. The first was a sixteen year old girl, Dorothy she had spent the day sorting bags of washing from a laundry at Guy's Hospital. She got a penny a bag. There had only been three bags that day and she put the three pennies on the table. Hard on her heels was the fourteen year old boy, Henry. He had been the whole day at Waterloo station begging passengers to let him carry their bags. He had earned nothing except the shoves and kicks of official porters. He had no shoes to his feet. There was a shuffling from upstairs and Dorothy said, 'Who's upstairs.?'

Her mother said, "it's your sister Joanne."

Dorothy was pleased to hear that her sister was home and without asking any other questions she trotted up the stairs to see her. They were good friends and Dorothy missed her elder sister now that she was away from home.

Mrs.Gallagher gave Henry two of the pennies from the table and told him to take the mug and to go down the street to get some milk, a half penny piece of margarine and a half a loaf of bread and a screw of tea and sugar enough for one mashing. Mr. Gallagher didn't put his one shilling wages on the table. That was to pay off rent arrears.

Joanne and Dorothy had been talking upstairs and Dorothy,after getting Joanne's news had told Joanne what a bad state the family were in with money. Joanne forgot her own problems for a minute when she remembered that she had money. She came down stairs and gave her mother the change from the five shillings Mrs. Reilly had given her plus some coins of her own. There were around four shillings.

The windfall was so unexpected and so spectacularly welcome that the question of Joanne's condition was momentarily dismissed. For Mrs. Gallagher It meant food on the table, the rent, and candles for over a week. Mrs. Gallagher could not believe hers eyes. The mood of the family changed so radically that it mollified Mr. Gallagher and he motioned for Joanne to come to him and he embraced her, stroked her hair and said that he would sort everything out for her and she wasn't to worry. He would go to see Mr. Reilly at the end of the week. He would see that something came out of it. The tears of relief she had shed and the flour from her father's face and clothes that had got on to her face and hair made a paste that later set like a crust.

Henry came back and was promptly sent out again with coins from Joanne's contribution for two pennorth of bacon bits from the butcher and an opened penny tin of plum and apple jam from the grocers . When he came back Mrs. Gallagher gave Dorothy the still snoring baby to hold and she mixed some of the flour with water and made patties of dough which she fried on a fire made up of more sticks . They ate that with fried bacon bits and supplemented it with bread, margarine, jam and hot tea with milk and sugar.

They sat round on the floor and drank the tea from the jam jars and tins. They looked at each other in the light from the almost burnt out candle and the almost burnt out fire. They were a family and seeing them from the outside an observer might have wondered how family love could survive in such conditions, but it did. Apart from Joanne who usually ate the Reilly left- overs in Mrs. Sawyer's kitchen, they had not eaten so well for a long time. They went to bed and slept all together like badgers in a set covered by the rags of old coats on two old flock mattresses. Mrs. Gallagher fed the baby again and as she cooed it to sleep she said, almost as if she was saying a prayer, 'Things will be alright in the morning.'

Sidney spent his morning arranging with the removal firm Carter Paterson to collect the luggage. When it was all ready he got news from a visiting courier that 'the office' would be taking possession of the house until such time as a tenant or a buyer was found. He took the courier aside and said he was concerned that someone might come to the house and try to blackmail. him. Could he ask Mr. Melville to deal with it if it happened? He hadn't any other details but it might concern an employee that they had just dismissed.' The courier made a short note in his book and said that Mr. Reilly could depend on him to deliver the message.'

There was nothing to do or worry about now except to get down to Victoria station and catch the train for New Haven. He would stay in The London and Paris Hotel there and wait for Margaret. He had all his effects, papers and cash stowed in his brief case. It wasn't going with Carter Paterson. Sidney had permitted Margaret to take everything. He didn't mind as he still had the same plans to leave her in St. Petersburg so he wouldn't be troubled by having to organize her luggage in Russia. It was only when he was describing to Margaret where she was to meet him that he realised that he had made a mistake in choosing the London and Paris Hotel Newhaven as a place to meet. The last time that she had stayed there she had been with her late husband The Reverend Hugh Thomas.

He calmed her down and reassured her by saying that they were not staying there together, she would arrive in Newhaven, he said, with just enough time to catch the 1.15 ferry to Dieppe if she caught a train from Victoria at around 10.15 in the morning he would be there to meet her. Sidney then dressed for his departure in a dark suit he had kept out of the luggage and he put into his Gladstone bag a change of clothes for the next night. As always his Japanese razor was in his top pocket. He said goodbye and left the house, caught a cab to Victoria station and arrived in good time for the train to Newhaven.

As he waited around for his train to come in, he browsed the WH. Smith bookstall in the station. There was a shelf of books on elocution. It seemed to be all the rage. As he did so he came across a booklet with the title 'Speak Oxford English in Six Easy Lessons.' By Professor D. Jonas. There was a time when he had not wanted to lose his foreign accent but a thought struck him and he wondered why it had not struck him before. He was supposed to be an English Business man travelling in Russia yet he had a Russian accent. Not a strong one but an accent nonetheless. Would questions be asked? According to his papers he was English with Irish ancestry. He would have to modify his Russian accent. There was not time to do anything more comprehensive. He was confident he could affect a change. He had a good ear and he learned quickly. He bought the booklet. Even as he waited for his train he began to repeat the exercises;

'In Hampstead, Hertfordshire and Hereford, Hurricanes Hardly Happen.'

' Fancy asking Alice to dance to that brass band when she'd rather sit on a grassy bank with a brandy glass in her hand'

'My papa has a motor car and pa drives rather fast. Fields and farms and draughty barns pa goes charging past.'

Chapter Fourteen

The time came for his train so along with his case he carried the booklet into his first class carriage and made himself comfortable and settled down to complete exercise one. He was alone in the carriage so was able to practice his exercises out loud.' Ghosts on Posts with crusts in their fists.'

Mr. Gallagher did not get the work he expected over the next days so one morning he rose and made up his mind to take Joanne back to Paddington 'to 'ave a word with this 'ere Reilly bloke.' He scrubbed himself using a sliver of carbolic soap with water in the bucket he had fetched from the standpipe and after dried himself on an old rag He tried to make himself look as presentable as possible. He had another shirt and most of the grime of his work had come out at the last washing so he put this on and combed his hair and his beard. He had only one coat and one pair of boots and both the boots and the coat had seen better days. Joanne put the clothes on that she had left the Reilly's in apart from her maid's pinafore. The dress had been supplied by Mrs. Reilly. They had burned the clothes she arrived at the house in.

They were going to walk to the station intending to catch a train but decided to walk all the way. They could not really afford the fare. Mr. Gallagher thought that it was only about four miles so it should not take them more than an hour and they could cut across parks and save time and shoe leather. They set off choosing to go to Lambeth and Southwark and over the bridge there. It was a fine day,

They arrived at 6 Westbourne terrace within the hour and both could have done with a sit down and a rest but the person who answered the door did not invite them in to do either. In fact he did not speak to them but turned and called to someone from the interior and left them at the door. They were surprised to see a tall thick set man in a policeman's uniform come striding up the hall towards them. He was very abrupt and said, 'What d'you want? And what do you mean by coming to the front.?The tradesman's entrance is round the back.'

Mr. Gallagher summoned up his courage. Believing the righteousness of his cause gave him confidence. He said. 'I want to talk to this 'ere Mr. Reilly what lives 'ere about my girl 'ere Joanne and 'im doin' right by 'er.'

All the policeman said was, 'Oh it's you. We've been expecting you. Wait there.' At that he closed the door.

Mr. Gallagher and Joanne waited for what seemed a long time Then, their interest was taken by a black police wagon drawn by two black horses that stopped at the curb behind them. The man in the uniform came again to the door but this time he had his helmet on. He walked out on to the porch and taking Mr. Gallagher vigorously by the arm took him down the steps.

Mr. Gallagher said.' 'ere what's your game what yer doin' I aint done nothin' wrong?' The driver of the van had got down from his seat and opened the door of the van. He motioned Mr. Gallagher to get in. 'What for? ' said Mr. Gallagher. The policeman said 'Are you getting in or do you want some help?' When he said this he pointed to his night stick. Mr. Gallagher got in.

Joanne was as much surprised and had no time to react before the driver of the van had taken her arm and pulled her down the steps and pushed her in the van. He then closed the door and locked it from the outside. The door had small barred window in it.

Mr. Gallagher and Joanne looked at each other as they both stood at the back of the van holding the bars and then looking out of the window in alarm. They then sat on the bench seats at each side and Mr. Gallagher said, 'What the bloody 'ell is this all about. I don't know.' He stepped across to Joanne who was looking very agitated and sat down and put his arm around her and said,' it's all right love don't fret yourself.' But he had no confidence in what he was saying and would have liked some reassurance himself.

Mr. Gallagher got up and looked through the barred window again to see where they were going but as he rarely if ever came into this part of London he had no idea. He did not have any more time to think on this as the van stopped and the door was opened. They saw as they looked out from the inside of the van that they were in a court yard. The police man who they had first met had ridden at the front with the driver and he had opened the doors. He told them to get out.

They stepped down still bewildered. He took Mr. Gallagher's arm and the driver got hold of Joanne. They were both led across the yard through a door in the wall into a corridor and into an open area past a desk with another policeman at it. They were in Paddington Police Station. It said it on a sign. The man at the desk said, 'Take them into the room there. The key's in the lock. Somebody will be along to see them soon". They were led, subdued into a room with a barred window high up the wall near the ceiling. There was a small table with two chairs on one side and one on the other. The window did not let in a lot of light. The walls were bare. They heard the door being locked.

Mr. Gallagher sat down in one of the two chairs and he held Joanne's as she sat on the other. Joanne began to cry and both of them began to think of what they could have done to be taken to a police station like this. Joanne thought it was something to do with her work at the Reilly's and if anything had been stolen. Mr. Gallagher felt sure it was to do with the minor pilfering off the dock that he had certainly been involved in.

They had been sitting for some time when the door was unlocked and a young very smartly dressed ' City Gent', as Mr. Gallagher might have described him, came into the room carrying papers. He was followed by the policeman in uniform who had in his hand an oil lamp with a green shade. He placed it on the table, turned up the wick so that it cast a bright light on the centre of the table and stood back against the wall. The 'City Gent' said to the policeman, without looking at him, as he consulted his papers which he had placed on the table, 'You may leave us.' The policeman said, 'We usually stays sir, just in case' The 'City Gent' then said very firmly again without looking at him' You may leave us,' The policeman went out and closed the door.

The immaculately dressed young man in his obviously very expensive clothes was in sharp contrast to the dress of the two people sitting across from him, especially the ragged and tramp- like Mr. Gallagher. If any more contrast was needed it came in the form of the young man's hand-made boots and their black polished lustre. As the 'City Gent' had sat down at the table Mr. Gallagher with an unconscious movement had shifted his dirty worn out boots out of the way under the table lest he contaminate the shiny black polished leather surfaces of his interviewer's hand- made footwear.

The 'City Gent' continued to look at the papers he had placed on the table. He turned the pages over and occasionally made a mark on a paper with a silver pencil he had taken from one of the pockets of his waistcoat. Then he looked up and said," Vincent Patrick Gallagher, born 10th. February 1855 in Brixton, Father Vincent Michael Gallagher arrested in May 1860 for allegedly assaulting a policeman. Bound over in the sum of ten shillings". Vincent had not heard of his father's crime before."Now what about you Vincent? Do you know Francis William Magee and Christopher James McSherry?"

Mr. Gallagher knew them as fellow workers at the docks. They had recently been sacked off the job and were barred from working there anymore,

Yes I know them said Mr. Gallagher.' Nice enough lads, good workers. I don't know why they were sacked.'

Did you know that they were Irish Nationalists or as they are sometimes called, Fenians?'

' I know there were always talking politics, but I don't think there was any harm in them.' Mr. Gallagher said.

"Now let me see, your job Mr. Gallagher is as a casual labourer on the docks. It depends on you presenting yourself each day to be selected for work by the ganger and if you are not selected then you don't work and those that are selected do, is that right?"

Mr. Gallagher was beginning to forget his bewilderment at being where he was and he entered now into what he thought was a conversation on working practices on the docks, a bone of contention with all dock casual workers."' You're right there Mr. if you are not the 'blue eyed boy' at the end of the gangway you're back on the bloody cobbles with your hands in your empty pockets and no mistake."

'Well, Mr. Gallagher, said the man,' Your pockets are really empty aren't they? You have five, maybe now six mouths to feed. eight weeks rent arrears, according to your landlord, Mr Rabinovitch and if you get into any more arrears he says he's going to evict you. Now you wouldn't want to be known as someone who is an associate of Irish Nationalists, would you? Someone who, shall we say, has been taken into a police station and questioned about his affiliations. That wouldn't go down well with the foreman would it? You wouldn't want to be known as a troublemaker would you? Then you would be on the cobbles. No work, no money, then what would become of you and your family? On the other hand if you keep your mouth shut and keep your daughter on a short leash and tell her to stop making these wild accusations about a respectable businessman, you might find yourself 'the blue-eyed boy' and not 'the gang-way ender.'"

Both Mr. Gallagher and Joanne wondered how this man knew so much about them, even the name of their landlord and as if reading their minds, he said, 'You would be surprised how much we know about you, both of you.'

Joanne became aware before her father did of what this was all about and she suddenly found the courage to say it.

"I don't know who you are and I don't want to know." she said."And I don't know where you get the right from to bring us and keep us here or to threaten my father in the way that you are doing when it's me you really ought to be talking to." Mr. Gallagher had never heard his daughter speak out so firmly. He had always thought she, like most young girls of her age, was something of a shrinking violet."We came to see Mr. Reilly in good faith expecting him to face up to his responsibilities. It's obvious he is not going to. I don't want anything from him now and my father doesn't want anything from you. So you should let us go to get back to our family and our home." Mr. Gallagher had always thought 'our Joanne has got a head on her shoulders."But although he would not have verbalized it in the same way, he was still surprised at her articulacy. Joanne had, as a lot of young women of her time, found her voice.

"Ah quite the little suffragette aren't we? We will see you at Hyde park Corner yet. But I will tell you this young lady, my advice to you is to forget Mr.Reilly. Forget you ever met him. Forget you ever had anything to do with him or you will be dealing with things you have no idea about and things you will not be able to control. I hope I am making myself clear for your sake and your father's sake, indeed for the sake of your whole family. You are much better out of it."

Joanne spoke up again. She grew in confidence." Have you had your say? Because if you have I want you to let us go now. We have done nothing that is against the law, so you have no right to keep us here. We don't want anything more to do with you. You have nothing to do with us."

Her courage in speaking out seemed to affect him. He did not have the same air of absolute authority that he had when he first came in. She felt that she had made a little victory. That she had drawn something out of this impossible situation that was theirs. He was doing something that was a reaction to what she had said. It was minor, but he was no longer the complete master.

He got up and said in a quieter but a coldly menacing voice." Remember what I have told you." He then turned and left the room and left the door open. Joanne and her father walked through it and out down the corridor and into the yard. The driver of the van was standing by his horse and the man was standing next to him saying a few words. Joanne said,"We want to be taken home." Her father tried to caution her not to go too far but Joanne had found her feet. 'You brought us here, you will take us home.' She saw the man nod and then move back into the building. The driver of the van indicated that they should get inside. They would arrive home in a police van, that was scandalous but they would ride and not walk. Before they got in Joanne told the driver the address and then said,' And don't lock the door.' He didn't. Joanne sat for the whole journey with her arm around the shoulder of her father as if protecting him from any further humiliation. Just as once he had done with her she was now doing with him.

Well before they arrived at Cancel Street Mr. Gallagher rapped on the roof of the van and shouted to the driver to set them down. The driver was very surly as he opened the doors and the Gallaghers stepped out. Joanne however was having none of it and she said cheekily, as if alighting from a carriage, 'Thank you my man.'

Although there were quite a few people in the street they found themselves in and they got many inquisitive looks, they did not recognize any faces. They were not their neighbours so the shame and ignominy of arriving on their own street in a police van was avoided and it was only a five minute walk home once they got their bearings.

When they did get home Joanne's mother was visibly agitated.' Where 'ave you been? I have been waiting for you. You have been a long time. I was getting worried that something had happened to you. A Mrs. Sawyer's been to see you Joanne.' Mrs. Gallagher could not contain herself and she held out her hand. In it was a little leather pouch. ' She brought this for you,Ten sovereigns, ten sovereigns, more than half a year of your wages. Mrs. Reilly gave it to Mrs. Sawyer for you. The Reilly's have gone abroad, something to do with his business. Mrs. Reilly says don't tell her husband. And Mrs.Sawyer's found a place for you, at least until you start to show and then they'll see. It's at the house she's working at. 'Es a foreigner, German I think. Its near Park Lane. She wrote the address on this piece of paper with your reference from Mrs. Reilly. You've got to go and see her as soon as you can.' Mrs. Gallagher held out the note and envelope then she sat down as if the giving of the news had exhausted her, She was also worried that she might drop the baby in her excitement.

When she heard what her mother had to say Joanne was only a little less excited. All three of them looked at each other and at four shining gold sovereigns that had spilled out from the dull suede leather pouch as Mrs. Gallagher had put it on the table. They were all three thinking the same thing, Ten gold sovereigns all at the same time and a new job. Against all the odds the Gallagher family had survived another crisis. Tonight there would be a candlelit fish supper eaten from newspaper for them all and whole milk for the baby.

Chapter Fifteen

Sidney Reilly arrived in Newhaven late in the afternoon and he got a cab for the short distance to the London and Paris Hotel. He had stayed there before and found it a bit of a rabbit warren. He booked in and went up to his room to wash and change and to continue with his exercises. He was pleased that he had managed to get away before anything unpleasant happened with Joanne and perhaps her father. He was sure that would all sort itself out one way or another. He settled down to an evening in which he would continue with his exercises in elocution and perhaps later he might go down for a spot of dinner and a drink at the bar and then an early night. He was to meet Margaret the next day and they had to make the journey to Paris and then there was the prospect of a brief holiday together to look forward to. He reminded himself that he had to meet her and take her straight to the ferry. He did not want to upset her by having to come back to the London and Paris as it had such bad memories for her. He had the dinner and drink he had promised himself and went to bed with his elocution lessons.

Back at Westbourne Terrace, Margaret ignored what Sidney had said before he left.' Don't be too generous with the staff, give them no more than a month's wages in lieu of notice'. She gave Mrs. Sawyer half her wages for a year, 'In lieu of notice she said.' And she gave her an envelope that had in it, a very favourable reference because I have been very pleased with your work and I want to you to do something for me'. 'What is it?'. Mrs. Sawyer said, feeling that she had been released from any obligation to say yes to whatever her ex employer asked. Mrs. Reilly said in a tone that she did not intend to sound condescending, but nevertheless it did. 'Well, I would like you to take this letter to Joanne's address, you know where it is don't you? I will pay your cab fare and this is also for her. ' She handed Mrs. Sawyer a little leather pouch.

What of course she hoped, was that there was someone looking down at her as she did her good works. Faith Hope and Charity and the greatest of these is Charity. Thirty sovereigns she thought would surely be more than enough to buy her an indulgence and so out of the purgatory she felt she was slipping into. Mrs. Sawyer did as she was asked but with a little more spontaneity. She already had the intention to visit Joanne's address to give her the news that her new employers wanted a house maid urgently. Mrs. Sawyer had 'been so bold' as to recommend Joanne and she had told her full story. They were willing to consider her in spite of everything.

Even before she left on the day that she had arranged to meet Sidney at Newhaven, Sidney's 'colleagues' from 'the office' arrived to take over the house. Margaret handed over the keys and she was gently reassured that the house, indeed all their property would be in good hands. They told her that they thought the best course of action was to lease the house and that they thought that they had already found someone suitable. She should they said pass on to Mr. Reilly that all rents and leasehold charges would be deposited in his bank account which they had details of. She was to go to catch her train and not to worry in the slightest. That was, with her guilty preoccupations almost overwhelming her, just what she wanted.

She had fortified herself with a good breakfast and she got to Victoria in good time for her train and was informed that as it was running precisely on time it would get her to Newhaven to catch the 1.15 Ferry to Dieppe. She hardly noticed the time passing for as she was sitting in a carriage by herself she was able to take an occasional nip from a half bottle of whisky that she had thought to carry with her. The quarter bottle that she consumed before the train had been running 30 minutes meant that she made the rest of the journey in a sleep undisturbed by passengers who got in and out of the same compartment without her noticing them.

Sidney was waiting for her at the station at Newhaven and as she got down somewhat unsteadily from her carriage to the platform, he took her elbow and said in a sing song voice from the side of his mouth, 'You've been drinking again,' Margaret gathered the hem of her dress up from the dusty platform and said, 'I needed something to calm my nerves with all the things I had to do. You left all the last-minute arrangements to me and it was quite a strain. I haven't had any lunch yet and the small drop of whisky I had has gone straight to my head.'

Sidney ignored her and simply added this incident to all the others that he was making a mental note of to use as reasons justifying leaving her in St, Petersburg.

They went out of the station to a cab that Sidney had waiting and he said that they would go first to check that their luggage had been delivered to the ferry and then board and perhaps have lunch in the dining saloon. Margaret did not object.

Sidney met with the representative of Carter Paterson and was given documentation relating to all the baggage of theirs that had gone on board. Sidney having left Margaret in the terminal waiting went back to her and they joined the line of passengers having tickets checked at the bottom of the gang way of the Newhaven Dieppe ferry. The ferryboat was 'The Tamise'. its two black funnels were gently smoking as it got up steam for the voyage.

Once on board Sidney had a steward lead them to their first class cabin booked for the afternoon and then give them directions to the restaurant. Sidney knew already, but for form he asked the steward how long it would take to get to Paris, sea crossing and rail journey together. Speaking with a strong provincial French accent the steward said that Madame and Monsieur would be in St Lazare station Paris by 7.15 that evening.

They settled themselves into their small but comfortably appointed cabin. It was paneled in a light wood with two bunks, one that if it was pulled from the wall converted to a small double bed. Sidney predicted that if Margaret wanted to go to bed for a nap in the afternoon she would be the worse for drink again so he suggested without implying that it was the reason for the choice, that she should sleep on the bottom bunk while he slept on the top. The motive he gave for not wanting to share a nuptial couch was because the shaped board at the side of the bunk would prevent her from rolling out should the crossing be rough.

Sidney had washed and bathed (There being no showers in the London and Paris) at the hotel so he gave the tiny cubicle in the cabin that housed a wash basin and WC over to Margaret for her to rinse away the dust of the journey she had just taken. While she did this Sidney went up on deck to watch the preparations being made for the crossing to France.

It took him back, for a few years before he had made the crossing in the opposite direction and he remembered with a thrill of anxiety how worried he had been that his pursuers might have got someone to follow him on board and to murder him while he was asleep and cast his body overboard. He had stayed awake for most of the night positioning himself with his back to a lifeboat, his razor at the ready, so that he couldn't be surprised. He had eventually succumbed to sleep and thought his moment had come when wakened cold and damp by a passing steward who enquired as to whether he was sea-sick.

Below in the cabin Margaret was having similar apocalyptic thoughts, She had made the crossing from France to England on the same Ferry after a tour of Europe with her first husband. She once more put the bottle to her lips in an attempt to erase the memory.

Sidney went into the restaurant and ordered lunch for two and then went below again to collect Margaret. They had a simple lunch of steak frites and salad but Sidney did take the opportunity to taste the wine and in spite of having started her day with spirits, Margaret managed a half bottle of the red Burgundy that Sidney ordered with the camembert cheese that he chose. They followed the cheese with fresh fruit and excellent French coffee and once again Margaret did not refuse another drink, namely the cognac that they both had as a digestive. Sidney then suggested a turn around the deck to get the breeze on their cheeks.

The sea was, as it sometimes is in the channel, as smooth as a mill-pond and as it is always, busy with shipping. There were French and English fishing boats from two man boats fishing with lines to medium sized steam trawlers with mizzen sails set and pleasure yachts with their white sails full in the wind. In the distance coasters chugged up to British sea ports and on the horizon there was the unmistakable line of a grey warship its four funnels pouring their smoke against the sky,

'The Tamise' now streaming thick plumes of grey smoke from her two black funnels was pushing aside the flat, glass- green sea in a dramatic bow wave as she made her 15 knot progress to La Belle France. Sidney felt the illusory romance that even the simplest sea voyage induces and as they together leaned against the rail of the port side bow quarter he put his arm round the waist of Margaret and smiled at her.' Are you looking forward to the journey?'. She wanted to say,"If only you knew how much I have wanted to get away from England these last weeks, and the memories it holds for me." But, she knew that she couldn't confide in him her fear and guilt. And she simply answered. 'Oh yes very much.'

It was a fine day so they passed the time on deck only going below, Sidney for his elocution booklet and Margaret for a magazine. The returned to the deck and found two deck-chairs and enjoyed the sunshine and the sea- breeze. After a time Sidney invited Margaret to help him with his exercises saying only that he wished to improve his English. She thought it very amusing hearing him repeating the verses, especially when he mispronounced the lines

They enjoyed themselves at this until they discovered and were surprised, that the French catering crew actually served English tea. They noticed that quite a few of the French passengers enjoyed their tea too.

They had not long finished their tea when the French coast came into view and very soon after they were entering the port of Dieppe, disembarking and crossing the port to reach the station where the train to Paris waited.

There was no dinner to be had on the train to Paris once they had disembarked from the 'Tamise'. It was too early for the French. So they had to be satisfied with a drink from the buffet car. Sidney ordered a bottle of Champagne and by the time they reached Paris they had consumed two bottles.

Chapter Sixteen

Outside the Paris Station of St Lazare, Sidney hailed one of the new gasoline powered taxis recently introduced to Paris Streets(in time in fact for the Exhibition) and indicated that they wanted to be taken to The Ritz Hotel, Sidney had heard that it was the newest and the grandest hotel in Paris.

Neither of them had ever ridden in a motor car before and its passage over the pave of the Paris streets they didn't think as comfortable as a hansom cab plus they thought the smell of petrol fumes distasteful.

The taxi driver had already got used to taking his fares, the ones he reckoned were visitors,the long way round to their destinations, ostensibly to see the sights but really so he could augment the fares. Picking Sidney and Margaret up from the station, he went to Madeline and then down Rue Royale to the Place De La Concorde and round in to the Champs Elysees.

The Champs Elysees and the Place de La Concorde rolled with traffic. Around Concorde it flowed like water down a drain and into the river of vehicles that ran up and down the great boulevard of the Champs Elysees.

On The Champs Elysees it was growing dusk so the pavements were crowded with people. There were workers on their way home, to whom Paris was an office or workshop and tourists looking for the magic everyone said Paris had. Sidney however had his eye on the new taximeter recording the fare and said to the driver in French that they were in a hurry to get to the hotel because they wanted dinner. They could see the sights later. Sidney told him to turn round and go back to the Vendome. The driver realized immediately from Sidney's imperious tone and fluent French that they weren't just a couple of tourists up from the sticks who did not know their way around.

When they got to the hotel and were shown to their luxurious suite they were told that their luggage had arrived and was in store with cases marked 'Paris' already waiting for them. Sidney asked Margaret to be quick changing as he intended taking her out to a cabaret after dinner. Sidney very quickly, showered and shaved and with the help of a valet, who went with the suite changed into evening dress, opera cape, shiny black top hat and all and Margaret with her ladies maid changed into a dress whose green was very much the colour of the dress that Sidney remembered Caroline had worn at their first meeting. The colour was in fashion that year. Margaret looked beautiful. Her blonde hair shone with a golden sheen and complimented her blue eyes. When she was sober Sidney found himself moving back to the affection he'd had for her the first time they had met.

They went out of the Ritz through its red carpeted and gold decorated entrance and the door man hailed one of the new yellow painted petrol powered taxicabs. Sidney and Margaret got in and he asked the cabbie to take them to Maxims. It was not very far away but they were not going to walk. The taxi turned right into the Rue de Rivoli and Sidney pointed out the Tuileries Gardens. Within a few minutes they were in front of Maxims. Sidney had made a reservation from England at the same time as booking the Ritz. It was Paris, at the time of the exhibition. He calculated that it might be impossible to get a table if he simply speculated.

Maxims was noted as perhaps the best restaurant in Paris and its clients were a gallery of the celebrated and the rich of Paris and Europe. For Sidney it was an imperative that he dine there and even better that he be seen with his beautiful partner. It could be that he would be envied by strangers. He also wanted to demonstrate that he was accustomed to good living and that he was completely at ease in such surroundings.

He did this to begin with by ordering an aperitif of Kir Royale, champagne and cassis liqueur. And then as Margaret had suggested that he order for them both, he chose from the menu a classic list of French gastronomy., Burgundy snails in parsley and garlic sauce, followed by a smoked salmon mousse, then steak Diane, a plain fresh green salad, a Roquefort cheese and, flambéed at the table, crepes suzette. He ordered a simple dry Bergerac white with the first two courses and a red Bordeaux from St Emilion with the steak and then again with cheese. Their dessert was accompanied with a young demi-sec champagne. When she saw how confidently he handled the waiters Margaret loved him again, as she saw him as the man of the world she had once known.

As they were having their coffee and cognac Sidney repeated his suggestion that they go on after dinner to the Moulin Rouge, a cabaret nightclub that had become very famous since the time that Sidney was in Paris. Sidney called for ' l'addition' and the total sum on the bill including service, would have kept the whole of the Gallagher family, fed clothed and housed for a twelve month.

When they arrived at The Moulin Rouge again by taxi, the frontage under the great red sign and the slowly turning illuminated sails of the windmill was a confusion of rich bourgeois top hats evening dress clothes, walking canes and beautiful women with superbly coiffeured hair jostling with the ordinary inhabitants of the night –life of Paris.

Sidney sent the taxi driver in with a generous tip for the doorman to ensure their entry. The taxi driver came back and pointed out a bald fat man in evening dress with a thin curling black moustache who was gesticulating for them to come to him. Sidney paid the fare for the cab and they walked in through the crush. The fat door man, impressed by his tip took Sidney's hat cape and cane and Margaret's shawl and led them half bowing for the whole of the way to a table into a an overcrowded hall. There was with a bar with a long mirror covering the length of the back wall and a raised stage at the other. The side walls were covered in gaily coloured posters with paintings of young women dancers in extravagantly styled dresses or with posters advertising the talents of thin young acrobatic men.

When they sat at their table they were squeezed in between other clients seated just as uncomfortably. There was a noise that was a mixture of the clink of glasses, the shouts of waiters, the popping of corks and the hum of animated conversation. There were mature if not old men with very young women and mature women with very young men. There were women embracing women and men embracing men and there were women whose profession could be guessed at as they passed from table to table going from one crowd of unaccompanied young men to the next. Over all this a pall of blue smoke hung halfway in the air, from the hundreds of cigars and cigarettes being smoked in the hall. The hall was a blaze of light from lamps on the ceiling. A waiter came to their table and Sidney ordered a bottle of Champagne. He asked for Russian but got a blank stare from the waiter. It was an indifferent bottle of the French variety that arrived.

Sidney gave a sovereign to the waiter who brought the champagne in its ice bucket and it was accepted as immediate payment. As he did this an orchestra drifted in after their interval for refreshment and the members of it arranged themselves in a space before the stage and began to tune up. A tall thin man appeared on the stage in a black tail suit with his top hat rakishly on one side of his head and he made an announcement, the words of which were lost in the hubbub of sound swirling up from the assemblage. The orchestra struck up with a very loud and vigorous rendering of music from Offenbach's Orpheus in the Underworld and a dozen girl dancers came in from separate sides of the stage, six from each wing.

They danced in holding their short skirts up to their bosoms, Underneath their black satin skirts they wore many frilly petticoats in pinks and blues and reds and whites. Their high-heeled boots were black, tied with red ribbons and their stockings were white with frilly red garters holding them up. They had their hair high on the head. The curls and waves of their hair were plaited with multi-coloured ribbons and most of them seemed to be red heads. They began a series of acrobatics as they took it in turns to cart wheel across the stage. Then in a row they high-kicked in time. They accompanied their dancing with cries and squeals as each seemed to be trying to outdo the other in acrobatics or kicking.

As the dance came to its close they lined up along the front of the stage with their backs to the audience and with a great shout they bent over and lifted their skirts way above their hips. They had no underwear on; no drawers or knickers. Their behinds were completely bare down to their white stockings and red garters. Twelve beautifully formed, round naked bottoms all in a row with just a hint between of the 'frizz' of their pubic hair.. A great cheer went up from the crowd. Sidney thought it the most erotic sight he had ever seen. Margaret gave a gasp and with her eyes open wide in amazement she put her hand to her mouth They ended the dance finally with one girl as a centre piece pirouetting on one foot and leg while she held the other foot and leg bent at the knee high against her head. She exposed herself completely. Her fellow dancers dashed from all the sides of the stage and for a finale leapt up in the air and came down on the floor of the stage in the splits, again with shouts and screams.

The applause for this act was tumultuous with many of the audience standing to show their appreciation. An old lady had been walking around the tables before the dance selling roses and some clients had bought them from her. These were thrown on to the stage. As the cheering died down the orchestra struck up again and the girls came on for a short encore and they performed what was definitely the favourite part of the act and that was the girls lining up and bending over again with their skirts and petticoats above their hips. The girls went backstage cheered to the echo and then some of them came out again and descended the steps from the stage and mingled with the crowd. It was obvious that they were very well known by their audience as they kissed and embraced obvious friends and accepted the many drinks offered to them.

Sidney saw the look of mild reproach on Margaret's frowning face and said, 'Well Margaret dear we are in France. This is the country where prime ministers die in the arms of their mistresses. Margaret looked puzzled.' Yes' continued Sidney, 'Felix Faure the P.M. of France died while making love to his mistress il flagrante dilecto. It happened in February. Good riddance for my money. He was too friendly with the Tsar. But I must say that when I suggested that we come here I wasn't expecting such a show. Here have another glass of champagne to cool you down.' Margaret said, as she held her glass out for the sparkling wine and she was almost chuckling."I think it is you who needs cooling down. I saw the way you looked at those girls or at least what we could see of them." This was just like old times she thought, they were having fun as they used to.

The orchestra struck up again and a young typically Parisian girl, diminutive and very pretty came on the stage in a dress with the skirt pinned up at the front revealing 'frou frou' petticoats black stockings and high buttoned up boots. She began to sing a song lamenting a lost love with a chorus that described her wandering the streets of Paris searching for him. Many of the spectators joined in which she did not discourage. When she had finished her performance there was a long interval that gave the thirsty and the more drunken members of the clientele a chance to either be served or serve themselves. Sidney also noticed that some sections of the audience were becoming more noisy and boisterous than was acceptable to the management and when the singer, after the interval was followed by a scantily clad female contortionist, Sidney decided that it was time to go.

They went out and although it was nearly midnight the Boulevard de Clichy was thronged with people. They walked along to the Place Pigalle and sat at the table of a pavement café, ordered a night-cap of cognac and watched the world and his wife (or someone else's wife, Sidney thought) pass in front of them.

After their night-cap Sidney suggested getting a cab back to the Ritz but Margaret wanted to walk on a little further not least to see the illuminations around the Place Pigalle powered by the new electric light. The lights lit up the boulevard and the square and the painted faces of the many girl prostitutes standing provocatively along the pavement. What surprised both Sidney and Margaret, as they made their promenade was that the girls, some who looked very young indeed, seemed to be indifferent to Margaret's presence and made their advances to Sidney anyway. Implying in their lewd expressions
that 'Madame might also want to join in.' it was not an idea that Sidney completely rejected.

They weren't able to get one of the new 'motor' cabs so hailed Paris' answer to the hansom. They did not have to wait long and when it came Margaret got in and Sidney stood on the step up to the cab with the door open and told the cabbie where they wanted to go, The Ritz. He described what he thought was the best route from Pigalle, Rue Jean Baptiste, Rue de la Chausee, Opera Garnier, Opera and on to Vendome making sure that any opportunism on the cabbie's part was disqualified. Sidney knew his way around and although he was a big tipper when it came to a waiter in a classy restaurant, he got his money's worth from cab drivers.

That night Sidney and Margaret made love so passionately that memories of their first association came back to both of them. The desire that Sidney expressed and the need for it that Margaret felt banished all feeling except the joyful physical satisfaction that Sidney inspired in her. Exhausted they fell both naked back onto the grandeur of their extravagantly decorated bed now a tangle sheets and covers. They lapsed into sleep, For Sidney this sleep only lasted an hour and when he woke he ordered onion soup from the hotel kitchen.

When it came and was served on a table in their room and the well rewarded night waiters had left, he woke Margaret and described the French tradition of the restorative and they ate the luscious hot brown soup with toasts covered in melted gruyere floating on its surface. Revitalised they fell back to making love again. And when at last they did sleep it was a sleep that lasted until eleven o' clock in the morning and they ordered coffee and fresh croissants in their suite. They ate their breakfast when it was brought and made love again. It was the first night for months that Margaret had not been troubled by the goblins of guilt and recrimination. It was a repeat, she thought of their honeymoon night.

When they did get up it was too late for the lunch that Sidney had planned. His intention had been to lunch at a restaurant called Chartier in the 9th Arrondisement on the Rue de Fauberg that he remembered from his previous time in Paris and then to go on to see the Tour d'Eiffel. The change of plan meant that they went straight to the Exhibition grounds.

Once dressed after a substantial sandwich snack in their suite they made for the electric tram to take them to the Galerie des Machines. Sidney was immaculate in chocolate brown suit with white spats and a jacket open to reveal a brocade waistcoat with a soft collared plain pink shirt and darker pink Chavet tie and Margaret in a long day dress in light lime green with only a relatively low neck-line and small white hat topping her golden hair that she had insisted should be dressed by the hotel coiffeuse even though it made them even later.

The exhibition was full of marvels. There was even a whole negro village imported from French Equatorial Africa. Margaret thought it not much of an advertisement of the progress that the French Empire had brought to such people if we were to be entertained by the basic level of life that the people in the village seemed to be enjoying. The image of the Empire of the United States was represented by a fairground cowboy, Buffalo Bill who had done a tour of England and entertained Queen Victoria.. He was supported in his demonstration of how the Americans had annihilated the Buffalo, tamed the Wild West and the Redskin by a lady sharp-shooter of the name of Annie Oakley. Margaret mentioned that it seemed hardly the profession of a respectable woman. Margaret forgot her past sometimes and saw herself as a respectable woman.

For Sidney the greatest achievement of the project was the Eiffel Tower. It was the centre piece and as such he thought it would be the one thing that would last beyond the exhibition itself but was disappointed when they got to it to find that it was built on grass-covered waste land with a couple of wooden shacks at its foot. They could not dine there that evening and could not go beyond the first level as it was not finished.

They spent the rest of the afternoon touring the grounds and exhibits and were still there in the early evening so Sidney suggested that they dine at Chartier and then go on to Folies Berger which was only around the corner from the restaurant. He didn't think it was necessary to go back to the hotel to change and after a short discussion in which he flattered Margaret on her appearance as she was, she agreed. He would make it a little more interesting if they travelled from the tower by Bateau Mouche on the river to Notre Dame and then wonder of wonders he would break the habit of years and as it was Paris go on the Metro to Chartier. Margaret had not enjoyed herself so much for a longtime and Sidney was beginning to rediscover his young wife but also significantly just why he was where he was.

Chartier was not the grand palace of gastronomy, wine, decoration and regal service that Maxims was but a place where poor poets, writers and their hangers on congregated,nicely typified thought Sidney as they now served absinthe. Margaret and Sidney were somewhat too expensively dressed, if not overdressed at the side of the other clientele, but Sidney had learned since the time of his last stay in the city when he was much less affluent that 'one should never be embarrassed by being too well-dressed.' It did not spoil his enjoyment of a good dinner as they were served by French garcons in wrap around black aprons and white shirts who wrote their order on the paper table cloth and each and everyone seemed to be wearing the same pencil thin moustache. Regular customers took their own napkins from little wooden numbered cubby holes arranged against the wall.

After dinner they walked the few steps to the Folies Berger and it was as it had been a few years ago. The long bar with the great mirrors behind it was staffed by beautiful, demure almost shy young women often girls who had come up to Paris from the provincial countryside.. But he let Margaret drink too much and before the entertainment of the evening had finished he felt he had to take her back to the hotel. Luckily they were not far from the Ritz as it took all her control not to be ill in the taxi or the foyer of the hotel, which would have been a disaster for Sidney.

He got her up to the suite in time and she deposited the days contents of her stomach in the bathroom of their suite. It was a pity. Things had been going so well. But untypically he blamed himself. He undressed her and put her to bed and she snored as he contemplated what he should do for the rest of the night. When he had first visited Paris it was as a refugee from his home country. If he bore any grudge against the Russia that he had fled from it was because of the overt anti-semitism of the Tsarist Establishment and he had found a fellow feeling with many of the people he had met in what were his formative years; those first short years in Paris. When reflecting on the rationale for his actions Sidney had a tendency to sentimentalise. The very people he had such a fellow feeling for were the ones he had been prepared to betray and steal from. That did not enter his head as a plan formed in his mind to revisit one or two of his old haunts as Margaret slept off her indulgence.

Chapter Seventeen

Sidney donned a simple plain suit, one he had planned to wear in Russia that might disguise his affluence and he asked the doorman to order him cab to take him to the first Arrondisement, Des Halles. The precise address being the café Petit Valet on the Rue Montorgueil. There Sidney had often arranged assignations with a young French girl he had thought he had truly fallen in love with but whom he had later abandoned to escape to England. It was also the place he had first met the Russian Anarchist girl he had given over to the Duexieme Bureau

When the cab dropped him off in front of the café it was as he remembered it, a plain window half covered by a checked curtain held by rings on a brass pole. The tables and chairs usually set out in front had been taken inside but the café was still open. He went in and ordered what had been his favourite drink in Paris, a Pastis de Marseilles. He added an order of French cigarettes. If anything brought back his memory of those times it was the smell of the strong home –grown tobacco of French cigarettes. The proprietor took the metal lid off a large glass jar and Sidney asked for ten which he counted out and Sidney packed them into a silver cigarette case. He didn't sit down at one of the half dozen tables in the café as each one had someone sitting at it; a solitary drinker or a couple of lovers engrossed in each other. He sat at the bar counter and took his drink, 'sur le zinc.'

He let his mind wander back to those times and was so lost in his memories as he sipped his drink and inhaled the smoke of nostalgia that he did not notice a young man of about his age staring at him curiously through the mirror on the wall at the back of the bar as if he recognized him. He was shabbily dressed with thick curly hair and a face and colouring more typical of central Europe than France. He was drawn to Sidney's attention when he got up from his seat and took a seat at the end of the bar. By the attention he gave Sidney it was obvious that he had moved so that he could look at him more closely.

Sidney cast a glance in his direction and Sidney's memory was immediately better than his for the young man was still puzzling over whether he had ever seen Sidney before. Sidney recognized him straightaway as a member of the same Anarchist cell that Sidney had been a clandestine informer in. The stranger had two small but very distinctive crescent shaped scars, one on each side of his mouth. They gave him a permanent sinister smile. Sidney remembered that he had got them when a French policeman had pushed his head through a window.

Sidney got up put on his hat which he pulled down over his forehead and shoved a few coins over the bar in payment. The café owner picked them up and was about to give Sidney his change when he saw that Sidney was already out of the door.

As Sidney left the door of the café in a hurry it dawned on the stranger who Sidney was. He immediately set of in pursuit cursing in Georgian Russian that he had not recognized him before as he could have had him cornered.

Once out on the street Sidney began to walk quickly and then he broke into a desperate run. In the quarter the café was in, Des Halles there were myriad systems of gas-lit alleys around a central market out of which came all the produce that Paris ate from day to day, vegetables, fish and varieties of meat that ranged from horse to pig to cow through the genres of poultry, rabbit, and game large and small. Even guinea pig and dog could be found if looked for.

Sidney dodged down the first alley he came to and the way was so narrow he had to squeeze past two brawny butchers with half pigs on their shoulders walking two abreast. Porters carrying cow carcasses, labourers hauling crates and porters pushing iron wheeled barrows loaded with hessian sacks, criss-crossed his hectic dash. The half-lit confusion plus cobblestones slimy with blood and waste water caused him to slip and fall full length and to slide with a crack to his head against a brick wall.

Two burly butchers, their aprons smeared with blood bent to pick him up commenting cheerfully that he should take more water with it and then were non comprehending when he wrenched himself from their solicitous grasp and ran pell-mell again into the mele of market workers. They shouted after him, 'Pick yourself up next time you drunken bastard.' In his head long dash, Sidney turned and saw the head and shoulders of his pursuer framed between two sides of a butchered horse being taken down from a wagon. He was only twenty paces away.

Sidney turned down one alleyway then another in the maze that was Des Halles but the man always saw him and followed, getting closer. Sidney could not shake him off. In desperation Sidney turned into what he thought was a butcher's shop. He would go in the front and leave by the back but he was mistaken it was a voie sans issue, a cul de sac. The bones he had mistaken for those thrown out of a butcher's shop were on a pile that was part of a rubbish dump for bones and vegetable refuse waiting for collection. The pile nearly filled the alley.

The methane stench of rotting green vegetables and the odour of putrefaction from the vestiges of hide, fat and flesh left on the great heaps of bones stacked against the wall was overpowering for Sidney. But it was not as strong as the smell of his own fear. He was trapped. Sidney had no skill as a street fighter. He needed the support of a weapon and preferably a pistol. He had his back to a great stack of bones that dripped with maggots and buzzed with blue flies. He stood and waited for what he thought was the inevitable.

There was one gas jet high up the wall but its guttering flare cast only a flickering light and it made the place look even more like a hellish charnel house. Sidney had one thought, 'What a place to die in.' Sidney saw his assailant at first, run straight past the opening to the infernal alley that Sidney had ensnared himself in and for a moment Sidney thought he might have given him the slip. But then he must have retraced his steps for within a few seconds he reappeared and blocked the passage and Sidney's escape route. He made a few slow menacing steps towards Sidney.

Sidney knew he was defenceless. He had thought it unnecessary to bring his pistol and his razor was in the top pocket of another suit.

The man spoke and in Georgian Russian, 'I thought I recognized you, you double-dyed, double-crossing son of a whore. We've been looking for you for these past five years. Don't worry I'm not going to kill you but I am going to hurt you. Then I'm going to take you back to meet some friends of mine who once thought they were friends no, comrades of yours. I think they will kill you, but slowly. You snake, we trusted you and all the time you were in the pocket of the flics. Do you remember Nikita? You sold her out you lying bastard.' Nikita was the girl he had informed on who had finished up with the Russian Secret Police. 'You know what she did in the end? She hanged herself under the Pont Neuf. You said you loved that girl and you betrayed her. Now for Nikita I am going to cut off your ears and slit your nose, then I am going to make you chew on one of your own bollocks.'

He drew a fat Spanish clasp knife out of a pocket and opened up a large sharp pointed blade shaped like a pike's head As he did this there was a commotion at the opening of the alley. There was the clattering rattling noise only bones can make as a market worker tipped another barrow load against one of the growing piles. The Georgian, distracted momentarily, turned his head. It was enough for Sidney. He reached for the only weapon available, a cow's leg bone. It was from the pile behind him. He grasped it and hit the man on the side of the head once and then as he staggered from that blow held the great bone high in both his hands and brought its rounded joint socket end down with an almighty crack on the young man's forehead. Sidney saw the life going from his eyes as they rolled into his head and he went down like a pole-axed beast and fell on his back. Sidney heard that he hadn't killed him for he began to snore as only the completely unconscious snore. His hair was a bloody mess where the bone had bashed him and a thick rivulet of blood was oozing down over his nose, into his open mouth, across his teeth and out down his chin.

Sidney was jubilant and he shouted out loud and almost danced antic with relief. 'You thought you had me didn't you? Well it will take more than you, you fucking Georgian barfly.' As he spoke Sidney took the knife the man had dropped and he used it to cut string from the bundles of rotten cabbage and leeks. Then taking a long length tied up his would be assassin.

He first tied both his hands behind him and then wound the thick string round his ankles Then he turned him over on to his front and pulled his legs so they bent at the knees. He then made a noose and put it round his neck. It was a trick a Sicilian had taught him in this very city. As his knees became stiff with bending he would, in reflex try to straighten them out and in so doing tighten the noose round his neck. If somebody didn't come across him in the next hour or so he would strangle himself.

Sidney didn't care one way or the other but he said to himself that the odds were on somebody, a worker or some scavenger, passing by and releasing him. By that time Sidney thought, I will be long gone. As a further precaution against him taking up the pursuit again, Sidney cut the laces of both the man's boots, took them off and then took off his holey socks leaving him bare feet. He tossed the boots and socks behind the piles of bones.

Sidney dodged out of the alley looking furtively left and right. There was still a profusion of traders and artisans moving this way and that seemingly at random but like bees at the entrance to a hive they each had their purpose. He retraced his steps as far as he could and as quick as he could and enquiring of a fellow standing against a wall having a minute with his pipe got a direction out of the teeming sprawl of Des Halles. Once out in the wider street he threw the knife away and he patted his waistcoat pockets with both hands for his watch but he must have lost it in his fall. That was a going to be a prize for someone. As he did this he looked himself up and down. His suit was covered from trouser bottoms to the lapels of his jacket in the filth of the stones he had fallen on and he could not see the dirt on his face. It would not have to matter he told himself, he had to get back to the Ritz and make arrangements as soon as possible to leave Paris. It had to be for St Petersburg by the earliest train available in the morning.

Having got his bearings he ran and then decided to only walk quickly towards the main boulevard in the quarter, Boulevard Sebastopol. The last thing he wanted to do was attract the attention of some gendarme on his beat. The streets were deserted so he might have aroused suspicion. At Sebastopol his wavings for a cab were ignored by the few that passed and he realised it must be his appearance that was putting them off. He took off his jacket and his waistcoat the waistcoat having protected his shirt from the dirtiest effects of the fall. He then took his handkerchief and dipped it in the water of a horse trough and washed his face as best he could. He then turned his jacket inside out and carried it with his waistcoat over his arm covering most of his filthy trousers. It worked. The next cab that passed stopped and he popped into the cabin of it as quick as he could and said, 'The Ritz and don't spare the horse.'

At the Ritz he knew he would have another problem and that was going in through the front entrance. He instructed the driver when they got near to take him around to the side where there was night porter's door. Paying off the cabbie he knocked on the porter's door and an old man answered. He gave him the details of his suite and the old man at first dubious was then persuaded by a generous 'pour boire' to let him in.

Sidney went straight up and threw off his dirty clothes and luxuriated in a hot shower which cleansed him of all the night's accumulation of dirt and danger and as after any such engagement he always felt elated, enervated and ravenously hungry. He called room-service for sandwiches and champagne. When his order was delivered he ate and drank and then he went to bed naked and without even attempting to wake her, invaded Margaret's somnambulant form.

Work went on at Des Halles as it did every day, for twenty four hours a day. But in the alley where they stored the rubbish nobody came to dump any more bones and no starving pauper came to dredge the crates of decomposing cabbages. The reflexes in the knees of the young man straightened the muscles of his legs and the noose round his neck tightened and slowly throttled him before he even regained consciousness. When he was found and the police were called a bright newly promoted brigadier said that the modus operandi was typically Sicilian and so the murder was put down to internecine strife between the Italian and Russian Anarchists. A score had been settled so revenge killings might be expected in the alien community and the case was closed. ' As long as they just kill each other who cares'? Said one hard -bitten cynical old gendarme who's beat was Des Halles. He had seen it all since he had walked over scores of corpses in his time especially those men, women and boys of the hundreds who were shot against the wall of Pere Lachaise Cemetery during the slaughter of the Paris Commune. 'I'll be satisfied if they don't shoot me before I draw my pension. je m'en fou'.

Even though Sidney had not gone to sleep until nearly four he was fully awake at six and shaking the shoulder of a still sleeping Margaret. He had asked for breakfast to be served in the suite at six thirty and it came promptly. Sidney had asked for scrambled eggs and toast which was the nearest at that time the Ritz got to an English Breakfast; toasted French bread leaving something to be desired.

Margaret did eventually wake up but could not understand the urgency.' Why did they have to leave? I thought we were to have a holiday in Paris. We have only been here two days.' Sidney invented a message he had received from London by telegraph. They had to leave today and they had to be on the twelve forty five train to Moscow changing at Warsaw. He had not yet told her they were going to St. Petersburg.

Sidney's was such prestigious accommodation at the Ritz that staff were sent up to do their packing for them and by ten all the cases were being consigned to the Gare de L'Est for the twelve forty five Warsaw Express.

Margaret was still grumbling but she dressed for the train and by eleven thirty she was waiting in the foyer as Sidney paid the bill.

Chapter Eighteen

Just before twelve they were walking along the quai past the carriages of the Paris -Warsaw Express to the wagon lit that Sidney had reserved at the Ritz. Sidney handed a sheaf of tickets to the guard and a white coated steward tried to take Sidney's hold -all from him. Sidney insisted on carrying it on board himself. Once in their compartment Sidney was less agitated and Margaret noticed his change in mood. 'You have had the air of being quite upset this morning, all this rushing for the train and cutting short our visit. Is there anything wrong that I should know about?' She said. 'No,' He assured her, 'I just hate having to make last minute arrangements but the message I got from the firm insisted on it.' In reality of course his change in mood was directly related to the fact that he now felt safe on the train. A paranoia had set in after the events of the night before and he felt sure he might have been followed back to the Ritz. He needn't have worried. Dead men tell no tales.

As they settled into their compartment, luxurious wood paneled suite by day and converted to bedroom by night, they heard all the noises of an international railway station, whistles and clanking wheels and then the massive roaring chuffing sound of steam and smoke expelled from its smoke stack as the great French locomotive heaved its long train of carriages out into the clear daylight spinning its great driving wheels until steel gripped iron and the Warsaw Express began to pick up speed on its transcontinental journey.

The eastern arrondisements of Paris moved past their carriage window like the film frames of the new cinematograph and soon they were heading north,north east across the cockpit of Europe, the ancient battlefields of Europe since the Gallo-Roman times of Vertingretorix, through Malplaquet to the Napoleonic wars and most recently if twenty years is recent, to the still open wound for France of the battlefields of the Franco-Prussian War and the annexation of Alsace, and Lorraine.

They heard a knock on their compartment door. Margaret looked up from her magazine and Sidney put his elocution text down and asked who was there. It was the carriage steward and the call for lunch. Sidney looked across the compartment to Margaret who sitting on the comfort of the upholstered cushioned seat had, to relax, unfastened her bodice. Her rounded breasts were of that palely blue white of fresh milk against the light blue day dress she had chosen to travel in and her blonde hair was in the disarray that had resulted from the impatient and urgent removal of her hat as she ensconced herself in the privacy of their compartment. Sidney looked at her and the brief lines he knew of an English poet, was it Herrick? 'A sweet disorder in the dress......' and the next line, he thought ended in 'wantoness'. Before he could think that he would eat lunch later Margaret said, 'Shall we have a simple lunch served in here or shall we go to the dining car?". Sidney looked at her and with the typical fickleness of his moods which indicated that he always meant what he said when he said it, stated, 'No, let's get freshened up and reserve a table. I want to show you off.' Margaret liked that flattery but she still said, 'Show me off indeed, don't be foolish and give me time to tidy my dress.' Sidney shouted through the door,'A table for two, with our backs to the engine.' Oui monsieur, was the reply and then confirmation' Un table pour deux'.

They had a good lunch but instead of returning to their compartment, Margaret went into the Ladies drawing room at the end of the dining car and Sidney went into the library to continue his exercises.

He chose a chair against a small mahogany desk and gave his book the concentration he thought he was capable of when he had set himself a task. He sat, took out his silver case, took a match from the cone of the dispenser on the desk, struck it against the ridged porcelain of the striker and lit one his last French cigarettes. However the hum of the train's speed and the rocking motion of the carriage combined with the almost musical sound of the four beats on one note and then after a brief pause the four beats on another of the wheels passing over the joints in the rails began to conspire to break his concentration. Added to this was a good lunch digesting and the half bottle of Beune plus a cognac digestif he had drunk. He stubbed out his half-finished cigarette and he was soon in a post prandial doze.

He woke to the sound of subdued voices. They were speaking in German. Two men had entered the library while he dozed. They were smartly dressed in the traditional suits of southern Germany, high buttoned and with collars trimmed with velvet. He had passed them in the dining car and they had bid him good day. He had pretended not to understand their greeting. He wanted to maintain the identity on his passport and not to give away his knowledge of languages apart from English. As he heard them speaking he did not immediately reveal that he was no longer asleep. As they spoke he became more and more interested. He was an inveterate 'picker up of other people's ill-considered trifles.'

The larger one of the two seemed to be continuing a conversation started in the dining-car.

'The British Empire is finished or at least it is in decline. It has been going down - hill since the 1870's. We will surpass and are surpassing them in all industrial production. It is the time for Germany's place in the sun. The British are finished and they will be out for the count when our beloved Kaiser tells the world of his plan for a navy that will more than rival the damned British Navy. It will be a navy of modern Dreadnoughts and the secret of its power will be.' Here he became more confidential and he bent his head towards Sidney.' His partner pursed his lips and shook his head. 'He's English, doesn't understand German.' The big one went on.

'Our navy will be powered by oil, coal is obsolete. The fuel that gave Britain its energy and economic power is out of date and they haven't got access to any oil reserves. Not one place on that pink map on which the sun never sets has any oil.'

His listener had a very perplexed look on his face and he spoke slowly when he did.

'But have we?'

'Yes we have.' Said the big fellow.

Sidney was wide awake by now but still maintaining a pretence of sleep.

'We will soon have The Baghdad to Berlin Railway. We at The Deutsche Bank have even persuaded the City of London and its financiers to assist us in investing in it. They think they are on to a good thing, but we have the full cooperation of the Ottoman Empire. We are training and fitting out their army. The British don't like this and hypocrites that they are they and their agents are interfering in the Balkans and encouraging a clique of western educated young Turks to revolt against The Sultan. But they do not know the half of it my friend and it is here that your knowledge of the middle east will be most important. You must use your contacts in Mosul, Kirkuk and Basra indeed your informants throughout Anatolia and Mesopotamia if the advantage we have gained is to be put to its fullest use.' He paused and then said in a voice so low that Sidney had to strain to hear him while not revealing his state of wakefulness.

'We have acquired the subsurface mineral rights for 20 kilometres on either side of the railway along the whole of its length from the Turkish border to Baghdad. As our geologists have prospected from the already exploited wells at Mosul and proved that oil is under the whole area The Reich will be assured of oil supplies for generations to come. It will prove that our strategy of Drang Nach Osten is the right one and confound our timid diplomats.'

At that moment a steward came in to the carriage and invited the company he saw to take tea or coffee either in their compartments or in the dining car. He effectively broke the spell for he delivered his message in German and Sidney intuitively responded. As he did and walked by the pair who had been so intently conversing he saw a cloud of doubt pass over the big man's brow. Sidney said jauntily in his best English accent as he left the carriage, 'Tea time ay. The same in any language.'

He didn't go to the dining car nor did he bother to order tea instead he went straight back to his compartment and there Margaret was sitting watching the now darkening world pass by the window. 'You have been a long time.' And she said ironically,' I thought you might have got off at the last stop.' Sidney was too pre-occupied to reply or to notice whether she had been drinking or not and without more ado he went straight to his case and took out a note book and recorded as much of the conversation in as much detail as he could remember. It would become a significant element in his final report. He thought twice about that later and decided to wire 'The Firm' in code from Warsaw.

They had dinner brought to their compartment that evening. Sidney said to Margaret that he wanted to be alone with her and to relax. In reality Sidney believed superstitiously that if he met the big Bavarian again he might in one way or another betray that he had understood every word of his conversation.

They had a good dinner and that put Stanley in a better mood so that when it was time for the steward to make up their bed and before they got in to sleep in it Sidney would not let Margaret take off her underclothes but made love to her in her stockings and unloosened corset taking her from behind through her opened drawers and making her gasp with pleasure at his passion. She hoped he knew how happy it made her to be lost in the eroticism of their love making. She didn't need drink for forgetfulness when prone on her his hands were clasped on the fullness of her breasts and his tongue was bringing her to climax in the cleft of her sex. She pressed his head between her open legs, drew up her knees, lifted her buttocks off the bed and smiled as she groaned and was lost in the spasms and delight of orgasm. She had no idea that his intention was to abandon her in St. Peters burg. His only thought on the matter being what he was to use as an excuse.

Two days later after stops at Berlin HauptBahnhof and Poznan the smoke and steam shooting express dragged its great tons of weighty rolling stock into Warsaw station. The passengers who were going on into Russia were transferred to waiting rooms while wider gauge engines and carriages were fitted for the journey. Sidney and Margaret waited with the others. As they did, Sidney saw in a Russian newspaper placed in a rack for travelers, the excuse he was seeking for leaving Margaret in St Petersburg. There was a cholera epidemic in the Caucasus. It was a perfect piece of serendipity. He was fully aware of his cynical intention to leave her behind because he believed she would be a hindrance. She would get in the way and not allow him, within a number of dimensions to do as he wished. It would transform that cynicism into a solicitous concern for her well being and welfare that would be difficult for her to gainsay.

He decided not to tell her until they got to St. Petersburg. The fact that they were going to St. Petersburg and not to Moscow he had not as yet revealed to her. The time might be right when the train left Warsaw and the line branched off north in the direction of Lithuania, Latvia and Estonia and not direct East to Moscow. He decided that the right moment might be as they passed through Byalistok not far from Warsaw on the line to St. Petersburg.

Chapter Nineteen

For the hour or so it took to make the engine and rolling stock transfer Sidney worked on putting his newly acquired information into code from the instructions in the book he had been given on leaving Melville. He then changed his mind and asked to be directed to a telephone. Taking the number from his notebook he rang the British Embassy in Warsaw and asked that an attaché be sent to the station. When the man arrived Sidney gave him his notes on the conversation he had overheard and asked that they be sent straight way in the diplomatic bag. He included a message that informed Melville that he was going to St. Petersburg first, as he was leaving his wife there to get her settled as far away from the cholera epidemic as he could and he would do that before he went south to the Caucasus. He also asked the attaché to use his contacts in St. Petersburg to arrange for the renting of an apartment for Margaret, of appropriate standard preferably on The Nevsky Prospekt. He saw the attaché on his way and then waited with Margaret for the train to make its departure.

When the train had reached Byalistok he decided to tell Margaret that their destination was St. Petersburg and not Moscow. He did not immediately tell her that he was leaving her there but thought that he would as soon as he got her settled in an apartment with perhaps a hired lady companion to keep her company and to look after her.

The train was not as comfortable as the Warsaw Express and although first-class it had seen some wear and tear and was perhaps evidence of the lack of investment in the Russian rail network and its rolling stock. Its great salt caked locomotive poured out black smoke from its stack. A sure sign that the fire box and boiler were worn out. Black smoke signaling wasteful and inefficient combustion. A lack of investment that was due no doubt to the economic decline that Tsarist Russia was experiencing at the time.

Sidney looked out of the window of the train at the peasants working in the fields and at the workers waiting in stations that the train passed through. Their poverty was obvious. Sidney knew that their living conditions were abysmal and that they lived under a system that made them pay criminally high taxes and deprived them of the land that was theirs. It was no wonder that there were strikes by industrial workers and that there were frequent agrarian disorders. However he thought the only way that things would change would be through Russia exploiting its vast reserves of raw materials and its even more extensive population.

It was a population that opportunistic politicians were wooing with a dubious democracy and some with an even more dubious socialism. As far as Sidney was concerned he would rather have The Romanovs. They could be brought into line and made to realize what responsibilities they had for Eternal Mother Russia that for Sidney, when overcome by his sentimental attachment to his homeland, was like Ancient Rome,

'An Idea in the Mind of God.'

As the train chugged through the provincial town of Byalistok it was almost time to go for dinner. The 200 or so kilometers the train had travelled from Warsaw was at a speed not exceeding much more than 30 kilometers an hour. As they took their places in the dining car Sidney thought it a good time to tell Margaret of the new plans.

As they began their indifferent food served by indifferent stewards. Sidney said to Margaret, 'You may or may not have noticed that we are heading north and not east.'

Margaret toyed with a serving of meat on her plate that she did not recognize although she had ordered beef. She was not in a good mood.

' Why would you expect me to know the difference?' She said, petulantly.

'Well, I say this.' Said Sidney patiently understanding the reasons for her demeanor and not wanting to irritate her more in case it made the question of her staying in St. Petersburg more difficult to manage. 'We are heading for St. Peters burg and not Moscow. I am going to give you the few days holiday I promised you in Paris and St. Petersburg I can promise you is as beautiful as Paris.'

As if to confirm his decision to tell her the train stopped at an isolated halt and two Russian border guards got on and began to go up and down the train checking papers and credentials. Had Sidney not told Margaret, the question asked by one of the guards regarding their destination as Sidney presented his and Margaret's identity papers would have.

There was a knock on the door of their compartment and Sidney opened it to the two black uniformed guards. With a salute and the clicking of heels that made the large polished brown holster of his pistol slap against his hip one of the guards said, 'What is the purpose of your journey to St. Petersburg.?'

As the guard looked from the British pass port that Sidney had handed to him to Sidney and then to Margaret, Sidney said that it was part pleasure but mostly business. On this he took out his Ozone Preparations correspondence and tried to explain briefly the purpose of his intention to travel on from St. Petersburg to the Caucasus and Baku. The guards moved on down the carriage without further questions.

That news of a short holiday changed Margaret's mood and allied with Sidney's attentiveness, night and day it made the relative discomfort of the rest of the long slow train journey more acceptable. Even Sidney looked forward to the somewhat careless carriage steward coming into their compartment to put down the bed so that he could get into it and keep Margaret happy, at least for the time being.

They were breakfasting in their compartment on the morning of the fourth day out of Warsaw when they trundled into Vitebeski Station, St. Petersburg. The guard walked the length of the train shouting out St. Petersburg in loud Russian as he passed.One of his colleagues stopped him for a few moments and had a brief word and then hurried past him and stopped to knock on the door of Sidney and Margaret's compartment. He had a telegram for Sidney from the Embassy in Warsaw with the details of the apartment in St. Petersburg.

In no less than twenty minutes they had vacated their compartment and Sidney was making arrangements in deliberately halting Russian with the luggage clerk and a porter for their bags and particularly Margaret's trunks to be sent to number 26 Nevsky Prospect. Sidney had done his homework well and so had the attaché. Sidney called a cab outside the station and he directed the driver of what was more a carriage than a cab to take them to a place where they could wait in comfort while last minute arrangements were made for the apartment. Sidney said to the driver, again in suitably halting Russian that they should be taken to Dominic's café, also on The Nevsky Prospect.

At Dominic's café Sidney ordered ice cold vodka and caviar with blinis and sour cream. Sidney's plan was to go from Dominic's to The Imperial Hotel and to stay there for a couple of days before moving Margaret into an apartment with the companion that Sidney would now set about finding.

The Imperial Hotel was comfortable to the point of luxury and it was a considerable relief to settle into their suite after the grubby basic conditions of the train from Warsaw. The first thing they both did was have a bath and Sidney broke the habit of years by soaking himself in the bath with Margaret. Before doing that he had ordered Russian Champagne and smoked salmon sandwiches from room service. It came and Sidney answered the door in an enormous white woollen dressing gown embroidered with the Imperial Arms. The waiter wheeled in the trolley with the ice bucket on it and a complimentary bouquet of flowers. He took the champagne and glasses into the bathroom and they both luxuriated in the hot water of the grandiose bath tub soaking off all the dust and grime of their journey.

They drank the bottle and then made love among the soap suds the eroticism of their embraces made more sensual by the lubricating effect of the water and soap as they slid off and on of each other's naked wet bellies. Then Sidney was almost overtaken by an impulse murderously and pathologically violent in its evil character. As Sidney brought Margaret to a climax so vigorous in its effect that her convulsions caused water to lap in waves over the side of the bath.

She was with her back against the end of the bath. She slipped and her breasts and head with its blonde hair went under the bath water. Sidney had his hands on her shoulders and he kept them there. Margaret's hair spread in fronds as she struggled sending gouts of bubbles to the surface. In the moments she was under water Sidney thought how easy it would be to simply keep up the pressure of his hands until she drowned so solving the problems he had with her.

Margaret kicked her feet in panic and caused the bathwater to cascade even more over the edge of the bath on to the towels surrounding it. Sidney conquered his homicidal urge and Margaret came up gasping, spluttering and thrashing in the throes of both drowning and orgasm. She was at one and the same time furious and scared to death and after thumping Sidney with both fists on his bare chest and calling him all the bastards under the sun. she began to cry. He tried to placate her by telling her that it was a joke that had gone too far but she was not to be reassured and it took the rest of the evening and an invitation to a promenade on the boulevards of St. Petersburg to get her into a receptive mood again.

After that fiasco Sidney tried as hard as he could to make the few days he knew he would be spending in St. Petersburg as enjoyable as possible for Margaret. The hotel suite was as luxurious as The Imperial could provide and for the few night they were there Sidney had romantic dinners, served by the staff in their rooms. Sidney let Margaret drink as much as she wanted of the heavy Russian wines of Georgia, Moldova and The Ukraine and The Russian Champagne of The Imperial Vinyards of Arau-Dyurso. And she was soon too, acquiring a taste for Russian vodka,drinking it as she did from a bottle frosted with ice and so as viscous as a syrup when it was poured. These evening ended happily for Margaret as they dissolved with her inebriation into the sensuality of their love-making.

During the day they took carriage rides along the Nevsky Prospekt by the river Neva and over the bridges of the many canals. And on one occasion they picnicked on the fringes of the Nevsky Forest. Sidney hired two Imperial Hotel staff members to accompany them in a separate carriage and to serve the picnic for them on the green grass of a clearing still dappled and lit by the yellow rays of the late summer sun.

Sidney remembered for a long time the image of Margaret reclining sun-lit on the grass, in a full, pale blue afternoon dress trimmed with white lace and intertwined with thin ribbons of black velvet. The sun shining on her blonde hair made it look like threads of gold and topped as it was by a simple dove white feathered hat and with a parasol over her shoulder she looked as if she was sitting for one of the new French Impressionist painters.

When they did go out in the evening it was to Dominic's Café Restaurant. If a Russian secret policeman or one of his aides had put Sidney under surveillance he might have wondered how this non-Russian speaking English businessman could cope so easily with a Russian restaurant menu as he ordered zakuski of cold borsch, considered choices for the main dish that ranged, as he advised Margaret from Palmeni (dumplings), Bigos (Chicken stew), Goloubtsy(cabbage stuffed with chicken), Pozharsky (chicken cutlets), to Golonka (braised pork) and Chanakhi (Roast Georgian lamb). As dessert he chose sweet pancakes for her topped with Smetana (Sour Cream). She loved him when he treated her like this. She was proud of him and she felt that she was envied by other diners as he represented so patently, the cosmopolitan traveler, so much at ease in every circumstance.

For Sidney there was another motive in going to Dominic's for it was at Dominic's that he had charged the head waiter with the task of finding a companion for Margaret. The Head waiter had suggested that it would be difficult but in fact many of the customers at the café side were young graduates of the university and so it was to be a relatively easy task for him and one he knew he would get a hefty tip for.

For one young woman he knew,the prospect of working as a companion to an

English woman approached the ideal for she was a student of English and saw it as an opportunity of having her room and board provided while significantly improving her language skills. She had left a photograph and the head waiter discretely showed it to Sidney and at the same time assured him of her suitability. Sidney gave him the address of the apartment and asked him to arrange an interview with the girl for ten in the morning two days hence. Sidney thought that by that time he would have persuaded Margaret of the wisdom of staying in St. Petersburg while he journeyed south.

Sidney looked at the photograph. It was of a young woman in her early twenties, wearing light, round gold-rimmed spectacles. Her hair was of the formal plaited 'earphone' style with one on each side of her head and with a fringe over a vaguely pretty face on which was a shy smile. She was wearing a man's shirt with a cravat at the collar. It was covered by a 'V' necked pull over. The girl's name was Karole Domskaya. She seemed to be just what Sidney was looking for, so Sidney decided that he would break the news of the cholera epidemic to Margaret the next morning and that it would be necessary for her to stay behind.

Chapter Twenty

Sidney woke early the next day and ordered morning tea for both he and Margaret. He drank his tea and caressed her when she had finished hers. He let her explore him with her mouth and embark upon an adventure to please him. He knew that this would put her in good mood. The idea that she could please him as much as he pleased her convinced her that she could keep him and that they could continue to return to their old passion as they had over the last weeks during their journey here. For him it was a ruse to prepare her for the news that he was going to leave her behind.

He called room service and asked for newspapers in English German and Russian. He knew he was being optimistic. There was no possibility that they would have The Times and anyway that would not have reported the cholera outbreak; the German paper might. The Russians certainly would. As it was when the steward came he only had, as Sidney expected, the Russian Papers. To make a show for the room steward Sidney threw the paper to the floor and said, 'What use is this to me? Haven't you got any English Papers? The steward replied in broken English, that he had not. Sidney gave him a grudging tip and then when he had gone picked up the paper and took a quick look. There on the second page was news of the outbreak of cholera in The Caucasas.

Sidney got back into bed and opened the newspaper. He looked at the front page and then casually opened it to the second page. He put on a horrified look and said. 'Good God.' Margaret put her second cup of tea on the table at the side of the bed and asked what was wrong.

"There's been a cholera outbreak in the south Caucasus, just where we are going."

"Does that mean we can't go?"

"Well I'll tell you this." Sidney was at his most solicitous. "It certainly means that you can't go. I am not having you exposed to such dangers. It is me that is on duty not you. There is no reason for you to put yourself at risk. I shall make arrangements for you and leave you here in good hands and get back to you as soon as the job is done. I should not take long, no more than a month or perhaps two."

Margaret was quite alarmed. Things seemed to be going upside down. She was looking forward to a nice long train journey while enjoying the attentions of Sidney as she had coming here.' But what shall I do here by myself? I don't know the language and I have no English friends. I will be so lonely and how will I look after myself? I don't know how to even shop for an egg"

"Don't worry, give me a little time and I will work things out for you. I will find you an apartment in a central position and recruit a suitable companion for you, who will see to your needs, perhaps someone near to your age and although I am going to a far flung 'outpost' it is not so far that I can't return and see you from time to time." Of course Sidney had no intention of coming back as he said but it was no effort for him to lie. He would have said anything to get Margaret to accept this new circumstance.

    Margaret sat up in bed looking confused and glum. She had the inevitable demeanor of someone who was expecting happiness and instead got disappointment.

    Sidney knew what to do at least to solve the immediate problem of Margaret's melancholy. He laid her back on the bed and as her head touched the pillow he leaned over her looking into her blue eyes. He took the curls of her hair, untidy with sleep on her forehead and stroked them over her right ear. Then with his left hand he reached down in the bed and drew the hem of her night dress until it was up over stomach, her navel. her breasts and to her neck. As he kissed her gently on the lips he whispered,' Now I am going to show you what you will miss most.'

    Sidney spent the rest of the day continuing his task of convincing Margaret that she should stay in St. Petersburg. He explained that the embassy would arrange the apartment and he would organize the employment of a companion, although of course he had already done that.

    The next day they went for lunch at Dominic's and the agent for the apartment house came into the café and enquired about Sidney and was pointed in his direction by the maitre d. Sidney having left a message to the effect that the agent was expected.

    Sidney and Margaret were taken in the carriage the agent had waiting to Number 2 Kazanskaya in St. Peters burg. The apartment the attaché had arranged to be rented was on the second floor and there was a concierge who lived in small rooms in the basement. The apartment completely furnished as it was had been recently decorated. It had two bedrooms, a reception room, a dining room and a kitchen, with a large bathroom and all the usual offices off the master bedroom. It was electrically lit. In the entrance hall there was a very large stove ornately tiled in green gold and white. It took over part of the hall from floor to ceiling. The agent pointed out that when it needed lighting and refueling, the concierge would perform that task. He also indicated that in the same apartment complex of different floors there were shops and salons that catered for every need. Residents in the apartment block did not have to venture out into St. Petersburg proper. Everything was literally on their doorstep.

    In other circumstances Margaret would have been impressed but she was not to be persuaded that she should stay until Sidney became quite firm and talked of her harming his career and that the sooner she was settled the sooner he could leave and therefore the sooner he would be back. In the end she saw that she was going to have to accept the inevitable but that did not stop her being miserable at the prospect.

    Sidney did not now consider that Margaret's objections were going to be an obstacle to his plans to go south alone so he engaged himself in the formalities of leaving the Imperial. He gave the desk the address of the apartment and instructed them to send Margaret's luggage to arrive the next day and his he said, he would make different arrangements for later, Margaret spent the day subdued and had no enthusiasm for any plans that Sidney might have had to entertain her. Her mood left Sidney unaffected. His ability to be unmoved by any scale of happiness or its opposite on the part of others insulated him from any feeling except those that he saw as his own. He was motivated completely by his own ego. If a situation impinged on that then he would react. If not. as he said to himself almost as a mantra, il n'existe pas. As the motto said on the letter head of the stationery and business cards printed for him and interpreted by him as 'no faith in any world but mine ' 'Nulla Mundo Fides'.

Karole Domskaya arrived at number 26 in good time and was there as the carriage Sidney had ordered to take him and Margaret from The Imperial arrived. As they stepped down from the carriage she introduced herself and Sidney presented Margaret whose hand she took smiling as she did. Karole was about the same stature but perhaps just a little shorter that Margaret. They both had the same slim figure. She was simply dressed in a short chocolate brown corduroy jacket fitted to her waist and bust which she wore over a darker brown skirt down to her brown high button boots. The cream blouse under her jacket had a lace frill collar at the neck.

Margaret was as Sidney expected, reticent but even she had to admit to herself that on first impressions she was struck by Karole's open and guileless personality. Karole's English was very good with her Russian accent adding to the sound of her speaking rather than detracting from it. As they walked up the stairs to the first floor she chatted to Margaret and asked her how she had enjoyed her stay in St. Petersburg and how there was so much more to see and so many places to visit that a few days stay could not do it justice and so on. Margaret's answers were monosyllabic but not unreceptive.

The agent was waiting on the landing in front of the imposing oak double-doors of the apartment and after opening the doors gave the key to Sidney. He then asked to be excused because of other business and saying in poor English as he descended the stairs, that he could be contacted at his office in the event of there being any problems. Karole switched immediately into her role and spoke to him in Russian translating his reply into a much more acceptable form.

Sidney ushered both Karole and Margaret into the hall and then into the drawing room 'Or whatever it is called.' Said Sidney in good humour as everything seemed to be going to plan. He indicated to Karole that she should sit down and he began the interview which he had already convinced himself was unnecessary, however for the sake of form he would conduct it anyway.

As she answered his questions Karole explained that she was a graduate of St. Petersburg University and had been one of the first young women to be accepted for studies in Faculty of Fine Art and had opted for English studies as a subsidiary subject. Her mother was a widow and she lived with her and her elder sister in what was known as The Kalininsky side of the city. Her father had been an official in the city's treasury before he died.

Sidney then explained her duties. She would act as companion to Margaret and so arrange everything associated with 'The Household' laundry, cleaning, commissions and cooking. It would be left to her to employ a daily housemaid and a cook but

Margaret would see to their wages."She would also see to yours Miss Domiskaya." Said Sidney." which will incidentally, be the equivalent of £4 pounds per month room and board included. You will have one half day free each week and the time of that can be arranged with Margaret."

Sidney pointed out that she was however, to make herself available to Margaret's wishes as requested, any time day or night. She would be asked to speak English at all times but if Margaret wished she could pass on a little of the Russian language. It was. Sidney added, a good opportunity for Karole to improve her English with a' native speaker.' The contract would be short term, no longer than three months and after that renegotiated as necessary. Here Margaret, who was sitting in an opposite arm chair listening, looked up, but she saw from Sidney's expression that she should say nothing.

Sidney turned again to Miss Domiskaya,' Did she find the terms acceptable? And if so when could she begin her duties?'

Karole did not have to think for long. Work was difficult to find in St. Petersburg for a newly graduated young woman and working for Mrs. Reilly and living in would take a financial burden off of her mother. Mrs. Reilly seemed a nice friendly woman with whom she could get on and if it didn't work well there was always the door.

'I would very much like to take up the position and I find the terms quite acceptable and if you are in agreement I could start right away.'

For Sidney the decision was made and for Margaret it was a fait accompli. He told Karole to go and get her things but she had come prepared she said; of the few things she had, she had brought them with her and she had left them with the concierge. She could move in right away.

Sidney said he would leave them to it as he had to organize his trip south and he left to arrange his train tickets. Karole went downstairs and Margaret, disconsolate and without the assistance of a maid began to unpack her luggage. When she came back and after depositing her few belongings in the smaller of the bedrooms Karole helped Margaret and she on her part could not be unaffected by Karole's charming friendliness and cheerfulness. 'Perhaps I should make the best of a bad job. 'Margaret said to herself. 'It may not be so unacceptable after all.'

Sidney busied himself over the next day or so with his luggage, final details and financial arrangements for Margaret at the Russo-Asiatic Bank. He assured her that there would be a healthy account to draw on but at the same time warned her that it was not a bottomless pit if she went on shopping sprees. He also had a quiet word about her drinking and he observed that she seemed not as dependent on it as before. Margaret thought privately that the reason she was 'off' the drink was because over the last weeks she had been so happy with Sidney. With him gone she thought maybe the depression would return.

Sidney wanted to travel light so he commanded The Imperial to have the major part of his luggage sent on by rail to the Hotel Europe in Baku. It was Baku's best hotel.

He left himself with enough to wear for the journey which might take three to four days and for a short stay in Moscow where he intended to stop off to check his bank account and to establish contact with the consul.

What he also did was send a telegraph message to 'Ozone Preparations' but in reality to Melville it was in plain language confirming the reasons why he was leaving Margaret in St. Petersburg and informing him that he was embarking on his project to gauge the commercial possibilities of any business associations The message was of course monitored by the Ochrana and that Sidney expected.

He didn't expect that through the innovation of wireless telegraphy a German telegraph operator on a trawler off the south coast of England would be picking it up in his earphones and relaying it to an address in Hackney London where electric blue flashes under the door of one of its rooms indicated the message's reception and showed to Caroline Belvedere, as she carried a breakfast tray along the corridor to Herr Mueller that he was still hard at work, Just as he had been, a short time before when Sidney's communication on The Berlin –Baghdad Railway had been leaked by telegraph via a Foreign Office double agent.

Caroline balanced the tray on one hand and knocked at the door.' 'Heirein' said the voice of Herr Mueller. 'Set it down there mein Leiblich. You are too good to me. I don't deserve you. Oh by the way I have just had something on the wire concerning your friend Mr. Rosenblum'. Caroline felt the tiniest twinge of a reflex in the lower reaches of her stomach as the sound of his name reminded her of the two nights Sidney and her had spent together. ' I am afraid we are going to have to deal with him before he gets too close to what we are up to in the Caucasus.' Caroline knew what that meant.

"But he is so low level." Said Caroline."Is he worth bothering about? It would be wasting time effort and resources that we could well use elsewhere."

'' No". Mueller continued, The order from H.Q. is that Mr. Rosenblum should suffer a nasty accident while conducting his 'researches.'

Caroline walked back along the landing reflecting on her experience with Sidney. She could not recall precisely the joy they had shared but she remembered with affection what charming and easy company he had been and how comfortable she had felt with him in and out of bed. What she was not aware of was Mueller's vindictiveness and jealousy with regard to his feelings for her and of how they had overridden his 'professional' attitude to Caroline's overt prostitution of herself in The Service of The Reich. His subjectivity in the matter of Caroline was a hidden flaw in what his superiors saw as the perfect Chrystal of him as agent of their covert and subversive foreign policy in England.

Chapter Twenty One

On the day of Sidney's departure, Margaret and Karole accompanied him to the Tsarskoe Selo station for the 10.30 train to Moscow. They both came into his first- class cabin past the inevitable old tea lady at the end of the compartment warming up her samovar in preparation for orders of black Georgian tea. Karole said goodbye to Sidney, promising to look after Margaret ' as if she was my own sister' and then left discretely so that Sidney and Margaret could say goodbye in private.

Sidney pulled down the blinds of the compartment and embraced Margaret and putting his right hand down the front of her corsage on to her left breast and he took its nipple between his index finger and thumb. He squeezed gently. With the other hand he lifted her skirts and petticoats and felt between her legs through the silk of her drawers. He pushed her back against the door and she lifted her right high heeled booted leg on the seat. He kissed her with a passion that infused her with desire and almost persuaded him that perhaps he would go on a later train.

"God I will miss you." He breathed through his kiss. But as she kissed him and thrust her lower belly against him she began to cry and to say, "Please don't go, what shall I do without you?"

He did not release her from his embrace but said simply "You know what to expect with my job. Think of my returning to you and how we both will feel by then?" Sidney knew his wife well and what he had to do convince her of his sincerity. She was not part of the prevailing culture of Edwardian sexual prudery. She recognized her needs and she knew how effectively Sidney fulfilled them. What she had not recognized yet as her stirred emotions always blinded her to the truth about Sidney was that every aspect of him was part of a manipulative scheme to get the world and its people to do what he wanted it to do. Once again it had worked with her.

"Now then my brave little girl dry your eyes and let's say goodbye without any more tears."

Margaret looked into the mirror on the mahogany paneling of the compartment and saw how her tears had affected her face. Her eyes were red and the blue eye cosmetic she used had run with her tears. The rouge on her cheeks was smudged where Sidney had put his face. She tidied herself, powdered her face as best she could and smoothed down her dress and then she went with Sidney out onto the quai where Karole was waiting. Sidney stood back in the doorway of the carriage and Margaret got down out of the train. Along the line of the train, at the head, the great black locomotive was letting out a regular mechanical beat while gently hissing steam in a jet while smokier wisps came from the heating and braking pipes in the spaces where the carriages where linked. A railway worker wearing a shiny peaked cap and oily overalls walked steadily along the length of the train tapping the wheels so that they gave a bell-like ring. Sidney looked down at Margaret and moved onto the step and said that he would write regularly.

The guard with his thick grey moustache, forked beard and uniformed more like a military man than a civilian employee passed them holding his staff with a roundel on it crying out in Russian that passengers should board. Sidney retreated to the interior of the carriage to let other passengers get on and a porter took the opportunity to close the door. Above in the iron work of the station roof the hour hand of the station clock was on 10 and the long black minute finger jerked to the figure 6. The guard looked at his watch and raised his staff and way up on the engine the engineer turned his head and disappeared under the hood of the engine to pull leavers, watch dials, release brakes and let valves force steam into pistons. The great driving wheels spun before getting a grip and grey black steamy smoke burst out of the engine chimney in great puffs and the train began to pull away and leave relatives, friends, colleagues and railway workers standing on the quai.

Margaret and Karole waved their handkerchiefs and they stood there and watched heads go back into open windows no longer sure which one was Sidney's. They stood there as the Moscow Express curved along its lines diminishing in perspective until the red light on the rear carriage disappeared into the great clouds of steam and smoke left in its wake. It took Sidney away and left Margaret wondering if he would ever come back.

The train journey to Moscow took nearly a day but Sidney was comfortable in his old fashioned sleeping compartment. He continued his elocution exercises and read up on McGregor's book on India. He had also his notes on oil and the Caucasus. He mused on the length of the journey he had yet to make to Baku. It was a bloody long way. He would have liked a companion but reconnaissance in the dining car did not give up information on any ladies.

In Moscow his first priority was to contact the consul and investigate his Moscow Bank account. He wanted to see what funds were in, what facilities there would be for getting money in Baku and how he could transfer funds for Margaret. He also wanted to deposit the large amount of 'rubles' he had brought with him from England. He was quite confident there would be no problems of acceptance. He was right. It was all sorted out by the afternoon Being with the British Consul in Moscow seemed to carry a lot of weight and his enquiries were answered immediately and the transfer formalities took only a little more time. Sidney did not want to spend too much time in Moscow so he declined the hospitality of the consul and instead accepted the advice about a hotel very close to the station where the consul said they spoke English and he reserved his room for two nights.

After his stay Sidney left the hotel and went to catch the train for the first part of his long journey to Baku. In front of him were railway lines that stretched for nearly two thousand kilometers. Even if there were no stops or breakdowns, very unlikely, it would be a journey of at least three days. Sidney decided to estimate around five.

His accommodation was in a 'soft' first class compartment that was really a double. Its upholstered seats converted into a double bed and Sidney settled in and made himself comfortable. As he was putting his feet up there was a knock on his door. He opened it to the guard and an official who was not only there to check his ticket but also his identity. There were the usual questions. Why are travelling to the Caucasus? Where have you come from? How long will you stay? Please present your papers. Your wife is on this passport, where is she? He wasn't an Ochrana man merely a local official.

Dinner on the first night was not too disappointing. He had not concerned himself much with eating during the day having ignored the breakfast offered at the hotel. He was still nostalgic for his favourite English breakfast. There was little chance of that being available in Russia. Even The Imperial in St. Petersburg had not been able to come up with even a passing imitation. the concept of soft boiled egg had yet to reach the countries near the Arctic Circle. His unsatisfied appetite made sure that he was able to do justice to the bottle of chilled vodka he ordered.

As he reflected on St.Petersburg he thought he would spend the rest of the evening writing a letter to Margaret. He had telephoned her from the hotel in Moscow and he had telegraphed her from the consulate. She seemed to have settled to her new circumstance.

In fact Margaret and Karole had, in the day or so that they had been together, become quite good friends. Margaret had never really known other women apart from those women that were in her family, her mother for instance and her aunts. She had never really had the friendship of a woman. The only female friends she had ever had were the girls she was at convent school with and they were never really close, the nuns did not encourage it, Besides the friendships of adolescence did not compare to the friendship of a relatively mature woman of one's own age. Someone one could share confidences with. someone who had had, although of a different culture, more or less the same experiences. Margaret was beginning to enjoy the company of Karole. She was successfully taking her mind off the departure of Sidney but also she was thinking less of the Rev. Thomas and her lost baby. Significantly, she was not drinking.

They took walks in the parks of the city. Karole knew her city well and she was able to introduce Margaret to museums and galleries and to the magnificent architecture of Peter the Great's great experiment in creating a European city for his New Russia.

One of the delights of their new friendship, certainly as far as Margaret was concerned was that she was able to share her wardrobe with Karole. They were near enough the same size as made no difference. Karole had never been able to afford the quality of workmanship and material of the dresses that Margaret now took for granted and she could not hide her pleasure at being allowed to try them on. This pleased Margaret very much. Margaret took the opportunity that she had to be generous very much to heart. She could not hide it from herself. It was part of her penance. She could not take communion at the moment. Karole had not yet been able to find a Roman Catholic Church in St. Petersburg.' There must be one.' she said. ' But until I do find one come with me to the Russian Orthodox Church that I attend. I will translate the service for you and the words that the priest says. What do you call it in English?' Margaret said, pleased at the invitation. 'I think you mean the sermon.'

Sidney went back to his compartment, He washed at the washstand that folded up conveniently after use and flushed out the used water as it did so and before he got into his pyjamas he called for the steward to put his bed down. That done he changed and got into bed and began to write his letter. Writing it brought back memories of Margaret and he felt somewhat lonely, added to his loneliness was a strong sense of desire for her. They were not feelings he was used to as he had trained himself to be self sufficient even in the matter of having to put up with solitude. The sensations he had of missing Margaret however were counterfeit. Had there been the opportunity to fill his bed with a desirable stranger memories of Margaret would have been dismissed immediately.

For Sidney the journey south seemed interminable. The train passed through featureless forest and plain and made stops at stations and halts whose names he was never again able to recall. He was struck by just how vast his country was and that within it there was a great variety of peoples,cultures and economies. Their world of work must have encompassed every trade, profession and labouring activity known on the earth. The only system capable of organizing the wealth these multitudes created was capitalism.

There were forces at large in the country that wanted to deliver to the masses of Imperial Russia and their governing institutions some political concept called social democracy and socialism. This for Sidney was anathema. Where ever he came across it he would oppose it.

How could such a land mass of lakes,hills, valleys, plains, mountains,forests, cities, towns. villages, peoples, cultures and tongues be governed other than by a political and economic system that relied on an authority drawn from the divine? The Tsar like the Pope was God's representative on earth. The application of a scientific political method could only work in the laboratory minds of academic university revolutionaries. This was Mother Russia, Holy Mother Russia,the gargantuan land that the greatest poets and novelists in the world were inspired to write about and he had been born into their same language.

The destiny of Russia was the destiny of the world and he saw himself as part of that destiny. What Russian author had written, 'If God is dead then everything is permissible'? No, it should read if Russia is dead then everything is permissible. 'He wanted to be proud of his heritage but his clandestine profession forced him in to the subterfuge of adopting another identity.

Chapter Twenty Two

As he looked through his carriage window it was only his boredom that made him lapse philosophical. It seemed that he was seeing an aspect of the infinity that Pushkin and Tolstoy wrote about. As if eternity might have this endless train journey in common with it. He was one man moving across a physical world of nature that was part of a regenerative cycle. He wasn't as other men however, within the inevitable entropy.In his psychopathological conceit he saw himself a part of this force of nature. His fate was as eternal and massively substantial as the great snow-capped mountains of the Caucasus range that was coming in to view. It did not alarm him that such egocentricity could have no room in it for the ordinary activity of human relationships or any possibility of an identification with the other. That experience for Sidney only came in the trivial but necessary daily business of looking into the mirror when he shaved.

At last the final part of Sidney's railway Odyssey was in view as the train halted at Grozny and he thought as he watched passengers get on and off that perhaps he had arrived in an Arab country. Women had their heads and hair covered, some even with a veil that allowed only the eyes to be seen. Men were mustached and heavily bearded and as they walked along a few paces in front of their women whom they allowed to carry their luggage parcels, they rolled small beads on a cord rather like a catholic rosary. There was something else to notice at Grozny; troops. They stood at intervals with rifles along the quai and there were many others coming and going. Maybe, thought Sidney, these are the troops I should be reporting on. It was a surprise also that he had to submit to having his papers checked again by two tough looking border guards whose pistol holsters had their leather flaps unfastened as if for speedy retrieval of the heavy revolvers they carried in them. After Grozny came Makhackala and the first view of the beautiful Caspian sea. Within no more now than three hundred kilometers or so now the train would pull in to Baku and, thought Sidney.' My work can begin'.

When the train at last reached Baku it was early evening.He was struck by the grimy desolation of what he was to learn was the Bibi –Eilat oil field with its forests of wooden derricks and antique rocking oil pumps that were known as 'nodding donkeys' by those in 'the trade.' Sidney saw that the beautiful blue of the Caspian sea on the Apsheron peninsula had been transformed into black sludge where leaking crude oil from the maze of oil pipe-lines from the wells in and around Baku had seeped into the sea for up to five hundred yards out. On the horizon to the west there was an enormous cloud of black smoke and flame that lit up the darkening sky like an infernal torch and it was possible to hear on the wind the roar of what was a blazing oil well. This area, exposed as the approach to Baku was made by train was most appropriately called 'Black Town'

As soon as Sidney left the station with the minimal luggage he carried he saw that there was a heavy pall of smoke over the town and that everywhere there was the sickly smell of petroleum. He asked a railway station functionary where the Hotel Europe was and instead of directing him there he called a carriage for him. When it arrived Sidney saw that the wheels were clogged with what looked like black clay but it was in fact a mixture of oil and mud. There were traces of oily mud all over the carriage and as Sidney was careful of his clothes he decided not to get in. There was an alternative and it was indicated to him, the electric street car,

The Hotel Europe was an oasis of luxury compared to the streets Sidney passed through on the way to book in. As he looked out of the tram car as it took him to the hotel, Baku seemed to have more in common with the shanty towns and frontier outposts that had sprung up in California or in the Klondike of Alaska during their gold rushes. Some streets had stepping stones across to avoid the oily mud and the sidewalks that fronted the many one storey buildings. They were thronged with workers whose oily work clothes had a shiny polished look while on their feet they wore boots that were caked in the same oily mud as on the wheels of the carriage.

At the hotel his room had been reserved and his luggage already delivered. He bathed and dressed for dinner and went down to the bar for an aperitif. The hotel was populated with oil speculators and oil prospectors whose origins were from all over the world apart from The USA. He was later to be told that the Russians didn't like their American competitor Rockefeller of Standard Oil.

The restaurant was so crowded that there was no possibility of dining alone so at dinner he had to sit at a table with a Frenchman, A Romanian, a Belgian and two Germans. They had all been in Baku for many months and were all geological experts of one kind or another. They were however quite interested in Sidney's questions and did not hesitate at all in giving Sidney advice and information on the oil industry in Baku.

Sidney did notice however that the Germans were just a little reticent when it came to describing what their activities were. Sidney picked up on this immediately."Those two fellows," he said to himself,,'Have got something to hide."The Frenchman and the Romanian were free with information on Baku's oil fired power station,the transportation of oil by rail, sea and the new developments of the pipeline. They were full of statistics on the volume of oil produced in Baku and the Caucasus region. Russia and its oils could light the world, it seemed and just one well was producing more than all North American output.

When it came to Sidney asking where new prospecting was being carried out their answers stopped and the Germans became even less talkative. That is where the secrets lie, thought Sidney. That is what is really important.; as he had thought in London, all the rest was statistics. He must make it his business to find out where new oil fields were being looked for

He lightened up the conversation by asking about the night life and what one did for fun. There were places to go where beautiful Georgian maidens could be found for company and there were parties if you could get an invitation. So said the Romanian. The venue for most high class parties as the Frenchman described them was The Villa Petrolia. And the next bit of information made Sidney sit up. The Villa Petrolia was owned by the Nobel family. Sidney feigned ignorance with regard to the Nobel family but he was soon enlightened. The Nobel's, with their innovatory approach had revolutionized the oil fields. They had introduced new drilling methods and methods of extraction that ensured less waste and that less oil stayed in the ground. Investment in railways and the carrying of oil in tanks on rail went hand in hand with the building of larger tankers for sea transportation and the use of oil for fuel in engines had been the result of new refining methods. And as for, Emanuel junior, he was an engineering genius and it was rumoured he was working on a secret project for the Russian Navy. Sidney did not betray any special interest in the Nobels but he did make a mental note to himself that he would endeavor to get an invitation to the next party or at least one of the parties at Villa Petrolia.

Dinner came. 'Cooked by French chefs imported from the best restaurants in Paris' Boasted the Frenchman.' You will not get cuisine like this anywhere else in Russia, even Moscow or St. Petersburg. Unfortunately you will have to drink Russian wine.' There followed a discussion on the relative merits of French Champagne as opposed to the Russian variety. Sidney in an attempt to draw attention from the more salient questions he was asking gave a valiant defence of the Russian variety. Really he wanted to ask questions more related to his investigations. He got round in the end to asking about the troops at Grozny and why The Russian Army found it necessary have such a presence in force.

The Frenchman and one of the Germans lighted on his query immediately and exposed quite lightheartedly the rationale behind Sidney asking it. He had not realized that his question was so obvious. Maybe he had drunk too much. ' You bloody English,' said one of the Germans,' Sidney found it difficult to avoid being offended by his rudeness and he wasn't an Englishman. He reflected on his reaction later and became worried that he really was losing his Russian identity. 'What do you think the troops are for? Don't bother answering that I know what you are worried about. You think the Russians have got their eye on your precious Raj.' Sidney. protested that his interest was just academic and he wasn't concerned with anything apart from his project. But his protests were dismissed by the bigger of the two Germans at the table.

" It's common knowledge my friend that your people think that Russia is building up an invasion force to move into India. I can tell you 'old boy", And here he put a sarcastic emphasis on the words, 'old boy,'"That the Russians have no intention of walking into India. They have enough on their plate with keeping in order the Armenians. The Azerbaijanis, Georgians and particularly the Tchetchins in Dagestan. They are certainly the ones who are as you English say, 'A pain in the necks.'"

The Belgian chimed in not having contributed much to what was becoming a lively and quite rewarding conversation for Sidney and said, 'Mr. Riley is it?' He gave the impression,in his Belgian way of politeness of apologizing for his German colleague."The troops you saw at Grozny are there to put down local revolts and spats between the various religious factions."It is always Religion." The Frenchman added." As our Montaigne has said, 'Never was a Kingdom given to so much blood, as The Kingdom of Heaven." The Belgian interjected."It is the same in Armenia but there the Turks are also interfering and murdering Armenian Christians at a rate that the Romans in the Coliseum would have envied.'

The German interrupted." Don't Criticize the Turks my Belgian friend when the echoes of the cries of those thousands who have disappeared in the 'Darkest Africa' of your Belgian Congo, have not yet died down. The Turks know best how to deal with the diversity of their Empire."How is that?" Sidney questioned wanting the conversation to go on as he was gathering so much from it and it looked as if it might degenerate, from the look on the Belgian's face into another Battle of Sedan. The Frenchman decided to answer the question laughing as he did so."There is no wonder the Turks are described as 'The Sick man of Europe.' When you ask a Turk how they manage to organize such an empire as they have he will tell you, 'That it is like carrying a sack of rats that are trying to gnaw their way out of the sack, Every now and again you give it a bloody great shake up."

This 'set the table on a roar.' Their laughter was heard so much above the hubbub of the noise the rest of the diners were making that heads turned to the table that was having so much fun To emphasis what a good time everyone was having, Sidney ordered another couple of bottles of champagne. The only aspect missing from this good time was a little female company so Sidney ordered that, as other tables seemed to be doing, from the Head Waiter.

He would, when requested, disappear from time to time to an upstairs room only to emerge within minutes with well dressed and attractive young women. This was a service that was as popular as the dry cleaning facility the hotel offered to those whose clothes were, in the filthy atmosphere and environment of Baku forever becoming oil stained.

Sidney called the Head Waiter over and said cheekily in the broken Russian that he affected for form, 'A round of girls please and make them your prettiest and I will see it is worth your while.' Within a few minutes the Head Waiter had returned with six very pretty girls. Not one of them more than twenty years old. Chairs were brought up and more glasses and more bottles and as Sidney's Russian was the best at the table (as the girls' command of English seemed to be restricted to the vocabulary of the bedroom) he was in the position he loved best, the centre of attention. It looked as if it was going to develop in to a good party and this was only his first night. It was only marred a little by how much the Head waiter wanted for the services of the girls, 'I assume it is for all of the night,' he whispered sotto voce in Sidney's ear.' It is cash on the nail, as you English say.' 'Yes all night.' Said Sidney paying out some hundreds of rubles. He consoled himself by commenting thoughtfully to himself that at least the rubles came from the wad of forged notes he had kept back from the packet, most of which he had deposited in the Russo-Asiatic Bank of Moscow.

The party did go on all night and his companions were most appreciative.' What is a gentleman's arm if it is not decorated with a pretty woman?' His new found French friend said and in the end towards two in the morning one by one The Belgian, the Romanian, the Frenchman, the two Germans drifted off to bed with their bought and paid for escorts. Before he went Sidney collected up the notes that they had to a man pressed on him as their share in the costs. Sidney was glad of that. He had thought himself a little impulsive in offering to pay for all the girls and he got genuine notes back in exchange for the counterfeit rubles he had paid with.

The two Germans took their girls to the room they shared. But the girls were a little disappointed. For a time their hosts insisted on ignoring them. The two Germans, one was a great six footer with a red face and a misshapen nose and ear that suggested he had been a pugilist at some time in his career. He described himself as from, 'Berlin, 'The Kaiser's sandbox.' The other, of smaller build came from Leipzig. They stood apart from the girls who were sitting on one of the beds and began to talk urgently to each other in German.

"It is him. He fits the description exactly and Reilly, that was the name we were given."

The big one from Berlin was more cautious, 'We have to make sure. We should check his identity credentials, his passport or something. If we get it wrong and Mueller learns he's the wrong man we'll be for the high jump.'

The shorter one began to speak again. 'I am convinced its him and I'm going to phone Tbilisi. I've got the number and there's a phone at the desk downstairs.'

Again the bigger man advised caution. 'Why not wait until morning and bribe the desk clerk to give you the information on him that you need. He will have registered and filled a form in for the police. Nothing could be easier and we will have all the information we want to get in touch with Tbilisi. Mueller, I can tell you is not a man to be trifled with. I have heard of his reputation and it is unsavory to say the least. Some say he is the company's, hatchet man and here he drew a flat hand across his throat.' But, not only did he not want to make any mistakes in this matter he also wanted to get into bed with the girl who was waiting for him and making her impatience obvious by frowning and pouting her lips.

This argument seemed to convince the smaller man and he accepted grudgingly the drink offered him from a bottle on the table. The two girls who were almost tired of waiting were at last able to demonstrate what charms they had and with professional alacrity they soon had their partners thinking of little else.

Chapter Twenty Three

Sidney spent the night with his girl but the experience was unremarkable. He had already decided to make the seeking out of military information as the first part of his brief. If the material he had gleaned from the previous night's conversation was of any significance he could wrap that part of his mission up in two or three weeks of visits to major centres and so confirm what his dinner companions had said. Because he had become committed to this, with his typical single-mindedness he was pre-occupied and so could not give all his attention and energies to pleasing the not unattractive girl he found himself with.

What that meant was, he did not make love to her for very long and though he had pleased her it was soon over and he turned to sleep. And so did she. For her part she was happy enough. Life was hard and demanding for a working girl at The Hotel Europe, Baku and she did not get enough sleep. So to be able to close her eyes before three in the morning was quite a treat for her.

The next morning Sidney was up fairly early. He took the girl down for breakfast and then arranged with the desk clerk to vacate his room paying a retainer and getting a promise that it would be available on his return. He decided to make Batum, on the relatively new railway line his first port of call and he saw that he was in luck as there was a train leaving just before noon. He took with him his minimum amount of luggage. But this time he packed his small camera. If he needed extra film, he told himself he would be able to buy it there. He was away therefore before his German comrades were even awake. The journey to Batum would take over thirty hours.

Margaret got Sidney's letter three days after he had posted it and it upset her. Karole had been diverting her so successfully with visits and outings that while she had not forgotten Sidney the sharp reminders of him not being with her that would have come with solitude did not arrive. She was beginning to tell herself that she had been away from him before and that she had been able to tolerate it and she was associating him less and less with the main agony of guilt that troubled her. Getting his letter brought it all back.

Karole was perceptive enough to gauge that Margaret was unhappy with the letter so she kept an eye on her that day lest she resort once again to the bottle for solace. Karole had been on her guard against this happening and although she had not been so patronizing as to keep drink out of sight, she in a sense interposed herself between Margaret and the bottle. What she could not do was be with Margaret in her dreams.

The night following the day she got Sidney's letter was particularly bad. Karole could hear Margaret's pathetic whimpering and cries at the distance she was from her bedroom. She got out of bed and saw from her clock that it was two in the morning. She went in her night dress into Margaret's room and she pulled back the covers and got in beside her. She felt straight way how hot Margaret's body was. She cradled her still sleeping head under her left arm and lay her right arm over Margaret's breast. Margaret intuitively turned in her sleep so that she faced Karole and moved towards her. Karole on impulse kissed Margaret on the lips her cheeks feeling the wetness of the tears that Margaret had shed in her dream.

Still asleep dreaming Margaret passionately responded and pulled Karole closer to her while pressing her abdomen against her. Margaret's night dress had with her movements ridden up and Karole's hand went down to Margaret's naked buttocks and then round to her sex. Karole had last done this with a one- time best friend in her final year at school. For Margaret it had been an experience embarked on with trepidation when she was at convent school. The nuns laid the tause on hard for such misdemeanors. Most surely because it reminded them of their own carnal, sinful hypocrisy.

Within a few minutes Margaret had flung her left leg over the Karole's right hip, pressed her breasts to Karole's and was near to climax and half awake. When she did awake she did not recoil with horror to find Karole in her bed but instead almost intoxicated with the eroticism of Karole's lesbian lovemaking she kissed Karole again and slipping Karole's night dress off her shoulders moved her lips to Karole's breasts and then down to the bush of her pubic hair.

They said very little to each other that first time. Karole whispered Margaret's name and as she breathed it there was contained within the simple statement of it, a query as to the necessity for an apology, a request for permission and an expression of submission.

For Margaret there was no confusion and significantly no guilt. She had awakened wanting love and Karole had been there. She had been there in such an excitingly new context of sensations; the softness of her skin, the delicacy of her touch, the tenderness of her kisses and the gentleness of her embrace. The desire she had felt for Karole Margaret thought, was almost musical. Her way of being in love and making love now had simply changed key from major to minor. Karole for her part felt that all these sensations had combined in one complete moment that was almost like a divine epiphany. Margaret seemed to have put her in touch with a sort of divinity. In the sexual fantasies she had involving Margaret she had seen her like a Venus, naked, rising from the sea, vulnerable, but prophetically available, waiting to be possessed, her hand over her pudenda her arm across her breast only symbolically hiding that of herself temporarily so as to be prepared for erotic revelation.

Karole had not before thought on manifesting her fantasies in reality or making Margaret aware of her desire to make love to her. Her fantasies had merely provided a stimulus to the satisfying of herself and anyway Karole had thought her preferences and Margaret's were for men. After they had made love for the first time Margaret reflected on her preference. She had not so much preferred but been preferred by the few men that there had been in her life. The Rev. Thomas had treated her like an acolyte, like a vestal virgin in his own personal temple and there were times in their sex life when he had merely used her as what she might have crudely described as a visual aid. Sidney was of course another matter. His love-making, she now saw enslaved her when she thought it had been a liberation.

That night was to be the first of many as Margaret and Karole moved from the emotional state of friendship to the emotional and physical plane of lovers. The memory of Sidney became more easy. It diminished and became less difficult to bear and when again the hobgoblins of guilt pursued Margaret in her Thanatos dominated dreams, she had the surety of waking up to Karole's comforting and passionately expressed erotic love-making. There was only one thought that horrified Margaret in what was becoming a new way of life, and she tried to dismiss it from her mind. In all her associations with Karole. as they lived together longer and became closer and as they knew each other better, Karole seemed to be such a force for life. Her optimism was not just infectious it was stimulating to a degree that energized Margaret's daily life. If Karole's love was a force for life, what had Sidney's love been?

Sidney did not go right on to Batum, he decided to break his journey at Tibilisi and to begin his researches there. He also stopped off at a hardware shop and bought a collection of small jars to keep his samples in. The Ironmonger also supplied him with a packet of sticky labels that Sidney intended to number and stick on the jars and so give his enterprise a genuine scientific look.

Tibilisi was about half way along the relatively new railway but the track it followed was centuries old. It ran along the ancient Silk Route into India so Raj watchers could be forgiven for believing that it was the first leg of an invasion road from Russia into India. But whether the Russians were building up a force to do that in modern times, was as Sidney's observations were to bear out, more than debatable.

Sidney's research methods were simple. First he toured oil installations and took samples of various sorts of rod-wax and at the same time kept his eyes open for military bases and then he frequented the 'water holes' of the wanton soldiery. For the price of a few drinks and with discrete questioning, and here he had the advantage of his Russian, he was able to get the most reticent squaddies to talk about their duties and the extent of the bases they occupied.

One of the first conclusions Sidney was able to come to was that in Tiblisi there were no front-line troops. There were no crack regiments coiled to pounce on British possessions with military efficiency or elan. The men who made up the battalions that were there to police the province of Georgia were to a man conscripts that would not have lasted five minutes against a crack British regiment, thin red line or not. The complaint he heard most was, 'I want to go home.'

It was the same story as he continued over the next weeks his long and tiring journey on the rail connections with Yarevan, Kars, Poti and then finally Batum. At each of the places he stopped off at there were troops in some concentration but they could not have combined into an invasion force. Well trained and equipped front-line brigades, to spear-head a campaign would be needed to break British Indian Army resistance and enable a military force to over-run and then occupy even a small part of the territory of the Raj.

He would categorically say in his dispatches that there were simply no troops of division strength or quality in the provinces of the southern Caucasas Added to these observations he could show most cogently that there was no evidence of essential supply emplacements or material dumps. And perhaps more important there were no transport lines. Hundreds of horses and the same of transports would have been needed to move an effective invasion force. There was no sign of them. It would have been difficult to hide such depots.

True there was a relatively efficient rail network on this side of the Caspian but troops would have to cross Persia were they to come from that region or cross the Caspian. But whether the invasion came from the Southern Caucasus or even from Turkmenistan on the other side of the Caspian its forces would still have to tackle the mountainous tracks and passes of Afghanistan before they got to the frontier.

Were the Russians to embark on such a strategy it would take them months to mobilize the men and material to mount it, It would be difficult if not impossible to do it without being discovered. The logistics of such a military expedition would be impossible to camouflage so there would be time for opposing forces to be ready and waiting. There was nothing he could have photographed so he did not have use for his camera. He was disappointed as he was looking forward to working with his new toy.

Sidney thought that he had sufficient detailed information to compile a comprehensive report without having to go to Grozny. He would simply imply that the same conclusions could be drawn with regard to the Tschechin and Dagistan. He wouldn't be falsifying his assertions. He had, after all passed through Grozny. It was having reached that decision that brought him back to Baku some weeks later and to the Hotel Europe and the room that they had kept vacant for him in a shorter time than he expected.

A few nights later still awake at midnight, he was quietly at the work of completing his report on Russian military dispositions, when he heard a tapping at his hotel bedroom door. Sidney rarely lost his sense of caution wherever he was. He put all his papers in a large leather wallet and locked them in a suitcase under the bed. He then checked that his razor was in the pocket of his shirt and felt for the comforting bulge of his pocket browning in its novel holster.

He went to the locked door and asked through it, 'Who is it?' A voice he recognized answered saying,' A telephone call for Mr. Sidney Reilly at the desk downstairs' it was the voice of the boy who serviced his room. He unlocked the door but as he turned the key, scarcely had the mortise lock slipped out of its metal tenon when the door was burst open and he was knocked unconscious by a blow from a rubber truncheon.

When he came to his arms were tied to his chair, his ankles tied together and a further rope round his neck secured his head to the back of the chair. There were two men standing over him. He could not make them out precisely as he was still recovering from the blow he had suffered to the head and they had their backs to the light. They were both broad shouldered and of a heavy build. One of them held his razor open in silouette.

They moved away from him and sat on the bed. Now he could see their faces. One had the large round red face topped with thinning fair hair, of someone who had been perhaps a boxer at some time. His nose looked as if it had been broken and one of his ears was unmistakably a cauliflower. He was one of the Germans he had met at dinner. The other had a longer thinner face with a high forehead. His head had been shaved. He had a scar on his right cheek that had all the characteristics of a dueling scar from a German fraternity house. He did not recognize scar-face.. They began to speak in German. They made the serious mistake of assuming that Sidney could not speak the language.

' Why the hell didn't we take him outside? How are we going to cover it up if we do him here. If we had taken him outside in the dark we could have dumped him in an oil pit.'

The thin faced of the two said in a voice of authority. 'I want to talk to him for a while, then we will take him outside by the back entrance to the hotel. I've got your colleague waiting with a cart and we are going to take him well away from the town and we'll dispose of him there.'

The shaven headed one came over to Sidney first and said in passable English," Well, we have been looking for you and we thought we had lost you, you have not been around for a while. So Mr. Bloody Sidney Reilly or whatever you call yourself we want a few words with you.'"

Sidney was still puzzling as to who had sent them and why they had been sent. They weren't Russians, so weren't after him for his recent bit of military espionage. They were Germans. He said to ' scar face'." I think you've got the wrong man. I'm just researching the quality of different oils that I have found." He indicated the jars that he had filled and labeled, and set in a row on the desk."I'm an English Business man. I can show you my credentials. Untie me and I'll get them for you. They are in that folder on the desk." Sidney was clutching at straws but a plan was forming in his mind. In the folder, as well as his 'Ozone Preparations' papers there was a small leather bag of gold sovereigns and a bundle of the forged ruble notes.

'You don't have to bother." Said the red-faced one." I can get them."

He went over to the desk opened the folder. He immediately ignored the papers as he lighted on the money and the sovereigns.

He said to scar-face, in German."Look what we have here chief." He held up the money and the leather bag.

Sidney gave no indication he understood until scar-face waved the money in front of his face.

" Yes. Yes, help yourself to that and there's more where that came from." He successfully introduced a note of panic into his voice.

Scar-face could not hide his interest in what Sidney said, and he took hold of Sidney's face and twisted Sidney's mouth."What are you talking about, you English bastard.There's more where this came from?" He said this in his English.

"As part of my work I have purchased a drilling rig in a derrick and for security I have secreted the other money I brought with me in the derrick shed. I didn't trust the hotel safe. There are two hundred sovereigns and a bundle of rubles in a locked box in the shed wall at the side of the derrick. You can have it all. Just let me go and I promise you will hear no more about this. I'm telling you, you have got the wrong man. Its plainly a case of mistaken identity." Sidney tried to sound as desperate as he could.

"OK," said red-face."Just tell us where it is and we'll collect it."

"Oh no. Oh no, Oh no I am not." Said Sidney."I may be your prisoner but I am not that much of a fool. I tell you where it is and you get rid of me. Oh no. You don't get its whereabouts and the key to the shed unless you take me there and let me go before you get the money. You can torture me but I can tell you, you will not get it out of me."

Scar-face hit Sidney across the mouth. Saying as he did."Don't underestimate us my friend, give me time and you will be begging to tell us" Sidney's teeth had cut into his lips with the blow. The taste of blood in his mouth gave him the resolve to consider what revenge he would extort for that indignity.

Red-face said in German." Why waste time boss. We take him in the cart, get the money,tell him he is free and then gun him down as we were going to anyway. What have we got to lose?"

Although irritated at having to agree with his subordinate, scar-face saw the wisdom of this and, using Sidney's razor cut the ropes that bound Sidney. As he did this red-face covered him with a large pistol the mark of which Sidney had not seen before. In a pretence at getting the circulation back into his limbs, Sidney brushed his hand against his groin and felt the reassuring bulge of his own pistol. The advice of that gnarled old Parisian recidivist had worked again. They had not felt there for hidden arms.

Red-face noticed Sidney's interest in the pistol."You like it do you? I shoot you with this and you'd think that you'd been hit by a train. It's a Mauser nine millimeter. It shoots like a Maxim and try running away and I can still hit you at two hundred yards." The pistol had a pear shaped grip and a magazine under a barrel that was untypically long for a hand gun. It certainly looked lethal.

As the three of them walked towards the door scar-face said."We are going out of the hotel by the back entrance, you walk with us as if everything was normal, OK?"For good measure scar-face punched Sidney on the side of the face.' Don't put a foot wrong or we'll plug you where you stand, money or no money, understand?" Sidney added this other blow to the bill that he had now convinced himself he would get them both to pay.

Sidney wanted to continue the impression that he was encouraging their sympathy as he asked. 'What about the boy? You didn't hurt him did you?"

Red face said. "Don't you worry about him, you've got enough to worry about. He's been well paid and threatened. He knows that if he opens his mouth we'll shut it for him."

The trio walked out of Sidney's room. Sidney felt the barrel of red-face's pistol in his back. They walked along the deserted hotel corridor of that floor and down the narrow stairs to the kitchens below. In the dimly lit kitchen there were one or two kitchen hands fetching and carrying among the stoves and cupboards but no one gave them any attention. All three walked out of the back door into the night.

In the darkness out into the yard behind the hotel a small horse drawn four wheeled cart with a canvas cover was standing. It was like a miniature covered-wagon. The driver, indistinct in the dark sat up on the front holding the reins of a patiently waiting horse.

Sidney was forced to climb inside through the canvas at the back and he sat on a crude bench across from red-face who menaced him with the Mauser. Scar-face sat next to the driver. Sidney saw that the driver was the other German from the hotel. Scar-face snarled,"Where to and don't try any tricks or he will shoot you where you sit."

Sidney said quietly in a submissive voice, that he hoped would lull them into thinking that he was completely subdued." Head for Black Town." He didn't know what he was going to do to extricate himself from this dangerous situation but ridiculously he thought of Mr. Micawber and his hope that 'something would turn up.' Usually Sidney did not believe in hope. His watchwords were 'think don't hope'.

The cart rocked backwards and forwards and creaked on its springs as it travelled on the pot-holed and muddy road out of Baku into the forest of derricks, nodding donkeys and landscape of oil pools and burning gas flares that was Black Town. For Sidney any one of the ramshackle clap-board wooden obelisks that they passed might have done, but he wanted to go into an abandoned quarter of the oil-field. The rigs they were passing betrayed activity. A clangorous noise came out of clapboard derrick towers as steam driven drills wound and turned their rock grinding bits deep beneath the earth.

When the wagon had travelled on for a further mile or so Sidney, now on the seat next to the driver giving directions, saw what he was looking for. It was a leaning Tower of Pisa of a derrick and with its almost roofless shack, that had once housed the workings, it was obviously abandoned.

Sidney shouted for the wagon to stop and said, 'This is the one.'

Scar-face was the first to get down from the wagon and he surveyed the wrecked buildings. As red-face pushed Sidney over the tail-board so that he only just managed not to fall on his face in the black mud, Scar –face said.' You have bought this?" And then with a sinister laugh, he said' 'We are not the only ones who have taken you for a ride. ' The three of them stood in the over grown oily grass in a gloom lit only by the dim flickering light of flares still burning off the gas of worked out wells all around and on the horizon. The driver of the cart stayed where he was on the seat, holding the reins of the horse.

Scar- face looked at the planks of crooked door, 'OK where's the key and you better not be up to any tricks or I shall cut your balls off?' Sidney went to the tumbledown wall of the shack as if retrieving something from a hole in the wall at the same time he fumbled with the front of his trousers.Red-face was behind him.

Sidney felt the comforting shape of the grip of the Browning and as second nature released the safety. In one deft movement he pulled out the pistol, turned round to red-face and shot him twice in the stomach causing him to stagger backwards, his hands clutching his wound. Blood was already seeping through his fingers. Scar face was mesmerized. Sidney, aiming for the bulk of Scar-face's torso, missed his chest and shot him in the right shoulder. Red-face and scar-face both fell down together groaning in pain.

The driver of the cart saw what happened. He had just enough time to turn the cart, gee up the horse and to begin moving. Sidney quickly picked up the Mauser that red-face had dropped and aiming it through the back covers of the cart squeezed the trigger and let off four automatic shots.The heavy sound of the shots echoed around the towers of the wooden derricks and then was lost. Three shots hit the driver in the back, one bursting his heart. He tumbled from his seat and was dead as he fell under the front wheels which ran over him. The rear wheels stopped against his body which acted as a brake as the horse although startled by the shots halted in its tracks and stood between the shafts, traces hanging as if waiting for further instructions.

Sidney now turned his attention to scar- face and red –face. He was as cool as if he was taking some minor decision like deciding the colour of one neck tie over another. He reminded himself of the old saying,' revenge is a dish best tasted cold.' He checked to see if scar-face had a weapon on him and all he found was his own razor.

He said, in German, much to scar-face's surprise, 'I'll have this back if you don't mind and this.' He took the bag of sovereigns and the rubles out of scar-face's pocket and put the rubles and the razor in to his own. He put the bag of sovereigns on the ground. He then walked to red-face and as he did he said to scar –face over his shoulder. I want you to watch very carefully what I am going to do for if you don't tell me what I want to know I shall do the same to you. However if you cooperate I shall consider letting you go.

Red -face was lying on his back groaning and pushing bubbles of blood out of his mouth. Sidney without any compunction took the Mauser and he said, as if repeating a nursery rhyme, 'Two in the chest and one in the head.' It was advice on how to make certain of a kill given to him by the same old criminal who had told him where to hide a gun. The one in the head destroys the nervous system and the two in the chest the respiratory system. So no chance of recovery. He then shot red-face three times. The bullet-hole in his head caused a small jet of blood to pulse out for four or five seconds and the consciousness could be seen passing from his eyes. At the same time his heels beat a tattoo on the oily grass and he was dead.

Scar-face watched in horror. Sidney returned to his side and he said, 'Now who sent you?'

Scar-face hesitated. He was plainly terrified. The reversal of fortunes had shocked him into incredulity. Sidney held the Mauser by its barrel and rested the hand grip on the, by know profusely bleeding, wounded shoulder. Scar-face screamed with pain.' Now who sent you?'Sidney said again.

Gritting his teeth through the agony he felt scar-face said. 'I don't know, I got my orders in a telegraph wire from Moscow, it had your name on it and these two Germans here, who were at the hotel with you, told me where you were. '

'Why were you after me?'

'Our unit in London said they wanted you out of the way before you got too close to what we are doing here.'

This was what Sidney really wanted to hear. He said, 'And what is it that you are doing here?'

Scar-face hesitated but only momentarily as Sidney held the Mauser up to torture him again. Scar-face said. 'We have formed a joint prospecting venture with the Russians and they have bought a franchise from the Persians to exploit oil-fields in Northern Persia. The Persians want to keep it secret because they know of British interest in negotiating the same agreement. We together with the Russians have come up with a better offer.'

Scar-face was becoming very talkative so Sidney went on to ask, 'How did your people know I was in the Caucasus?'

'They got the information from an agent in England. Someone who had met you in England, somewhere on the coast,' He stopped, and said.' I can't talk any more. Get me to a doctor. I am losing a lot of blood.'

Sidney said. 'I'll get you to a doctor, just tell me who the agent was in England on the coast?'

Scar-face was desperate, but he thought he was buying his life. Almost weeping with pain he said.' I don't know the name of who it was except that it was something to do with a woman who works for us.'

The revelation hit Sidney like a bucket of cold water in the face and he said her name out loud, 'Caroline.'

Scar-face was almost fainting with pain. He didn't hear what Sidney was saying. He groaned.' Oh for god's sake get me to a doctor.'

Sidney hardly heard him. All he could do was repeat her name, 'Caroline.' He checked the magazine of the Browning. It had two cartridges in it and one in the chamber.

He said to scar-face, in an almost distracted tone.' What's the coded message you have to send to say you have done the job of killing me off?'

Scar-face struggled to reply.'I have to send a wire to the German Embassy in St. Petersburg, marked for the attention of K.F.M., message B-A-R-K.'

Sidney looked very thoughtful and said. 'Is that all? I warn you for your own sake, don't keep anything back.'

The scarred face of the man lying before him was livid with loss of blood and the eyes in it seemed on fire. The Browning pistol was already cocked. Sidney pointed the barrel close to the fore head of scar-face. Scar-face, almost whimpering said, 'I swear to you on the eyes of my mother, that's all there is."

Sidney then pressed the pistol to scar- face's left temple so that it touched his skin. With the sudden realization that he was looking death in the face, the man screamed. 'You said you would let me go. I trusted you. I've told you everything I know. For God's sake man, please, please I beg you don't do it. Oh for God's sake you'll never hear from me again. Oh my God Oh please, please. please.' As he began to blubber, with his good hand scar-face clutched at the legs of Sidney's trousers.

Sidney could not understand his pleas. Had the situation been reversed he would now be drinking oil in one of the black pools. Sidney could not see his way to spare him. These were the rules of the game. You were either killed or you killed. It was as simple as that. If you didn't know that much then you shouldn't be playing the game. It puzzled Sidney that the man did not seem to understand.'

'Yes I did.' Sidney said.' But your trust was misplaced.' Sidney then said his mantra, 'two in the chest and one in the head.' With that Sidney shot scar-face three times at close range.

The man's last reflexes were juddering away as Sidney went over to the body of the driver of the cart and dragged it to the edge of one of the many deep oil pools around. He pushed it in and there was hardly a disturbance on the surface as it slipped in to disappear in oily blackness below. He then did the same with the bodies of scar-face and red-face. His effort was eased by the oil on the grass lubricating the slide of the bodies as he dragged them.

He then picked up the empty brass cartridge cases around that were glinting in the light of the gas flares and tossed them in the pool. He replaced the now empty Browning in its intimate holster, fastened his trousers and picked up the Mauser. He would keep that as a souvenir and have a shoulder holster made for it. Then, before he climbed up onto the wagon, he picked up the bag of coins. As the horse trotted slowly out of Black Town and pulled Sidney and the wagon back to Baku, all Sidney could keep on repeating to himself was the name, 'Caroline.'

Chapter Twenty Four

Dawn was almost breaking when Sidney got back to the hotel. He parked the wagon in the back yard again and thought that he would confiscate it. He went up the back stairs to his room and ran a hot bath to wash off the filth that had accumulated on him in the night. A shower wouldn't get near it. His clothes were ruined so he thought he would throw them away. He dressed in plain clothes and packed all the things he had in his room. He took his lighter luggage with him when he went downstairs to the desk and checked out of the Hotel Europe arranging for the more substantial part of his luggage to be taken out to the wagon. He then drove the wagon down to the telegraph office at the station and sent a wire to the German Embassy in St. Petersburg. He mounted up again, turned the wagon round and headed out of town towards Villa Petrola.

Two days later in the back room of a flat in Hackney Karl Frederick Mueller got the signal on his telegraph equipment that warned of an incoming message. The message had travelled a long way. It had begun its electric journey from Baku along the copper wire that now linked the Caucasus with the German Embassy in St. Petersburg. Then on more copper wire to a receiving station in Antwerp and then across the sea to the wireless shack of a trawler without any fish. From the trawler's ariel a signal went to London and it caused Mueller's Morse key to tap out ' For eyes only of KFM. B-A-R-K stop B-A-R-K stop B-A-R-K.. Mueller decoded that as,' Britischer Agent Reilly Kaput.' He could hardly contain his glee. He got up from his seat and dragged off his earphones and rushed along the landing to Caroline's bedroom with the thin strip of ticker tape that had the message on it. He went straight in.

Caroline was in the middle of the room in front of the large mirror of her dressing table. She had one foot on a stool and her long hair was in damp strands down her back. She was naked, toweling herself dry with a large, thick white towel after her morning bath.

She turned to him mildly irritated and said, 'I wish you would learn to knock.'

He waved the thin piece of white paper at her like a child with a piece of bunting. 'They've done for him, they've eliminated him. They've put him out of the way.'

She wasn't in the mood for guessing games. She was just preparing for another assignment and not looking forward to it.

She sat down on the stool. She began to rub her hair dry with the towel, taking it in fronds looking in to the mirror as she did it. She was indifferent to what he was saying, 'They've put who away? What on earth are you talking about.?'She was not prepared for his answer.

He shouted at her as if she was deaf. 'Reilly, Reilly. Our man in Tiblisi has done him in. He's dead.'

She saw Mueller's grinning face looking in the mirror over her shoulder. She didn't turn but stopped drying her hair and held the towel still and looked at her own face and said slowly, 'Who did you say?'

He replied as he turned and left the room. 'Bloody Reilly, Sidney Bloody Reilly, What a coup, the British will be put out poor things.'

Caroline sat as she was for a long time and in spite of herself she began to shed great tears that ran down her cheeks and splashed onto the plate glass that protected the polished wood of her dressing table. She sat so long that she began to cool down and was quite uncomfortable with her wet hair cold and lank. She didn't move but let the towel drop to her feet and with her hands on her naked thighs and her head slightly bowed, she continued to weep and then to say quietly to herself. 'This bloody business, I have had enough of this bloody business.'

Mueller's triumphalism was premature and he was to suffer significant sanction for what he thought was the assassination of 'Sidney Bloody Reilly.' Because of a failure in communication the instruction had not come through that a system of cooperation was in the process of being established between the Special Branch of Great Britain and the Secret Service of Imperial Germany.

Sidney decided against going into another hotel and thought that he would investigate the possibility of renting a villa for the time he needed to get access to Villa Petrolia. The side of the town the Nobels' residence was in was a suburb that was much cleaner than the immediate environs of Baku and he thought he would look there. He was already working out a strategy for his plan to photograph the engine designs and it didn't involve waiting for an invitation to a party.

He bought a newspaper and looked in the 'To let' columns and found what he was looking for. A new development of suburban houses had started to serve the growing population of the middle-classes of Baku. The houses were in various stages of completion but a few were finished and only their gardens needed tidying. It was one of these houses that Sidney was to lease. It was a small detached house built in traditional Russian style and it was advertised as being to let on a short term lease, furnished, with a housekeeper and a maid servant. He visited the address which was marked as 'No six plot' and was directed by the housekeeper in residence to the agent. He quickly arranged the formalities of the leasehold and he moved in. He could now begin to form his plan.

For the next few days Sidney went down to the livery stables where the horse and wagon were kept for him and he trotted out with his wagon and kept the Villa Petrolia under observation. His idea was that he would see who it was who worked there. His interest, particularly was in the female staff and how they performed such tasks as getting in supplies, shopping etc and whether there were female staff who didn't live in but visited the house each day.

What he did see was a nurse or governess who regularly took a child out in a baby carriage with another older child holding her hand while they had a daily walk. He decided that she would be his first target. He noted that she visited, with the children, a small grassed area with shrubs and pathways. It was not far away from the villa. That he decided would be where he would lie in wait to meet her. He also decided for the purpose of the next part of the operation that he would adopt another identity at least temporarily. He would call himself Michael St John Devereux PhD. He would be a history professor from the University of London.

The next day he rose, had the morning tea he had arranged with the housekeeper and got dressed in his linen suit with waistcoat and a duck-egg blue shirt and blue striped Chavet tie and brown elastic sided hand-made boots. He chose a handkerchief of blue silk for his pocket and he went down to a simple breakfast of omelette bread and coffee. He had noted that the governess commenced her walk around ten in the morning, so he planned to be in 'the park' by nine forty five. He chose a dove grey homburg hat and an ebony stick trimmed with silver. He took half a dozen plain white visiting cards from his writing case and in his best copperplate hand wrote Michael St.. John Devereux PhD. University of London on one side and his address here, which was simply 'No. six plot' on the other. He then went out into a day that was fine with a blue sky accommodating some pillows of white clouds.

In' the park' there was a small ornamental lake and around it for the benefit of visitors were benches to sit on. He sat waiting and while he did he read his book of elocution exercises. The governess was on time and surely enough at around ten she walked through the gates with her charges, the baby in the perambulator and the little boy dressed in the fashion for children, boys or girls, a sailor suit.

The little boy was presented with a ball to play with by the governess and he began to roll it on the grass. As the young woman got close he saw that she was around thirty or thirty five or so with a slim figure but was rather plain of face and she wore spectacles that were rather too heavy for her. She was wearing a brown dress with a black woollen cape on her shoulders. On her head she had a tam o'shanter hat of almost the same colour as her dress. Her hair was fair and piled on her head like a cottage loaf.

The little boy presented Sidney with the perfect opportunity to approach the young woman for the ball he was playing with got away from him and rolled towards the pond. Sidney caught it before it went in and taking off his hat he gave the ball to the young woman. Then something happened that he had not anticipated. As he raised his hat and gave the ball to the woman and prepared to engage her in conversation a shaven headed broad-shouldered thick set man of medium height of about twenty five years old stepped out of the bushes around the pond and stood obviously near to the woman, visibly as a protection. The Nobel's governess had a body guard.

Sidney turned to the young man just as he said to Sidney in Russian, 'Can I help you your honour?' Sidney maintained his pretence that he couldn't speak the language.

Sidney deliberately avoided talking to the young woman and said to him in English, 'I do beg your pardon, I hope I have not given the wrong impression. I was returning the little boy's ball and then I would have passed the time of day with the young lady.'

The governess smiled shyly and she said in the English of a native English person. 'I'm afraid he doesn't understand English only Russian." She then spoke to the body-guard in Russian, assuring him that all was well. He stepped back a little way. She turned again to Sidney.' Don't be alarmed my employers insist on him accompanying me on my morning walk with the children. They consider Baku to be a bit of a wild place and they are afraid we might be molested or even, perish the thought, kidnapped.' The little boy in the sailor suit still holding his governess' hand was aged about five. He looked at Sidney with apprehension. He was not used to strangers.

'Oh dear.' Said Sidney. ' My morning constitutional is getting a little complicated, Let me introduce myself.' He gave her the card he had written that morning. 'As you see my name is Michael St. John Devereux. I am a history professor from London. England and I am here in Baku researching the story of the development of the oil industry with a view to writing a series of articles or maybe even a book on the subject. I have rented a villa nearby and I thought this little park might serve for my morning walk although I see that there are few who use it. We seem to have it to ourselves."

The governess introduced herself as Miss Gwendolyn Hoyle and she walked on a little way, pushing the perambulator and still holding the little boy's hand. Sidney took the liberty of walking on with her. The body-guard maintained a discrete distance behind.

Sidney said, "Where are you from in England. Have you been here long?" The young woman seemed awkward in his company and he wanted to put her at her ease. Then it dawned on Sidney. The body guard was not only watching him he was watching her too. If her employers, the Nobels were any thing like English employers of domestic servant they did not encourage gentlemen callers. The woman was embarrassed to be talking to Sidney under the eyes of the body guard who would certainly report back.

Sidney didn't wait for an answer to his questions but instead said, "It is such a pleasure to be talking to someone from the old country. I do wish you would do me the honour of treating you to tea sometime on your day off. You do have a day off don't you? My address here is on the card it isn't far away. I do hope you won't stand on ceremony and go all formal. We really aren't in stuffy old England. Let's adopt some modern Russian manners and break down the social barriers. Do say you will come and visit me. If it makes you feel any better I have a housemaid and a house keeper who will keep an eye on me if I start acting like a cad."

To Sidney's surprise, the woman blurted out, "Oh I wouldn't think you would behave like that at all Dr. St. John Devereux." Sidney noticed that she pronounced it in the conventional way 'Sinjun'. "It's just that we don't know each other and…."

Before she could finish her sentence Sidney said, 'And there's no chance we will get to know each other if we behave as if we are in Kensington or Hyde Park. Oh do say you will come. I don't know the language and you do. You might even be able to give me some insights. I seem to have bitten off more than I can chew. It would as well be such a treat to have an intelligent conversation in English with a pretty girl like you." He had saved the last part of the phrase till the end and he said it slowly and looked at her with his eyes cast down a little.

She blushed. No man she had ever met, but then she had met so few, had ever called her pretty. She said shyly and politely in a way that Sidney found quite charming. 'It is a very kind offer Mr. St. John Devereux er Dr. and I don't know if I should accept but I promise I will think about it. Now if you will excuse me I must return to the house. The baby will soon need feeding. His nurse will be waiting and the little boy has a nap after his morning milk.'

Sidney offered his hand to her and she took off her glove before she held it. Sidney then kissed the back of her hand and said. 'I think I am picking up some Russian habits. Good morning to you, until we meet again.'

As she pushed the perambulator with the baby in it back to the Villa Petrolia Miss Hoyle could think of nothing else but her brief meeting with 'Mr. St. John Devereux or Dr. St John Devereux', to give him his proper title. She hardly noticed that she was holding the hand of the little boy and at one point when he stopped to examine a dead beetle on the ground she continued walking and dragged his little feet along until he cried out. She was really most distracted and later on when she had her dinner in the kitchen with the rest of the staff even they noticed that she was even less-communicative than usual.

Miss Hoyle had her pre bed -time bath in the servants' bathroom. It was plumbed for hot and cold water. She undressed thinking about Dr. St John Devereux. She was thinking about him when she looked in the long mirror on the wall at her nakedness. She thought to herself that she still had a slim and firm figure and that her breasts had maintained that slight tilt upwards and her stomach, though rounded was not fat. She turned and looked over her shoulder at her heart shaped bottom and her thighs. Her fair hair came down past her shoulders and she brushed it vigorously and curled a portion of it with her hand and chewed it in her mouth as she sat before the hinged mirror of her dressing table in her room.

She was still thinking of her meeting with him as she got into bed in her night dress and pulled the hem right up to her neck imagining Dr. St John Devereux doing it for her. She decided that she would see him on her next day off, 'Why shouldn't she?' She said to herself. 'What possible harm could she come to? He was quite obviously a gentleman and an English gentleman at that.' She did decide however not to tell anyone of her proposed assignation. It was nobody else's business but her own. It was her own time after all and she was a grown woman.

She was also as she excitedly reminded herself as she put her fingers into her pubic hair, still a virgin. She then did something that even scandalized herself when she thought of it afterwards. She sat up in bed and cupped each of her bare breasts in her hands and leaned forward as if she were offering them to him.

Chapter Twenty Five

Sidney was so sure of himself that he simply waited in for a few days. He was convinced that she would come and she did on the afternoon of the next Thursday.

He welcomed her in the unkempt garden having seen her walking down the unmade road strewn with builders' detritus that led to the small group of houses. She was holding up her skirts, revealing her petticoats and her high-heeled boots as she negotiated the clods of earth and rubble.

'Miss Hoyle how good of you to come. How good of you to give up your time off to come and see me. Please come in and I will have to make tea as I am afraid the housekeeper and the housemaid are like you having an afternoon off. I hope you don't mind that.' They would on all his future meetings with Miss Hoyle, be having their day or afternoon off. He would see to that.' It won't be an English tea or even a Yorkshire high tea for I think that is the kind of tea you know.' He had noted when he first spoke to her in the little park that there was a slight northern burr to her English accent.' I see that you haven't brought your body-guard with you today.'

No, that was true Miss Gwendoline Hoyle had not brought the body-guard but then she thought, she had not brought her customary caution or conventions either. 'To be meeting a strange man in his house alone with not even a housemaid as chaperone, how scandalous, what were things coming to?'

She hesitated on the wooden steps that led up to the small verandah and she looked at her boots which had some mud on them. Without thinking she undid the laces and took them off so that she walked up to the house in her stocking feet. Sidney observed this and added it to his thoughts on the fact that she had broken convention by coming to see him. For Sidney the process of the conquest that he intended to make had already begun

Miss Hoyle was still smiling at Sidney's mild teasing on the subject of the body-guard when she took the cane chair that Sidney offered her on the verandah. Sidney went into the house and came out with a pair of his own slippers. 'It's a warm day but I don't want your feet to be cold.' A few moments later he went in and came out this time with a tray of tea glasses, a tea pot and a plate of rather clumsily made smoked salmon sandwiches.' I'm sorry about the state of the sandwiches.' Sidney said. She at last said something. ' I know, it is so difficult to make proper sandwiches. It's the Russian bread around here, those little brown loaves of rye bread. I think it's only made for dipping into soup.'

Sidney poured the tea and apologized for it being Georgian tea but Miss Hoyle said that she had grown to like it and now preferred it, black with a little sugar and sometimes lemon but if there was no lemon that was alright.

They chatted together and Miss Hoyle felt herself more and more at ease. She had never met a man before who paid such singular attention to her. Sidney was exercising his usual skill at persuading the women who found themselves in his company that they were the centre of his universe. He was right she was from the north, West Yorkshire, near Leeds and her parents had paid for her to go to a good school there and she had left when she was eighteen and gone into service and found that she was very good at looking after children. She had taken up work in London and after some years found employment with the family of a minor aristocrat. His family were friends of the Nobel family and she went to Oslo, Norway with them on holiday which is where she met the Nobel family and was eventually offered a position with them and she had been with them ever since.

The afternoon passed very quickly and it was soon time for Miss Hoyle to return. Sidney fetched her boots from the bottom of the steps and insisted on putting them on for her. In spite of her reservation she allowed him to do it. There was after all no one else looking. He took the opportunity of feeling her calves well beyond the tops of her boots and it did not escape his notice that she gave a sharp intake of breath as his hand caressed her stocking covered leg. She asked him not to accompany her to the villa. She preferred her visit to him to be confidential.

Over the next few weeks she spent all her free time with Sidney. The housekeeper and the maid were always taking their days off when she visited Sidney and they found themselves alone in the house. It was late summer but the days were still warm so they often went into the countryside for picnics where they sat together in sunlit glades and ate blinis and caviar and drank Sidney's favourite Russian Champagne, Sitting side by side on the wagon as the horse plodded along forest paths or country lanes, Miss Hoyle's dress became less and less formal. One day she sat on the wagon in an off the shoulder blouse Sidney had bought for her. He told her that the embroidery of small red roses and golden buttercups where the lace was tied was Hungarian. She was in her bare feet and with her long fair hair unbraided and over her shoulders. It was hair that Sidney said was the most beautiful hair he had ever seen. It was scandalous but she said, she felt like a gypsy. She felt that she had become prettier.

Then on one long day off they stopped in the forest by a tumbledown charcoal burner's hut. Miss Hoyle was much embarrassed because she wanted to relieve herself. She went inside for privacy. Sidney waited outside for a few minutes and then after securing the horse he went in just as Miss Hoyle was rearranging her clothes. Sidney took off her spectacles. The world then became indistinct for Gwendolyn, myopic that she was and everything condensed into a blur.

Sidney embraced her and kissed her and after a very brief hesitation she returned his kiss and kisses. He took her to the other side of the hut and lay her down on the fern covered floor. He opened the lace neck of her blouse to reveal her breasts and kissed them and then lifted her skirts to her waist. He gently took down her underwear and she did not resist indeed she lifted herself to make his undressing of her easier.

As she felt the prickle of the dry fern on her bare bottom and bare legs she whispered to him, 'I have never done this before, please don't hurt me. I won't have babies will I?' He was as tender in loving her for the first time as he had ever been with anybody but, inevitably there was hurt and she was surprised at how uncomfortable it was. The experience was not at all as she expected It to be and there was blood. Sidney had to say that he would promise that the next time would be much better.

The next time was in his bed at the house, in the afternoon and it was much better. As it was much better the time after that and the times also after that. It was so much better then that one of the times after that would be, Sidney intended, secretly in Miss Hoyle's own bed at night in the Villa Petrolia. He would by then have persuaded her to take the risk. He would be one long step closer to completing his plan.

So it was on one afternoon when once more the servants were out that Gwendolyn Hoyle found herself naked in bed again with 'Dr. St John Devereux.' Sidney had to admit to himself that Gwendolyn's voluptuousness had taken him by surprise. She gave herself over totally to bodily pleasure and would consent to any sensual excess. She was even prepared to submit herself to 'The Chastisement of Love' so captivated was she by Sidney. For her part it seemed that Sidney dedicated himself completely to giving her pleasure. She then impressed Sidney by quoting Shakespeare;

"I am your spaniel;

The more you beat me, I will fawn on you;

Use me as your spaniel, spurn me, strike me'

Neglect me, lose me only give me leave,

Unworthy as I am, to follow you".

The transformation from shy, prudish, virginal, spinster English governess to luxuriating, breathless, perspiring lover was complete. As the old saying had it thought Sidney, 'cast off the clouts and guilt and shame are cast off with them.'

Sidney told her that photography was his hobby and that he wanted to take some studies of her. In her total submission of herself to him, she consented to Sidney taking photographs of her in various stages of undress and photographs of her in provocative poses of complete nudity. She found the experience enervating and was amazed at the degree of lasciviousness she felt. It was as if, she thought, she was being caressed by the lens of the camera.

It was when the portfolio of erotic prints of her had been collected from a studio in Baku, whose proprietor had been well rewarded for his discretion after developing and printing them that Sidney showed them to her on one of her afternoons off. She was shocked at the realisation of what she had done. He convinced her that they were only for him and that they were important practice for him in the use of artificial light and he promised that the negatives would not fall into the wrong hands and that he would keep them in a safe place. "Oh Michael", "She said if my employers should see them I would be ruined. My reputation would be in tatters. I would never be able to work again."

It was on that same afternoon that Sidney introduced the idea of them sleeping together in her bed at the Villa Petrolia.' We shall spend the night together like true lovers. We will not have to wait for your afternoons off to make love' He would not come he said until she went to bed and he would surely be gone before dawn. 'We will be like Romeo and Juliet.' He said.

At first she would not entertain the idea. She thought it out of the question, It was certain she said, that they would be discovered. In spite of her qualms he asked her to draw a rough plan of the house and grounds. She did and what she drew was a walled garden with a gatehouse. That she said was where the body guard he had seen in the park slept. The villa was on a small mound with steps leading up to the front entrance.

Sidney asked her to describe where her room was in relation to the rooms of others and where the doors were to get in. He didn't tell her but he had no need for keys. His case of tool steel lock picks would open ninety nine percent of locks he came up against.

She told him that her room was at the back of the house on the ground floor. The house had an orangery that ran the length of the back of the house and her room was at the end of the orangery and could be entered from there. It was one room away from the nursery but she did not have responsibility for the children in the nursery. They were for the nurse to look after in the evening and at night and she slept in a room next door to the nursery on the other side. All the other bedrooms were on the first floor where the family slept. The other servants had their rooms under the roof.

Sidney asked her where Emanuel Nobel's work room was. She asked him why he wanted to know that. His answer was that he supposed that he worked late and he didn't want to arrive when he was still up and working. She told him that he usually worked until ten o' clock or thereabouts and that his work room was at the opposite end of the orangery. The house, she said was usually quiet by eleven o' clock, she herself going to bed by around nine thirty. He asked her to keep a light burning in her room and he said much to her consternation that he would come that night. She begged him not to but he 'stopped her mouth' with a kiss and before long she had forgotten her objections and was reveling in the passion of his embraces.

Gwendolyn undressed for bed that night full of trepidation. The Villa Petrolia had been wired for electricity which was generated by an oil fired independent generator. That was switched off late at night so Gwendolyn lit a small chamber candle and put it in the window as Michael had insisted upon. She saw through the window that the night was cloudless and that there was a bright moon just rising.

She lay awake for what seemed a long time but eventually succumbed to sleep. She was awakened by finding' Michael' on her bed already naked. She saw his body and face pale in the moonlight shining through the window. 'How did you get in?' She said. He pressed his finger to her lips as she started at discovering him with her and heard him whisper in the moon beamed darkness, 'I have put your candle out. Shush, I found it very easy to get in. Let me make love to you.' He did and she found it almost impossible to suppress her moans and cries of pleasure and thought she would wake the household.

After about an hour she fell to sleep again, exhausted by 'Michael's' energy and her own responses.

Sidney waited until he was sure she was asleep and putting on his trousers and shirt he quietly let himself out of her room and into the shadowy darkness of the moon lit orangery. He crossed the cold tiled floor in bare feet passing through the shadows of the alien tropical plants and trees that lined each side of and filled the glass-covered space. The air was heavy with the scents of exotic blossoms. When he reached the door to Nobel senior's workshop he stooped down for the bag of equipment that he had secreted when he first gained entry before going into Gwendolyn's room. He had left it there behind one of the larger plant-pots. He took out his case of lock-picks and within a minute the door opened to him.

The room was not large and was served by only one window. Sidney covered this widow by fixing with pins a large towel he had brought with him for the purpose. He retrieved from his bag the hand lamp he intended to use for the photographs he was going to take and lit the oil lamp in it. He saw by its bright white light beam that the room was almost taken up a by an inclined drawing board on a stand and a piece of furniture rather like a desk but made up of a series of large drawers that covered its length. There were other small cupboards and wall fittings around. Sidney guessed that the drawings he was looking for would be in those drawers. Each drawer had a substantial lock on it.

He set to work on the first drawer lock and it was some minutes before he heard the satisfying click of the mortise being withdrawn. The others opened more easily as the first lock had a mechanism that corresponded with the other drawers. He looked through each drawer and found the drawings he wanted in the third one down. They had a title in Russian Cyrillic writing with the Russian Navy emblem on the top that referred to the Imperial Russian Admiralty and with the Russian words 'TOP SECRET' stamped in a red rectangle. He took out some six blue-print drawings and saw that they were not just of an innovatory oil refining process and engines as he had expected but the elevations and plans of a complete ship. It was a design he had not seen before. The Heading stated in Russian Cyrillic capitals, 'TORPEDO BOAT DESTROYER'

The side elevation on one blue-print showed a low sinister looking hull, with four squat funnels. It had a high bridge with a searchlight platform forward that was nearly as high as the funnels. Its armament was four 88 millimetre quick firing guns with 7.62 and 20 millimetre machine guns and four 50 millimetre torpedo tubes. The engine specification was for an oil-fired turbine generating 27.500 horse power turning three shafts and six propellers to give a top speed of 35 knots. Nobel had not just designed a revolutionary engine for the Imperial Russian Navy but a completely revolutionary new type of naval vessel that it was designed to fit into. With a tonnage of 1.500 it was three times as big as the latest Royal Naval vessel of its type and 15 knots an hour faster. Sidney could hardly contain his excitement as he prepared to photograph the large midnight blue white-lined sheets full of mathematical formulae, dimensions and technical specifications.

Remembering all that H.T. Edwards had told him, he set up the Nydia camera by screwing the right-angled cramp to the desk top and moved the drawing board to a measured five feet from the lens and put the board vertical and pinned the first drawing to it. There were a number of auxiliary oil lamps around and he lit them and arranged them so that he got the maximum amount of light on his subject. He then added the light from his hand lamp and having recharged the camera with fresh film after photographing Gwendolyn. He checked the image through the view finder. Then he saw to it that the aperture was at its fullest and the shutter speed at one fiftieth of a second and carefully pressed the button on the shutter release cable and photographed each of the six drawings twice as he pinned them one after the other to the board.

The operation was over much more quickly than he expected and within half an hour he had, having obtained the record he wanted, replaced the drawings in their drawers, secured the locks and put the board and lamps back where they had been. There was no evidence that anyone had been in the room at all. He blew out the light of his hand lamp and picked up the bag with his equipment in it and slung it over his shoulder.

Then as he was taking down the towel from the window which he had used as a blind, he heard a noise outside. With his hand on the razor he had made sure was in his pocket he crept to the door. He expected to see the bulk of the Russian body guard but instead he opened it to Gwendolyn standing there in her night-dress. Her hair fell to her shoulders, she was bare-foot and she was wearing her large spectacles. Bright moon-light shone through the windows of the orangery. It was so bright Gwendolyn's nakedness could be seen outlined through the lace of her night clothes.

'Michael' she said with a gasp. 'I woke up to find you weren't in bed and I heard a noise. What are you doing in there? It is Mr. Emmanuel's private work-room. No one is allowed in there without his express permission.'

Sidney put his back to her to relock the door with his picks. He dismissed her concerns by saying that he was just having a look around because he was curious. That's all there was to it. He then turned to her and hoarsely whispered, 'Let's get back to bed. It is nearly dawn and you know your vampire has to return to his crypt before the sun rises and he needs to refresh himself with the blood of a young virgin or be condemned to roam the everlasting night for eternity.' He then whisked her night-dress over her head and carried her naked back to her bedroom, her white night dress made almost transparent by the moon light, floating behind like ectoplasm brushing aside the great black leaves of the ferns and forest plants in the orangery.

Chapter Twenty Six

Sidney left Gwendolyn fast asleep in her bed and he let himself out and locked her door behind him. The dawn was just breaking over the smoke and fog of Baku as he left the grounds of Villa Petrolia as he had entered, via the back wall. It had all been much easier than he had expected and the relationship with Gwendolyn had been the real key to him entering the Villa Petrolia and that had not been as messy as he thought it might have been. He congratulated himself on how well it had all gone.

He was lucky. He mused to himself, "That's what you need, luck. You either have it or you haven't. That's what Napoleon asked about his Generals, were they lucky?" He walked back to the villa clutching his bag of equipment and tried to think of a faster way of getting his reports on Oil and the Caucasus, The Military dispositions of Russian troops and most significantly the film of the blue prints back to Melville. He thought of delivering them to Urquhart the vice-consul but dismissed that as he was too low level. He had no intention of delivering them to his contact in Moscow. There was a leak somewhere on the line. He wanted to place everything in Melville's hands personally if at all possible.

Back at his leased villa he treated himself to a shower and then sleep for a couple of hours. He rose and breakfasted and then began to pack up his things to leave. He had given the maid and the housemaid a day off again. They saw him as a very generous employer. By midday he had collected the horse and wagon from the livery stables and he had his luggage stowed in it by the hostler and he told him to take it from the station where he would leave it empty. He told him the lie that he would be back for it shortly. He left a note for the housekeeper in accurate Russian that said that he was relinquishing the rest of the lease. It was paid up and she should so inform the agent. He also left a small package on a table in the kitchen marked for the attention of Gwendolyn. He had not told her that he was to be leaving. He decided that it would be best that she should discover that after he had gone. He locked the door and put the key in the mail-box for the housekeeper to collect.

At the railway office his enquiry on how to get to England by sea did not result in any positive conclusion. It would be the train north. Then he lighted upon the idea of Melville meeting him in Stockholm. He knew that some of the 'State's' Russian business was done from a bureau in the British Embassy in Stockholm. He would wire Melville when he was well on the way of his railway journey to St. Petersburg and arrange a meeting in Stockholm where he could pass over what he thought was priceless information. With the thought of St. Petersburg came the thought of Margaret. He had not had the degree of contact with her that he would have liked but her letters, when they infrequently came did not suggest that she thought that this was untoward. She accepted that he had been very busy. Really for Sidney as the train chugged its slow way to Grozny and beyond his one thought was on the reception of his 'prizes'.

On the day he left, though Sidney did not know it he caught one of the last trains to leave Baku for some time. In his preoccupation with his own affairs he had not noticed as he boarded his train, the knot of railway and oil field workers gathering in the station forecourt. It was the beginning of industrial action and a series of strikes that was to close down the activities of Baku for quite a few days. The strikes spread and took in all the oil fields. Although oil production and so profits had soared wages hadn't moved and new production methods were resulting in unemployment. The strikes weren't sporadic or isolated they were well organized. By one of those extraordinary coincidences of history one of the strikers and organizers was a young Georgian by the name of Dugasvili. He was as time passed to become Sidney's nemesis. He was later to adopt the nom de guerre of 'Josef Stalin.'

A few days after Sidney had spent the night with her Gwendolyn took her afternoon off and walked down to where Sidney had leased the villa. In spite of her misgivings she had waited for him to come again to her room after dark but she had waited in vain. As she picked her way across broken tiles and discarded scraps of wood that littered the unmade track that was the approach to the villa she could see that she was being watched by two faces looking through the window. She went as usual to the steps to the verandah behind and by the time she got there both the housemaid and the maid were waiting at the door to the verandah. They asked her in polite formal Russian what they could do to help her and she replied that she wished to see Dr. St John Devereux.

The housekeeper who was obviously in authority said, 'I am afraid Miss that there is no one of that name living here and in fact the gentleman who was living here left for the north by train two days ago.'

Gwendolyn was nonplussed, 'But', pleaded Gwendolyn, 'I know Dr. St. John Devereux was living here,' Gwendolyn hesitated, even Russian domestic servants were aware of the decorum regarding an unattached young woman visiting a bachelor gentleman alone.' The gentlemen in question invited me to take tea with him here on one occasion. I wasn't able to but I did borrow a book from him and I would like to return it.'

'I'm sorry Miss er did you give your name?'

' No I didn't, I'm sorry, my name is Gwendolyn Hoyle. I am an employed as a governess by the Nobel family at Villa Petrolia.'

At this the maid took it upon herself to go into the house and she returned with the parcel Sidney had marked for Gwendolyn.

'If your name is Gwendolyn Hoyle then this for you, here look it says your name on it.'

Gwendolyn took the parcel and asked again, 'But Dr. St.John Devereux, do you know where he has gone?'

The housekeeper acting on the information on Gwendolyn's status, assumed her position as being just below that of Gwendolyn's, delivered a somewhat tart reply. 'I've already told you he don't live here and never has nor am I at liberty to say the name of the gentleman what did live here so if you don't mind there are those of us who has work to do and can't spare the time to answer any more questions' With that she almost pushed the maid into the house and closed the door behind her.

Gwendolyn was confused and miserable and as her glasses began to mist up she had to take care as she walked back up the rutted track that led away from the house. As she did she opened the packet. In it was the sheaf of negatives from the photographs Sidney had taken of her. She cleaned her glasses with a handkerchief and she saw herself in the gelatin squares like the picture of a ghost reclining naked and darkly translucent on a chaise longue. Her hair was white, below were thin dashes of white that were her eyebrows and there was a small triangle of white at the junction of her lower abdomen and thighs. In the parcel was an enigmatic note. It said, 'I didn't need these after all and I hope you don't mind but I have kept the prints as a souvenir of our days together. Until the time that we may meet again Dastvidanya. M.'

Gwendolyn Hoyle began to cry. The tears she shed ran down her face under the rims of her spectacles. Although it was very hard for her to come to the conclusion she had to admit to herself that she had just been used but for what purpose she wasn't sure. She had been so happy and he had seemed to be just as much happy as she. Before she got back to the Villa Petrolia, she said aloud 'He used me.' And she repeated it just as often as she sobbed out her disappointment and the realization that he was lost to her and she convinced herself that she would probably never make love with anyone else ever again. ' What.' She thought in her misery, 'is to become of me?'

Within the next weeks Sidney was in St.Petersburg. He had stopped off at Moscow between trains and given himself enough time to check his very healthy bank account there. When he arrived in St. Petersburg he went straight to Margaret's apartment but not only was she not there, the place was rented to another tenant. The mystery was to some extent resolved when he went to the Embassy and learned that some ten days previously Margaret had asked for documentation to get her back to England. The Embassy had also assisted, at Margaret's request with the arrangement of an exit visa for her companion. They were able arrange this quickly through their joint contacts with the Russian authorities. Margaret had not left a forwarding address.

Sidney was puzzled but not distressed by the information about Margaret. He was sure that news of her could be got from Melville if he managed to meet with him successfully in Stockholm. To facilitate this he wired Melville a coded message and asked for a meeting at the British Embassy in Stockholm as soon as possible. He booked in at the Imperial for a few days and waited. He didn't get a wire back from Melville saying he would meet him in Stockholm but a telephone call from the Embassy in St Petersburg to expect a call from Melville on what the attaché said was a secure line from London. Sidney still didn't trust the telephone line but he went to the Embassy anyway to wait for it.

When it did come Sidney gave Melville chapter and verse on his achievements and the details of his brush with the German agents in Baku. Melville's instructions were that the whole package should be placed in the Diplomatic Bag as soon as possible. Melville said it was not possible for him to leave England at this time. Melville assured Sidney that he would be waiting for the bag at the other end and that no one else would have access to it except him and no less a person than the Foreign Secretary. Sidney was further instructed to wait in St. Petersburg for the next two weeks. On the question of Margaret's whereabouts Melville said she had set up house with her companion at an address in Westminster. The precise place Melville said he would have for Sidney with his reply.

For the next two weeks Sidney was able to enjoy something of a holiday. He was free of his 'responsibilities' as far as Melville was concerned and he could indulge himself with further philandering as Margaret was not as he had expected her to be 'at home'. There was plenty of entertainment to be had in St. Petersburg for those with money to spend and Sidney was not slow to avail himself of it. He knew the night life that St. Petersburg had to offer and he knew which cafes and restaurants had the best reputation.

He was already a frequenter of Dominic's but to ring the changes he had choices such as the Café de Paris or Kiuba's as it was more affectionately known as by St. Petersburg's lovers of French Cuisine. The chefs were brought in from Paris. Kiuba was the renowned owner. The Café de Paris was at 16 Bolshaya Morikaya. Or, he could choose to go to the Vienna Restaurant on Mitsa Gogolya. For more enlivening diversion there was the anciently established English Club at 16 Dvortsovara Naberezhnaia.

If this was not sufficient distraction there was gambling at The English Club either card or casino and it was well known as a place where the well-heeled of St. Petersburg could meet with pretty girls and there would be no questions asked. Sidney saw to it that he did not go short of this opportunity. He loved having a woman on his arm, even if he had to pay for her.

Sidney eventually got the call to revisit the embassy. There was a diplomatic letter 'for his eyes only' from England and it was this time from Melville. It was formal and bureaucratic in tone but it was comprehensive in its congratulation of Sidney and stated how the questions his discoveries had raised had been very well received by the agencies concerned. The Foreign Office had taken all his findings on board with reference to the military disposition of troops in the Caucasus There was even reference to how pleased those 'At the palace' were. Melville ended by saying that Sidney should expect a coded communication within the next few days.

Sidney returned to the Embassy a couple of days later after another telephone call and the coded message was waiting for him. He was given a small office to decode it and read the message. It was from Melville and generally it said that the material he had supplied could not be underestimated and that as predicted he was a 'made' man and he could expect a bankers draft for £5000 to be sent to his account in Moscow plus he had to add all the expenses he had incurred.

It was quite obvious from the tone of the message that Melville's reputation had also gone up dramatically for it hinted that he, Melville might well be acquiring a different status in the not too distant future. The message ended by saying that there was another brief for Sidney on its way in the diplomatic bag. But until it arrived Sidney could consider himself still on leave. There was however interestingly, no reference to an address for Margaret.

His leave lasted more than was promised and it was nearly a month after Melville's coded message that the desk clerk at the hotel said that there had been a telephone call for him. He saw from the note that the Embassy had called. He asked the front entrance porter to get him a carriage and he arrived at the gates of The British Embassy on Nevsky Prospekt just before ten.

The cold St. Petersburg autumn had ended and there was a flurry of winter snow blowing into the Embassy gardens as he showed his identity papers to the guard on the gate. He had not put on any gloves and as he waited for the guard to return he reflected on the winter in this region and hoped his next assignment would take him to warmer climes.

The frosts in the city were so fierce that it was perfectly acceptable for complete strangers to approach you in the street and tell you that there was a white spot appearing on your nose or that the bottoms of your ear lobes were turning white. These were dangerous signs of the beginning of frostbite. Before going out it was necessary to consult the thermometer on the outside of the window to see how far below freezing the streets were No, Sidney said to himself. I don't want to have to endure an arctic winter here no matter how entertaining St. Petersburg is. He wouldn't have to, the brief that was waiting for him would see to that.

The guard came back and Sidney was led up the steps of The Embassy and through its great oaken doors into the magnificently tiled entrance hall. Waiting for him there was one of the Ambassador's secretaries. He was perfunctory in his reception of Sidney.

The Ambassador was no better than his minion in welcoming Sidney. As he went into his office he didn't look up but carried on writing whatever missive he was concerned with and he motioned with his left hand that Sidney should sit down in the chair that had obviously been placed for him in front of the desk.

He did look up eventually and he pushed a large foolscap envelope towards Sidney. It had a red wax seal and was tied with red ribbon impressed with same wax. Sidney noted that The Ambassador was dressed in the standard F.O. 'uniform', wing collar and 'club' tie. Sidney was not yet expert enough to say which club. He had a black jacket on with similarly black waistcoat under it. Across the chest of the waistcoat was a light gold watch chain. Sidney could see under the desk that his trousers were grey pinstripe. He was a man in his late forties with steel grey hair and what Sidney liked to call 'the well-fed look'. He could see that his shoes were highly polished and protected by gray spats. He gave the strong impression that he already knew what was in the official envelope. His demeanor was quite different to the previous time that he had visited the Embassy.

'I've been instructed to give this to you and I want to say as I do so, I do not approve of the methods you people use and I wish to caution you on a significant point. We in the diplomatic service have been working hard over many months for a rapprochement with our Russian counter parts. If you compromise my position and those of my officials by one jot with the Imperial Government of His Majesty The Tsar I shall do all in my power to discredit you to the extent that you will be persona non grata in all the territories of the Russian Empire.'

Sidney ignored his remarks but thought, if I put a foot wrong with Melville I am stymied and now it's the same with this fellow. He took the envelope and merely expressed his thanks and asked for a place where he might read the letter the envelope contained. The Ambassador turned in his chair adjusted his pince-nez and rang a bell on his desk. The same secretary came into the doorway.

The Ambassador said airily with a wave of his hand, 'Put this person in the vestibule near the door. He then turned to Sidney and said, 'I bid you good day sir.'

Sidney was ushered into a small ante-room with a little desk and a chair. He sat down and then got up again because the secretary who had shown him where to sit had left the door open.

Sidney broke the seal of the envelope and began to read its contents. He was to travel to Port Arthur on the Liaotung Peninsula in the Far East where the Russians had established a warm water Naval Base for their pacific fleet. Vladivostok where the fleet was usually stationed could not be used in the winter so the Russians prior to the debacle of The Boxer Rebellion had negotiated a lease with the Chinese whose territory it was.

The action of the Russians had upset the Japanese because the Russians were using the advantage not only to shelter their fleet but they were also extending their influence in Manchuria, and Korea. Russia and Japan had their eyes on the natural resources and strategic positions of both countries vis a vis influence in The Pacific. Further to this the Russians had started to extend their railway network into Manchuria. As a rider to this, reference to the Americans and their Pacific ambitions had been added.

As if to confirm the remarks of the Ambassador notes had been written in red ink in the margin to the effect that considerable Diplomatic efforts were being exercised by HMG's representatives in Japan, Russia and the USA to stave off the possibility of relations in the region degenerating to the point of confrontation and perhaps even armed conflict.

Sidney's brief was simple it was that he was to use all means possible to discover any circumstances whatever that might be inimical to the interests of Her Majesty's Government of the British Empire and to report on such and also he was to give his full cooperation to The Japanese if requested. He was to report as regularly as time allowed by Indian Army Wireless Stations and by Lloyds Maritime Intelligence Service signal stations in Malaya and China. The Station locations and contact codes were enclosed. The letter concluded with a request to Sidney to have an interview with the Commercial Attache of the Embassy and a note to say that his retainer had been increased to £350 per month.

Sidney left the vestibule and asked to see the Commercial Attaché. He was shown into an office much smaller than that of the ambassador. Sidney was not surprised to be confronted by an attitude he was by now getting used to.

The young man had a parcel of material that had been prepared for Sidney and he went through its contents without attempting to hide a patronizing and supercilious tone.

Sidney was to travel to Port Arthur by the Danische Compagnie Est-Asiatic Shipping line which had offices in St. Petersburg. He was to maintain his responsibility as the London representative of the British/Far Eastern Chambers of Commerce along with his position of Director of Ozone Preparations. Once in Port Arthur he was to make contact with one, Moise Akimovitch Ginsburg who was chandler to the Russian Navy. Ginsburg would provide him with employment and commercial bona fides. The tickets for his journey and the addresses he needed were contained in the package.

Sidney got up and took the parcel and left the office with a polite thank you. He walked from The Embassy and out into the chilly street with a feeling of relief. He would soon be on the move again. A condition he relished.

Chapter Twenty Seven

Sidney took ship with the East Asiatic shipping company on their vessel 'Malaya 'at the end of September just as the St. Petersburg winter was settling in for its long frosty occupation and the snow was already being swept into frozen piles on pavements and streets by the battalions of Russian women whose job it always seemed to be. He fastened up his overcoat and kicked his boots as he mounted the gangway of what he immediately observed was a cargo ship and not a passenger boat.

Weeks of cramped accommodation were ahead with unpalatable meals eaten with the captain and officers and unbearable bouts of cabin fever. Sidney had thought of ignoring instructions as to travel arrangements and risking the long train journey to Vladivostok and its frequent identity checks. Now as he put his minimal luggage on the bottom bunk of a cabin he would be sharing with the second engineer he wished he had risked it.

It was a round the world voyage that was with its many ports of call interminable. The Malaya sailed out of the Baltic across the North Sea first to Newcastle in England and then to Hull. From Hull the next destination was London. Here Sidney thought of jumping ship and making contact with Melville or even Margaret but before he could make a serious attempt the ship left Tilbury and sailed down the Thames and round into the English Channel where she sailed on to Le Havre. Sidney was a good sailor but he was not prepared for the Bay of Biscay and he spent some days either against the rail or in the heads suffering the trials of sea-sickness.

Once in the Mediterranean the voyage did take on the quality of a cruise and the only thing to mar the seven days that were spent in Alexandria that 'Pearl of the Mediterranean' he noted, was news of the death of the old Queen. He would now, in a sense, be working for someone else, Edward the Seventh.

The stopover, all too short that it was nonetheless enabled Sidney to refill the emptied reserves of his personality and to avail himself of the charms of a very beautiful but relatively expensive young woman recommended to him by Emin the Armenian barman of the Hotel Caesareum on the Medaan Saad Zaghlu where he stayed rather than on board ship. She told him as she undressed for him for the first time that the Caesareum Hotel was named after the retreat that Cleopatra had built where she could entertain her lover Mark Anthony at the beginning of the First Century BC. Their lovemaking therefore followed in the footsteps of a long tradition. They were not only making love but making history as well.

The girl like the barman was also an Armenian She was a Christian whose family had disappeared in a Turkish purge. All her relatives had been massacred to second cousins. She had been in Egypt when it happened, sent there by her father, a lawyer, to learn English. She told Sidney that news of her family came to her from a 'sympathetic'

Turk or so she thought. His intentions it turned out were less than honourable and his real aim was to attach her to a 'string' of women he already had 'under his wing.'

With no one to look after her she had hired her own bodyguard and gone independent. She told Sidney all this one very warm afternoon in his hotel bedroom, louvered shutters closed against the sun as they lay together side by side in the darkened room after having made love. Both their bodies were bathed in sweat, bare under one blanched white cotton sheet like twin patients on an operating table. Her name was, she whispered to him on that sultry afternoon, Anahid Moulmeinian. Anahid she said meant 'the immaculate one, the virgin or the goddess Diana.' She smiled at the irony of it when she told him.

Sidney asked if she would be with him during the short time that he was in port and she agreed. She excused herself for a few minutes from the dinner table they were sitting at in the hotel in order she said, to dismiss her guardian. 'I won't need him, as you being the English gentleman that you are will be my guardian.'

They spent the next few days exploring Alexandria and their nights making love until dawn then sleeping until breakfast was served for them in Sidney's suite. They would then take a walk along the sands of the Mediterranean and call in to a beach side shack for a late lunch of fresh fish cooked on the coals of a rudimentary stove and served by the fisherman who had caught it fresh that morning. They ate the delicate flakes of white fish flesh with their fingers on flat Egyptian bread. 'We are like the multitude when Jesus fed them with loaves and fishes' said Anahid.

Sidney said."If that is what we are like, I shall compose a new Beattitude. And verily I say unto thee it shall be this, 'Blessed are those who find joy in making love for they shall find love in eternity." Anahid was just a little shocked and told Sidney that he should not blaspheme. 'I thought Christianity was all about love' Sidney said, and he then went on with a mischievous smile as he kissed Anahid's fishy tasting fingers,' Mary Magdalene knew all about making love.' Anahid thought she had lost the capacity to blush, but she did as she said, 'Now you are teasing me you rascal.'

Although Alexandria was not Anahid's home town she enjoyed showing Sidney its history. She took him to the cross-roads of Al Horreya and el Nabu Damil where she said Alexander the Great was buried. On the next evening they enjoyed a fiacre ride in the moonlight along the palm fringed road by the East Harbour that led to the Turkish Quarter and beyond to the old town of Ras el Tin. Sidney had to tip the driver heavily to take that journey as the Turkish Quarter had a notorious reputation and Anahid was uneasy about going there. Sidney took it as a challenge and his confidence reassured Anahid. After Ras el Tin their carriage trotted along the causeway to the site of what had been once a wonder of the world, The Lighthouse at Pharos. Its place was now built over by the lowering Fortress of Qait Bey.

Anahid had never had a client as attentive, solicitous and polite as Sidney. He was, she thought, more like a lover in his gentleness and consideration and she liked his company more and more each day of the short time they had together.

On the last morning of their being together before Sidney went back on board for the rest of his voyage, she woke him up at dawn and he found the whole of the bed covered in blood red rose petals. She had bought roses and asked that the petals be taken off and put into a basket. She had then strewn them on the bed while he was still asleep.

As he woke she quoted to him a verse which she said was from the work of one of Armenia's most celebrated poets, 'Dawn' by Khoren Nar Bey de Lusignan.

"Roses upon Roses spread in sheets below,

In the high blue ether Clouds that shine like Snow,

Lightly, brightly, softly. Spread before thy feet,

In this tranquil season wait thy face to greet,

Waits in hope all nature, O Aurora sweet!"

Sidney came out from under the covers and lay naked amongst the rose petals and Anahid did the same. She said as she did so, "You are Cupid to my Aurora."

As they loved each other the petals adhered to their skin as they perspired. They filled the division between Anahid's breasts and Sidney kissed them away so that his mouth was filled with the petals as he put his lips on Anahid. 'You have made me a bed of roses.' He said. What she did not tell him was that strewing a bed with flowers was the custom reserved for the nuptial couch after Armenian weddings.

Then came the time for Sidney to sail and he had become so enamored with Anahid that he asked her if she would come with him to the Far East. She did not directly refuse but said that he had given her so little time to consider it. As he left her to mount the gangway up to the deck of the ship he said that it might take time but he would come back to see her. As she waved him away and the ship moved from the quay and she felt the tears welling in her eyes of parting from a man she had, even in the attenuated time they had been together, fallen in love with. She brought herself back to the reality it was necessary for her to live in, and thought how she had heard that kind of promise before.

After the Suez canal and millenniums of Egyptian masonry the ship sailed through a new dam that was drowning many ancient temples on it banks.

Across the Red Sea it was not as with the Peninsular and Oriental line, Port Side out Starboard Home, on board Sidney's ship the heat was unbearable. Sidney spent the journey to Aden where the ship put in either drenched in the cooling effects of sea water from a hose on deck or in his own perspiration.

From Aden they then sailed across the Indian Ocean to Colombo in Ceylon and here began the final leg of the journey for after Colombo there was Penang and the ship began to know its way home to Singapore, Hong Kong and Shanghai.

Sidney changed ships in Shanghai and before he did that he made contact with one of Lloyd's wireless listening stations on the Chinese mainland that he was to use to pass on information. It meant that he did not arrive in Port Arthur until March 1901.

As he walked to the bottom of the gangplank there waiting for Sidney was the man who was to be Sidney's business partner for the next two years or so, Moisie Akimovitch Ginsburg.

"How do you do Mr. Reilly. It is good to meet you. I hope you had a pleasant trip. I have arranged for your luggage to be delivered to your accommodation as I have a place for you to stay already set up. I hope it meets with your approval. I have my carriage waiting and as it nearly lunch time I thought we would visit a little inn that I know so that we can get to know each other over a good lunch and one or two bottles of wine. How does that suit you?"

Sidney found all that quite acceptable but he was a little preoccupied with how much Ginsburg knew about him. If he knew his real Russian identity then that meant he, Sidney had been delivered into someone else's hands. Ginsburg was obviously Jewish. Did he know that Sidney was too? As the horses clip-clopped along the crowded streets Sidney forgot about the long sea voyage he had just endured and remembered that he was still to all intents and purposes on Russian territory and a territory that he was in no doubt would be well policed by the Ochrana.

In the restaurant Ginsburg ordered three main courses, Pelmeni, Bigos and Gloubtsy with a serving of Sevruga Caviar and chilled vodka. Sidney noticed that when he ordered from the Chinese waiter his Chinese was understood. When the caviar came Ginsburg toasted their new partnership and said, 'Where I come from, we have an old saying, 'Always start a new friendship with a good meal.'

'Begging your pardon Mr. Ginsburg,' said Sidney, 'But where are you from if I may ask?

'I'm from The Ukraine,' said Ginsburg. 'And you're from Odessa in The Crimea.'

Ginsburg saw Sidney's change of expression and added quickly but quietly, tapping the side of his nose at the same time with a smiling frown that screwed up his face.

'Don't worry I know all about you but you can be assured your secret is safe with me.'

But Sidney did worry. He was an adherent of the maxim that 'three people can keep a secret as long as two of them are dead.' Ginsburg's assurance was no comfort. The only consolation that Sidney could bring to mind was that St. Petersburg was a long way off.

Ginsburg could see that Sidney was still uneasy. 'Look' said Ginsburg,' What if I were to give you an earnest of good faith and then you will see where I stand. You will be able to pass it on to your people, put your stock up with them and at the same time it will show you that we are on the same side so that we can start as we mean to go on. What if I were to tell you that the Russians have bought a submarine from a German manufacturer and that they are having it shipped in parts by rail to Vladivostok? Apart from the fact that they already have problems with torpedoes and are likely to have the same problems into the foreseeable future that is all I have for the moment but I may be able to fill in the details later. What do you think of that?"

Sidney had to admit that it was the kind of information that he was looking for and that Ginsburg was right, it would put his stock up with Melville and he would get the message to him as soon as possible using the signal station on the mainland. It would show too that he had started work right away. The other important point was that Ginsburg was now just as much in Sidney's hands as Sidney was in his. Ginsburg reached over and took Sidney's hand and shook it as if completing a bargain. Sidney had the feeling that the two of them were going to get on very well together.

The courses were good when they came and Sidney began to relax his anxieties a little when on the outside of ice cold vodka, good red wine and Russian Champagne. It was such a change from the boat. He was also beginning to warm towards Ginsburg who gave the impression of having an open easy going personality. As the meal went on. Ginsburg talked of Russia, Port Arthur, business and the Russian Navy.

He said. 'The Russians have been in Port Arthur for over two years and have not really consolidated their position. That is to our advantage as their main, if not their only source of supply is Ginsbug and Co. Everything they want from an anchor to a smoke stack I boast, we can supply. I know you have other responsibilities but there is money to be made here especially for a bright young chap like you with your linguistic talents and experience. The Russians are disorganized and the Chinese are only just recovering from that Boxer business and as for the Japanese they are so furious at Russia getting the concession they can't see the wood for the trees. There is, without putting too fine a point on it, much talk of war here and that brings a great deal of confusion and where there is confusion there is profit.'

"Where would you say I fitted in to all this Mr.Ginsburg?"Said Sidney.

"Look, let's start as we mean to go on, Call me Moisie and I'll call you Sidney. Let's drop this Mr. business, far too formal. I want you to handle, once you have settled in of course, the purchasing of Timber from the States, some real estate deals that are in the offing and one or two aspects of shipping between here and two trading companies we have in Nagasaki and Yokohama." Sidney had cocked his head on one side and made a little of a grimace. Ginsburg went on."I know it sounds like a tall order but yours will be an executive role keeping an eye on the many staff we have to handle the ordinary day to day affairs of that side of the company. What do you think?"

Sidney was prepared to take on the responsibilities that Ginsburg listed. He had been forewarned that Ginsburg would be offering him employment but he had not expected that the offer would be in the form of a partnership. Ginsburg must be, he thought getting some advantage from the British Government. Perhaps he was, Sidney thought, in the same business as me." If he was that was all to the good, they would be scratching each other's backs."

Sidney decided to move the conversation in another direction by asking about what entertainment he would have access to in Port Arthur.

"You can have a nice life here if you set your stall out," Said Moisie." There is quite a lot to occupy your mind outside business. There is a thriving European community and a good club where you can meet up with people, make contacts and if you like a flutter on the tables there is a casino and there is always a good game of cards going on somewhere. Accommodation is cheap but as I have said you don't have to worry about that but then so are man servants." And, here he paused."and maid servants, if you know what I mean." He gave a knowing wink."The Chinese girls in Port Arthur are the prettiest and the most obliging on the peninsula. Mrs. Reilly is not with you I understand. We are all men of the world aren't we, what the eye doesn't see the heart has no concern for, yes?"

After the meal Ginsburg took Sidney to the apartment that had been arranged for him. It was on the first floor of an four storey house. It had a balcony, two bedrooms, a kitchen and bathroom. The water closet, such as it was, was in the garden 'dans un petit cabinet.' Main drainage and sewage collection had not yet arrived in Port Arthur and anyway the Chinese always built their privies next to the pig-sty; nothing should go to waste. The house was conveniently located. It fronted the main street and was only a walk away from the company offices. His luggage had already been delivered from the boat so all that remained was for Sidney to employ a man servant and he could begin his new life in Port Arthur. He did this the next day and the china man he employed brought his wife with him who he said was a very good cook.

Sidney settled quickly into his new accommodation, his new job and his new life in Port Arthur. He was well used to change. The occupation that Ginsburg had provided for him was, as he had said one of an exclusively executive nature. He took the decisions and others did the real work and as Gins burg and Co had an effective monopoly on trade, particularly with the Russian Navy the decisions necessary were not difficult to take.

His work also involved him in frequent travel to the cities of Yokohama and Nagasaki across the Yellow Sea to Japan sailing on the East Asiatic line. Japan was a complete surprise to Sidney. He had heard it described as being a country that was emerging from a totally medieval culture into a modernity that was like a butterfly coming out of its chrysalis. He thought it was more like someone being coerced into taking off one set of clothes whose design and size fitted perfectly and being forced to don a costume that not only was too big and so did not fit, no time was going to be given to grow into it.

Ginsburg had also told Sidney that if he saw an opportunity to make some money for himself, he was to take it. That kind of opportunity did present itself often particularly in the area of real estate. There was much ignorance on the part of the Chinese as to the value of land and property that they owned when in the context of Russian Military and Naval needs. Sidney and Ginsburg were in a very good position to know more about them than the average Chinese peasant on The Laiotung Peninsula. Fair dealing in business is much less profitable than the cynical exploitation of the ignorant by the entrepreneurial and so Sidney saw a very good return on the investments he made while at the same time furthering the interests of Ginsburg and Co. and reaping copious commissions as a result.

That is how Sidney spent that next year but while being involved in the commercial he did not neglect his social life. The sudden influx of military and naval personnel into Port Arthur had created a market for prostitution that had to be supplied with women and girls and they were to be drawn from most levels of a society that had a long tradition of the concubine. Sidney found that he had access to young women of culture who had been trained in the art of entertaining men and he developed associations with a number of Chinese young women whose company was not only the source of great pleasure it introduced him to an ancient culture of sexuality that added new dimensions to his experience. The sexual adventures Sidney availed himself of were quite different in degree and quality to anything he had ever had before and one discovery fascinated him, Chinese girls have little or no body hair.

Sidney's had an interest in gambling. It was also the interest of many others in the European community. To serve that interest there had been, when the Russians arrived in Port Arthur, the rapid growth of gaming clubs and gambling houses. With that growth a system of organized crime took control of such establishments and offered them protection not only against interlopers but also against bad debts. The Russian Administration should have provided a police force and legal process to counter this but it was not one of their high priorities.

The Chinese, historically a community dedicated to superstition, it follows were also inveterate gamblers. Unfortunately some of them, clients of these new iniquitous dens of vice, when they failed to honour their bets were found, sometimes whole and sometimes in pieces floating in the bay. The Triad, the name every Chinese knew as the movement behind all organized crime were ruthless in their treatment of transgression.

Chapter Twenty Eight

In late January 1902 Sidney took one of his regular trips to the Japanese mainland to organize a consignment of provisions that were destined for a Battalion of Siberian riflemen in the hinterland of the Liaotung. The competition between Russia and Japan did not extend itself, at the time to interfering with the ordinary currency of commerce. He had more or less finished the business of ordering the victualling of these troops from warehouses in Nagasaki when he was approached by a member of the Japanese Military who introduced himself as a Colonel. The Colonel asked Sidney to accompany him to his Headquarters. Sidney thought at first that he had not bribed the officials at the warehouse to the extent they expected and they were therefore contriving that obstacles be placed in his way but it transpired that there was another reason for the Colonel's interest in him.

When the Colonel with customary politeness sat Sidney down in his office and offered him a glass of Saki he introduced himself as Colonel Akashi Motojiro. He was that member of the Japanese Secret Service Sidney should have met up with in Paris.

Colonel Motojiro passed to him a dispatch which he asked Sidney to read. It was in English and it came from The Foreign Office in London. It stated that a treaty had been organized between His Britannic Majesty's Government and The Imperial Government of Japan. To describe it as baldly as that was to vastly understate it. It was one of the most comprehensive agreements between two sovereign nations in the history of diplomacy. Future members of the diplomatic profession, whatever nationality they were, would study its content as an example of what diplomacy, that reconciling of the irreconcilable, given the right joint international conditions, could achieve.

Britain would have preferred to have come to some sort of arrangement with the Russian Empire and in fact British diplomats had been working for some time to this end. Russia was closer in geography, culture, history and even Royal Blood than Japan but the sticking point in any discussions regarding closer relations with the British Empire was always Russia's Naval ambitions. Russia's wish was to have a navy that would rival any in the world. That to the Senior Service, His Majesty's Ships was anathema so a treaty with Japan was concluded and one of its most important and complex codicils was that Britain or Japan would assist and aid the other in the event of an act of war against them by more than one of the Great Powers. That meant that if the growing and pernicious competition in the Far East between Japan and Russia could not be solved by Japan's diplomats, Japan could consider war with Russia as a last resort knowing that Britain would prevent any other great power from intervening to assist the Russians.

There was an additional protocol and that was The Anglo-Japanese Naval Treaty. Japan would have its Navy ships built in British yards and the crews for the ships trained by The Royal Navy. It formalized, made official and extended a process that had been in operation for some six years.

What it meant for Sidney as Colonel Motojioro was quick to offer as soon as Sidney realised the implications for himself and Ginsburg and Co. was a job working for Japanese Military Intelligence and this with the full support of his British employers, For Sidney it was only a question of asking how much he would be paid.

Once Colonel Motojiro and Sidney had come to an agreement the colonel drew up a list of the priorities in terms of the information he wanted. So Sidney returned to Port Arthur with a joint responsibility. He was to act as an agent for Motojiro and for Melville. What he didn't do was to tell Ginsburg of his new attachment.

At the top of the Motojiro's list was reference to the disposition of capital ships in Port Arthur's harbour, any fortifications either constructed or under construction and their armament, generator and search light locations and most importantly what mine fields had been laid down. In short as comprehensive a description of the harbour's defence plans as could be obtained.

When he returned to Port Arthur Sidney with his usual single-mindedness began to make enquiries regarding what would be his best course of action. Through his contacts in the East Asiatic shipping company he soon came to the conclusion that much of what he was looking for might well be found in the Offices of the Head Marine Architect. It now became a question of how he could gain access to these offices and the information that was in them.

The partial solution to his problem came by the happy chance of his dalliance with a young Korean woman who worked in one of 'The houses' frequented by Russians and Chinese who were employed by the harbour authorities. He decided that he would cultivate a closer acquaintance with her and try to discover if any of her other clients were involved with the bureaucracy that organized and controlled port installations.

The girl Sidney had met was one of a 'consignment' of girls delivered to Port Arthur from Korea by a Chinese contractor who set them up in 'concubine houses' to service the needs of the Russians and their employees. They were more or less sex slaves and were bound to their employer by convention and by the fact that they had been bought from their families in the countryside. Peasant families with too many girls and not able to marry them off sold them as prostitutes or domestic workers; usually the former. They would be from a family that had not practiced the post natal birth control custom of strangling them a minute or two after delivery, often the fate of girl babies in Korea and China.

He had come across the girl some months before after a night out on the town and one of the party recommended the particular house where she worked as being worth a visit.

The 'house' where he found her was built in Chinese style. A building with a tiled pagoda roof around a courtyard with a garden and a pool and fountain in the middle. The supporting pillars and ornate doors were decorated in red and gold and grand stylised lion sculptures in wood guarded the steps up to the entrance. He and the company he was with were welcomed by the Chinese 'keeper' of the house, madam Key Chui. With all the customary if not ceremonial politeness of her culture she introduced 'her' girls. Sidney's eyes alighted immediately upon a diminutive young girl of, as he saw it unusual prettiness and chose her without any further consideration of the others on offer. Madame Key Chui pointed out to him that she was Korean and not Chinese.

She first offered Sidney an opium pipe,"to Chase the Dragon." He refused. She then offered to bathe him which he accepted and he insisted that she share the tub with him and although it was not the custom she had agreed. He found the experience of soaping her nakedness delightfully exciting as when she did the same for him. He had never been with a Korean girl before and he was struck by how physically different she was to the Chinese girls that he usually found himself with. They were light of frame and delicate in their responses.

He was very much seduced by her modesty and reserve when undressing. As she had been trained she made it into an erotic ritual until the voyeur was overcome by the desire the final sight of her nudity stimulated. She was like Chinese girls without any body hair. And there was a vigorousness about her love making. It was more robust, almost, with her short hair and muscular thighs like being with a youth. Sidney also found out her name, Chun Souk. This was unusual. The girls were normally anonymous.

Each time he went to 'the house' he asked for Chun Souk and he got to know her well. He brought her simple presents of candy and chocolate but these impressed her. She wasn't used to such treatment nor were her 'colleagues' and some became a little jealous of Sidney's attention. She didn't mind this and she began to look forward to his visits and she became very affectionate towards him. For his part he was able to get her to talk more. To begin she told him about herself, where she came from and how old she was although she couldn't be quite sure about that. She thought she was ' about eighteen or twenty.' Then very gradually Sidney began to get her to talk about her other clients especially those who were employed in the port and harbour.

At first she seemed only to have had clients who were in junior positions; she was after all a relatively new girl. But as time passed and her reputation was enhanced by her being a 'favorite ' of a European namely Sidney, more senior executives from the Military Government and the Harbour Administration asked for her services.

Months passed and Sidney found himself with little he was able to report to Melville or Motojiro. The Russians had become increasingly sensitive over their relations with Japan and there was 'spy' hysteria in Port Arthur. They began to see Japanese spies everywhere and particularly amongst the European community. He knew that they had those in Port Arthur who had Japanese connections under surveillance and as he had suspicions that someone in Ginsberg and co. was in the pay of the Russians Sidney was keeping his head down. He began to feel concern that his principals might be losing confidence in him.

Then there was a breakthrough. On one of his now regular visits to Chun Souk and after a more than stimulating session with her wherein she confided to him afterwards as they both relaxed naked drinking the tea she made, that one recent 'visitor' had got himself into trouble as he was not able to pay his account. He was a regular Chinese client and he worked as an engineer in The Head Marine Architect's office.

He was in trouble, not only because he had not paid his bill at 'the house' but he had large debts with the gambling house subsidiary that ran its business parallel with the 'concubine house.' His debts were so large he was being threatened with violence by the Triads that controlled all the gambling in Port Arthur as part of a cartel.

This man was just the subject Sidney was looking for. If he had anything like a position in the Architect's Office he might have access to the plans for the harbour's defence or he would know who had and he seemed a perfect subject for blackmail and or bribery. Sidney asked Chun Souk to find out his name and where he lived.

It was just around Christmas time 1903 that Sidney made his next visit to Chun Souk. He had not seen her for some time as he had been to Nagasaki secretly having been summoned by Col. Motojiro. He went to see her in response to a message she had sent to him requesting that he come to her. That was unusual as it was difficult for her to get a message out. It had come to Sidney at the office in the hands of a sea captain of one of East Asiatic's cargo boats.

She was waiting for him and had bathed and dressed especially for him she had also made up her face with white face powder and very red lip stick. Her oriental almond eyes were carefully lined with kohl. Her hair which she had grown longer at Sidney's bidding, as black as a black cat was piled on her head and tied with white satin ribbon and she wore a shirt of bright yellow silk, below this a crimson red skirt, also silk over light white cotton trousers. Her feet clad in white cotton stockings were in black slippers trimmed with gold thread the toes of which turned up slightly. She looked beautiful. She had worn such dress before and Sidney had admired her. She never wore any petticoats or underwear. There was a small table in front of her as she sat cross-legged and waited for him. It was set with a teapot and two tea dishes their china glaze decorated with blue chrysanthemums.

'I came as soon as I got your message.' Sydney said, 'Is anything wrong?' it was not uncommon for the girls to find themselves pregnant and then they were evicted from the house for the duration of their pregnancy. This possibility had passed through Sidney's mind.

He sat in front of her and took her little hands and she said quietly in the halting English Sidney had taught her, not wanting to be overheard as clients expected confidentiality, 'I have the name of the gentleman we talked about, it is Ho Liang Shang. He came in to discuss his debts with Madame Key Chui. He came to talk to me as he was once one of my guests but I did not know his name. I told him of you and said that you wished to speak to him on a matter that he might find to his advantage. All this you asked me to tell him, Yes? He would not tell me where he lived.' Her discretion as far as her beloved Sidney was concerned did not permit her to ask why he wanted the information.

Sidney was very pleased and she could see this. She was happy that she pleased him. He was in the mood for being pleased more and he took her to one of the private chambers in the house. There he ordered that a meal be fetched from outside with sparkling Russian wines and they ate and drank reclining on brightly coloured cushions with the air around them heavy with the burning incense that had been set for them. The bed provided had chiffon curtains and the lamps they left lit shone through and showed Chun Souk ravishing in her nakedness as she gave Sidney every pleasure that she knew. She prepared him with the exquisite sensations of a foot massage then she asked him to put himself in every part of her. She put her fingers in him and took him in her mouth and he ejaculated as he had never done before.

As they lay together afterwards Sidney turned and leaning on his left elbow looked down at Chung Souk, her head on the pillow, and said, 'A great English poet wrote about two lovers like us, listen to some of his lines;

'Licence my roving hands and let them go,

Before, behind, between, above below.'

As he recited the lines he moved his hands and showed her the meaning of the words.

Sidney had once read a poem by John Donne but as on previous occasions when he had recited it he had not been able to recall the name of the poet or the title of the poem.

As he finished, she reached into her clothes, which were in disarray by the side of the bed, and Chun Souk brought out a small piece of pale blue rice paper on which there was black Korean script.

'I have written you a poem.' She said, ' May I read it to you?'

'Of course', said Sidney, 'I love poetry. Let me read it.'

Chun Souk whispered. 'No I wish to read it to you first in Korean if I may.'

In her sweet little girl's voice she quoted the lines with very obvious sincerity.

'I am like the willow tree.

The winds that blow from all the corners of the world

Are free to caress my tender leaves,

As is the rain falling down below the heavens.

In the spring birds of so many different feathers

May sit in my branches.

But hidden deep inside me,

As the roots of the willow are in the earth,

Is my heart that only you may touch. '

When she told him as far as she could what the lines meant in English he kissed her passionately and they made love again.

She had often asked him if she made him happy and he had said she did. She had been overheard asking such questions of Sidney and it was clear to the more mature and experienced women in 'the concubine house' that she was in love. They warned her against becoming emotionally attached to her clients. No good would come of it they all said. She was told that they, their 'guests' had wives and if they were white men they would eventually leave. Chun Souk could not contemplate this possibility. Sidney was someone who would not go away ever. His work was here and he didn't have a wife he only had her, Chun Souk.

What Chun Souk did not know was that, for Sidney there was someone else. She was someone that he had met as a result of a social gathering organized for the staff of Ginsburg and co and the East-Asiatic company. Her name was Anna Grigoryevna Collins. She was the Russian born wife of an Englishman named Horace Collins. When Sidney first met the couple he had been mostly interested in her husband. Although he found Mrs. Collins quite strikingly attractive and he considered from their first meeting the possibility of an affair with her, other priorities were forced upon him.

For some time he had suspected that someone in the Danische Compagnie East Asiatic was leaking information to the Russians and these were partially confirmed when after a visit to Japan, Col. Motojiro had informed him that a person in the pay of the Russians in Port Arthur had been unearthed by The Japanese Secret Service.

The brief information he was able to pass on was that the suspect was a European, a Japanese speaker and had once worked in the Imperial Stables.

Sidney knew from company gossip that Mr. Collins had been a jockey in England and was a consultant on horses in Port Arthur for the shipping company. He could speak Japanese and had represented the East-Asiatic company in trading horses in China, Korea, Japan and even on the Russian mainland where his wife had acted as translator. He had visited Japan almost as often as Sidney. He also knew from the same grapevine of gossip that Collins was in financial trouble. He put two and two together and decided he would seek to have his suspicions confirmed by an association with the man's wife.

He thought that Anna would be an easy conquest; after all he was also Russian, he didn't reveal that to her however. Although it did not take long for Sidney to discover that like many European wives in the ex patriot community of Port Arthur she was bored and neglected, she did not submit to his charms as easily as he thought she might.

Why the wives were neglected was easy to discover. Beautiful diminutive Chinese girls taught from childhood to submit themselves totally to the male had their attractions. Combined with the many other distractions that were present in the free -wheeling life of the Port Arthur of that time, these caused the joys of domestic married life, for European husbands to be second best. Anna it was true was childless, sexually frustrated and at that dangerous age of thirty..There was certainly a vacuum in her life but if Sidney, sexual predator and opportunist that he was thought that filling that personal void was going to be as easy as other conquests, he was to be disappointed.

He thought he would have an erotic romance while at the same time investigating the activities of her, as he suspected, informer husband. His affair however did not go as he expected. He found himself within a very short time powerfully attracted to her. One of the reasons being that she had been so difficult for him to get when he prided himself on being always the successful lothario. She was beautiful in face and form and it was also possibly the fact of her Russianness that caused Sidney to feel a strong affinity with her. In the end even he had to recognise that he had become strongly infatuated with her. Initially the purpose of wooing her had been to expose Collins not to desire her to the point of erotic love. Exposing an informer ceased to be the prime priority. Now he found that thoughts of her preoccupied him. He had found a woman to whom he had to submit rather than the other way. He had never before had to pursue a woman. Before It had always been the woman that did the chasing.

Chapter Twenty Nine

As it happened it was not Anna who was to reveal that Collins was in the pay of The Russians. It was by coincidence Sidney's contact with Ho-Liang-Shung that exposed Horace Collins.

Once Sidney had Ho-Liang- Shung's name and the facts about his gambling activities his first port of call was the gambling house connected with 'the house of concubines'. He knew the manager as a customer who bought his supplies of wine and liquor from Ginsburg and Co. so it was not difficult to find out that Shung owed some many thousands of rubles and he had left a number of promissory notes as his luck had completely run out at the same rate as his credit rating. Sidney was in a position, with the guarantees he had from Melville and Motojiro, to buy up all of Shung's debts and to lift the threat of more violent retribution that was descending on him from the Triads. He did this on condition that Shung was not informed directly. Sidney decided to break the news through a meeting with him arranged by telephone. He used the pretext of a delay problem arising over construction materials. Ho-Liang-Shung wished initially to send a subordinate but his attendance was insisted upon.

A private room in the offices of Ginsburg and Co. was reserved. Shung when he came was shown in. He was an educated, professional class Chinese of around fifty years old, slim and of average height He was dressed very smartly, in an obviously well-cut suit, as a westerner. Sidney introduced himself, requested him to sit and then instructed his juniors that he did not want to be disturbed on any account.

Ho-Liang-Shung had been placed in front of a desk whose surface was bare apart from a large square of white cloth. Under the cloth Sidney had arranged the promissory notes that Shung had left. Having already introduced himself to the somewhat confused Shung, he spoke to him in Russian. Shung, he found out later spoke also English and Japanese. Sidney sat down on a chair behind the desk.

Sidney did not beat about the bush when he said,"I have to admit Mr. Shung that I have brought you here on a pretext. You like to gamble don't you Mr Shung? What card game is it you like? Is it Vingt et Une or do you call it Blackjack? You are not however very good at it are you and you are having a run of very bad luck at the moment, true?'

Shung's typically and usually inscrutable oriental almond eyes opened wide with surprise at what Sidney said but then he was even more surprised, if not visibly shocked when Sidney lifted the cloth and showed the twenty or so I.O.U. notes.

Sidney said," Would you like to estimate how much those are worth?' Sidney continued quickly. He did not want to give Shung time to think."Never mind, the important thing is that I have bought them from your creditors. Without putting too fine a point on it Mr. Shung, I now own you lock stock and barrel. You probably know that as far as some of them are concerned I have probably saved your life or at least fairly important parts of your anatomy. Now you have a choice, I am going to make one or two suggestions to you. If you agree not only will all these notes be returned to you so that you can destroy them, but all your other debts will be paid in full and on top of that a considerable sum will be paid into a bank account or delivered in cash according to your instructions. However if you disagree, first of all the notes belonging to the Triads will be returned to them and the rest of your unsuccessful gambling affairs will be communicated to your employers. I do not have to emphasise what effect this will have on your family. It will be impossible for them to save face. You of course, given my previous comments on the ownership of some of your debts will have ceased to care.

Having said this Sidney took a great wad of rubles from a drawer in the desk and placed it within reach of Shung." In front of you is an example of my good faith. There are over six thousand rubles there, the approximate equivalent of one thousand English pounds. I shall give you a short time to consider my offer but I want you to be under no illusions, it will only be a short time." Sidney gathered up the notes leaving the wad of money where it was. He then left the room taking the bundles of I.O.U.'s with him.

Within minutes Mr. Shung appeared at the barely open door and whispered for Sidney to come back in. Sidney sat down and waited for Shung to speak first. He did and he said, 'What is it you want from me?'

Sidney began to speak quickly but quietly in a confidential tone."The situation is this, Japanese and Russian Diplomats are working together at this very moment to try to find a solution to the differences that exist between the two countries. Before we go any further I want to assure you that the information I am going to ask you to give to me will only be used as a diplomatic lever to persuade the Russians here in Port Arthur to be more flexible in their approach to overtures from the Japanese. The wish of the Japanese is that Imperial Russia should concede part of the Liotang peninsula to Japanese control and to consent to joint talks on Russian influence in Korea and Manchuria. If the information is forthcoming it will enable the Japanese to negotiate from a position of strength and it will certainly avoid any dangerous confrontation between Russia and Japan to materialize. The possibility of the war that everyone is afraid of will have been averted and you will have played your part. Sidney then coolly took out a small sheet of paper from the left pocket of his waist coat and began to read from it.' I want you to provide me with information on the following.

The disposition in the harbour of Russian Capital ships.

All Fortifications, constructed and under construction.

Armament types and emplacements.

Generator and searchlight installations.

Mine field Maps of harbour defences."

Shung blanched under his Chinese skin and stuttered out,' But, But if I disclose all that to you it will leave Port Arthur defenceless.'

Sidney's first thoughts were triumphant.' He is able to supply the information.' Then he leaned over and sympathetically touched Shung's left hand which was on the desk top and said, 'No, no, no, Mr. Shung you have not listened to what I said.There are negotiations taking place at precisely this time between the Russians and the Japanese. This information will be used only for a diplomatic advantage, not for a military one, I do assure you. I wouldn't want Port Arthur to be exposed in such a way. Like you I and my friends live here.This is where like you,I earn my living. I would make myself destitute. Why would I want to do that? My father had many Russian friend s and business associates. I would not betray his memory."

Shung looked at the pile of money and at his promissory notes. For the last few weeks he had been at the end of his tether. His wife was threatening to kill herself and the children. He did not know which way to turn. He had tried to recoup his losses but only succeeded in getting into more debt. It was only going to be a matter of time before Svinsky the Chief Marine Architect of Port Arthur found out about his circumstances. The only consolation for him was that he would by then be in the hands of the Triad. He sat for a few minutes and gradually convinced himself that he had nothing left to lose and if what he divulged was only going to used by diplomats….well…….was that so serious?

The answer Sidney gave to his next question convinced him completely.

Shung was perspiring and wiping his face with a large white handkerchief. He had a look of apprehension about him, almost like a child about to burst into tears, as he said."If do what you are asking what will be the details of my reward and in the event of my being found out how will I and my family be protected?"

Sidney replied quickly."As I have said all these promissory notes will be given to you plus another twelve thousand rubles making eighteen thousand in all, added to that you will receive one thousand British gold sovereigns. As for the other factors you are guaranteed 100% confidentiality. But in the unlikely event of discovery you and your family will be given a new life, with financial independence in any country of your choosing. This is not an empty promise. I have access to the resources.'

Shung did not hesitate any longer and said he would accept the offer. He had already worked out that if Sidney did not keep his promise he would contrive to say that the information had been stolen and a Japanese Spy, namely Sidney had been responsible. As he thought on this he spoke again.

'In protecting my confidentiality, there is something you should know before we finalise this agreement. There is a man in The Danische Compagnie Est-Asiatic who is in the pay of the Russians. If he should hear of this it would be disaster for me and I suppose for you. His name is Horace Collins."

Sidney congratulated himself straightaway. His suspicions were right and his assessment of the evidence had been accurate. It flattered his ego to have his intelligent judgment confirmed. Now, that it looked as if Shung was sorted out there would be time to deal with Mr. Horace Collins.

Sidney turned back to Ho-Liang-Shung." There is obviously some urgency over this matter. How long will it take you to get the information I am looking for? You can be sure there will be no delay, all things being equal, in seeing to it that get your reward. Don't worry about the other matter. We will deal with Collins."

Ho-Liang-Shung was desperate to get himself out of the financial mess he was in so he said. 'I am sure I can have all the information you require by the first week in January that is in five days time, if that is I do not encounter any problems that are not of my making.'

Sidney got up and offered his hand which Shung hesitated in taking but he took it in the end. Shung then left and Sidney became preoccupied with the problem of Collins. He found out later when he met Anna that he needn't have worried. The problem had solved itself. Collins was in Korea on trading business and would not be back until the end of the month. By then thought, Sidney I shall be well on my way. What he had to do now was make contact with Motojiro so that he could collect the information and bring the money for Shung. It would have to be through a message passed on by the listening station on the Chinese mainland and it would have to be soon as it would take Motojiro a little time to get from Japan.

Sidney took the train up country to the listening station and sent the message and arranged to meet Motojiro. He was to come ashore secretly in six days time at midnight in an isolated cove a few miles to the north of Port Arthur co-ordinates 39' 48 N 122'14E..The signal from the shore was to be three long dashes and one short by lamp and also from the shore, as the boat arrived there would be three short identifying blasts on a whistle. Motojiro was to come by fast torpedo boat and to bring the money for Shung in rubles and sovereigns. He was to be prepared to take back on board en route for Japan, four adults with their luggage, Sidney, Anna, Shung and his wife and their two little children. Sidney made this arrangement without consulting Shung or Anna but thought it expedient to send the request in the same signal.

On his return Sidney arranged to meet Anna and to take her out to an inn they had often visited in the countryside outside Port Arthur where they were not known but she changed the arrangement and sent him a message to say that she was alone at home.

When he got to the house she had instructed her house keeper to prepare dinner and then dismissed her for the evening. Anna was looking, thought Sidney more than usually beautiful. She was from east of Moscow and had the high cheekbones and slightly Asiatic cast of the eyes typical of peoples in that region. The rouge on her lips was carmine red over her white teeth. She was almost as tall as Sidney, slender but with a full bosom. She wore her black hair down whenever she met Sidney and this night was no exception. Her dress was of the chim sung Chinese style. It was of gold thread embroidered crimson satin with a high collar and it was slit to the waist

After dinner she got up and taking the bottle of Champagne Sidney had brought she went with her glass into the bedroom and without any preamble she undressed and lay on the bed. It was this kind of behavior on the part of Anna that captivated Sidney. She always took the initiative. Sidney lay by the side of her and she made love to him insisting that she mounted on top of him.

Sidney watched fascinated as she pleasured herself on him, her black hair falling over her face and touching his. She came to her climax before him and rolled off him to lie breathing by the side of him. She let him come into her but she seemed detached although she embraced him fiercely.

When it came to telling Anna of his intention to leave and take her with him without explaining to her the reasons why and the means whereby he was to leave Port Arthur, much to his surprise she declined the offer almost casually. He was devastated. He had even planned to ask her to marry him, bigamous though the marriage would have been.

She told him that although she had enjoyed their brief affair, her place was with her husband and she intended to stay with him. Sidney could not persuade her even though he hinted that there was likely to be a dangerous clash between the Japanese and the Russians. This was no surprise to her she said,' My husband has been warning of it for some time.' Horace had obviously been keeping his ear to the ground, but then that, Sidney thought, wryly is what the Russians were paying him for.

They spent the rest of the evening although still in bed together naked, arguing and their exchange became quite heated. He used all his powers of persuasion, telling her that he would be able to keep her in a style of life much superior to the one she had. He said that they would travel the world and live in the best of hotels and that she should want for nothing.

She was adamant. She would not be persuaded by any incentive he could offer. As he tried to embrace her again while assuring her that they would marry, she angered him by avoiding his arms and dismissing his offer of marriage in a derisory way.

She got up from him and dressed. He did the same and left the house much earlier than he intended. He was in a fit of pique. His pride was blunted and his ego bruised. He could not remember when a woman had turned him down so unequivocally. As he sat in a rickshaw on his way back to his house he decided that he would not take no for an answer and that before he left he would return to Anna's house and begin the process of persuading her again.

He didn't tell Chun Souk he was leaving even though he visited her three days later nor did he give any kind of warning to her about what might be coming if war broke out between the Russians and the Japanese. The last time the Japanese had occupied Port Arthur (or as they called it Ryojun) when at war with the Chinese in the late 1890s they had left the streets running with blood and strewn with the thousands of heads and bodies of the men, women and children they massacred.

The one thing he did powerfully regret was telling Anna of his plans as she had not consented to coming with him. For some time it concerned him that she might pass the information on to her husband. As things turned out she kept her counsel, or at least she did until he was out of the country.

Sidney made his own preparations for leaving. He chose a livery stable out of town and he hired two horses one as a mount and the other as a pack animal. He did not tell the stableman that he would not be bringing them back. He gave his household staff the day off and he packed what things he thought he would need, mostly clothes but also a few provisions and water just in case the unexpected happened. He had provided himself with a detailed map of the peninsula and a prismatic Verner compass. He had his oil hand lamp and he bought a whistle from a market store. Taking all his money out of the bank did not raise any questions as he often had to have access to large sums for cash transactions involving the company. He told his manager that he was going up country to see a stand of timber that he wanted to buy. That he was sure would be passed onto Ginsberg.

On the morning of the fifth day after the first interview with Shung a young Chinese boy came with a message to say that Mr. Shung was waiting in a tea house just a short way from Sidney's offices. Sidney went to his strong box and took out all of Shung's I.O.U.s and the rubles he had placed in there. He put them into a large envelope and walked the hundred yards or so down the crowded street to the tea house. He was cautious. He had his pistol in its usual place and he had the German Mauser in a leather shoulder holster a Chinese cobbler had made up for him. They were both loaded with the safeties off. The possibility of Shung having communicated Sidney's demands to his employers was an eventuality that Sidney had considered. For all he knew he might be walking into a trap. He looked carefully around but in the confusion of the pavement and road saw only street urchins, beggars, Chinese coolies carting goods or carrying as usual the loads that would break the backs of ordinary mortals. If there had been Russian Military police waiting for him they would have stuck out like sore thumbs. The Ochrana were a different matter. He did not, however as one important point, see any Europeans in his short walk.

When Sidney arrived,Shung, dressed as smartly as before, was waiting in the tea house. Sidney sat down and Shung poured out tea into two earthenware cups from a big brown pot with a bamboo handle. Sidney considered the other people in the shop. There were only six and they looked like ordinary clients. Sidney also assessed how he would get away if an arrest was tried or if there was a shoot out. One thing was certain in his mind, he would shoot Shung first.

All the precautions Sydney had taken in thought and deed were unnecessary, Shung, though most decidedly of very nervous demeanor had all the information he had been asked to supply. He looked up from his tea, glanced furtively around and pushed towards Sydney a string tied folder of the type that legal documents were generally contained in.

Sydney left it on the table and didn't open it but asked Shung if it was everything that had been asked for.

Shung looked down at his tea and said, in a voice that Sidney could hardly hear.' All the details of the list you gave me have been recorded in writing and on maps. You have a comprehensive description of the harbour in all its aspects, from commercial.," here he lowered his voice even further so that Sidney had to strain to hear what Shung said,"to military".

Sydney took it and without taking the papers out of the folder, carefully perused each page as if slowly counting bank notes. It took him some minutes. Shung had been as good as his word. It was all there.

Closing the folder and retying the string Sidney gave Shung his envelope and waited for him to examine the contents. Then without waiting for Shung to ask, He said,." You will get the rest tomorrow." Then he explained the arrangements for leaving that he had made with Motojiro.

Shung looked shocked. 'Oh no he said I will not be going to Japan. I have made other arrangements. Myself and my family will be going back to where we came from,Shanghai.'

'Well,' said Sydney, successfully hiding his surprise,"That is all one to me but you will have to come with me tomorrow to collect your money. I am not able to return to Port Arthur." Shung reluctantly agreed and they planned a meeting the next day in the morning to make the trek the little way north. Sydney pointing out that Shung would have to provide for himself and also hire a horse. As they parted Sydney said he should also, arm himself."You will be returning with a considerable amount of money. You will need to be prepared to defend yourself if you come across any bandits." They arranged to meet at nine the next morning. Their rendezvous would be on the outskirts of town outside the ruins of an old Christian church that they both knew.

Sidney went back to his apartment and opened the folder to lay out all the papers and documents in it on a table. Shung had earned his corn. He had followed the instructions to the letter, dispositions of capital ships with their names in Russian, searchlight positions the generator house, heavy and light machine gun pill boxes and block houses. Shung had noted that these had been built by the German company Krupp so they were substantial. Shore batteries, harbor installations and a highly detailed pattern in black dots had been laid out on a map where mines were placed in the sound and the harbor entrance. Sidney thought,"I have supplied the Japanese with the keys to the kingdom. Port Arthur is wide open." He could not wait to put it into the hands of the Japanese or more accurately he could not wait to get his hands on the fortune they had promised as reward.

That evening having completed all his preparations Sidney went to see Anna again. He felt sure that he had not given her enough time to consider his offer. He wanted to assure her that their liaison had a substantial basis and that he was prepared to marry her. He was convinced that she would in the end agree to what he wanted her to do.

He hadn't made an assignation with her but he wanted to see her. There was a deeper psychological reason that motivated him and that was the strong sense of rejection that he felt. He had convinced himself that her attraction to him and him to her was of a strength that made him irresistible. That she had said no was a significant blow to his idea of himself.

When his hired carriage arrived at her house and dropped him off he saw that there were lamps lit. He walked around the back of the house through the garden as they had both agreed he should for discretion but when he got to the main window at the back on the ground floor he saw through it that she wasn't alone. She was with a man he did not recognize; a European. They were embracing and after a few seconds he saw them both move towards the room that he knew as the bedroom because he had shared it with her on the numerous occasions that her husband had been away on business. She had lied to him. The reason for her refusing to join him on the voyage to Japan was not because of her husband but because she had another lover. Sidney was consumed with jealousy. He contemplated barging in and confronting them both but he reconsidered as there was too much at stake.

He waited for some time in the garden. The privy was outside and he seriously considered for some time that he would ambush one or other of them when they came out.

The wait calmed him down and when he thought on what there was to lose he decided that it was her loss so he left and walked a long way before he finally got into one of the many rickshaws that had passed him seeking a fare. But when he got back to his apartment he spent the rest of the night, fuming with frustrated anger, drinking Chinese rice wine and smoking the very strong Georgian tobacco of the Russian papyrosa cigarettes he had developed a taste for. Had Anna been within arms reach he would, he thought have done her a powerful mischief.

Chapter Thirty

Colonel Motojiro representing the Japanese Secret Service made his way along the dock in Nagazaki and asked the Marine Officer at the gate the way to the Japanese Navy destroyer Inazuma. She was in Nagazaki Naval Yard after a complete refit. He was carrying over his shoulder a large obviously heavy leather satchel that was hand –cuffed to his wrist on a chain. Colonel Motoiro was not looking forward to the sea voyage he was about set out on. He had been to sea a number of times but he had been, on each occasion, violently sea-sick.

He found the Inazuma, with its ultra modern high forecastle and sleek grey shape topped with four slowly smoking funnels, anchored along the far end of the dock. He presented his identity credentials to the marine at the foot of the gang- plank walked up it and turned to salute the poop deck and was personally welcomed on board by the commander of the ship a man who could have been Motojiro's brother they were so a like in age stature and colouring.

Captain Surogoshi immediately took Colonel Motojiro to the bridge. On the way there Col. Motojiro noticed that every nook and cranny of the ship he passed seemed to be occupied with a crew member. There were hammocks under gangways and in gun turrets and even slung across walkways. Captain Surogoshi noted his interest and said," I am afraid that the Ikazuchi class destroyer was not built with the crew's comfort in mind. The makers were more interested in space for high performance engines and boilers. We have ordinarily fifty five crew members and the ten extra marines that arrived before you have not aided the situation. You will share my quarters and though I have to ask you to excuse my lack of hospitality it should not be much of a hardship for the two or three days we will be at sea."

They arrived on the bridge and they were alone except for the white uniformed quarter master attending the wheel and he came smartly and loudly to attention when Surogoshi and Motojiro entered. Surogoshi motioned him brusquely to leave and turned to Motojiro. Behind him and above his head on the bulkhead was a Samurai sword on brackets and just below on the same bulkhead was a brass plaque about ten inches by five inches, engraved on it were the words,' IKAZUCHI Class Destroyer, 'Lightning,' Built 1897 Yarrow Shipbuilders, Poplar, London, England. Displacement 410 tons.' Surogoshi was opening a locked safe and he said without looking up."The sword was my fathers, he was a Samurai, a Knight of the Bushido under the code of the sword. When they cut off his top-knot he committed Hari Kari. The sword was passed on to me. He was a man like your father born into a feudal Japan. We are, you and I, Japanese of a

New World His son is now the captain of a modern warship. This ship is my sword. You are a soldier in The Emperor's Army, you carry your sword still. You have something for me I think?"

Colonel Motojiro took a key from a pocket in his uniform and unlocked the handcuff on his right wrist, loosened the chain and opened the leather satchel and took out an envelope of thick blue paper tied with black ribbon and where it crossed there was a red wax seal with the Imperial insignia on it."Please put this satchel in your safe with your sealed orders." He said." I am instructed to inform you by your own Admiralty Intelligence Service that your orders are not to be opened until we have been at sea for two hours heading east."

Captain Surogoshi gave the con of the ship to the white-suited Quarter Master and asked his Number One to escort Colonel Motojiro to his quarters. As they descended ladders to the deck below ratings ran past them to their stations and there were the sounds all around them of a ship being made ready for sea. The officer noted Colonel Motojiro's unease and recognized the symtoms. He said."Begging your pardon sir but we all get seasick. I have a remedy first given to me when I was in training with the British Royal Navy during sea trials of the 'Inazuma". I will order it from the steward." When it came it was Bovril and sherry, hot.

As the ship weighed anchor, ropes were cast off forard and then aft and the 'Inazuma' pushing steam and grey smoke from all four funnels made out to sea and Colonel Motojiro could feel the throb of her 6000 horsepower reciprocating engine under his feet. Neither the Bovril nor the ship under way made him feel any better.

Sidney got up washed and breakfasted and tidied away all evidence of himself in the apartment. He put all the stuff he was not taking in cupboards and drawers and left on the desk, a sealed letter addressed for the express personal attention of Ginsburg that simply said."Horace Collins of Danische Compagnie Est Asiatic is a paid informer for the Russians."

He put on cavalry trousers, calf length brown leather boots a thick Russian soldiers' shirt and dressed in a waterproof riding coat, he locked up and went into the yard carrying bulging saddle-bags. He had already put two trunks on either side of the pack horse. He mounted his horse and tied the reins of the pack horse to the pommel of his saddle. He fastened the top button of his coat and pulled up the collar and adjusting his broad brimmed hat well down against what was a cold morning he checked his saddle bags and set out to meet Shung The streets were already busy but he was only another traveler in the traffic and he was soon on the road out of the town.

The ruined Christian Church where Sydney had arranged to meet Shung was just outside the precincts of Port Arthur because before it had been leased to the Russians its Chinese name had been Lushun and Christian Churches had not been permitted in the town. When the Japanese invaded the peninsula of Liaotung in 1894, the priest, a

European had declared himself and his largely converted Chinese congregation neutral. The Japanese beheaded him his wife and family and every man woman and child in his 'flock' anyway, and then burned the Church.

Sydney, as he approached down the road could now see against the sky, the skeleton of its charred rafters and he could also see the shape of a horse and rider by one of the ruined stone walls.

As he got closer Sidney saw that it was Shung. When they met they exchanged pleasantries and then set off, Shung following on his horse behind Sydney, along the road to the coast. Sydney knew the way having been there before buying land on behalf of the company. It was not to be a long trek but Sydney wanted to get there before nightfall so that they could be in position for midnight and not clambering around in the black dark looking for the track down from the cliffs to the beach and the cove.

On board the 'Inazuma', well over two hours out of Nagazaki Captain Surogoshi had opened his sealed orders and had commanded the Quarter Master at the wheel to steer on a heading east north east bearing on the co-ordinates 39' 48 North 122' 12 East. The engine room telegraph had been rung to full ahead and though there was something of a sea running the 'Inazuma', bearings fresh, boilers copper bright, shaft straight, true and freshly oiled, propellers balanced to a penny weight after her refit was 'shipping it green' over her bows and though coal-fired by a watch of sixteen sweating, shirtless stokers was making her full speed of twenty five knots

Colonel Motojiro came on to the bridge with another mug of hot Bovril mixed with sherry and Surogoshi assured him that they would be on schedule even though the weather forecast was not good with a force eight gale predicted off the coast of the Liaotung peninsula. It was not the weather that Surogoshi was concerned about. He confided in Motojiro that they had received intelligence by wireless that there was some Russian patrol boat activity in the vicinity of their rendezvous point. 'It wasn't." Said Surogoshi."A question of not being able to see off the Russian Navy," 'The Inazuma' could out gun and out run all but a Russian capital ship, he boasted confidently it was because he didn't want anything to go wrong with the pick -up.

Sydney and Shung's trip to the cove had been uneventful. They arrived on the cliff-top just after sunset and made their way down the beach, walking their horses by a track that was neither too steep or too narrow. But it was as well that they had been able to negotiate it more less in the light. There were rocks on the beach and they tied up the horses and prepared themselves for a wait of a few hours.

Sydney checked their position as accurately as he could by his Verner prismatic compass and opened the lamp and looked to see that there was adequate oil in it. He had brought meat and bread and a bottle of water which he shared with Shung. He had also a supply of cigarettes and a small bottle of rum. After a noggin of rum and a Russian papyrosa cigarette Sidney took the blanket off his horse and lay it on the sandy ground and said that he would sleep for a little. It was not that the journey had tired him but because, in the lack of anything else to do it passed the time. Shung was quite obviously too agitated to sleep.

Sydney woke to Shung shaking his shoulder. It had started to rain and the wind had got up. 'What is it?' questioned Sydney not quite awake. Shung said."'I think I can hear engines out there." He pointed to his left in the blackness out to sea. Sydney took out,from a little case he retrieved from a pocket, a vesta and struck it against the cross hatched side. It flared only briefly before being extinguished by the wind but the light lasted long enough for Sidney to see by his watch that It was eleven thirty." If it is them." He said." They are early."

On the bridge of the 'Inazuma' Surogoshi had ordered an oil-skinned and souwestered yeoman signaler out on to the searchlight platform to man the Aldis lamp. The signalman stood there hand on the lamp handle waiting for instruction. The rain was torrential but the wind was not yet gale force. Surogoshi said to Motojiro whom he had summoned from below by speaking tube. 'According to my reckoning we are in position."As he said this he looked over to the navigating officer who was leaning over a map table at the other side of the bridge drawing two coordinating pencil lines on a map under the dim light of a bulkhead lamp. The navigation officer gave a look of confirmation and the said,'"Aye Aye Captain 39'48.45 north, 122'12.30 east." Surogoshi then ordered, 'Half ahead both'. That was repeated and the telegraph rang in the engine room and the chief engineer wiped his hands on an oily rag and levered the regulator down. Four of the stokers took a welcome rest and leaned on their shovels mopping their sweating brows their perspiring torsos glistening red in the light of the furnace fires. Up on the bridge Surogoshi unlocked the safe again and lifted out Motojiro's leather satchel. He then took the bung out of the speaking tube and barked orders into it that the long boat should be prepared for lowering overboard and the marines should make themselves ready and that the ship should be darkened.

Sydney took up the blanket and with the help of Shung made a shelter that protected the next match from the wind and Sydney was able to light the lamp. He closed the back and opened the visor and a bright white light shone out and illuminated the wind lashed bushes, and grasses that were growing on the cliff pathway. Sydney closed the visor and pointed the lamp out in the direction the noise of the engines had come from. He opened the visor three times, pausing and giving each beam about three seconds and then a beam of only one second. He repeated this three times.

On the searchlight platform of the 'Inazuma' the yeoman signaler barked out,"Lights on the starboard quarter." Surogoshi ordered,"Acknowledge, Acknowledge.'" The signaler flashed three long flashes and one short and then repeated. Below the bridge on the lower boat deck the ten marines in waterproof capes all equipped with Meiji Type 26.35 calibre side arms in white leather holsters shipped aboard the boat swinging on its davits in the wind. Its ropes were held secure by two ratings. Colonel Motojiro similarly attired climbed over into the boat and sat on the thwart in the stern the satchel handcuffed to his wrist again. It made him think that if they went down he would sink like a stone with the over seven kilogram weight of one thousand gold sovereigns securely attached to him.

Lights again flashed from the coast as Sydney and his companion responded to the Aldis blinking in the pitch blackness. The order came to lower the boat and as it bounced on the waves the marines dipped their oars into the swirling sea and pulled for the shore, a distance of about half a mile.

Sydney took his baggage boxes off the yoke on the pack horse and dragged them down to the shore line and sat on the larger one and began to blow on the whistle. He sat there for some time and then opened the visor of the lamp again. The light immediately caught the long boat coming in on the surf and within minutes the marines were shipping their oars and they were over the side and had the boat's prow ploughing up the sand. Motojiro walked a little unsteadily up the boat and climbed out on to the beach. He recognized Sydney in the light of the electric flash light he was carrying and then Shung came forward.

Motojiro shouted over the gathering wind."Where are the others?" Sydney replied." There are no others, only me and Shung." Sidney gave Motojior the package with the harbor plans in it and he held the lamp while Motojiro checked the contents. It took him some minutes.To say that he was pleased with what he saw was understatement, He saw promotions, decorations, and other rewards coming to himself for this night's work. He didn't unfasten the satchel from his wrist but took out a two stoutly wrapped parcels one much heavier than the other and replaced them with the plans Sydney beckoned Shung to come forward and said to Motojiro."This is the man you should reward." He took the parcels from Motojiro and gave them to Shung.

Shung placed the packages on the sand and opened the end of each one. He saw by the light of Motojiro's flash light, wads of rubles, with their bank wrappers still on in one and brown paper tubes of sovereigns in the other. Sydney said."If you had consented to come with us you could have counted it on the boat. In this weather and at this time of night you are going to have to take our word that it is all there, twelve thousand in rubles and one thousand gold sovereigns." Motojiro stepped forward and incongruously saluted, tried to click his heels, but his boots were inhibited by the sand and he said."You have the word of his Imperial Majesty The Emperor of Japan that what was promised you is all there." Shung said nothing but stuffed the parcel of rubles into one of his bags and the heavy parcel of gold into the other and quickly untied his horse. He was obviously eager to get away.

Sidney did not want to waste any time either and he asked Motojiro to get one or two of the marines to lift his luggage into the boat. He turned to say goodbye to Shung but he was already holding the reins of his horse, leading it by the head and trying to find the path back up to the top. Sidney shouted to him over the wind."Here have my lamp". Turning, he told one of the marines to take it to him. The marine came back and all that could be seen then of Shung was the beam of the lamp picking out the rocks and pebbles of the cliff track and the noise could be heard on them of the hooves of his horse scrabbling to find purchase as it made its way up the cliff.

With four marines up to their white pipe-clayed leg guards in the surf on either side of it the boat was pushed off the sand and floated in the shallows. Sidney went to his horses and checked to see that he had not left anything on them that would identify him. He saw that they were securely tied and thought that they would make a nice present for anyone who might find them. He had paid a big enough advance to cover their value.

Motojiro waited for Sidney to wade knee deep through waves that were now coming in on the changing tide and then to climb into the yawing boat over his luggage which had been stowed amidships. He then got in himself and went to the stern. The marines got in over the side, settled down on the thwarts, took up their oars and together rowed for the darkened 'Inazuma'. With the tide there was quite a sea running but the Marines soon covered the half mile or so to where the 'Inazuma' with steam up was standing off ready to sail. The rendezvous had been completed successfully in only just over an hour.

When they did come alongside it was obvious that there was some urgency to get them shipped on board. Even before the long boat had been hauled up on the davits and swung in board the 'Inazuma' was under way and at full speed. And then just as Sidney was being helped out of the secured long boat by two marines, with a suddenness that made Sydney catch his breath the incandescent beam of a searchlight rushed out of the darkness and seemed to materially smash into the superstructure of the 'Inazuma.' It lit brilliantly all along her decks the ratings who were running to stations, hoisting the flag of the Rising Sun, while machine gunners were taking the covers off their weapons and gun crews were winding up barrel elevations. In the bows two artificers were setting the fuses of two torpedoes. The small propellers on their noses protruding from their launching tubes. The 'Inazuma' had been spotted by a Russian Navy patrol boat. As suddenly as the searchlight had lit the sea and the ship it went out and there was darkness once more.

Sydney went below thinking that all the trouble he had gone to would come to naught if they were taken or even sunk. Motojiro went up on the bridge to see that the documents and plans he had were put away for safe keeping and to wireless Nagazaki that the mission had been a success. It was coded as 'Katagatami'. Surogoshi had just ordered the 'Inazuma's search light on,"To see what we are up against." He said. For only a second a great white beam of light shot from the bow platform of the 'Inazuma' and showed up all white a little model ship some way off in a foam crested sea like the projected image of a magic lantern. It was lit up enough and long enough for Surogoshi to go his file of photographs of Russian Navy ships and shout to his gunnery officer."it's a Sokul class torpedo boat and she has one Quick- Firer forward."

The end of his sentence was punctuated by the bang of an explosion and then the rushing tearing noise of a shell crashing through the air across the bows of the 'Inazuma,'" She's put one across our bows." Shouted a look-out on the deck. Surogoshi blew down the speaking tube to the engine room. The chief engineer heard the whistle and put his ear to his end of the tube and heard the captain say,"Get us out of this chief. Let's show 'em a clean pair of heels". Surogoshi put the plug back into the tube and turned to Motojiro and said." We have orders not to engage unless absolutely forced to defend ourselves." As he said this there was another bang and a shell landed in the sea just astern."They are aiming to hit now." He turned to the speaking tube again and shouted down it."Come on chiefy show us what she can do." He had developed the custom of familiarity with his chief engineer as a result of his Royal Navy associations.

Below in the engine room the chief engineer was looking at the brass ringed main steam gauge indicator needle as it moved into maximum and watching the propeller shaft revolution counter vibrate on the borders of red. The grills and steel plates of the engine room floor were gently shaking under his boots.In the boiler room the boilers were throbbing with super-heated steam and two watches of stokers, their naked torsos glistening with sweat in the red firelight were rhythmically and with perfect expert timing, turn by turn placing each of their shovelfuls of anthracite, accurately right into the fire boxes so that the concave surfaces of the glowing boiler fires were maintained for optimum efficiency.

The 'Inazuma' was moving at 26 knots and the chief knew that there wasn't a ship in the Pacific that could match her speed but he also knew that she could only be relied upon to maintain it for half an hour before she would need another overhaul of her bearings and boiler tubes. Had he been able to see the ship's bow wave he would have been even more proud of his ship than he already was. The graceful lines of the bows of a ship that was rightly called Inazuma', (Lightning) were speedily turning the sea aside like the sharpest plough turns the most friable soil. The Russian ship was fast falling astern in the blackness of the sea with no chance of being in range for a hit on the decks of the 'Inazuma ' or for getting off a torpedo.

When the 'Inazuma came into Nagazaki in the late evening of the next day Motojiro wanted to get off quickly for two reasons, His sea sickness had not been improved by the dash at speed through rough seas to elude the Russian patrol boat. Most importantly the documents on Port Arthur's defences needed to be delivered to Japanese Imperial Navy headquarters as quickly as transport permitted. Sidney followed him down the gangplank close behind not wanting to let Motojiro out of his sight before the substantial reward he expected was paid to him. Surogoshi accompanied them both to the dock gates and with great formality bid them goodbye saluting them with the words," Long Live the Emperor, Long Live King Edward, Long Live The British Navy."

Motojiro did not have to travel far because a special meeting had been convened in his absence in the Nagasaki Navy Dock Offices when his coded wireless message had been received. Sidney went with him in the automobile that was waiting at the dock gates. When they were shown in to the main office there were representatives from the Imperial Admiralty, The Emperor's Diplomatic Service, The Japanese Army and an aide from The Emperor sitting at a long mahogany table on which were two telephones. Their wires snaked across the table to connections in the wall. Behind the group of men, on the same wall was a large picture of the Emperor, its frame decorated with red drapes on each side, the Japanese National Flag and the Admiral of the Fleet's Ensign. No one said a word as Motojiro and Sidney came in and stood before the assemblage.

Motojiro in his uniform held the handle of the sword he wore at his belt and bowed very low. Sidney gave a nod of his head towards a line of men sitting so still and expressionless it could have been a group photograph. It was then indicated by a junior naval officer who came in and stood to attention at the end of the table that they should sit in the two chairs that had been set for them in front of the table. The same officer approached Motojiro and again without a word took the packet of documents from him and laid them before the admiralty representative first. He opened the folder and spread all the papers in it out on the polished surface of the table. In the only action that betrayed any impression of his humanity he reached in to a pocket in his uniform and took out another pair of spectacles and changed them for the ones on his nose. He then looked very closely at the papers and he did this attentively for some minutes.

Having finished he passed them on to the diplomatic representative who was in western dress of black jacket, waistcoat, watch chain, black tie and wing collar. He also wore spectacles. The admiralty representative waited until he had finished looking at the papers. Then he waved his hand to the junior officer and beckoned him to the telephone. He knew just what to do,. He wound the magneto handle vigorously, lifted the handset and spoke Japanese into it and then passed it to the admiralty representative. He then did the same with the other telephone and passed it to the diplomat. The junior naval officer then came to Sidney and whispered in English that he should wait outside. Puzzled, Sidney went to the door, it was opened for him and he sat in a chair by it on the other side.

Sidney sat there and the time passed. Darkness had already fallen and Sidney was desperately trying to keep awake being somewhat tired after a sea voyage that had not been conducive to sleep. He came out of his doze to find the entrance hall that he was in full of light and standing before him the young naval officer and a man he recognized as the diplomatic representative. The diplomat handed him two sealed envelopes both with his name on and he went back into the office. Sidney opened the first to find a cheque written to him, Sidney Reilly drawn on Barings Bank of Hong Kong. It was for a very, very large sum of money in English pounds. Added to the considerable fortune he had made profiteering with Ginsburg and Co. Sidney's stay in Port Arthur had been very profitable indeed. He was now a rich man.

The second envelope was for Sidney something of a mild shock for it carried a message in it from the British Embassy in Kyoto it to say that William Melville had resigned as superintendent of Special Branch and that he had taken up another position. There was an enigmatic post script from 'W.M'. It stated simply,' Contact British Embassy in Paris as early as it is possible to do so'.

Sidney left the Navy Offices with the young naval officer who arranged accommodation for him in the officer's quarters and the next day he set about organizing his trip back to Europe stopping first of course at Hong Kong.

When the Japanese Foreign office in Kyoto got the telephone call from their representative at the Navy Offices meeting in Nagazaki the first thing that was done was to send a wireless message to the Japanese diplomats in Port Arthur ordering them to suspend the negotiations they were involved in with the Russians. The next message that was sent to them contained a series of instructions whereby the Russians were to be offered an ultimatum; either they were to agree to terms or a state of war would exist between the two nations. The information Sidney had delivered had given the Japanese the whip hand.

The other telephone call was to the Head Quarters of Admiral Heihachiro Togo. What he and his staff immediately prepared for was a pre-emptive strike by the Imperial Japanese Navy against The Russian Pacific Fleet in the shelter of Port Arthur. Admiral Togo had a complete picture of the harbour defences but most importantly he had the design of the protecting minefield. The strategy that Togo formulated was to be a surprise attack with six battleships supported by five armoured cruisers, fifteen destroyers and twenty torpedo boats. He was confident that with such a force, manned by well-trained crews in well-armed vessels plus the element of surprise, he would devastate the Russian fleet. This attack would be carried out after the breakdown of diplomatic relations without a declaration of war.

Diplomatic relations were suspended and an ultimatum was delivered to the Russians by the Japanese. But the Russians had hardly time to read it when on the night of the eighth of February 1904 around ten thirty Admiral Togo put his plan into action and ordered his fleet to attack Port Arthur. When the engagement ended by around two in the morning of the ninth of February two prize Russian battleships and an armed cruiser had been torpedoed and Port Arthur had been bombarded. The Russo-Japanese War began in earnest and Port Arthur was besieged.

In that siege some 71.000 Japanese, Russians and Chinese people died, troops and civilians. One of them was little Chun Souk. She waited for Sidney but he didn't come as he had promised and she pined for him. Madame Kay Chui got very angry with her as clients began to complain that she was not giving value for money. She ordered her to work cleaning the bathhouse and the latrines until she came to her senses. So, there she was on the night of the eighth of February scrubbing the wood of the bathtubs and romantically recalling the times when she had bathed and loved with Sidney when a splinter from the explosion of a stray shell fired by a Japanese warship against Port Arthur eviscerated the lovely body that she had worshipped her beloved Sidney with.

As she bled out her life she was quite unaware that her fate had been determined by the man she had so much love for. But then Sidney being Sidney he was just as much unaware. In fact he was on board The Annam a cargo and passenger ship of The East Asiatic Line scheduled to sail out of Nagazaki before the Japanese attack. He was bound for Hong Kong and beyond to The Middle East, Marseilles, Europe and eventually England.

Chapter Thirty One

Sidney stayed a little time in Hong Kong, in order to arrange bank accounts at home and abroad for the cash, cheques, bonds and securities he had accrued in Port Arthur and Japan. His ship then set off for Europe. When the ship had passed through The Suez Canal and docked in Alexandria for a stay of five days he decided to renew his acquaintance with Anahid Moulmanian the Armenian girl he had met there on his last visit three years before. He therefore, without wasting any time got a fiacre and went straight to the Caesereum Hotel on the Maldaan Saad Zaghlu.

Little had changed there except that Anahid no longer lived at her old address but in a villa in the Greek Quarter. It was possible now to call her on the telephone. He asked the barman, the same man who had originally made their introduction to arrange a meeting with her in the hotel that evening. In the meantime he thought to go to the bureau of the British Protectorate in Alexandria to get a wire to the Foreign Office in London to say that he would be in Paris in two or three weeks.'"All being well." The English functionaries at the office betrayed their usual standoffishness but were wary at what Sidney's standing with the FO might be, so arranged the contact with little question.

In besieged Port Arthur Japan's surprise attack put Horace Collins in a different context as an informer for the Russians and he was protected. There was no point in him being denounced by Ginsburg and Co. indeed if they had they would have been compromised as anti-Russian and automatically considered as pro -Japanese.

On learning that Sidney Reilly had fled to Japan Collins put two and two together and surmised that it was Reilly who had leaked information to Ginsburg and Co. He had also learned of the affair between Sidney and his wife. It was only a step from this to put Reilly into the frame as a spy for Japan. This he could not prove but in his bitterness at being cuckolded and exposed he was incensed enough to put an independent plan into operation to try to wreak his revenge on Reilly. His plan was to contact the Annam and arrange for Reilly to be 'dealt' with. To arrange it he would have to leave Port Arthur and somehow get through the siege lines to a wireless station so that he could send a message to the Annam.

With his connections it was not difficult for Collins to get through the Russian lines of the siege and with his comprehensive knowledge of Japanese and with the forged papers he had used in his work before he was able to convince the Japanese soldiery he encountered of his bona fides. He travelled north by rail to Pulantien where he knew there was a wireless station. He was playing a hunch that Reilly would have left on the Annam. Collins knew that it was the last ship of the East-Asiatic line to sail from Nagazaki before the Japanese attack. He also knew its ports of call. The first officer on the Annam was a contact of his and he also worked clandestinely along with Collins for the Russians and Collins intention was to engage him in a scheme whereby Reilly could be 'intercepted 'in Alexandria if Reilly was still on the ship.

Collins sent a personal wireless message for the attention of the first officer of the Annam. The message did get through when the Annam was barely underway and the contact interpreted 'intercepted' as meaning that he should arrange for someone to deal with Reilly. He knew Reilly as an employee of Ginsburg and Co. and as an agent for the East Asiatic Line.

Collins waited around for a day in Pulantien for a reply and confirmation and he got it. As far as Collins saw it, if all things became equal, Reilly would be repaid in spades for his treachery and his dalliance with his wife. It was probably the last condition that motivated Collins the most. Unfortunately he had underestimated his wife for, as the poet says, 'Nowhere lives a woman true, and fair.' Anna was already deceiving Horace with another lover.

The first officer of the Annam a man of Russian extract and colleague of Horace Collins, Leonid Gregorovitch kept Reilly under observation for the whole of the voyage. At Hong Kong he thought he had lost him when he went ashore and it didn't seem he was to return before the Annam sailed again. But Sidney did come back and he stayed on board throughout the trip to Penang, Singapore, Columbo and through the Indian Ocean to Aden and the Red Sea and the Suez Canal to Alexandria.

Sidney enjoyed the voyage as the Annam was fitted out to carry passengers as well as cargo. Sidney had very comfortable quarters and he dined in the passenger dining room or with the ships officers as he chose. It was good to relax on the deck after what had been stressful months of work and when the ship passed up the Red Sea to Aden like its rival company P.and O. the Annam of East Asiatic line could offer starboard side home and shelter from the searing heat of the day.

When the Annam docked in the Eastern Harbour of Alexandria her first officer Leonid Gregorovitch was quick to observe Sidney Reilly's departure down the gangplank. Gregorovitch also noted that Sidney had informed the Purser that if he should be needed or if the ship should leave earlier than scheduled he could be found at the Caesareum Hotel on the Maldaan Saad Zaghlu. Gregorovitch took a few hours leave and went into the old town of Ras el Tin in the Turkish Quarter to look up an old acquaintance that he knew he could rely on to carry out the task that Collins had allotted to him.

As Sidney had done years before, Leonid hailed a fiacre and gave the driver an address in the Turkish Quarter. To get to the Turkish Quarter meant driving along the mole that joined Alexandria with the island of Pharos but the driver would not take him all the way. The district was still notorious as a place of thieves and vagabonds. A number of his fellow drivers had been robbed when taking fares right into the maze of narrow streets and alleys that made up the Turkish Quarter. The driver warned him to be extra careful as he dropped him off short of his destination. Gregorovitch had already taken precautions. He had armed himself with a Webley Mark 1V Boer war model revolver of 4.55 calibre and with an automatic pistol, a Bergman-Bayard 9mm. He had bought both weapons in Tokyo during a stay there on leave. The Bergman had been expensive as it was modern and new. The Webley Mark 1V was a piece of second-hand British Army surplus but in good condition and order as it had been little used in its five years since manufacture. His intention was to present the Bergman-Bayard to Georgio Ekrem his Turkish contact to help him in the process of 'intercepting' Reilly. As well as the boxes of cartridges for the firearms Leonid had a chamois leather bag of twenty gold sovereigns to reward Georgio for his work.

Leonid Gregorovitch walked in the hot sun the few hundred yards there were left to go into the Turkish Quarter with the blue of the Mediterranean on his right and West Harbour on his left. He was not thinking of ancient history as he walked along, his strong whitened leather boots rapping the ancient stones, but about the meeting with Ekrem. He had met him before on visits to Alexandria when the ship he was on docked here but he had not yet been to his address. He didn't like the idea.

He entered the Turkish Quarter by an archway that led into the stalls and shop fronts of a souk and he was immediately beset by traders offering him copperware goods and carpets and silk and handmade leather slippers. His white merchant navy uniform and cap had singled him out straightaway as, if not a tourist, then certainly a non-resident. He showed one of the traders a piece of paper with the address on it of Georgio Ekrem and the trader called his little son from the back of the shop to go with Leonid as a guide.

Within a few minutes the little boy, an urchin of no more than six or seven years old had walked him through alleyways that turned and twisted to the right and the left and brought him to a small green-painted oaken planked door studded with the round heads of great nails set in a whitewashed wall. Above the door was an ornate grill behind which was a rectangular window of dirty and dusty glass. Leonid gave the little boy some coins and he grabbed them, clutched them in his fist and ran back the way they had come. Leonid banged hard three times on the black cast iron knocker that hung hinged in the middle of the door. The knocker was in the heavy molded shape of the hand and ringed fingers of a woman. The sound of the three raps echoed loudly on the walls and stones of the deserted alley. For quite a few seconds nothing happened and then the shadowy face of a bearded man appeared through the grime of the glass on the window.

The door was opened by a girl more than a woman. She had tousled black hair around a face that had once had the edge of beauty before the scourge of small-pox had marked it. Her eyes were dark brown with long lashes and they shone in a smile that through red lips showed gapped white teeth. She had on a blue waistcoat whose looped buttons strained over a full bosom. It was embroidered with designs in obviously Arabic writing and she was wearing voluminous and transparent blue pantaloons that tightened at the ankles below which were red leather slippers. She gave a bow and indicated to Gregorovitch that he should come over the threshold into a small room. It had the smell of burnt cooking oil in it.

There was a wooden ladder in the corner that led to an upper floor down the rungs of it appeared the booted legs, clad in worn brown corduroy trousers of a heavily built man. His trunk and broad shirt covered shoulders followed and he turned as he reached the ground and showed a swarthy face with a large flattish nose, a furrowed brow, expressionless narrow eyes with a faint yellowish tinge and a heavy black beard. He was about six feet tall. He held out his arms and both gnarled hands with fingers like sausages, seemed to give a step back, cocked his head to one side, tucked his chin into his chest and said in heavily accented English.

"Gregorovitch my old friend, what brings you to my humble dwelling, where you have not yet been offered coffee and sweetmeats."

With that he barked out commands in Turkish to the girl and gave her a massive slap on a bottom that round and protuberant as it was seemed too big for the legs that carried it. She gave a squeal and went into a corner where on an octagonal table inlaid with brass there was a large ebony handled long spouted copper coffee pot bubbling over the flickering flame of a spirit stove. In a minute she had poured thick black Turkish coffee into two tiny cups and added sugar. She came forward with the coffee and a saucer on which were dates and white dusted lumps of pink lakum.

Gregorovitch betrayed by his manner, that he was not quite as pleased to be where he was as the welcome of his host suggested. He sipped his coffee and refused the offer of dates and lakum. He said moodily, glancing his eyes to the right and giving a slight jerk to his head in the same direction.

'Get rid of the girl.'

Ekrem tossed his head back and indicated that Gregorovitch should sit on a couch that was against the wall and said,

'Don't worry she can't understand English.'

'Get rid of her anyway.' Said Gregorovitch comparing the grubby state of the couch with his white uniform before he accepted the offer to sit.

Ekrem barked at the girl, again in Turkish and she made a reply in the same language that caused Ekrem to put on an angry face and to raise a fist as if he would strike her down. She scurried out picking up a shawl that she covered her hair with and had opened and was through the door as Ekrem lumbered after her in what seemed genuine fury. He shouted some Turkish curse after her as she ran down the alley and away.

He answered a question that Gregorovitch didn't ask.' You don't know what she said we were going to do when she had gone the bitch. You say you have a job for me, what is it?"

Gregorovitch took out the Bergman-Bayard and put it on the couch next to him. He then held out his left hand and carefully emptied out ten sovereigns into his palm from the chamois leather bag held in his right.

"We want you to get rid of somebody. You will get ten sovereigns now and another ten when you have done it. His name is Sidney Reilly he is an Englishman and he is staying at the Caesrarum Hotel." He handed Ekrem a piece of paper. "This will give you a precise description of him but I would suggest that you get close to him first so as to make no mistake in recognising him. It has to be done in the next five days because we sail then and I don't want him onboard when we cast off, do you understand?"

"Will he be alone? I mean does he have a protector, a bodyguard of some sort?"

" No, no bodyguard but he might be with an Armenian woman of about twenty five or thirty."

Sidney had talked untypically and rather indiscreetly of his first meeting with Anahid over the dinner table in the officers' mess on board the Annam and of his intention of trying to see her again.

Ekrem scowled and said."Do you want the Armenian whore dealing with as well?"

Gregorovitch dismissed his question with an irritated wave of his hand and looked down at the Bergman –Bayard self-loader."You do what you like with her. We are only interested in Reilly. Now this is the pistol that I want you to use. Its new but lethal in its effect. It is of a nine millimeter calibre. It could stop a charging bull and you don't have to get too close. Being the good shot that I know you are you could get him from across the street with this. Press the trigger on this, that's all you have to do. The gun does the rest. You can empty a magazine of six cartridges in a few seconds and he will be gone before he hits the ground then you can safely make your getaway before any bystanders have recovered from the shock. Just make sure you aim for the chest and the head. We don't want the uncertainty of him dying in hospital like the last time. I have brought you some spare cartridges so that you can have some practice and you load it simply like this." Gregorovitch held the pistol in his left hand, pressed the finger and thumb of his right hand on a knurled steel button under the barrel and the magazine slid out. He then thumbed six cartridges into the magazine and slotted it with a click back into the body of the pistol."When you've finished with it." Gregorovitch said." I want it back."

A few months before Ekrem had been given the job of killing the young mistress of a Japanese Diplomat. She had been murdered by Ekrem on instructions from Collins as a warning to the diplomat that he should be more positive in his negotiations with a Russian counterpart. Ekrem had cut her throat but not quite effectively enough, for it took her three days to die in Alexandria' s Hospital for Women and Children.

Gregorovitch had no more to say and he left Ekrem with the pistol, the description of Reilly and with ten sovereigns, saying to Ekrem that he would see him here again at his address in two days time to give him the rest of the gold after he had done the job.

Chapter Thrity Two

In his suite at the Caesereum Sidney dressed in a white evening jacket and black trousers that had been tailored for him in Nagazaki. He had a white starched shirt and collar on with a black tie. The shoes he wore were hand made by a Chinese shoemaker in Port Arthur. They were buttoned on one side and shone shiny black. He looked at himself in the mirror as he splashed cologne on his smooth shaved face and went down to the Caesereum bar on the first night of his stay and to his intense pleasure he saw that Anahid was there talking to her friend Emin the barman. It was he who had passed on the message about Sidney being in the hotel.

She looked as beautiful as when he had last seen her almost three years before. She wore her hair long to her shoulders and as she turned to look at him he saw the red lips of her full mouth, her high cheek bones her untypically blue eyes that he had suggested had come from an English crusader somewhere in her line and the smooth front of her high forehead was accentuated by the luxuriant waves of her hair above it.

She had the same voluptuous figure as when he had last met her and she had for this evening of their meeting clothed it in a cool suit of golden material. The jacket flared slightly at her rounded hips and it was open at the top just enough to see the rise of her breasts. The long skirt that she had on came down to red high button boots from a waist that he knew was not corseted. The arms that she held out to him were clad in black silk elbow length gloves.

'Sidney darling,' she said,' How absolutely wonderful to see you.' He remembered as he heard her voice how the slight accent she carried, for him had an erotic quality. It had taken him a long time to forget it.

Sidney for his part became immediately his typical charming self. It was as if some switch had been turned in him on being in the vicinity of an attractive woman. He strode towards Anahid quickly and took her gloved right hand and gently pressed his lips to the back of it. '

"Anahid my true and my only love, how kind and generous of you to come. I do not deserve such generosity. Although I have been far away from you for such a long time you have never been out of my thoughts and I have been as celibate as a novice priest as I cherished the memory of our brief association. I told you I would come back one day and I have kept my promise and I have brought a present from the exotic east." He presented her with a small parcel.

Anahid giggled like a schoolgirl at this declaration and the sound of her gentle laugh stirred Sidney's loins.

'Yes Sidney, so have I but in my case a novice nun. Come let us sit down and drink together and you can tell me lies about your adventures in China but I do agree you have kept your promise." She took the present and with his left arm in both of hers in a way that Sidney knew was a sign of her sincerely welcoming him and she walked him, her head slightly inclined, almost skipping to a table near to a window that overlooked the harbour and the sea that were now in the twilight of the dark blue evening twinkling from lights on the shore.

Sidney ordered a bottle of champagne and they sat facing each other over the table. Anahid took off her gloves and held Sidney's hand in both of hers and said in a tone of utter sincerity,

"I knew you such a short time but I have missed you. What did you do to me that I could not for some time forget you and I mooned about for weeks like a young girl in love for the very first time? I am not used to being infatuated by my clients. It is not good for me and the way I earn my living."

They decided to have dinner in the hotel and the time passed too quickly for both of them. She unwrapped the present he had brought for her. It was a small sculpture in Jade of a crouching tiger. She thought it beautiful. Sidney said,"Jade is considered by the Chinese to be symbolic of a long and happy life." Anahid took his hand and kissed his fingers as she said," I shall treasure it and always think of you when I see it."

As they were served their digestive of French cognac Anahid said,

"How long is your stay to be this time? I suppose it is to be as fleeting as the last time."

With digestive had come coffee and as Sidney drank his he said to Anahid.

"Like my last invitation to you so long ago, I had thought to ask you to come with me when I go. After Alexandria I am going to Marseilles and then on to Paris. You have never been to Paris. It is a city you will love and a city that will love you. I am not a poor man Anahid. We shall stay at the best hotel in Europe, The Ritz in Paris and I will seek out all the city's spectacular entertainment for you. I will give you a generous allowance so that you will not feel that you are losing anything by leaving with me.'

Anahid took up Sidney's hand and kissed the tops of his fingers. She looked more serious than she had all evening.

'I have to tell you Sidney that I have a patron and 'protector'. He is a minister in the British Protectorate Government. He is English and a very influential man. I live in comparative luxury in a villa in the Greek Quarter thanks to him. He understands that I am not his exclusively and he makes few demands on me but I must say that I owe my style of life to him. Without his 'protection' I would be back to the precarious business of working independently and I can tell you my dear, dear Sidney that things have changed in Egypt and in Alexandria., largely the result of your British 'protection'. Have you not heard of the outrages and disturbances here instigated by the Turks and Muslims? The Turks want Egypt in The Ottoman Empire and The Muslims want Islamic Law to cover the whole of the Arab world. As usual the religious fanatics who believe in a paradise in the afterlife will make a hell on earth for those who don't agree with them down here."

"I would even caution you to be careful during your stay as there have been vicious attacks on foreigners particularly the 'infidel' English. There has even been pressure put on me as an Armenian. I have been threatened with deportation for immorality. You British can be so puritanical. Of course you do not ask how many young girls and women it takes to gentle the frustrations of your Puritanism. So Sidney I am damned three times. The Egyptians hate me because I am a Christian, The Turks because I am an Armenian and the British because I am a whore."

Sidney so much wanted to say that he wasn't British, but Russian. Instead he said."You are not a whore. Don't call yourself that but if you insist I say we are all whores from Prince to pauper. We all have our price you can depend on it. The only difference is that Princes are usually more expensive than paupers."

Anahid went on to say. "I do not have to ask you to think what would happen to me if I was deported to Armenia; a woman alone without a man or a family to look after her. I would be friendless and terribly vulnerable. I would probably finish up in some sordid Turkish brothel, if I were lucky. If unlucky I would probably share the fate of the rest of my family."

Sidney leaned forward across the table and took Anahid's left hand in his right and caressed her silky smooth cheek with the back of his left hand.

"My dear Anahid stay with me tonight and give my suggestion some thought. You could if you wish make it a short holiday and explain this to your friend. That would give me time to persuade you that mine would be a long term commitment but you would be free to go whenever you decided it was in your best interests to do so. Think about it and stay with me while you are doing that. I shall love you so much tonight you will not want me to leave without you."

Sidney and Anahid were so preoccupied with each other they failed to notice a tall heavily built bearded man come into the bar. It was Gergio Ekrem. He was dressed in a crumpled linen suit and he had oiled his somewhat unruly hair, combed his beard put on a new shirt and cleaned his shoes. Had any of the customers he elbowed his way through to get to the bar seen him earlier they would have been aware that he had made an effort to tidy himself up to come out into society.

He ordered an Araq lit a cigarette and as he sipped the Araq he looked in the large mirror over the bar and strove to try to recognize Sidney's face in the reflections as Gregorovitch had described it. His gaze passed over those standing at the bar and further to the few tables he could see in the restaurant. He caught sight of Sidney and Anahid at their table by the window. They were still engrossed in the pleasure of each other's company. He recognized Anahid as an Armenian immediately but he had to have Sidney's identity confirmed. He beckoned the barman over and asked if Mr.Sidney Reilly was in the hotel as he had some business to discuss with him. The barman replied that he was and indicated Sidney and Anahid over by the window. Ekrem's only thought was,"Reilly's a Jew. Unmistakably. Why didn't Gregorovitch tell me.? I would have known him anywhere."

The barman asked Ekrem if he should send one of the boys over to tell Sidney, but Ekrem declined the offer saying, that it wasn't so important that it wouldn't wait until the next day and anyway the gentleman seemed to have something else on his mind at the moment. Ekrem downed his drink, paid and walked out.

The evening passed into dark and Anahid agreed to stay the night with Sidney. As he accompanied her up the stairs to his suite she did say that she had to be back at her own address by eleven as she had a lunch engagement with her 'patron'. Unfortunately she could not postpone it much as she wanted to stay to show Sidney around the town again like the last time they had been together.

When they got to his suite Sidney embraced Anahid and kissed her with all the tenderness he could summon from what he felt was his damaged soul after Anna's rejection of him. He felt as he caressed her form and flanks under her clothes that the desire that he felt for her could be like a baptism that would absolve him from the sins of his past. It was a past that increasingly bothered him as recollections of it passed through his thoughts these days. His rejection by Anna had caused him to reflect on how lonely he felt without the company of women. For Sidney the love of women was approaching the only religious and spiritual experience worth considering and making love he felt, cleansed the very nature of his being.

Anahid responded to his embrace and began to undress him as if preparing him for the cleansing. Sidney did the same for her and when they were naked they bathed together and then folded themselves into the covers of the bed and explored the most intimate recesses of each other as if newly discovered. They then made by turns, gentle and passionate love and at last fell exhausted in each other's arms and slept still connected.

He awoke with a terror he had never had before. He was bathed in perspiration. He had dreamed but had already forgotten the content. The lovely Anahid still lay sweetly sleeping beside him. He got out of bed and looked out of the window at the deserted square in front of the hotel. There were no street lights and it seemed that the only illumination came from the thousands of stars that littered the black velvet cloth of the Mediterranean night. Sidney felt uneasy. The dream had disturbed him but more importantly for him he was confused by the stirrings of a conscience he was not accustomed to feeling.

Sidney awoke again at around eight and shook Anahid by the shoulder to wake her to ask her what she wanted ordering for breakfast from the hotel kitchens. Anahid opened her eyes, stretched and yawned like an awakening cat put her arms round Sidney's middle and then threw the covers off lay on her back exposing all her nakedness to him. Sidney sat up in bed and she put her head in his lap and looked up at him. She said that she was ravenous and would have an Armenian breakfast of scrambled eggs and tomatoes.

"Its name is "dzvadzegh." She said, "And I want to eat it with Armenian lavash bread, and French croissants, butter, confiture, French coffee and fruit. Turkish coffee is not for breakfasts. I also want you to know," she said, her blue eyes shining and her red lips smiling open over her white teeth,"That as well as being hungry I am so happy." Sidney leaned down and gently kissed her."I hope I have had something to do with that.'"He said.

Sidney decided that he would have the same breakfast and she pronounced the words for him so that he could order it."But I am going to have mine with fresh figs for my digestion."He went to the door and called the boy who was standing in the hallway waiting for such orders. He gave him a few piastres and he scampered along the carpeted hall and down the stairs. Sidney then returned to bed and Anahid did what he loved his women for, like others he had known, she took the initiative and she aroused him and began to make love to him sliding him in and out of her and as she did so she said,

" I have been thinking in my sleep and I have decided that I would like to come with you."

She was astride him with the flat of both her hands on his chest; her breasts swinging gently with her movements and her hair down around her face. He made to move and lift her off of him so that he could embrace her in his enthusiasm at her decision,but she held him and moved against him so that he climaxed in an ecstasy that caused his eyes to roll into his head.

The breakfast came and they sat up in bed and ate it off two trays with much passing to each other of croissants, butter and jam and the pouring of fresh French coffee with steaming hot milk. And then they got up bathed and dressed. Anahid was in something of a hurry because of the appointment she had. Sidney insisted that he should take her to the Greek Quarter because not only would it save time it would also give him longer to be with her.

He watched her putting on her clothes, covering her nakedness in movements that were as erotic to him as, when she took her clothes off for him. He did this until, as she was carefully putting on her hat, she chided him to finish dressing as she did not want to be late.

For his part Sidney went to the cupboard in his suite where he kept the one day suit that he had brought from his luggage on board the Annam. He had remembered as well the 'souvenir' Mauser in the shoulder holster he had ordered to be made by the shoemaker in Port Arthur. In the light of Anahid's comments the night before and motivated by his usual caution he slipped the elasticated straps over his shoulders, checked the magazine of the pistol and put it in place in its holster adjusting it so that it did not create too much of a bulge under his suit jacket.

Anahid did not comment at all on the fact that he carried a gun. She had said during their conversation the night before that her protector, whenever he came to see her slept with one under his pillow. As he had slipped on the trousers of his suit he remembered that he had left the Browning stowed in a trunk on board ship.

"Are you ready to leave my love?" she said." We must go or I will be late. Why don't you stay here and I will come later, I promise? You still have to finish dressing." Sidney assured her that he was nearly ready and said."I don't want to let you out of my sight even for a moment. He will wait for you a few minutes this 'protector' of yours surely? I am beginning to become Jealous of him that you don't want to keep him waiting."

"It is not that I don't want to keep him waiting my silly jealous boy," she said." I have to bathe again and I don't want him to arrive when I am in the middle of changing my clothes and I must put different clothes on for lunch. Do hurry please, are you ready now?"

Sidney nodded his assent and as he did so he lit a Russian papyrosa cigarette.

As they walked down the stairs of the hotel and out into the sunshine of the square she said, with good humour.

"I am not in the habit of congratulating the Turks for anything but, their tobacco certainly smells better than that Russian brand you smoke."

Across from the hotel and by the side of the square there was a small pavement café. Sitting at one of the tables under the café's awning was a thick set bearded man smoking a Turkish cigarette with its distinctive oval shape and sipping a small cup of Turkish coffee. It was Georgio Ekrem. He had been there an hour waiting for Sidney to come out down the Hotel steps. He stood up and walked a few paces towards Sidney and Anahid but they did not notice him. When he was some six or seven yards from the couple he pulled the Bergman-Bayard from inside his jacket and shouted in English in a very loud voice,

'Sidney Reilly I have something for you.'

Sidney half turned at the sound of his name and the first thing he saw held in Ekrem's great paw was the leveled pistol. In one movement he thrust Anahid behind him with his left arm and withdrew the Mauser from its holster with his right hand. When he reflected on it later it seemed to him that he had performed the operation in slow motion. Ekrem squeezed the trigger of the Bergman-Bayard self- loader and six shots were fired from it in a rattle of sound in half as many seconds. Luckily for Sidney Ekrem had not taken the advice of Gregorovitch and tried out the reaction of the pistol with some practice shots. Ekrem was over confident. He had done jobs like this before and had always hit his man. He did however seriously under estimate the Bergman-Bayard and its powerful cartridge. With every shot the pistol bucked in his fist with the recoil.

Not one of the bullets hit Sidney. They all went wild ricocheting off cobbles and street furniture. When he saw that he had missed his target, Ekrem turned on his heel to run but Sidney was already down on one knee with the Mauser's under barrel magazine resting on his bent left arm coolly taking careful aim at the bulk of Ekrem's retreating back. Sidney loosed off three shots on automatic. The first missed and grazed the leg of a horse standing in the shafts of a fiacre one hundred yards down the road which reared up and out of control, galloped down the causeway.

The second bullet hit Ekrem on the right shoulder blade, flattened with the impact to a disc almost as big as a half crown and zigzagged through his spinal column and out of his left chest taking with it a portion of lung, rib and flesh as big as a saucer when it exited. The third bullet hit him square on the back of the head. On entry it made a hole only the size of the diameter of a pencil. When it left, after passing through his skull brains and head it took most of his face off splashing the air with dark red blood and grey brain matter. He dropped to the pavement like a felled tree and most of his blood was out of his body in seconds forming a large purple puddle around him. He was dead as he hit the stones.

There was mayhem in the street and two fez capped Egyptian policemen, with carbines raised were already dashing towards Sidney. He dropped the Mauser and went on both knees and held his hands high above his head at the same time he looked around for Anahid He could not see where she was in the confusion of people running hither and thither.

When they had walked across the square from the hotel the street had been deserted now there seemed to be scores of people. Then he saw what looked at first sight like a bundle of clothes that someone had discarded in the gutter. A few feet from the clothes was the hat that Anahid had so carefully placed on her head only minutes before.

In spite of warnings in Arabic from the policemen who were now standing in front and behind him as guards, he got up and staggered apprehensively towards the bundle that he now saw as he stood was the body of Anahid. With one policeman shoving his carbine into his face and the other prodding his back he knelt and cradled Anahid's beautiful head and hair in his arms.

It was too late. As he gently moved her disheveled hair out of her eyes he saw the light of her life in them fading to a glazed, blank. death stare. One of Ekrem's maverick 9mm shots had ricocheted off an iron horse trough and turning in the air like a miniature circular saw it had torn through Anahid's beautiful breasts and sliced her heart in two. As he held her the last gouts of blood from the dreadful wound in her breast soaked his suit, waistcoat and shirt. Sidney looked up at the policeman standing in front of him and with an expression of childlike misery, that he had not worn on his face since a little boy, he said, through tears that he had also not shed since then,

"They have murdered my Diana."

He did not have time to say or do any other thing for with one brutal downward thrust of the butt of his carbine on Sidney's forehead the policeman in front of him clubbed him unconscious.

Chapter Thirty Three

Sidney came round looking at the bright light in the ceiling of what gradually seemed to him to be a hospital ward. He was lying prone under the white sheets of a single iron bed. His head ached and he reached up and found a dressing on his nose. His nose was quite swollen and giving him a lot of pain. He turned and saw that sitting by the side of the bed was a man of about the same age as him dressed in a very smart white linen suit and waistcoat with a red flower in his button hole. The man was fair-skinned with fair hair and even in his semi-conscious state Sidney would have said that he was English.

The man spoke in the modulated tones of an Oxford or Cambridge college. Sidney was right, he was English.

"Ah Mr. Reilly, you have come back to the land of the living. Let me introduce myself. I am Sir Hilary Vernon -Cumming. I am His Britannic Majesty's representative in Alexandria of The Government of The British Protectorate; what a business. The whole affair has been a most unfortunate circumstance. I am afraid the policeman went a little bit too far. He has been disciplined. He said, Good God, that he thought you were an Arab. The man you shot, whose aim was obviously to shoot you, was known to the Egyptian police as a member of the Turkish criminal classes and you have done a job for them that has been needed doing for some time. The policeman who bashed you did not know of course that you were British and in the position that we know you now to be. My office has sorted everything out with the authorities and with the press. Reports of it did not reach even the ears of the most junior magistrate I can assure you. Officially the incident never happened. My people can be relied upon. As far as anyone who matters is concerned the business is closed. You will hear no more of it.

Sidney was now almost completely himself and the memory of what had happened came back to him. He sat up in bed although wincing at the discomfort it caused his head which still had a banging in it like someone striking an anvil with a hammer and he said,

"Anahid, what has happened to Anahid?" Sidney lifted himself as if to get out of bed.

His visitor looked puzzled and said,

"Do be careful Mr. Reilly you have had a very bad blow on the head and according to the doctors here you are suffering from concussion. You really do need to take it easy for a little while. You will be well looked after I can assure you. Who is this person you are referring to? I am afraid I am not aware of any one by the name of er, whom did you say it was?"

"Miss Moulmeinian, Miss Anahid Moulmeinian she was the girl who was shot down. What has happened to her?"

"Ah yes I understand now."Said the visitor."The passerby who was the unfortunate accidental victim of the shooting. She was taken away and no one was able to discover just who she was. She did not seem to have any family but it was then found out that she was Armenian and the Armenian Christian Church took care of the funeral arrangements and she has been buried in an Armenian Church cemetery. A most unfortunate accident and she was quite a young woman I believe".

"She wasn't just a passerby, she was with me and a dear friend of mine. How long ago was that? How long have I been here? How long have I been out?"

Sir Hilary Vernon Cumming paused and reflected." Oh I see we didn't know of the er em lady's association with you. Had we known of course we would have handled the matter of her er em funeral. I hope you don't feel we have to apologise? We did all we could. You have been here for two days. You were certainly out for the count when they took you to the cells. We soon got you out of there of course, awful places, not fit for dogs and then with a sedative and the anesthetic used to set your nose you have been lost to us for that time. But don't worry, the doctors and nurses here will soon have you on your feet."

Sidney threw the sheets off of him and got out of the bed. He was unsteady on his feet and clutched at the iron bed end for support.

Vernon-Cumming said."I don't think you should be getting up old boy. The doctors say you have a concussion and the nose is not quite right yet."

" I have to get up." Said Sidney,"I have a boat to catch."

He certainly had a boat to catch but what he most wanted to do though it could do little good now, was to visit the place where Anahid had been buried.

At that point a nurse came in but in spite of her protests she had, on Sidney's insistence, to find his clothes and she found them and they had been washed and cleaned of Anahid's blood. He was more or less dressed when the doctor came to advise him not to discharge himself. The doctor said that he had suffered a severe blow to the head and with the concussion that ensued he might well get very painful headaches and there was even the possibility of periodic blackouts.

Sidney thanked them for their care but said that he had to get out and he added that he was sure he would recover quickly because he had been looked after so well. He then asked how he should pay for his treatment but Sir Hilary waved his request away and said that the bill would be settled by his office. He was not to worry about that at all. Sir Hilary did go on however to ask him if he would reconsider his decision to leave.

Sidney shook hands with the doctor and with Sir Hilary and he walked out into glaring sunshine that dazzled him with its bright light and hurt his eyes and made his head throb even more than it was doing already. He was also a little puzzled at the looks and stares of people who passed by. There seemed to be something about him that they found curious.

He had left the hospital somewhat impulsively and he was now faced with the problem of finding where Anahid had been taken. Fiacre drivers it was said, knew every place in Alexandria so he hailed one from the pavement. But none stopped so he walked until he found a rank of fiacres waiting for fares. He asked the first one where the nearest Armenian Church was. He was told in halting English that the nearest was The Paul and Peter Apostolic Church. He told the driver to take him there.

When he reached the church it was closed but there was an old man in residence as a guardian. He spoke only Arabic and Armenian so Sidney told his driver to ask him where Anahid might have been taken if he knew. The driver spoke to him for a minute or so and came back saying that,"A woman, not old placed here before today in after morning. Not family, one mourners." Sidney motioned the guardian to take him to the grave.

The burial ground to the church had a wall around it and close against the wall near the entrance was a mound of newly dug sandy Alexandrian earth. This, Sidney felt sure was Anahid's last resting place. Sidney had no religion. He had shrugged off his Jewish heritage years before and replaced it with his own brand of extreme individualism. He could think of nothing to say as he stood there. The guardian for his part crossed himself. Finally Sidney said to the earth, to the wall and to the sky."If there is a place somewhere that something of us goes after we have passed away and it is a good place then something of this girl deserves to be there." He couldn't say any more, he couldn't think any more and he couldn't feel anything much anymore. He had not really recovered from the whole business. The shooting of Ekrem had not moved him at all. It was a job he had to do and he had done it and he had escaped hurt. The beating by the policeman had been incidental. He would have rather it hadn't happened but, but it had.

The death of Anahid was another order of things for Sidney. He felt a rising bitterness. What did anything matter? He dismissed now completely the pangs of conscience that he had reflected upon. There was nothing worth feeling guilty about even though it involved him considering that if Anahid had not been with him she might still be alive. He was a killer. It was dangerous to be associated with him. He should have told her that. But then if Ekrem had used a revolver he would be dead now and not Anahid. What he could not include in his assessment of the circumstance was that if he had allowed her to go back to her villa alone instead of egocentrically insisting on accompanying her then quite decidedly she would still be alive.

Sidney went back to the fiacre musing on just who the one mourner could have been. It was not likely to have been her 'influential' protector. He would have wanted anonymity. But then of course Sidney knew immediately who it was, Emin the Armenian barman. He told the driver to take him to the Caesereum.

There were few people in the Caeserum and Emin wasn't in the bar. He was in the kitchens taking a break and he came up when he heard that Sidney had come back. He welcomed him warmly and commented on Sidney's nose. That is when Sidney looked in the long bar mirror and saw that he had two black eyes and a dressing covered swollen nose.

Emin said," I came out of the hotel when the shooting stopped and I saw the police taking you and the Turk away. I then looked for Anahid and saw a few people round her body. I told the police she was Armenian and they let me get on with getting a priest and moving her. They did not want to be concerned. I went with her and the priest in a fiacre to the Church of Paul and Peter and she lay there until I could arrange for her to be buried. They did that yesterday."

Emin went on,"I told the British Authorities about you being taken away by the police but I didn't know what happened to you after that, the police would not say."

Sidney knew that he owed a lot to Emin but he would not take any money but then he asked Emin if he would arrange a headstone to mark the place where Anahid was. Emin said that he would do that and that he would perform the rituals necessary. He said,"I must visit the grave in a week's time and then again in forty days time and eat ritual cakes and sweetmeats over it. It is our custom and Anahid has no family to do it for her."

Sidney went upstairs to his suite and busied himself packing the few things that he had brought when he came to stay. He had decided to go back to the ship and stay in his quarters until she sailed. He could not bear the idea of sleeping another night in the bed that he and Anahid had shared. He went downstairs afterwards and took five sovereigns to give to Emin for the headstone. He said to Emin that he wanted Anahid's name on it, the day she died and the first verse of 'Dawn'. Emin knew the poem he said but five sovereigns was too much. Sidney would not take any back and he took Emin by the hand and Emin embraced him and they said goodbye. Emin was sincere in wishing Sidney a good journey on but in his heart he wished he had never introduced Anahid to him.

Sidney had his luggage put in a fiacre and he went out to the East Harbour to the ship and went on board. The explanation for his appearance that he gave to the captain and the officers who were on watch was that he had been involved in an accident with a fiacre.

Leonid Gregorovitch had taken leave again and made his way to the Turkish quarter but he couldn't persuade the fiacre driver to go any closer so he got off at the same place as before and again walked the last hundred yards or so. He had to ask again that one of the traders tell him where Ekrem's address was and the same little boy took him for the same few piastres tip.

When he got to Ekrem's nail-studded door there was no need to lift up the iron lady's hand to knock for he saw that it was open. There was the same smell of burnt cooking oil and the same grimy floor but lying on the couch that he had been, in his white uniform, cautious of, was the girl who had been there before. She was dressed in the same grubby waistcoat and the same transparent pantaloons. She did not hear him come in but he could hear the sound of her sobbing as she lay there. He stood by the side of the couch and she saw him and gave a great scream and leapt on him like a wild cat. She folded her legs round him and pulled at his hair so that his cap fell off. She put her ravaged face up to his and he could see from redness of her eyes that she had been weeping a long time. When she tried to get at his eyes with her fingernails he threw her off and she landed on the floor with a thud. 'Where is Ekrem? Leonid said. 'Where is Georgio'?

She curled up into an embryonic ball and wailed with grief. Gregorovitch bent down and took her by the shoulders 'Where is Ekrem?' He shouted although he already knew the answer. She confirmed it by drawing her hand across her throat in the absence of any possibility of replying in English. She then sobbed out what Gregorovitch guessed was the same answer in Turkish. Gregorovitch took two of the ten sovereigns he had brought to settle Ekrem's fee and put them on the floor next her as she continued to be wracked with sobs. Picking up his cap he then turned on his heel and walked out of the door quickly, his urgency encouraged by the realization that if Ekrem was dead then Reilly was still alive.

He had not gone ten yards when Ekrem's girl appeared framed in the door, a living banshee of grief as she screamed what he supposed were the vilest of Turkish curses. He moved even quicker putting on his cap and straightening his uniform that she had twisted in her assault on him. He noticed that one or two neighbours had come to doors and windows. The question might be being asked 'What has this European done to one of our Turkish girls?'

He was soon out of the souk leaving her and disappointed traders behind. But his intention was not to go back to the ship. He was already planning to go adrift. It would cost a month's pay in fines and maybe a year's seniority but in no way could he see himself returning after his leave to the Annam if Reilly was to be sailing on it.

On board the Annam Sidney was giving no thought at all to any of the considerations that preoccupied Gregorovitch. He was, as he settled into his cabin, nursing his broken nose and his black eyes. But the most part of his preoccupation was that he was still much beset by thoughts of Anahid. It was a tragedy and the normal one in this indifferent universe as Sidney saw it, the death of innocence. It was almost the case Sidney thought, that the more 'guilty' one was of the sins of all the world, then the more one was protected from the tragic consequences of having to live in the world. Sin and Guilt armoured the sinful against the world of man, flesh and the Devil. Innocence was left naked 'to suffer the slings and arrows of outrageous fortune.' In his renewed bitterness Sidney vowed in the future to be more than ever sinful and guilt free.

Sidney didn't give any thought to Leonid Gregorovitch until the captain said that they might have to stay in port a day longer because the first officer had gone missing and there was no explanation for his disappearance. The captain could not understand his absence as he was usually so reliable. Regulations said that they couldn't sail without a first officer.

Sidney had seen Grgorovitch at table when he taken his meals in the saloon used by the officers. He had been aware of him more because of his reticence when it came to conversation than anything else and not really given him much thought.Now his being absent without leave began to raise Sidney's suspicions. Once Sidney had collected himself after the trauma of events he had begun to wonder just how Ekrem knew where he was and who he was. Only the office of Danische Compagnie Est-Asiatic knew the ports of call the Annam would make and who of the company's employees was likely to be the person most interested in where Sidney might arrive? Only one man came to mind as far as Sidney was concerned, Horace Collins. Could it be that Collins had arranged with Gregorovitch, obviously a Russian to enlist Ekrem in Sidney's assassination? Things had not gone according to plan and Gregorovitch had scooted. The name of Leonid Gregorovitch went into Sidney's book for future reference.

Chapter Thirty Four

The usual ports of call across the Mediterranean were not made by the Annam. The temporary first officer recruited from the pool in Alexandria was an Egyptian and only spoke Arabic so the Annam went direct to Marseilles and so to find an appropriate replacement. Sidney stayed in his cabin and had his meals served there. He wanted his eyes and nose to at least be on the mend when he set off for his next destination, Paris.

By the time the Annam sailed into the old port of Marseilles around four days later Sidney had more or less recovered. His eyes were back to normal and his nose had ceased to ache and apart from a little bend in it now and that might have been his imagination. He looked at it in the mirror over his cabin wash basin while shaving. His nose was healed.

He said goodbye to the captain and crew and after arranging for the larger part of his luggage to go by freight to Paris and the Ritz. He caught one of Marseilles' new gasoline taxis to the Station and within the hour he had boarded the Marseilles-Paris express. Five and one half hours later he was walking out of Monparnasse in Paris and into a taxi to the Ritz. At the desk where he confirmed his reservation there was a message waiting for him from Melville. He would see him there the next day as he was en route for the South of France on business that Sidney might be able to assist with.

Melville arrived in Paris and Sidney entertained him to lunch in the Ritz restaurant. They had not met for over three years and Melville had some important news to impart.

"Well it is good to meet you again after all this time Sidney, a lot of water etcetera, I heard about the incident in Alex. I'm sorry about the girl but you came out of it OK. We also know about Collins and his wife and a joint operation between us and the Japanese has been mounted to sort him out and to put him out of harm's way. I don't think it includes the wife but I don't think either, we will have any control over what happens if the Japanese Secret service get their hands on them before our boys do; but to other matters. The Japanese were more than pleased with your work in Port Arthur and that's an understatement. They were so satisfied that they have another assignment for you not unconnected but I will come to that.

"Look" said Melville and he leaned forward so that the waiter putting dishes on the table was obstructed. Melville ignored him." I have some business in Provence you might be able to help me with but first I want to tell you about my new situation. I have resigned from the S.B. I resigned in December '03. I think you got the message in Japan. I am now with a completely new but totally secret Government sponsored

Organisation. It is for the moment, until the ministries come to some sort of agreement a loosely combined effort between Military Intelligence and Admiralty Intelligence and associated with other information gathering agencies."

"However I am guaranteed one hundred percent support and once it is formally established I can assure you it will have a quality of significant importance in the service it will perform for the State. We even have the full backing of the Palace. I have been made the head of it but my activities are completely clandestine. I operate for the moment with the identity of an ordinary business man from this commercial address." Melville slipped a simple business card past the silverware and across the white linen table cloth to Sidney with the address Washington Chambers 13 Victoria Street London and the title 'William Morgan Esq., General Agent'.

"I want you to come in with me. You will get a twenty-five percent increase in your retainer. All expenses will be chargeable and there will be new incentives, pension rights, official leaves, health and sickness benefits for you and your dependents and all these benefits transfer in the event of death or accident in the field while on duty. The contract I can offer you will be cast-iron plus total and utter anonymity but once in you are in for life, there will be no contracting yourself out."

"Now that brings me back to the Japanese. They have had intelligence, vague for the moment, that the Russian Baltic Fleet is to be sent to the Far-East. If it gets there all the advantage they gained at Port Arthur will evaporate. They want as full a picture on the situation as you can give them. It means you going back to England for a few months. I shall be back in London in August and I want you to contact me then at the address I have given to you. It will be the Japanese who will pay you, and as you know they are not ungenerous, but I have sanction under the Treaty we have with them to give all the covert support I can. I tell you Sidney this new role gives me carte-blanche to organize and initiate as my judgment takes me. I'll give you time to consider Sidney, but what do you say for now, do you think you will be with me?"

Sidney looked at Melville and the business card and turned it in his fingers for a few seconds and then said." I don't have to consider. Will it really be a big change for me? I will still be working with you and that has not been unsuccessful. Will you see to the formal transfer or will I have to resign from the S.B.? And as for going back to England I planned to anyway. I have a score to settle with the German parties I told you about who tried to plug me when I was in Baku."

"Good, good," Melville said,"I thought I could count on you. Don't worry about the formalities. You were never on the strength of the S.B. as a policeman so the transfer will be seamless. With this new organization you will however have a much more official role. You will be an employee of H.M. Government and you will have to sign a contract and an undertaking not to communicate Official State Secrets."

"There is something I must point out," Here Melville shook his head slowly as he spoke."There will be no thinking about the settling of scores and not at all concerning the Germans. We are working with them and exchanging a range of intelligence material. We know about their station in Hackney and the people running it. The Baku business was a miscalculation but you got out from under. I can tell you now it had nothing to do with the woman there. Forget about it until I tell you otherwise. Now about the business in Provence…."

The bond with the Germans had been successfully cemented when Melville, Reilly's boss worked with Gustav Steinhauer of the German Reich's Secret Intelligence Service to thwart a plot to kill Kaiser Wilhelm the Second when he attended the State funeral of Queen Victoria on January the 22nd 1901. William Melville organized the British agents who had tracked down the émigré German terrorists who had been planning the assassination. He then passed on all the information gained to the Germans, and Melville's success provided the platform for further cooperation. That cooperation began to significantly relate to the activities of the Russians and their Navy.

The new responsibility Melville had was head of the secret Government Department that became later in the century The Secret Intelligence Service or as it was dubbed,MI5 and MI6. Sidney Reilly was one of the first agents to be recruited.

The 'business in Provence' concerned an Australian financier with the name of William Knox D'Arcy, The French branch of the De Rothschild family, The Shah of Persia Muzzafar-al-Din and oil concessions in Persia that the British Admiralty were trying to get their hands on.

Sidney Reilly decided to accompany Melville back to the South of France where in Cannes in a joint effort they persuaded William Knox D'Arcy to sell the concession he had gained, not to the De Rothchilds but to British interests. Knox D'Arcy 's reward was the The Anglo-Persian Oil Company. The Oleum Syndicate That Hozier, Rollit and Wilson had set up got a spectacular return on their investments and The British Admiralty got an assured supply of oil for its new generation of oil-fired warships. The Shah of Persia got the British Order of the Garter. Edward V11 had denied it to the Shah in a fit of pique because Lord Lansdowne the Foreign Secretary had presented it to The Shah without consulting Edward as King. Such honours were the King's prerogative to bestow. Melville was sent as a special envoy to deliver it.The Shah was mollified and Persian oil flowed towards Britain. The de Rothschild's didn't go short. The family exploited oil in Baku and then founded Royal Dutch Shell a joint Dutch and British venture to capitalizes on oil reserves in the Dutch East Indies and in a variety of drilling and exploitation expeditions round the world. Saltend near Hull became the site one of the biggest refineries of Royal Dutch Shell.

When 'the business was finished' Melville and Reilly spent the rest of the summer until the beginning of September on the Cote D'Azure. Then Melville went back to London and Sidney Reilly had a brief sojourn in Brussels before he returned to England by the Zeebruges to Hull Ferry. Brussels in 1904 was the centre of international espionage. Sidney has been instructed to make contact there with an old associate who had returned to Europe to take up his position again as the Japanese Secret Agent in France and Belgium, Col.Akashi Motojiro.They went into immediate conference together.

Sidney's and Col Akashi's discussions centered around the new rapprochement between Britain and France. 'The Entente Cordiale' as the accord was described, had been signed only a short time before in April. It had implications for the Treaty that had been arrived at between Britain and Japan. That treaty had already been working successfully for two years, particularly The Anglo- Japanese Naval Treaty. The new question that Melville had raised in Paris of The Baltic Fleet's possible departure for The Far East, was not left off the Agenda.

As Sidney's Ferry came into Hull Sidney reflected on the stories he had heard of immigrants from the Baltic arriving in Hull and Grimsby. They wouldn't get in as easily these days. To get into Britain now you needed a pass-port. Gone were the days of open borders. They had disappeared with The Aliens Act. Sidney caught the train taking passengers west and got off in Hull Paragon.

Sidney did not intend staying in Hull for very long and as he arrived in Hull's grand refurbished Victorian Station The Paragon after showing his papers he was glad that he had only the shortest of walks to the Royal Station Hotel. Although he hadn't been able to reserve a place he found a room and looked out of the window onto what looked like one big building site. So much building was going on in Hull the air was full of stone dust and sand. He would stay one night and then catch a train to London, get his brief and then on perhaps back to Russia and St. Petersburg.

During the time that Reilly and Melville were in The South of France there had been a very significant deterioration in relations between Imperial Britain and the Tsarist Empire of Russia. It had begun with Russia exercising International Laws of the sea in wartime in connection with neutral ships carrying war contraband. Russia believed she had"Belligerent Rights". Initially warships of a Russian fleet coming out of the Black Sea had seized a British P & O Steamer 'The Malacca'. She was suspected of having a cargo of war material destined for a Japanese port. The Russians boardered her and then impounded her, sailing her away with a prize crew. Although there were protests in Parliament and the British Press stirred up public opinion the matter was in the process, although with difficulties, of being resolved. The ship had been returned but its cargo was confiscated.

As the scandal of that subsided, on the 24th of July 1904 detachments of the Russian Vladivostok fleet challenged another British ship. 'The Knight Commander'. Again she was suspected of carrying a cargo for the Japanese and the Russians wanted to stop and search her. They fired a blank shell to get her to heave to but she refused and her captain sailed her on. The Russians opened fire with live rounds and disabled her.

There was barely enough time for the passengers and crew to get into lifeboats before she sank. Luckily there were no lives lost. They were taken on board the Russian ships. The Russian Bear was certainly twisting the tail of the British Lion

The furor that caused reached such a pitch that there were calls for an ultimatum to be presented to the Russians. Parliament was in an uproar and the hysteria whipped up by the press had not died down even by early September and The Royal Navy were being called upon to take on The Tsar's Navy and to protect British Shipping. There were strong elements in the Royal Navy who wanted to do just that.

Sidney was reading press reports on the incidents as he went downstairs the next morning after a fairly pleasant night's sleep but he did not have time to think about breakfast before the desk clerk said that there was a message for him. It was from a Mr. 'M' and Mr. Reilly was to ring him at a London number as a matter of urgency. Sidney decided that it wasn't urgent enough for him to miss his favourite hotel meal, The English Breakfast. He wasn't disappointed and he was still savoring it when he went to the hotel telephone and asked them to get the telephone number that 'M' had left.

It was as he thought, Melville and it was the first time that Sidney had 'phoned Melville in his new identity, so he thought he had the wrong number when a girl's voice said,"Good Morning Morgan and company who is calling please?" Sidney checked himself and said,"May I speak to Mr. Morgan please. My name is Sidney Reilly"

William Morgan aka William Melville came on the line."Is that you Reilly? Answer me a question, When did we last meet and who was involved?"Sidney realized that Melville was checking his identity."I last saw you in Cannes and we were concerned with the affairs of William Knox D'Arcy."

Melville said."That will do I thought it was you anyway Sidney, can you talk?

Sidney said," I Suppose this line is as secure as any, it depends on what you have to say. Is it about 'The Malacca' and 'The Knight Commander"?

Sidney heard 'M' say," No, we can discuss the implications of that later. I want you to go to Newcastle."

"But I thought you wanted me in London to be briefed."

'M''s reply was,"I think the job has been done for you. Our people have detained a Russian at the port in Newcastle. They think he is deserter from the Russian Navy. You are the one who can question him. If he is a Russian Naval seaman then he is just the type we want to talk to, if you get my meaning. He is being detained in the Customs House. He came over from Christiansand in Norway. The only thing they can get out of him that they can understand is"Sailor on Aurora." We know that the" Aurora" is an armoured Cruiser in the Baltic fleet so we are putting two and two together. I want you to get up there and confirm that it comes to four."

Sidney got the train from Hull to York and then to Newcastle. There he questioned the"illegal immigrant" When he returned to Hull the next day he prepared his report and set it down on paper.

The sailor was a deserter from The Baltic Fleet, a rating on board the Aurora. He was a boy of eighteen conscripted and previously a factory worker. From Kronstadt, where the fleet was based, he jumped ship and he travelled Finland and across to Sweden by sea and then over Sweden and Norway by train. When his money ran out he had stowed away on the Christiansand to Newcastle Ferry.

He gave himself up at Newcastle having hidden himself in a lifeboat. He had expected to enter England without any problems but he had been unaware of the new regulations in force at the border and so had been detained.

According to him The Baltic Fleet was in a chaos of disorganization. The majority of the officers were incompetent and inexperienced. They had no control over their men and there were major problems of drink and drugs within the crews of many of the Fleet's ships. When news of the Japanese successes at Port Arthur had been received a great wave of demoralization swept through the fleet and now the Japanese were seen as supermen who were invincible. Information or rather rumour regarding the presence of Japanese Torpedo boats and mines in the north sea on the course that the fleet intended to follow when it sailed had caused near panic that had bordered on mutiny in some ships. This near hysteria had been compounded when it was realized just how far the fleet would have to sail to successfully join with the Pacific Fleet.

Following on from that the problems that came with storing the extra quantities of food and fuel and ammunition needed for such a voyage had further strained relationships between the lower decks and the ward room because crews quarters were annexed for storage room.

Generally the fleet is ill-equipped for what is thought to be an impossibly long voyage of near 18.000 miles and many of the ships are not considered seaworthy. Our man had deserted when Z.P. Rozhdestvensky The Admiral of The Fleet had flown into one of his regular uncontrolled rages and threatened every tenth man to a flogging with the knout.

Sidney added his comments, It was difficult to estimate when the Fleet would sail because the deserter was of such low level he was not privy to such important information. But, time being of the essence, to be effective in supporting The Pacific Fleet, against the Japanese Navy, The Baltic Fleet, comprising according to his uninformed estimation between twenty and thirty ships, would have to set sail somewhere in the early weeks of October.

The course they are going to take has already been communicated to all the countries the fleet will pass on its voyage to the east. It has been set away from established sea-lanes and out of sea areas where there might be fishing fleets to avoid other vessels. It's a Fleet on war alert so Rozhdestvensky has ordered an exclusion zone of some five miles depending on the channel. It is thought, but unconfirmed, that he has also ordered that any ships entering this exclusion zone and not being properly identified might be fired upon.

To send his report to 'M' Sidney had been instructed to contact a Mr. Oswald Sanderson at the Hull Offices of the Wilson Shipping Line where Lloyd's Intelligence Division had a wireless transmitting station. However when he began to transmit he got an immediate cancellation of his outgoing message and an incoming telling him to bring the report in person to London as soon as possible. Reilly booked out of the Royal Station Hotel and caught the 12.30 direct train from Hull to London Kings Cross.

When Reilly arrived at Kings Cross station, it was late evening. He decided against going into central London so he walked through the crowded concourse and out to take the short walk to the Midland Grand Hotel at St. Pancras and booked in for the night. He ignored the barefoot ragamuffins pestering to carry his bags and instead enlisted the help of a porter to wheel his luggage up the wide cobbled drive to the hotel and gave him a silver three penny piece for his trouble.

As soon as he was shown his suite he regretted his decision ;there was no bathroom in it. He took some time arranging a change to a recently updated suite and then from the hotel he telephoned"M" and was told that there was to be a conference the next day at"M's" office in Victoria Street. The conference was to start at ten and then he could deliver his report.

While on the 'phone Reilly asked if any news had been received regarding Margaret's whereabouts."M" gave him the last address he had for her in Kensington.

After dinner that night Reilly caught a cab to Kensington and went to the apartment house he had the address of. Margaret was not there. She and her companion seemed to have gone underground. She was still around somewhere for when he visited his bank on his way to Victoria Street the next day, he saw that a number of withdrawals had been made from the account he had opened for her. However the bank would not give any details of her postal address.

The next morning after his breakfast he caught a cab. The streets of London he passed through to"M"'s Victoria Street offices had much changed in the almost five years since his last stay. There was a lot of new building going on and as with Hull stone dust filling the air in places and there was more traffic and some of it petrol driven; buses, taxis and private vehicles like motor cars and motor bicycles puffed out blue sweet smelling smoke that reminded him of the atmosphere in Baku. There was still however plenty of horse dung littering the highways giving out London's typical dirty stable smell. There were more people on the streets too, men and women and they had a prosperous air about them. His cab trotted past shops and shop windows that were full of all sorts of goods and all sorts of customers.

Chapter Thirty Five

13 Washington Chambers Victoria street was not a particularly imposing address. Melville's new offices were on the second floor of a plain building whose only decoration seemed to be the highly polished brass plate screwed to the stone of the entrance porch.

Sidney got down from his cab, paid the cabbie and walked off the crowded afternoon pavement and climbed the stairs to the second floor and knocked on the half glass of a door painted in curling black letters with the sign;

"William Morgan and Company, General Agent. Please knock and wait."

Miss Lukerstone came to the door. She recognised Sidney immediately.

"Mr. Reilly, after all this time, how are you ?"

Reilly switched on a charm that he had not engaged for some time and replied."Miss Lukerstone, if only I had known you would be here…"

With a good humoured giggle, Miss Lukerstone cut him short and said."Yes Mr. Reilly, of course Mr. Reilly you haven't changed. You are not late but the conference has convened. Let me take your coat and hat. Everyone is in there."

She indicated a grand polished wood door with a sign in gold letters above it that proclaimed 'Board room.'

With a smile Sidney gave his hat and coat to her, adjusted his tie, straightened his jacket, passed his left hand over his hair and opened the door, went through it and closed it behind him.

The 'Board room' was oak-paneled on each wall to an ornate ceiling of plaster moldings and hanging from a ceiling rose was a chandelier recently converted from gas to electricity. Although there was bright sunlight coming from Victoria Street, the lamps were on. In mid-air there was a cloudy layer of grey, blue smoke from the pipes cigars and cigarettes being smoked by the occupants of the room

In the room, taking up most part of the space was a large oval table of the same wood as the panels. Around it sat five men. One of them was William Melville, now known as William Morgan. He hadn't changed much since their last meeting in France. Behind Morgan AKA Melville was a school blackboard with a white chalk drawing of

The British Isles the North Sea with The Dogger Bank and the coast-line of Norway, Sweden and Denmark out -lined in different coloured chalks. A red chalk, dotted line ran out of the Baltic through the Skagerack, off the south western coast of Sweden down past the western coast of Denmark and east of the Dogger Bank. The red chalk dotted line ended with an arrow head on bearing 55* 18* North -5* East. It indicated the course that Russian sources had made available to all countries,as Melville was to say later that Admiral Rozhdestvensky intended his fleet to steer on. It very much described a middle way between the waters of Denmark, Germany and Holland in the east and the sacred waters of the British Navy in the west, at least until they narrowed for the English Channel.

The men in the room were all in street clothes that in an age of rapidly changed fashion were just slightly behind the times. There was a predominance of waistcoats stretched over well -fed stomachs with expensive gold watch chains looped from button to pocket. There was one monocle and three sets of spectacles. Their four owners looked through them and eyed Reilly as he came in giving him the look only Englishmen of a certain class have perfected for individuals they regard as foreign. Reilly recognized only William Melville.

Melville began to speak as soon as Sidney entered the room.

"Ah there you, sit here." He indicated a chair next to him."I will make the points I have already covered for the sake of new arrivals. This is a meeting where it will not be necessary to identify those present. There will be no notes taken and it will not be minuted. Without putting too fine a point on it, I repeat, to all intents and purposes, as it is necessary to preserve complete confidentiality, and without wishing to sound absurd, this meeting is not taking place. I think everyone here understands that, agreed?" Melville pointedly looked at each face for a brief second in turn.

Monocle spoke up,"What about the woman in the office. She saw us all arrive. Can she be relied on?"

Melville did not try to hide his irritation."The woman in the office, as you describe her, only knows the identity of two people in this room. She is completely unaware of yours or the purposes of this meeting. She will see you again shortly because she will be serving you tea. She can be relied on absolutely. Now let's get on I would like you to listen to this report, But before I ask the gentleman who has just arrived to read it I want to make some reference to the recent developments regarding"The Malacca" and particularly"The Knight Commander". You will all be aware of the gravity of the international situation that these two incidents have created but it makes it all the more imperative that our plans come to fruition totally in the best interests of The British Empire and her allies." It was quite obvious who had the authority in the meeting. He nodded in Sidney's direction. Sidney read his report. Its substance was his meeting with, and observations on the Russian Naval deserter.

After he had read it Melville took the notes from him, folded them and put them in his pocket and said,"I shall destroy these notes later." He went on. We can add a few points to the report just read out to you. We now know the fleet numbers some fifty ships but only four of the modern Borodino Class. These are, As far as we can ascertain. The Borodino, The Alexandre III, The Orel and The Kniaz. The rest of this fleet is made up of, in the main obsolete and even unseaworthy vessels. When it sails into the North Sea we have learned from our intelligence gatherers that it will be, as ordered by Admiral Z.P. Rozhdestvensky who is in overall command, organized in two squadrons, one following slightly behind the other. He no doubt expects some sort of interference with the passage of his ships.

The Russians have changed the name from the Baltic Fleet to The Second Pacific Fleet. If it gets to Japanese waters, the main body of the fleet will be used to draw fire away from the modern capital ships and to provide cover for the same. However in spite of all that has been said, it is believed, by the Japanese that if these ships arrive in the East they could tip the balance in favour of the Russians We also have information from our Swedish connections that the fleet intends to sail one day earlier than originally planned. It will sail on the sixteenth of October instead of the seventeenth. Today is the first of October so we only have just over two weeks to carry out the request of our Japanese Allies, that we should use any means available short of outright naval engagement to delay the passage of the Russian Second Pacific Fleet during the time that it is in proximity to British waters."

" I expect this meeting to deliver information that will help in forming tactics and strategies to fulfill the request of our ally. I can inform you that H, M.G has given us tacit authority to proceed.The F.O. has also pointed out the sensitivity of this matter as far as The Palace is concerned. I suppose what is meant by that refers to the family relationship there is between Czar Nicholas and H.M. However I can confidentially report without fear of contradiction that H.M. is totally committed, one, to the alliance and two, to The Royal Navy." Here he paused for emphasis and said," We have carte blanche to proceed, as long as none of our actions could be interpreted as 'Acts of War.' So now let's get down to our business."

The four men seated at the table looked at each other through the smoke of their cigarettes, pipes and cheroots and as if by common consent one of them raised his eyebrows, briefly indicated himself and left his chair to stand in front of the blackboard picking up a thin baton from the table as he did so.

He was a man of average height, his fair hair slightly receding. He was the one with the monocle. He stood to one side of the board so that the assemblage could see what he was doing. Then he looked carefully at the board and marked a cross in white chalk well to the east of the Firth of Forth towards the coast of Norway but slightly to the west of the red chalk dotted line already drawn on the board. He spoke in the English accent, Sidney would like to have acquired.

"This is the approximate position of 'The Zero'. She is a cargo vessel owned by The Wilson Shipping line of Hull and is more or less on permanent station in these northern waters monitoring the passage of shipping around the Scottish coast and vessels passing to and fro in Norwegian and Scandinavian waters and through these sea lanes,into and out of the Baltic She is in Wireless Telegraph contact with the Lloyd's Intelligence Listening Station at Wilson's Offices in the port of Hull and she will count out the number of ships in the Russian Fleet as they pass.

She should be able to chart any change in course the fleet might make and give a more or less accurate estimate of its speed. She will also be able to tell us what weather to expect and give an estimate of visibility. Signals communicated from the ship will within a margin of only a few hours give intelligence on when the fleet will arrive at the position indicated."

He replaced the chalk and the baton on the ledge beneath the board, blew the chalk dust off his fingers, rubbed his hands together and returned to his seat, picking up as he did so the cigarette he had left burning in the ashtray on the table. As he sat down he put the cigarette to his lips, inhaled and blew a plume of smoke into the air and leaned back in his chair.

The next person to rise and leave the table to place himself next to the blackboard was a large man with a well fed stomach that his waistcoat buttons strained over. He was balding but had a thick greying moustache that was not particularly well-trimmed. He was smoking a pipe whose stem curved down to a large bowl. He kept it in his mouth under those whiskers whose ends had a yellowish tinge from the tobacco he smoked. He hooked the fingers of his left hand into the lapel of the brown tweed jacket of the suit he was wearing and taking the pipe from his mouth with his right hand he used its stem to punctuate the points he made as he looked at the map's outline.

"This is Hull on the Humber Estuary (Hull he marked with a small white chalk circle)and here is Grimsby." He jabbed his pipe at a vague position on the south- eastern coast-line of The Humber estuary."It is from these two British ports that the largest fishing fleets in the world set sail into the North Sea fishing grounds to catch the fish that feeds the nation." Sidney could see that"M" was already getting a little impatient at the"commercial geography" lesson the man seemed to be about to deliver. Luckily the man noticed it too and he moved quickly on.

"The now steam driven fishing boats from the two ports fish off The Dogger Bank in fleets called 'Boxers'. There is always one fleet at sea fishing at any one time. There can be anything from eighty to one hundred boats engaged catching fish under the instruction of a man who is called 'The Admiral'. The smaller vessels usually about 100 feet in length, catch the fish in trawls and then it is transferred by hand from rowing boats to larger fast steam-powered cutters who take it back to the Humber and to markets all along the east coast down even as far as Billingsgate on the Thames. When it is unloaded onshore, the fresh fish is transported inland by rail.

The area of The Bank that is fished is usually about one hundred and fifty miles or so East by North of Spurn Point which is here." He stabbed the end of his pipe on a spit of land that stuck out almost like a lid that might close over the Humber estuary."That does depend on where the shoals of fish are migrating to but for the last few years this is where they have been most found". Once again he tapped his pipe on the board, this time on the chalk line that was the western border of the area marked as The Dogger Bank."There is a fleet being prepared in the Humber as I stand here. By the time it is gathered together and ready to set sail it will be around the 19th of October. The fleets sail under different flags. This one will be known as 'The Gamecock' Fleet.

I should add that the sea area marked as that through which the Fleet of Russian War ships will pass is well to the east of where The Gamecock Fleet will do its fishing. That fleet will drop its trawl nets more than twenty miles west of the course drawn here. The course that the Imperial Russian Fleet will take is off the eastern edge of The Dogger Bank. That is a ground that is fished (and it must be said has been over fished) by European and Scandinavian fishing boats as it is in their waters, though there is no official demarcation and the sea-bed is between five and ten fathoms deeper than the trawl depths of where the Hull and Grimsby fishing vessels will be."

He half turned to go back to his seat and then as an afterthought he added." It might be of interest to this gathering, in the light of circumstances, for me to say that a number of fishing boats with Japanese names like 'The Mikado' and 'Geisha' have been launched in the last couple of years from ship builders on the River Hull down from the minster town of Beverley. That town is about eight or nine miles from Hull."

By the time he had finished his discourse, his pipe had gone out and he lit it using a tobacco-pipe lighter puffing out clouds of blue smoke in his wake while on his way back to his seat.

The next man to stand hardly waited for the previous contributor to settle before he was up and striding to the front of the 'class'. He was relatively tall and slim with thick gingerish hair and what is called in 'The Senior Service' as a 'full-set' on his suntanned face and chin. His carefully 'coiffeured beard and curly moustache were the same colour as the hair on his head. He was wearing a blue serge suit which he buttoned as double-breasted as he stood. He removed his glasses and began to speak.

"What has just been described will not be the only activity in this part of the North Sea in the time leading up to the passage of the two squadrons of Russian Warships The Home Fleet of The Royal Navy will also be present in these waters. The Home Fleet sails at one time or another all the sea areas around The British Isles, three times a year. It is either involved in exercises or courtesy visits or both. This last month The fleet has. I believe, been visiting The River Tyne. The ships of The Fleet will be returning to their Home Port around the 19th. 20th. Or 21st. of October. I can be no more accurate than that.

Such precise information is classified by The Royal Naval Intelligence Division.

It should be noted that the Fleet's Commander chooses to order that the captains on board his ships organize 'War Footing' conditions when involved in exercises and at night the order is 'Darken Ship'. Because of these circumstances the normal formalities of signal identification are suspended at the discretion of individual masters or generally ordered by the Fleet Commander. There should be no confusion as far as fishing boats are concerned as information on the approximate position of the fleet's activities has over the last two years or so been communicated by Wireless Telegraphy to 'The Admirals' of fishing fleets putting to sea in the vicinity of 'The Home Fleet's' manoeuvres. I am sure that the previous speaker can confirm that." He cast a glance in direction of the previous speaker who frowned, pursing his lips and nodded in assent while giving vigorous puffs on his pipe that made as he did so, distinct popping sounds.

"The other important reference to naval activity in these waters concerns HMS Devonshire. She is a four funneled approximately 11.000 ton County Class Armoured Cruiser. She was launched in April of this year and is at present, although the details of her exact whereabouts are not of course in the public domain, undergoing fitting out and sea trials in The North Sea. Her Commander has been made aware of the movement into our waters of The Second Pacific Fleet of the Imperial Russian Navy and the possible proximity of The Home Fleet. That will include information as to the position of the Hull and Grimsby Gamecock Fishing Fleet" He returned to his seat, and relit the cheroot that he had left smoldering in an ashtray.

The last person to speak did not approach the black-board but said what he had to say still sitting at the table. He did lean forward however and gesture in the direction of the map drawn on it.

"Since the 1890's and especially since the Anglo-Japanese Naval Treaty of 1902 a goodly number of vessels destined for The Japanese Imperial Navy have been constructed in British Yards, notably on The Clyde, at Blackwell and Poplar on the Thames and significantly in the context of The North Sea, shipyards up and down the River Tyne Here is a brief general list." He took up the piece of note paper he had been writing on. As he did so he returned to a pocket in his waistcoat the silver propelling pencil he had been using. He read from the pencil written list he had prepared.

"6 battleships, 4 armoured cruisers, 2 cruisers, 16 destroyers and 10 torpedo boats plus auxiliary and service craft." Having read the list he went on to say,"The contracts signed for the building of these war ships of course included clauses, post-launching,relating to repair, maintenance, servicing and re-fitting. As we speak there are Japanese Navy destroyers and Japanese Navy torpedo boats undergoing this type of work in the same yards that constructed them. Without putting too fine a point on it a deal of this work is being carried on now at shipyards on the River Tyne with its obvious outlet to the North Sea for fitting out and sea trials."

At this point, Melville looked around the room and his look gave the chance for other contributions but as none were forthcoming he got up from his chair at the front and covered the blackboard with a sheet that had, during the proceeding hung over the back of it. He then pressed a bell under the edge of his desk and said."If there is no more to report I shall bring our meeting to a close. I would like to thank everyone involved for their work and for the information that has been passed on. I can assure you all that it will be put to good use. I have just ordered tea and light refreshments to be brought in."

Almost exactly as he finished, there was a knock at the door. Melville called out,"Come" and Miss Lukserstone entered with a tray of tea-cups, sugar bowl, milk jug and a large plate of cake, bread and butter and biscuits. She set it down on the table, went out of the room and came in again almost immediately with a catering size tea-pot. She asked Mr. Melville if she should pour but he thanked her and told her that it would not be necessary. She left and the bearded ginger-haired man got out of his seat and said,"Shall I be Mother?"

The gentlemen at the table got to their tea and during the hubbub of conversation they set up, Melville told Sidney that he wanted him to stay behind after the others had left. As for Sidney, a plan of action was already forming in his mind and he began to suggest it to Melville but he motioned him to be quiet and said, sotto voce"We'll talk about it when they have gone. For the moment I want to tell you that there will be a message waiting for you at your hotel." Sidney did not question how Melville knew where he was staying. It had been obvious to Sidney for some time now that Melville had eyes and ears everywhere. Melville went on,"The message is an invitation to dinner tonight. I want you to accept it before you go back up north. The invitation is for you to have dinner at the house of the commercial attaché at the German Embassy. There will also be an old friend of yours there and I want you to remember what I told you in Paris, there will be no settling of old scores and take my assurance that this 'old friend' had nothing to do with the incident in Baku. In fact she is also working for us. She will, if all has gone well, have important information for you that is related to the business we have been working on here today. The details of where you are to go are in the note."

Some fifteen minutes later Melville noticed that the others, having had their tea were making preparations to go. They were shaking hands and putting on coats.

Melville got up and said his goodbyes, shaking hands with each in turn and thanking them again. In a short time, they had gone and all that remained were the crumbs of their tea and empty tea-cups on the tray and Melville was left in the smoky room alone with Sidney. Melville poured out two cups of tea and said,"I think it's still hot enough. You don't take sugar do you?" Sidney shook his head."I thought not," said Melville."Here have some cake." Sidney took the tea, refused the cake and instead began to speak.

"Well according to all that, there are certainly the ingredients for increasing the confusion already present in the Russian Fleet if the constituent parts can be organized and timed properly. If that comes about ships might be dispersed away from their fleet so increasing the possibility of delay. If things were done properly it could be weeks before the fleet is reassembled and add to that resulting breakdowns and we will have done a good job and one that might well satisfy our ally."

Melville nodded in agreement and then said, over the edge of his cup which he had raised to his lips,"I should remind you about something I mentioned in Paris when we last met, you will be contracted to the Japanese. I have taken the liberty of seconding you to them. They will pay you and they will pay you well, don't worry about that. You working for the Japanese will speed the plough." As Melville expected, Sidney didn't raise any objections. Melville knew Sidney of old. He didn't care who he worked for as long as the pay was good. Melville went on," Have you got some ideas already? I shall have to say that I will be disappointed if you haven't." He said this, put his empty teacup down and leaned back in his chair and looked expectantly at Sidney.

Sidney went up to the blackboard and lifted the sheet and folded it over the back."The first thing that I would want to do is see if we can get any of the Japanese ships laid up in yards on the Tyne out into the north sea and when it is appropriate sail them within binocular range of the Russian ships. Any class will do but ideally if they were torpedo boats or torpedo boat destroyers that would, as you English say 'put the wind up' the Russian Admiral and his commanders. They wouldn't need at all to get closer than say between three and five thousand yards to have an effect. Any closer and its almost certain they would be fired on. Two thousand yards is considered by the experts to be effective torpedo range. I have done my homework on that one. Melville interrupted him here and said,"That could well be arranged. An old friend of yours is in Brussels Colonel Motojiro and I can put you in cable contact with him. He should be able to set in motion what you suggest. That is as far as the Japanese will go. They have not sent anyone to Britain to work on this project.There are skeleton crews for the vessels you refer to but that would be the extent of their contribution"

Sidney went on," Yes I know. I met with Col Akashi recently. I will contact him and I am sure he will do all in his power to cooperate. The other set of events I would like to engineer concerns the trawlers. They would make a perfect obstruction. Imagine it, mixing a hundred fishing boats up with warships on war alert steaming on a collision course? Such a circumstance would completely disrupt the passage of any fleet never mind one whose commanders are as"jumpy" as Rozdevensky or as"trigger happy" as his crews are reported to be. The problem, and it should not be underestimated, is how to persuade the Admiral of the Gamecock fleet, that's what he called him wasn't it? He has obviously overall responsibility. How to persuade him to change the course and position of his fleet. I have an idea but it would require such a degree of cooperation from the Admiralty and The Royal Navy that I am not sure that it would be forthcoming." Melville was eager and he didn't hide his eagerness.

"Well what is it? Come on out with it, what do you propose?" Melville insisted, Sidney had concentrated on what had been delivered in the meeting and even as the members of the meeting had been talking a plan had been forming in Sidney's mind.

Sidney turned again to the blackboard pointed at the position where it had been indicated the 'Gamecock Fleet' would be and said,"if we can get the Royal Navy, for it seems to me that's the only authority the fishermen would obey, to order the 'Gamecock Fleet' to sail east into the course the Russians will take, there would be so much confusion the job would be done. What if we could get the captain of 'HMS Devonshire', the war ship that will be in those waters, to intercept the fishermen to say that the 'Home Fleet' is steaming into their fishing grounds and in order to avoid it they have to steer twenty miles East to 55* 18 North. 5* East? They could be instructed and so convinced that it is only a temporary measure until the 'Home Fleet' has passed and then they could return? The timing of such a venture might be, for propaganda purposes, ideal."

Melville looked quizzical and asked," Why do you say that?"

Sidney risked impertinence and replied,"Do I have to teach an Englishman his history? It looks to me, that if everything coincides, the time when the 'Gamecock Fleet' sails, the progress of The Russian Fleet and if we could organize them coming together, the whole business would take place on the 21st. Of October, the anniversary of The Battle of Trafalgar, 'Trafalgar Day', 'The Nelson Touch', 'England Expects,' and all that."

Melville opened his mouth in surprise, and exclaimed,"Of course, how the hell did I miss that." But he then lapsed into despondency and said," Damn the man, you are right it would be perfect timing but there is a problem. I have it on good authority from my counterparts in The Royal Naval Intelligence Division that the First Lord wants generally nothing to do with the mission. He has made it plain that he does not want 'HIS' navy to be involved in any, to quote,' jiggerypokery '. We could not get him to consent to ordering one of his commanders to do anything like that. Your idea is a good one but it is I'm afraid a non-starter."

Sidney, though obviously disappointed, nodded in agreement and said," Well, yes, I understand so tomorrow I shall take a quick look round the shipyards at Poplar in East London then I'll catch the train in the evening for the North East. I shall make contact with Motojiro by cable and after any arrangements I can make there are in place I will return to Hull. Although I haven't got it completely worked out yet I intend to hire a boat there and I shall go and see the progress of The Second Pacific Fleet for myself."

Melville said,"Good I shall leave it to you and you know we have people in Hull that you can contact. But, you will have to keep them at arms length. Nonetheless It has been guaranteed that assistance will be forthcoming if you should need it. Up there they have not forgotten how much you contributed to the work of the Oleum Syndicate so one good turn deserves another but I re emphasise if it is necessary to do so, in the time you are dealing with the matter of Russian Fleet you will be working for the Japanese."

Melville took another piece of cake and while munching on it said,"That brings me to the next bit of business that concerns you. I have left one matter to the last so that you can be totally assured that your identity is protected if the Russians come sniffing around especially as the Horace Collins matter raised its ugly head in Egypt. First off I can tell you that Mr. and Mrs. Collins have disappeared without trace. Not even the Russians know where they are but to put the Russians completely off the scent and to provide you with bona fide credentials for being in the north-east of England we have introduced one of our people into The Kensington School of Mines. We have given him a name that is so sufficiently close to yours it will confuse anyone searching for your identity and you will be able to adopt, for the time you are in the north his status as a Mines Inspector. His name is Stanilaus George Reilly."

If Sidney was surprised at this last piece of information he did not show it. Truth to tell he had ceased to be surprised at anything that Melville sprung on him. It was interesting enough that he had information on Horace and his wife but creating a new personality in the shape of Stanilaus George Relly"took the biscuit". Melville seemed to be able to do anything that he thought expedient in the new role that had been given to him.

"So," Sidney queried," So until further notice, I am to be known as Stanilaus George Reilly. Mines Inspector?"

"Exactly," Said Melville pushing a folder of documentation towards Sidney as he spoke."You get the picture. It should protect your real identity from prying eyes." Then Melville expressed a rare flash of humour when he said," The only thing is don't go looking down any coal-mines or you will really upset the apple cart. Mind you, knowing you as I do, you could probably even pull that one off." Both men laughed out loud but Sidney's laughter had a ruminative quality to it. He was already considering the possibility that if necessary he would pose as a Mines Inspector and get away with it.

Chapter Thirty Six

Back at The Midland Hotel Sidney retrieved the message that had been left for him. As Melville had said it was an invitation to dine at the residence of the commercial attaché to the Imperial German Embassy. His address was on the eastern side of Park Lane towards Bond street.

It was to be a formal affair as he of course expected and it occurred to him as he passed one of the electric light lit glass display cabinets in the hotel foyer with a tailor's dummy modeling a new design of evening dress in it, that he might hire the now fashionable dinner jacket with its white starched shirt front and black tie. The jacket was said to have been an innovation of Edward V11 when as Prince of Wales he had told his tailor to style an evening wear jacket for him without tails.

Sidney instructed the receptionist at the desk to send up the hotel tailor to get his measurement. The tailor, with his mouth already full of pins, his tape over his shoulders and with French chalk prepared came up to Sidney's room with a selection, in different sizes, of the new jacket, over his arm. With an eye inherited and then trained the first black jacket that he unfolded fitted Sidney as if cut for his form. Sidney rarely wore 'off the peg' but on this occasion he was satisfied and it pleased him that he would be just right in fashion. As he posed for the fitting in the mirror he reflected on how little his figure had changed in the last few years of exotic foods and erratic meal times.

After the visit of the tailor he went downstairs and into the Midland's smoking salon. He was surprised to find an inordinate number of generally young women there indulging in the cigarette and tobacco habit. The hotel had opened one of the few spaces around where women in London could smoke in public. The experience almost put him off his own habit. He tolerated it for a while and as he did he called for a Whisky and water with ice. He sipped it and read newspaper reports about the Second Russian Baltic Fleet and the Siege of Port Arthur in what was now being called,"The Russo-Japanese War".

By the time he had returned to his room bathed, shaved, perfumed and changed it was time for him to have the doorman call a cab for him. He walked down the steps of the hotel in an overcoat, hat and gloves against an unseasonably October cold and gave driver the address. The cabbie was heavily muffled against the same cold but for more reason. He had to sit in front of only a glass windshield to shelter his open seat as he peered through the foggy air to the yellow glimmer of street lamps.

After a honking, rattling trip flavoured with whiffs of sweet exhausted gasoline through the surprisingly thick Central London traffic, the house he was set down in front of was one of a grand white painted neo-classical terrace. A stone balustraded balcony ran all along the first floor. At the top of every set of steps, curving wrought iron railings guarded on each side the drop down to the paved ravine of a basement. The railings were in the design of a rack of spears. Each polished black, brass-knockered door was under an impressive pillared entrance portico.

On a flag pole jutting out from the wall the banner of the Imperial German Reich drooped in the still foggy night and every window in the house was bright with the new electric light including the half-circle above the door. But the bell-pull he yanked with its retained wooden handle had not yet been touched by that modernity and he heard its mechanical clanging below stairs summoning the white- tied and tail- coated butler who opened the door to him only seconds later.

Sidney said that he hadn't a card but stated that his surname was Reilly and the butler said,"Good evening Mr. Reilly, you are expected, Von Schonenberg and his other guests are in the drawing room."After taking his coat hat and gloves he was shown by the manservant past the warming flames of a great fire in the foyer chimney and down a wide entrance hall tiled in large black and white squares. He was escorted past gilt-framed portraits, a Prussian coat of arms, under another Imperial German flag, hanging from an ornately decorated landing above, and through grand double mahogany doors. Then he was shown into a room where men in evening dress were standing aloof and poised and women, expertly coiffeurred in expensive high fashion sat with aperitif glasses in graceful jeweled hands.

Sidney hardly heard his introduction to the rest of the guests. He got a general impression from his host, a Prussian aristocrat, with monocle, dueling scar and shaven head that the dinner party was to be made up of the usual list of businessmen,national politicians from home and abroad, Empire civil servants and servants of the Raj along with of course their wives. Where the person he was most concerned with fitted into this social gathering he wasn't sure. All he was aware of was a beautiful woman with green eyes, glorious red hair piled in natural curls and in an off the shoulder ultra-marine blue evening dress with long gloves to the elbow. She looked like a model for a French painter. It was Caroline Belvedere.

As Sidney was introduced to her she could hardly contain herself and it caused the gentleman she was accompanying, a balding man, with pince-nez and a goatee beard to ask if she had met Sidney before. She lied and said,"No, I thought I had but I was mistaken." He was not convinced.

At the table Sidney found himself placed next, on one side to the unmarried daughter in her late twenties of a West Riding woollen manufacture and on the other to the wife of a physician who had once prescribed a cold cure for one of the late Queen Victoria's children. As the evening wore on and he ate through the interminable courses of the modern society dinner party he realized from the reaction to his conversation with the younger woman at his side that a word in the right place and he might find himself in the running for a worsted mill inheritance in Leeds which might include a Jacobean mansion in the Yorkshire Dales. He did not think he was misinterpreting the discrete looks of encouragement he intercepted that were being sent across the table to her spinster daughter from a large woman who was obviously the matchmaking mother.

Although Sidney had enough social graces not to neglect the guests who had been placed either side of him, he could not resist making glances down the table to where Caroline seemed in animated discussion with the men she was in between. He found himself devising ways and means to have her to himself at some point in the evening. His murderous intentions towards her had all but evaporated especially as he was under orders that they should and had been replaced by the desire for her that he had felt from their first meeting.

His chance came with the brandy and cigars and the usual exit of the ladies. He excused himself and on the way to the garden that he had asked a minion the way to, walked past the still open door of the room the ladies had departed to. He figured correctly that Caroline would be watching for him and within a few seconds she joined him at the back of the house in the chill air on the stone paved walled circle of a terrace above misty shadows of bushes and trees that shrouded the formal garden. She rushed into his arms and he accepted her embrace aware that no one he had ever met had ever received him with such spontaneous enthusiasm. She almost jumped to him and put her arms around him and she held him so tight that the memory of her nakedness against him was quickly recalled even through the folds of her voluminous dress, in spite of the fact that it had been some years since he had felt her body or the touch of her skin.

When she had finished covering his face with kisses, she said,"There was a time, an awful time when I thought you were dead. I am so, so pleased to see you again. It has been such a long time. Where…." He interrupted her and said,"Yes, as someone else said, rumours of my demise have been very much overstated, or words to that effect and I thought you were involved. I must tell you I planned the most terrible revenge."

"Sidney, love," Caroline said tenderly, stroking his cheek, looking up at him, her eyes glistening with the beginning of tears,"Please believe me I had nothing to do with the affair. Mueller was behind it all and his motives were not just"matters of state". She said this as if, had they been, that might have excused Mueller's actions."He was jealous of you and very uncomfortably obsessive about me. He has been recalled to Berlin and I have not heard anything of him since then and you know what my work is now. She hesitated then and looked over her shoulder. I must go back in now. I will be missed. Where are you staying? I will come to see you tonight no matter how late it is. You are aware that I have information for you but as well as that, your people should know what the man I am with is arranging with the Germans."

Sidney said hastily," Suite 36 The Midland Hotel St. Pancras, I will wait up for you and be a good girl."

She laughed and said,"If I can't be good I will be careful I promise." Then she turned and as she walked back into the house, blew him a kiss,"A Bientot".

He would wait up for her,yes and if she came he would sleep with her and they would make love. But, as for believing what she had said, that was altogether another matter. She was a double agent now, working for the Germans and for the British. He was in the same trade. He knew in himself that it was not an activity that generated trustworthiness and veracity. His borrowed motto remained the same 'Mundo Nulla Fides' Have no faith in the world, or to translate it less precisely, Trust no one.

Sidney stood for a little while on the terrace and lit one of the last of his papyrossa cigarettes. He inhaled and blew out the smoke from the strong tobacco and in whirls and curls it mixed with the developing fog closing round the house and garden. He had become aware since Anahad that his need for the company of women had gone beyond what he thought he had looked for in the past. It had, he thought moved into his emotions. As he stood, the lighted cigarette glowing in his fingers,reflecting on his meeting with Caroline and the effect she had on him he consciously resolved to check its progress into areas of himself that perhaps he had less control of.

He turned to go already planning an excuse to leave the occasion early but he found his way through the French windows that led to the terrace impeded by the figure of a little boy of around two or three years of age. He was in a little night-shirt. His feet were bare showing his little toes and one of his hands was clutching a knitted doll, which he held close against his cheek and the thumb of the other was in his mouth. With an intuitive paternalism that when he thought of it later surprised him, Sidney bent his knees so that he was at the child's height and said."Hello, who's little boy are you?"

As he looked at the pretty face of the boy with its shock of dark wavy hair over a tiny brow, there was something about the set of the boy's eyes. They had a familiarity that strangely disturbed him. He quickly dismissed the feeling and holding the child's hand he walked him towards one of the household staff already presenting herself as in search of the boy. She had a shape like a cottage loaf and in her white cap and apron he would have guessed, had he been asked, that she was the cook. She gathered the baby boy up in her arms and said."So there you are you little rascal, I don't know what we are going to do with you, wondering about as you do. Say thank you to the nice gentle man for holding your hand." Protocol demanding that she did not speak to the guests she carried the boy away and he looked at Sidney over the shoulder of the woman and taking his thumb out of his mouth, waved goodbye with a tiny hand while still holding tightly to his knitted toy with the other.

Because Sidney had almost returned to the smoking room to join his fellow diners he did not hear the cook as she entered the below stairs kitchen with the boy shouting to one of the housemaids."Joanne, Joanne, If the mistress, out of the goodness of her heart is going to let you bring the boy into the house with you when you are at your work, you must see that he stays in his cot and he doesn't stray about the place getting in my way and in the way of the guests."

Sidney stayed long enough, before making his excuses,to observe the man that Caroline was with cast a suspicious eye over him and to hear sufficient conversation among the other cigar holding male figures, some with swelling waistcoats, stretching comfortably in their chairs or lolling confidently on the table's edge, to confirm his prejudices about"democracy." Sidney mused on the idea that ordinary voters believed that in that Mother of Parliamentary Democracy, The House of Commons it was adversarial debate between the voices of elected members in the chamber that decided the great matters of pith and moment involved in steering a nation's destiny.

How wrong they were. One could say that not even the smoky corridors and vestibules of The House heard the real reckoning up of policy criteria. No, it was here in the cloisters of High Society where a perspicacious hostess, her dinner-table seating arrangements underwritten by an ambitious and/ or influential politician husband, could arrange that plutocrat might rub shoulders with entrepreneur and aristocrat converse confidentially with High Ranking Civil servant then move on to put the right word in a Ministerial ear. Policy was thus formed, largely in favour of the ruling class with perhaps a few crumbs falling from the rich man's table to satisfy the mob. So a country and its people were governed. As Sidney saw it that was the true definition of"democracy".

As he made his excuses, in immaculately delivered High German, it was plain from the reaction of his host and hostess that he had done all that had been asked of him by Melville. He had shown his face and it had been accepted. After much clicking of heels and kissing of hands he walked down the steps to his waiting cab and it amused him to think that, rather than being a business of the secret and the clandestine, this affair of"espionage" was instead one in which everybody seemed to know everyone else. It did not matter so long as it was known whose side one was on. He did doubt however that the Germans were on the side he"played for". The information that Caroline was to deliver later on that night would confirm his view.

When he got back to his hotel he undressed, bathed and then relaxed with a night-cap of single malt whisky before getting into bed to wait for Caroline's promised arrival. It was already late and he dozed until a knocking at the door of his suite roused him to wakefulness. Ever cautious he slipped his 9mm Browning in to a pocket of the dressing gown he put on when he answered the door to the uniformed hotel night-porter standing there with his cap in his hand.

"Begging your pardon sir for waking you at this hour" Sidney looked at a clock on a wall over head in the half-lit corridor, it was two-thirty. The head porter went on,"But there's a.." Here he coughed and put the word into parenthesis,"There's a" lady" downstairs who wishes to see you."

Sidney hid his anger at the man and decided the less said the better. He didn't reply to him but went inside to his desk put the pistol on it and retrieved a half crown from a purse he kept there. He simply pressed it into the man's hand and said," Bring the lady up to my suite and if you don't make a fuss there will be the other half for you in the morning before you finish your shift." The night porter touched his forelock and padded off down the carpeted stairs and minutes later he returned escorting Caroline. Sidney had waited at his door and he held out his hand to her and led her in, closing the door on the porter who was attempting to say thank you and good-night.

Immediately she was inside Sidney embraced her and began kissing her neck and the hair round her ears. He was already aroused and she felt him pressing against her. Caroline took his head in her hands and kissed his forehead and said," Wait, wait, please wait Sidney I have important things to say to you. I must tell you what I have to before anything else. Please wait and please understand I have to deliver my report."

Sidney feigned disappointment and in a mock sulky tone he said."Oh very well, business before, how does the phrase go? I forget. May I get the lady a drink?"

Caroline smiled and asked for a soda water.

She sat at his desk and picked up a pencil and paper from the stationery rack. As Sidney squirted soda into a glass, Caroline began to write. When she had finished she sipped the water and gave the note to Sidney and said,"Please see that your chief gets this as soon as possible. The first part referring to the plan the Germans have for supplying the Second Pacific Fleet with coal by enlisting the assistance of 60 Hamburg Amerika Line colliers will soon be released to the press. It will be in the public domain. The second section sets out that Zaharoff is to be involved in the German"dreadnought" building plan and that he is planning the reconstruction of the Russian Fleet. That is a state secret. At the attaché's house, when he wasn't jealously guarding me he was meeting with a representative of Blohm and Voss the German Shipbuilders."

Sidney's mood changed when he read what Caroline had written. He would get it coded and transmitted when he went to Poplar the next day. The man who had been on Caroline's arm that night at the German attaché's dinner party was Basil Zaharoff A notorious International Arms dealer. He was according to Caroline's report negotiating a secret agreement that would put The Imperial German Navy into direct competition with His Majesty's Royal Navy. The agreement was for the building of a new fleet of modern dreadnoughts. For Sidney it recalled the conversation he had heard on the train to Russia.It might initiate an arms race that could have the most serious consequences for relationships between the two nations and might even lead to war.

Sidney turned to Caroline and put his arms around her. He felt an untypical tenderness towards her that related, through knowledge of his own work, to the risks he knew she must have taken to get the information she had delivered. He kissed her and said,"I am worried for you. This is dangerous work. If Mueller gets wind of it he will be after you as he was after me."

Caroline looked at him with a puzzled expression on her face and she drew away from him a half pace with her arms round his waist. She inclined her head a little to one side and put an amazed tone in her voice and said,"Well Sidney, you old romantic, what has come over you. I am in this for the same reason as you are, I am being well paid for it."

They both fell laughing on to the bed and began feverishly to undress each other until Caroline jumped up and said giggling with glee,"Just a minute, just a minute, all that you are going to crush is a pair of silk pyjamas, this is a one off model and it cost a couple of weeks of my dressmaker's life and me a large handful of sovereigns. Help me off with it please."

Sidney helped her unhook the back of her dress and she stepped out of it revealing her lace underwear and camisole. She was not wearing a corset. Then they made love with her still in her underwear; the eroticism of Caroline's lacy half undress titillating and arousing both of them to passionate embraces and sensual kisses. And both of them then with joint judicious premeditation made love in their nakedness. Their mutual perspiring of sweat caused them to adhere to each other and when he was over her it dripped from his brow into her limpid eyes and it made her blink with its saltiness. She was as voluptuous as he remembered her in Brighton and he was as adept in his foreplay as she had recalled many times since when just before sleep she had caressed herself as the memory of him returned.

As Sidney awoke just before eight the next morning he remembered that they had both fallen into an exhausted sleep after a couple of hours of delightful love-making. He carefully disentangled the limbs of his that were entwined in hers and made to slide out of the bed. He hesitated when he saw, as she slept on, her beautiful chestnut hair laying over the arm her head was resting on, the fall of her breasts and the swell of her belly above her bent knees. He desired her again but that would have to wait. He had to go to Poplar and Blackwell Dock on the Thames in East London and then north to the Tyne. He bathed and dressed quickly. He had already arranged that the bulk of his luggage be on the 5.30 train to Hull. He would travel on to Newcastle. All there was left to do was pay his hotel bill The suit he had hired could be left for collection in the suite and he had to leave a note for Caroline. He wrote it and left it on the desk.

" My Dearest Caroline. I have to travel north for some days. However I shall be in the Hotel Metropole in Brussels by at least the 26th of October. I have reserved a suite there. Please come and join me. I shall arrange for the hotel here to buy you a ticket on the ferry from Dover to Ostende and then onwards by train to Brussels. When you get there ask any cabbie, they will know the Metropole. I shall expect to see you there and we shall carry on where we left off but over a bottle of Russian champagne with caviar and blinis. I am, Your Sidney."

Sidney packed an overnight bag and quietly left his suite. Placing a "Do not Disturb" notice on the door handle he went downstairs. He paid his bill, confirmed the business of his luggage, bought Caroline's tickets and had them placed for her attention behind the desk. He paid the porter his other half crown and went to the outside to get a cab from the rank. It was a foggy London day and as he placed his foot on the step of the cab to mount up in to it, he thought it was the only city in the world that one left with the acrid taste of sulphur in the back of the throat and the smell of horse-shit in the nostrils.

Caroline woke an hour later and saw his note. Without having to think about it she decided that she would go to meet him in Brussells.

When Sidney got to the shipyard at Poplar in East London he recognized that he had been there some years before. Then he had been given a brief to report to Melville on the building of two Japanese battleships, The Shikishuma and The Fuji. That was at a time when Imperial Japanese Naval expansion was being viewed with suspicion; not like now. He also remembered that his surveillance duties coincided with the tragedy of the armoured cruiser, HMS Albion. She had been launched on the Blackwell bank of the river. The launch, in an almighty cock-up, drowned dozens of civilian onlookers. Warships, it occurred to him then, were just as effective in killing people in peacetime as in war.

Before he did anything else he coded the message Caroline had delivered and sent it off via the signal station the Japanese were using. Sidney's visit to the crew of the Japanese destroyer in dock for repairs and maintenance turned out for him to be superfluous. The Captain of the skeleton crew manning the vessel had already had a signal from Colonel Motojiro that they were to cruise the waters the Baltic Fleet (Now known as The Second Pacific Fleet) were to pass through in the North Sea, but were to remain out of range of both the Fleet's guns and its torpedoes.

As Sidney left the ship, down the gang plank and past the two Japanese marines guarding it, the thought struck him that the same signal might well have been received by the Japanese Navy people on the Tyne. In which case his journey up there would also be a waste of time. Not only that, but the Inspector of Mines credentials that had been arranged for him would be a waste. The important and effective work he had the intention of doing was going to be in Hull and at his last observation of its environs there were no coal-mines at all to be had in the city. He said to himself,"not even for ready money." He would still do that work however under his new identity of Stanilaus George Reilly.

His business at Poplar taking less time than he expected enabled him to get a much earlier train and it was an express making only one or two stops before Doncaster and then only at York before pulling into Newcastle.

It was the journey to Palmer's Ship Building Yard at Jarrow on The River Tyne that took the time and it was early evening before he was able to meet the Japanese there. He had a wide choice because there were a number of Japanese ships in the yards, some undergoing modification and others in various stages of construction. There was a wide variety of vessel types from Torpedo Boat Destroyers to what the British called in the days of Nelson,"Ships of the Line." And one of these was a Battleship. It was easy to get the impression that it was Britain building the Imperial Japanese Navy.

The Royal Navy seemed much more in evidence than at Poplar and it was a Royal Naval Lieutenant who escorted him to the ward room of a British Destroyer docked for a re-fit in order to introduce him to the Japanese Commander who was in charge of the Japanese skeleton crews stationed on the ships in the docks.

After the introductions and Sidney's presentation of his "new" credentials the Naval Lieutenant bowed out discretely and left Sidney to talk with the commander. It was the same story from the Japanese Naval officer, create a presence in the North Sea, have the Fleet under observation but keep out of range and don't under any circumstances engage. Motojiro had signaled a duplication of the orders given at Poplar.

Chapter Thirty Seven

For Sidney the whole day had been wasted and he had to recoup it. He did not want to pass the night in Newcastle so he urged his cabbie to get him to the Station in Newcastle early enough for him to make a train to York where he would just be in time to catch a connection that would take him via Selby to Hull. It was the Milk Train and it did not chug into Hull Paragon Station until 4.30 on a dull day with a light drizzle wetting the dark early morning streets. Sidney walked into the back entrance to The Royal Station Hotel and he was shown to his room by a porter where his luggage was waiting for him He was so much in need of sleep that he did not even wash before undressing to his underwear and getting into bed. He slept until ten.

At ten when he awoke he ordered a late breakfast in his room. It came just as he was donning his bathrobe after his shower and shave. He ate it voraciously not having had a meal since a lunch on the train up to the north. He had foregone dinner in Newcastle to save time.

When he had finished eating he looked at his diary and noted that it was the fourth of October. That left him with just over two weeks to organize, and set into motion the plan he had been working on since the meeting in"M's" office. He was going to take it upon himself to hire a fishing boat and to observe the passing of The Imperial Russian Second Pacific Fleet at close quarters.

He dressed simply in the plain suit he kept when he wanted to look unobtrusively business like and after enquiring at the desk where the nearest reference library was. He was told by the clerk and he walked out into main Paragon Square to ask the way to Hull's Central Library in Albion Street.

He walked through the entrance porch to leave the hotel and was just about to ask the doorman for further directions when he spoke first.

"So that's all they are going to get."

Sidney was non-plussed."Excuse me did you say something?"

The doorman, Sidney guessed he would be in his sixties, was dressed in a brass-buttoned bottle-green uniform with a top hat of the same colour that was trimmed with an equally green cockade of feathers. He touched the rim of his hat in a salute and said," Begging your pardon sir, I was thinking aloud. I was referring to what they are building over there." He pointed across the road in front of the hotel to a square that looked like a construction site. Around it were the walls of demolished dwellings and shops, their staircases and fireplaces exposed as if in cross-section.

The doorman went on."They're putting up a memorial to our lads that didn't come back from the Boer War. There were around sixty of 'em. They'd be better off givin' the money to the widows and orphans. They don't need memorials, they needs food and rent."

Sidney looked over to the square that had being cleared. There was a plinth covered in a tarpaulin under which presumably the monument in question was standing, protected and he reflected on the part he had played in that particular Imperial adventure, albeit at a distance.

What Sidney saw as well, overlooking the memorial site were large signs in enormous white letters painted on one of the surrounding walls. They were so dominant that it seemed as if the square had been cleared not for remembrance of war dead but for the better observance of the advertisement of OXO, NESTLES MILK and VIM.

Sidney did not pass on his thoughts to the doorman regarding the irony of that commercial advertisement or to what extent his interference as an agent provocateur and informer during the war that was being commemorated, was equally ironic. He only remembered Moshie Ginsberg's, words"War brings confusion and confusion means profit." Sidney then added his own words, and said to himself," As advertising's use is to beat the competition and to profit then war is the ultimate expression of competition. It would seem fitting that they should go together"

Instead Sidney made what he thought were the appropriate noises required of him, "Hm. Yes, quite, I wonder if you could help me? I am a stranger to the city. I am looking for Albion Street and the library."

The doorman immediately shrugged off his charitable considerations and virtually jumped to his duties. He indicated that, as it was only a step to walk and not at all necessary to get a cab, Sidney should turn right, walk for around fifty yards then cross the road and turn right, walk along and pass The Royal Infirmary,"(You can't miss it) and the Library and Albion Street will be in front of you across the road." Sidney tipped him a silver three penny piece and was rewarded with"Only too happy to oblige sir."

With such precise directions and as it took only five minutes Sidney was soon perusing the photographs of fishing boats from the library's reference section brought to him by a very pretty library assistant whom he noticed responded quite positively to his now, cultivated foreign accent. Sidney was immediately attracted to her with her English Rose complexion, blue eyes and her wavy fair hair swept to the top her head and flowing down past her shoulders. She was fashionably dressed in a batiste blouse with it high neck, a fashion introduced because Queen Alexandra had a blemish on her throat, and a 'trumpet' shaped skirt.

He was certainly distracted for a few minutes by his lascivious desire to know her better but quickly returned to his 'duty' and he soon confirmed the words of the whiskered worthy who had pontificated in the meeting at"M's" offices that not only was Hull a centre for fishing but it was also important as a place where fishing boats were built or at least the River Hull was, right up to the Minster Town of Beverley.

The photographs that he looked at showed that they were pretty boats with a high bow and graceful lines of about one hundred feet long with a mizzen sail and as it said in the notes with the photographs,"Good sea boats." The first generation of fishing boats had been sailing smacks but sail had given way to steam and they were now Steam Trawlers fuelled, as the black smoke from their funnels illustrated, by coal.

As he turned over the pages of the dozens of photographs he had access to a thought that was exciting to Sidney came to his mind. To emphasise and expand it he asked the same and very willing young woman who said her name was Miss Newsam who had already helped him, to bring photographs of navy ships. Once he had these he turned to images of early torpedo boats and thought how much their lines and superstructure resembled a modern steam trawler. The funnel on the first torpedo boats was more amidships and of course they had torpedo tubes either on their decks for launching or arranged so that a torpedo could pass through the bows for the target. But, how easy it would be, Sidney thought with pathological imagination, for a steam trawler, with certain simple modifications to be mistaken, at a distance of course, for a torpedo boat possibly about to make an attack.

As his thoughts morphologised he concluded that It might not be that he would simply observe the passing of the fleet, his original intention, he would provoke it into belligerent action. Sidney did not subscribe to the Tolstoyian view that individuals could not shape history. For Sidney it was only individuals that made history. The mob, as far as he was concerned only made the noise that accompanied history.

The next problem to be surmounted was where and how to hire the fishing boat that he could use in such a ruse. That would have to be followed on by the other problem of a crew to man it. He saw as the most pressing priority the hiring of a crew. He knew nothing about fishing boats, the hiring of them the sailing of them, or the manning of them. He must search out people who did and do it quickly.

An address in P:arliament Street was what he had for one of his Hull contacts and he asked the obliging library assistant how to find it. She went to the trouble of drawing him a map that showed it was in what was called "The Old Town". It was, she assured him, only a short walk away.

His preoccupation with the plan he was working out did not prevent him from noticing what an attractive provincial town Hull was with its mix of neo-classical architecture of pediments and columns and modern facades. As he had observed before, there was much new building taking place. He passed an almost completed fine civic hall and following his map walked through a brand new square dedicated to the late queen and saw in front of him a great column in the style of the one erected to Nelson but not so high. There was a figure on it however and the monumental engraving at its base told that it was to William Wilberforce the renowned liberator of slaves. Hull obviously had an historical claim to fame.

Then he was presented with the sight of a grand building with a semicircular frontage and imposing domes and of many fishing boats of the same sort as he had seen pictures of in the library. The building according to his map was The Dock Offices and the boats filled the two docks that were on each side of the bridge he was walking over. In the dock on his left there were so many moored it might have been possible to walk on them from one side of the dock to the other. And as he walked on his path took him actually under the bows of the boats that were moored in the dock on his right. In that dock there were not only steam trawlers but cargo boats and tall ships their masts reaching scores of feet high and their rigging, sheets and drooping sails festooned spars and yards. Around all this was such a business of traffic that one might have thought that it was a metropolis being passed through rather than a provincial town.

With the building of some grand construction on his left, the street he had been directed to had on each side, a neo-Georgian terrace of houses running its length. He climbed the steps in front and entered the open door of the address he had been given and was confronted by a desk in the entrance hall at which sat a young man dressed in a smart city suit. It was less of a house and more of a temporary office. The young man got up to greet Sidney but without speaking he presented him with a card on which was written,"The London and British Chambers of Commerce." When he saw the card Sidney thought wryly,"I have done business with these people before."

Sidney gave his name as George Stanilaus Reilly. The young man offered Sidney a chair and got up to walk through a door into another room. Within a few minutes another man somewhat older, balder and in the conventional dress of perhaps a solicitor, black jacket, pinstriped trousers and watch chained waistcoat with a pair of pince-nez on his nose came out and said."We have been expecting you Mr. Reilly. What is it that we can do for you?" Sidney pulled his chair closer to the desk and described just what he wanted to do; to hire a fishing boat. Sidney described the type and said that he wished to engage a crew to man it. As he did this the man carefully noted, what he said.

When he had finished writing he said,"As far as the boat is concerned, we may be able to help although that may present its problems given the demand for fishing boats at this time. The hiring of the crew is a different matter. That will be an enterprise you may have to organize yourself. However we shall seek advice on the ways and means and let you know. We don't want to discuss the matter by telephone or deliver material to you at your hotel so we would like to arrange to see you say four days from hence here at this address. Does that find favour with you? Sidney nodded in agreement but at the same time he had the date of the 19th. In his head and thought coming back on the

8th. Of October was beginning to cut things fine. In spite of his reservations he got up and left, walking out once again into Hull's streets.

When he had asked directions of the girl in the library he had also asked where a good place for a drink might be. She had described 'as he seemed to be interested in history,' an inn not far from the offices he had just visited,"The Olde White Harte" and when she had drawn him the map she had, rather pointedly he thought, added the telephone number of the library."What would be more pleasant than to have the company of a pretty girl for luncheon?" he said to himself.

He walked down the thoroughfare from Parliament Street, It was called Whitefriargate and he followed her directions into a little alley. Hidden in the middle of the alley was what looked like an ancient and imposing town house. It was in fact a public house and on the wall outside he saw hanging the sign of the bell that said he would be able telephone from inside. He entered what was the classic English public house of large"ingle-nook" blue"Delph" tiled fireplaces and beamed ceilings and he gave the barman a silver three penny piece and asked to use the telephone and then for the library's number, then he asked to speak to Miss Newsam. After the usual telephone formalities of requesting the name of the caller, she came to the telephone.

As Sidney heard her say hello in the earpiece he told her that he was the gentleman that she had helped so much earlier that morning and he went on to say, that to show his appreciation he would like to invite her out to lunch. She was, as he expected hesitant at first, she wasn't she said really supposed to take personal telephone calls, but very slowly, as he also expected she responded to his charm and powers of persuasion and agreed to meet him. But when he suggested that he should meet her in The Olde White Harte she very quickly said,"Oh yes they do lunches at that hostelry. I would prefer however, 'The George', which is around the corner off Bowl Alley Lane in The land of Green Ginger. I shall be there in just a few minutes" The chief librarian usually dined at 'The Olde White Harte' along with member of the library committee of the corporation. She did not wish to meet him or them.

Momentarily Sidney thought he had entered the world of 'Alice in Wonderland' as Miss Newsam described where they should meet and as he passed the telephone back to the barman he queried the street names she had given him."No sir." The barman said,"They really are the names of streets in this quarter. 'Bowl Alley Lane' is just outside and it leads to 'The Land of Green Ginger". Leave this house and turn left, when you come out of the alley turn left and left again." Hull, Sidney thought has that memorable quality of 'Les Pays de Marveilles.'

He walked around the corner to a street in which was a classic coaching inn complete with large wooden double doors that at one time obviously welcomed the mail coach from London. It was the rear entrance of a larger hotel whose frontage was in the Whitefriargate.

Going through the doors at the entrance he passed into the bar, noisy with midday drinkers and went into the dining room where he motioned to a black aproned waiter and asked to sit at one of the vacant tables already laid with crockery, cutlery and starched white cloths. When the waiter came with a menu Sidney said that he would order when the friend he was expecting came but in the meantime he would have a large schooner of dry sherry.

His sherry came and Sidney sipped it and then he got up, told the waiter to reserve his table and he walked out into the street again. It occurred to him that Miss Newsam would prefer for him to meet her outside rather than having to come into a crowded pub, a young lady alone.

Almost as soon as he stepped outside Miss Newsam arrived. She had put on a blue-ribbon trimmed straw boater pinned on top of her hair and a pale blue soft leather jacket over her blouse. He doffed his hat and offered his hand to her. She took it and with a continental flair he brushed his lips over the top of her glove. Sidney, said as they stood on the pavement now busy with shoppers and workers taking their lunch break,"I really should introduce myself. My name is George Stanilaus Reilly and I am here in Hull on business to do with the fishing industry. I must say I am most pleased that you have accepted my invitation. I do hope you don't think I was being impertinent in asking you."

Miss Newsam had experienced misgiving when she thought that perhaps she had been somewhat impulsive in accepting Sidney' offer. Even on the walk to 'The George' she had thought that she was stepping outside convention. But Miss Newsam regarded herself as a modern independent young woman and as she considered the situation she answered the questions she asked herself with an a affirmative,"Why shouldn't I?" But, when she met Sidney again and he performed the gesture of kissing her hand all her doubts evaporated and she simply said,"No not at all Mr. Reilly it is very kind of you to invite me. Permit me to introduce myself. My name is Miss Chloe Newsam."

Sidney smiled at her and took her arm and escorted he into the dining room where he asked her if she wanted anything to drink. This she did reply to in the negative for only a few months before in a campaign organized by the local Band of Hope she had signed the pledge. She asked him to order a saspirella.

Sidney ordered the lunch of mixed grill that Miss Newsam had selected from the menu and for himself a portion of steak and kidney pudding and applying a favourite technique he used when charming women he had just met he persuaded her to talk about herself.

She was twenty four and unmarried and she had worked as a library assistant since leaving school when she was sixteen. Her parents had paid for her to go on from her elementary education to a private school and she had nursed ambitions at one time to go away to university or to be a teacher but her father had died and so such plans had to be shelved. Now she lived with her mother who suffered somewhat from "nerves" and she was making her career in the library and in fact was waiting for an appointment at a new library donated by the philanthropist Andrew Carnegie that was in the process of being built in the suburbs of the city where she would be the junior librarian.

As she talked and ate, and Sidney loved to watch his women eat, he saw that her breasts rose and fell under her lacey blouse and he thought to himself that perhaps he would not be satisfied quite with just a luncheon with this attractive girl.

Sidney said to Miss Newsam when she had finished her meal and the ice-cream that she ordered as a dessert."Have you time for coffee?"

Miss Newsam said to his surprise that she had plenty of time because his invitation had coincided with her afternoon off."In that case," Sidney said." you can show me round the town a little and answer one or two queries I have regarding the location of various places, that is if you don't mind and have nothing else that I might be keeping you from."

Miss Newsam was beginning to enjoy herself. It was not often she got the chance to walk out with such a presentable gentleman as she thought Sidney was. He seemed such a man of the world and with that hint of the mysterious foreigner about him, Miss Newsam had found herself quite attracted to him from the time he asked for her help in the library.

Miss Newsam had planned to do the household chores for the week, the laundry and the cleaning but she thought Mr. Reilly's offer much more attractive."Oh I would be more than pleased to. I have a little shopping to do for my mother but it is just for one or two things and it should not take long."

They had their coffee and Sidney paid the bill politely dismissing Miss Newsam's profuse thanks and they walked out into the autumn sunshine with Miss Newsam adding that Hull got more sunshine sometimes than anywhere else in the country. It had she said its own special climate surrounded as it was with the estuary and the river and being so close to the sea.

Within a few minutes Miss Newsam had walked Sidney to see Hull's Holy Trinity Parish Church and described its ancient brickwork and what little medieval glass it had having been smashed in The English Civil war which she proudly pointed out had begun in the city,"In the very public house you were in before lunch." She said."The town worthies having hatched a plot to exclude King Charles the First by closing the gates against him, and the conspiracy took place in a room above the bar. Then of course it wasn't a public house but the house of the Governor of the city, Sir John Hotham."He later betrayed The Parliamentary cause and was executed for it."

Sidney let her talk on, knowing that the more interest he showed in what she knew the closer to persuading her to extend her interest in him would come to the point where she would permit more erotic intimacies. He also reflected on the view he had that it was never the man who did the choosing. It was always the woman. Granted he had made the first move but it was acceptance that counted. She could quite simply have said"no" to his advances. She didn't. She said yes

Miss Newsam did not need encouraging to continue her description of Hull's historical reference.

"Here," she said,"Is the building that was once the Old Grammar School." She had stopped in front of an old two storey brick and slate building with mullioned windows."William Wilberforce was a pupil at this school."

Sidney made a contribution."Oh yes, I saw his monument on my way across the town guided by your very accurate map." Even the briefest and gentlest flattery, Sidney knew could work its effect.

"Yes". Miss Newsam enthused,"He was instrumental in liberating all the slaves in The British Empire. If you like I can show you the house in which he was born. It is not far away from here. In fact nowhere is very far away in Hull and it is after all so flat." She smiled at what she had said and Sidney nodded his assent.

But Miss Newsam was not finished with The Old Grammar School and it was her reference to another old boy of the school that convinced Sidney there and then that he would, in the next few days have his way with her.

"Andrew Marvell went to school in this building." She said it with a pride which indicated that she had often thought about the fact."He was born just outside the town and became its Member of Parliament in the seventeenth century. I think he is one of the greatest poets in the English Language. Sidney was not prepared to admit that he had never heard of him.

Miss Newsam's lecture on local history and its part in English Literature went on."I think if he had written only one poem he still deserves his place."

"Which poem is that ?" Sidney enquired.

" His poem, 'Ode to a Coy Mistress.'" Quite near to the old school there were benches. Taking her arm Sidney guided Miss Newsam to one of them and they sat down and Sidney said,"Do you know it? If you do recite it to me. I love poetry."

Miss Newsam could not believe her good fortune, she had met a man, a man not much above her own age, an attractive man, a charming man, a very presentable man and he liked poetry. She didn't know then that he was a cad and a predatory cynic and a murderously dangerous cynic at that. She also underestimated Marvell's verse. It had been written two hundred and fifty years before to persuade a maid to give up her virtue and its power of persuasion was still potent. She began;

"Had we but world enough and time

This coyness lady were no crime

We would sit down and think which way

To walk and pass our long love's day.

Thou by Indian Ganges would rubies find,

I by the tide of Humber would complain

As she went on repeating Marvell's complex system of Hyperbole, metaphore and simile moving as it does in verse like a lover exploring the body of his beloved to lines like;

"Now, therefore while the youthful hue

sits on thy skin like morning dew"

and beyond to

Through the iron gates of life

and finally,

Thus though we cannot make our sun stand still yet we will make him run."

Miss Newsam, thought Sidney, in quoting the poem had all but put him into bed with her and poor deluded girl, from now on her fate was sealed. Marvell had done Sidney's work for him.

Sidney said"Bravo, Bravo." And he applauded."That was really well recited."

Miss Newsam felt quite hot and the blush that was on her cheeks had begun at her breasts. They, under her batiste blouse, were now quite pink. Their rosy hue had seeped upwards to her neck and above. Had she been a more experienced young woman she would have known that the heat she felt was more desire than embarrassment but she would have had difficulty acknowledging that to herself so early in her relationship with Sidney. For his part Sidney had taken less time in the past to exercise his seductive art but he was honest enough in these matters to admit to himself that money had often speeded up the process.

Recovering herself Miss Newsam walked Sidney round the corner into Hull's Market Place, and by this time Sidney had taken her arm. She wanted him to see the golden statue of William the Second erected by the city's grateful Protestants for his"Bloodless Revolution" in 1688 and as there was enough autumn sunshine to see him at his best Sidney wasn't or rather Miss Newsam wasn't disappointed. There he stood glistening in his guise of a Roman Conqueror, laurels and all, on his stirrup-less horse erected over a public convenience.

Sidney was, getting bored with this guided tour. He had things to do, places to go and people to find so it was only when Miss Newsam said that the river Hull was over to her left and the estuary straight ahead down to Victoria Pier and the ferry that, Sidney revived his interest.

Miss Newsam was eager to point out that the River Hull was crossed by a number of lifting bridges that cut the city into two, the east and the west very much like St. Petersburg it was said and she asked as she guided Sidney in the direction of the High Street passing as they did the last lifting bridge over the River Hull before it flowed into the Humber, As they negotiated quite a busy road she asked,"Have you ever been to St.Petersburg, Mr. Reilly?"

"Oh yes, Miss Newsam, Oh yes, a few times. But I did want to ask you a question about the area of the city where the fisher folk live. Is that area near the river here where I can see what looks like fishing boats moored?"

" No, no Mr. Reilly." Miss Newsam said with the authority of local knowledge,"The neighbourhood where most of those people live is in the west of the city along a thoroughfare called Hessle Road. It is not a very attractive part of the city and not a district I would advise you to visit, especially at night."

Sidney was of course going to ignore this advice. If Hessle Road was where he would find fishermen it was just the place he wanted to be. Sidney tried to put an apologetic tone into his voice when he replied, "I am afraid my business will inevitably take me there but I do assure you Miss Newsam that I will be cautious in my associations if it is as you suggest, something of a 'not quite respectable quarter' of your fair town."

He modified his irony and his reaction to Miss Newsam's somewhat patronizing suggestion that he might not be able to take care of himself by drawing her quite close to him, so close she thought he might have kissed her face and then patting the back of her hand."Now let us find somewhere to have tea so that I may sit you down to discuss the possibility of asking you out tonight and if your response is positive to receive your suggestions as to where I should take you."

Miss Newsam felt 'swept off her feet.' She even felt a physical sensation when he used an expression like"sit you down." And now he was stating his intention to take her out for the evening and they had not yet been formally introduced. Things were moving faster than she could control but she was reckless enough to say to herself that she didn't care.

Sidney looked up the River Hull and right towards the Humber Estuary. He mused on what it would be like in a fishing boat on water that looked too wide to be a river.

His thoughts were interrupted by Miss Newsam suddenly swinging round in front of him, still holding his hand and bursting into the girlish chatter of a little schoolgirl. She almost danced around him in her gaiety.

"I know what we should do." She said as she jumped up and down, now clapping her hands together in her excitement." Let's have tea on the ferry." Her sudden expression of innocent child-like gaiety inspired in him a lascivious desire for her there and then but it was not the time or place unfortunately for the manifestation of the eroticism of innocence.

Sidney was non-comprehending."What was the girl on about?" He said to himself." The ferry to where, Belgium, Holland, France? How could there be time for that?

He successfully hid his desire for her when he said," I don't understand, what ferry and where to?"

Miss Newsam was still happily chattering and she was almost tugging him along the pavement in the direction of the great river as if she were a little child. As she did it she said,"There is a ferryboat that crosses the Humber to New Holland. We can buy tickets at the railway station that there is there, but it does not have any trains of course as it is on Victoria Pier and then we will stay on the ferry for the return voyage and have tea in the salon. It will be so exciting."

With railway stations without trains and talk of 'New' Hollands Sidney was once again in wonderland."New Holland, that must be too far." He said.

"No, No," she said." Not at all. It is just across the river."

As they turned a corner the Humber Estuary confronted them like a sea. It was busy with all types of craft. Wind -blown black smoke shrouded the steamers and coasters that were chugging up the middle of the river and down it. Paddle steamers splashed as they turned on the water and steam cargo boats were anchored off and tall sailing ships with their sails drooping or flapping in the breeze waited on the wind and tide and smaller ships and boats weaved between them.Some of them were like the fishing boat pictures that Sidney had looked at in the library and had seen moored in the town docks. Directly across the café au lait coloured wide water was the pale green misty line of the other bank with the hardly distinct red brick buildings of what must be, Sidney thought, the"New Holland" Miss Newsam was talking about. Above all was a great wide bowl of cloudy bright blue sky that because of the flat horizon was the biggest sky he had ever seen.

Tied up at a floating pontoon pier was a paddle steamer with grey, white smoke curling from its funnel. There was a queue of people waiting to buy tickets at a building that Miss Newsam told him was the station and passengers were walking to the boat down a gangway on the pier. Small horse drawn carts were being driven carefully through an opening onto a wide space in the bows reserved for that traffic.

Sidney bought return tickets and they went on board and stood on the deck for a while and before they went below to escape the quite cold autumn wind, blowing off the river they watched sailors casting off and heard the engines as they turned the paddle wheels, churning up into muddy foam the boat's shallow anchorage.

In the brown varnished wood and brass fitting of the boat's saloon there was the press of other passengers ordering beer and strong drink from the bar. At Miss Newsam's asking Sidney requested a less potent pot of tea for two and cakes."Refreshment enough, the drink that cheers but does not inebriate." As Miss Newsam said this Sidney thought that he would enjoy causing her to discover that in the matter of physical love she would be much less abstemious.

After their tea they braved the now very cold wind and walked on the deck and were in time to watch the boat dock on the other side and to see passengers get on and off and the boat set sail once again for Victoria pier and Hull.

Miss Newsam was so pleased with their little adventure. As they came on shore she clung to Sidney's right arm with both hers and so walked very close to him. Sidney was immediately convinced that had he been able to take her somewhere comfortable and private such as his hotel room he could have had her there and then with little resistance. She was completely in love with the moment and so it followed with him. But for Sidney her seduction would have to wait. Miss Newsam had to go home to mother. For herself this was the first time that she had not felt like fulfilling her obligation. She wanted to continue the rest of the day with Sidney but she knew her mother would not only be wanting her evening meal she would also need the medicaments that her daughter had been charged with obtaining.

Sidney accompanied her to a pharmacy where she bought a patent bottle of tonic wine and pills that were to assist her mother in sleeping. As the shop assistant packaged Miss Newsam's purchases. Sidney enquired as to whether Miss Newsam's mother drank alcohol. Miss Newsam expressed an emphatic"No". The reason for Sidney's enquiry was to observe to himself, as someone who had peddled the same kind of stuff, that the tonic was made up of more than 45% alcohol plus an essence of cocaine and the pills were a basic opiate and with a more refined heroin mixture in a box with an impressive label.

Sidney walked Miss Newsam to her tram car stop and he waited until her foot was on the iron step of the tram before he asked her if he could see her again. As she was in such a state of nervous tension waiting for his request she blurted out so impulsively that other passengers boarding turned to see,"In a week's time I will finish at one in the afternoon and then I have two days leave."

Sidney shouted to her as the tram moved off," I will telephone you at the library."

She passed down the car and sat down on a slatted wooden seat and waved to him through the window. As her car moved out of the square she could think of nothing else but her afternoon with Sidney and now there was the prospect of seeing him again. In the darkening early evening electric blue sparks spat and crackled from the trolley overhead filling the bay on the upper deck with an eerie pale metallic light. The tram car carrying Miss Newsam clanged its iron wheels on its railed route as the black-uniformed driver wound the brass resistance handle and the tram's speed increased with a low hum and the conductor called"Fares Please" and rang the bell on his ticket machine.

Chapter Thirty Eight

When she got home, not even the petulant questions of her mother, sitting up in the bed that had been moved downstairs, irritated that she had been kept waiting both for her tea and her"medicaments" especially her tonic could spoil Miss Newsam's mood. She poured a liberal draught from the bottle of tonic into a glass on the bedside table and passed it to her mother. She took a gulp from it and licked her lips."I've used the commode." Her mother said."I had to get out of bed myself as you were late. I could have fallen and no one would have known."

Miss Newsam took the chamber pot from under the commode chair and laid a serviette over it and then took it and emptied the contents in the outside privy. She rinsed the pot under a brass tap on the wall. She returned to the house, replaced the pot and went to the hall mirror to take the pin out of her hat and tidy her fair hair. She also took off her jacket and as she did she looked at her reflection in the glass and smoothed down her blouse letting the palms of her hands pass over the rise of her breasts as she did so. She moved both her hands down to her waist and hips even to the smooth tops of her thighs under her skirt. She imagined that it was Sidney caressing her.

Miss Newsam was a librarian and so more literary than most. She read a lot of books. She was au fait with and enthusiastic about the works of the celebrated pacifist writer, The Countess Bertha von Suttner. They were on the book shelves of all thinking young women. She had read and been inspired by her anti-war fiction but the novel she had to confess she was most engrossed in at this time perfectly fitted her feelings, George DuMauriers's"Trilby". She indentified with the central character completely. She had taken the book off the shelf and had not yet returned it in spite of multiple requests from the reading public. She would have liked to model herself on Dorethea Baird, the actress who had made the role of Trilby her own in the stage version.

By the time that Miss Newsam's tram-car had turned the corner, Sidney's preoccupation had shifted back to his plan to interfere with the Imperial Russian Second Pacific Fleet. On his walk back to the hotel he called in at a stationery shop and bought cartridge paper, tracing paper, ruler, pencils, pens, inks and technical drawing instruments. His intention was to make the designs of a fishing trawler that would, at a distance have all the appearance of an attacking torpedo boat.The seduction of Miss Newsam, significant and anticipated though it was, would have to wait for other priorities. Psychopathological as he no doubt was, Sidney still had that intellectual capacity of being able to hold two opposing concepts in his scheming mind at one and the same time. And maybe given Sidney's particular turn of mind, they weren't in opposition. Both would involve a programme of organized deception and both would result, given success, in the not inconsiderable pleasure of egocentric satisfaction.

When he got back to his hotel there was a note at the desk waiting for him. It stated quite simply," URGENT, Contact Parliament Street tomorrow."

Before he went up to his room he ordered sandwiches and coffee to be sent up as he would not be eating dinner in the dining room. He intended spending the evening in the neighbourhood Miss Newsam had warned him not to go to, Hessle Road. If he was to find a crew for the boat he thought, quite rightly as it happened, to find them there. The best person to consult on how to arrive there he felt was the doorman.

He ate his sandwiches when they came and he then spent the next few hours making rudimentary sketches of the cylinders he thought would appear at a distance to a ship's lookout as torpedo tubes when fixed on the deck of a fishing boat. He had decided that he would adopt the persona of a fish scientist from a University department of Fishing and Agriculture and declare that the tubes when they were manufactured and fixed port, starboard and stern would serve the purpose of holding tanks for examples of fish species. He drew three examples with a small hinged lid on each and with front and back ends blanked off. He decided that for his ruse the length of the tubes was not critical but the diameter would have to be of the standard size that torpedoes were from 15", 18" and 21".

When he was satisfied that he had the primary designs he could base an order on to a sheet metal fabricators he put on his jacket and went down stairs to ask the doorman to call him a cab. He did not think it necessary to change his shirt.

The cabbie said that he didn't often get requests to go to Hessle Road adding that even the police were known to patrol in threes. To Sidney's enquiry as to where fishermen congregated the cabbie said that the 'Star and Garter' was the most notorious venue for fishermen who came back from fishing trips with money in their pockets but as there was a public house on nearly every corner, he could 'take his pick'.

The cabby dropped him off at the door of a very large public house built on the corner of a street off the main tram –lined thoroughfare. Even from the outside it was possible to see through windows, lit by yellow gas lamp light, that it was well frequented. He stopped at the door and as he did so a customer came out on a gust of warm air. He was obviously, by his clothes a working man. As he passed Sidney he took his appearance in one look touched the flat cap he was wearing and said deferentially," not the kind of place you should be going in, if I might say so Mister."

Sidney smiled and replied,"Thanks all the same, but let me be the judge of that if you don't mind." And he walked in through the door that the man had held open.

Inside it was crowded by men with drinks in their hands standing at a long bar that went from one wall to the other or they were sitting in half dozens at pint pot strewn tables cramped together across floorboards that had been liberally spread with sawdust. The atmosphere was thick with grey tobacco smoke and the strong smell of beer. There were women too, young and indeterminately old. They revealed their dubious morality by calling to each other as Sidney entered or soliciting him with questions as to whether he wanted company.

Sidney ignored the reference to him being a 'toff' and the ribald reassurance shouted from one table that,"Molly and Jesse always wears clean knickers when stepping out with a gentleman" and he walked straight up to the bar and called on one of the burly barmen at it to serve him with a whisky. When it came Sidney didn't beat about the bush but simply enquired as to where he could hire a crew for a fishing boat. The barman didn't reply but looked at the crush of men standing shoulder to shoulder on each side of Sidney and they all burst into roars of laughter.

One of the group was a large powerfully built man in a ginger suit and waistcoat stretched over a round beer-filled stomach. He was wearing a Brown Derby hat He was clean shaven at the chin but with a moustache as ginger as his suit. He took the pipe out of his mouth and said, as he touched Sidney's arm in a gesture of friendliness that Sidney did not expect,"Don't mind them, it's just their bit of soft. You'll find no crews for hire at this time. They are either all on trips or waiting to go on one. We don't get no more than three or four days in port before we are off again. Besides what would a young gentlemen like you be wanting with a fishing boat crew? If you don't mind me saying so you look more like a chap who is used to the city life. You're not going to sea for pleasure are your?" When he said this he looked round at his audience."Because if you are, around here we've got a saying about that, He who would go to sea for pleasure would go to Hades for a holiday." There was much hmming and aahing at his wise remark.

Sidney told the man it was not a pleasure trip and recounted the story he had invented about himself. He was a fisheries scientist and wanted to take a boat and a crew to collect samples of various species of fish off the Dogger Bank so that breeding and migration information could be collected. He had not thought, he said, that it would be so difficult to recruit a crew. He himself, he added had no experience of fishing and fisheries beyond the university laboratory.

Suitably impressed, the fisherman said," Ah you're a university man are you, well what do you want to know? I have been fishing for twenty five years and the last fifteen years as a skipper." Standing next to him was a thin little man with a flat cap and a watch chain on his waistcoat. He put his pint pot down and drew his hand across his moustache and volunteered a contribution, looking up with eyes as watery and dull as an oyster at the brown derby hat of his companion," What he doesn't know about fishing ain't worth knowing and that's a fact."

With the unerring good fortune that Sidney in his conceit expected to be the lot of his life he had once again, at first hit, scored. He had found the right man.

Sidney said with assurance,"I have made arrangement to hire a fishing boat of the sort that sails out of The Humber and it will be ready to sail in the next few days. However the owners say that I will have to hire my own crew. I will of course pay them well and I should add, anyone who helps me find them."

At the mention of"pay" the big man detached himself from the group and motioned Sidney to follow him. He passed along the bar and he gave a nod in the direction of a man standing behind the bar whose demeanor and dress indicated that he was one apart from the barmen, probably the landlord, Sidney thought. The big man opened a door with a frosted glass half window. It had the sign"Private" painted in black across it. He walked in and Sidney followed him.

Sidney found himself in a small ante room used as a store for bar equipment and furniture. It had one window high up on the wall. There was another plain door that Sidney guessed led out to the street. The big man turned up the gas light and then took two chairs from a stack against the wall and placed them at a round marble bar table with cast iron legs.

"Here," he said,"Sit yourself down. Do you want another drink?" Sidney shook his head." Now you say you want a crew, well I'll tell you what you will, at a minimum, need, to man your hired fishing boat. And then I will see what I can do about finding the men for you. He then went on to say, not all that successfully hiding the opportunism that had persuaded him to deny his initial pessimistic remarks,"It will cost you though."

Sidney took out from an inside pocket a notebook with a pencil attached. He opened it and waited for the man to speak again.

"My advice is don't be fobbed off with a boat any less than a 100 foot steam trawler. Any less and you'll have trouble if the weather comes on to blow. Now to man such a boat you will need a Skipper, a Bosun, a Chief Engineer, a 2nd Engineer, a Third Hand, a Deck Hand, a Trimmer and last, but I will tell you not by any means least, somebody who can rustle up a good pan of"shackles", a Cook. I am expecting you to say that you will be at sea for a few days, right?" Sidney nodded his assent and decided not to ask what"shackles" were.

The big man noticed as well, that there was a look of non-comprehension on Sidney's face. And he said,"Don't you worry about their duties. I shall find you a skipper that will know what they have to do and he will see to it, mark my words, that they will do a good job for you. Now, when do you think you will want 'em?"

Sidney told him that he expected to pick up the boat in the next few days but it had to have certain simple modifications done to it. He then went on to indicate that he would like to have a little time on board to get used to being at sea but all in all if things could be arranged he would like to set off for"The Bank" around the 19th. Of October. So if possible if they could be found in the next week that would give enough time." What did you think?" Sidney questioned

When Sidney said this the big man raised his eyebrows and said,"Well if you set off then, you won't be short of company for that's when, what we call "The Game -Cock Fishing Fleet" will sail out of the Humber heading for the same place as you"The Dogger Bank." And because you want a crew for then It's going to make my job of finding one for you all that more difficult." It went without saying, Sidney thought, that it would be even more expensive.

When the big man got up that signaled the end of the interview. He led Sidney to the other door out to the street and said."Come back in two days at the same time and I will be here. Ask for Big Albert. Don't make it any later or I will be gone. I will have a crew for you. But I warn you it will be the best I can get because the others will be out fishing or ready to go out. Don't have any worries, they will sail your boat for you if you keep an eye on them."

He opened the door and before letting Sidney out he shook his hand saying,"If you can't get a cab any tram going up that line," he pointed towards the way Sidney had come,"will take you back into town." But as he went out Sidney turned to him and said,"The research work I am to do and the results I think I will obtain from it have certain commercial implications so I would be grateful if you could be as discrete as possible in the arrangements I am asking you to make."Big Albert" Said simply, touching the side of his nose with his index finger."You can rely on me."

As the door was closed behind him, Sidney walked across the street dodging only one or two carts and bicycles. He stood around for a few minutes before he came to the conclusion that Hessle Road was not a thoroughfare that many taxi cabs might pass along. He decided to break the habit of years and to use public transport. He caught a tram-car. He stepped on the first one that came and asked the conductor if it would take him into town and got the affirmative. He paid and climbed to the top deck and as the car passed within a few score of yards of the docks and the river, he sat thinking on his plans and on how they seemed to be coming together.

The next morning, dressed and breakfasted for 8.30. Sidney had an idea that the message he had received was to do with the hiring of the boat so he picked up the rudimentary drawings he had sketched and made his way to Parliament Street. Once there he was shown into a room where sitting at a desk was the man he had met before. He stood up as Sidney came in and held out his hand."Good morning, I see you got our note. We have some good news for you. We have been able to find you a suitable boat and it is waiting for you at a wharf just up the river at a place called Hessle Haven. Have you managed to hire a suitable crew?"

After shaking the man's hand, Sidney sat down and replied to his question by saying that the question of hiring a crew was well in hand and that he would be able to report on its successful hiring in the next few days. What he did want to do was see the boat, he said and to arrange for one or two simple modifications if that was possible. He did not think it necessary to explain to him what he wanted to do beyond that.

The man took out a set of drawings from a drawer under his desk and he lay them on the table and invited Sidney to look at them as he said,"These are the details of the boat that we have hired for you. All financial arrangements have already been made, hire fees, insurance, bunkering, etc. As I said to you before, the rest is up to you."

Sidney saw in front of him professional drawings of the front, side and end elevation of the same sort of fishing boat that he had seen pictures of when in the library with Miss Newsam. Printed down the margin was the name of the boat and brief technical specifications. Sidney did not understand what they meant beyond the obviousness of the name.

Steam Trawler."JANUS" H 133. 171 ton/63 ton. 110 feet length. 20' – 9 beam. Draught 11'. T.3 Cylinder and boiler. (New Boiler fitted 1903).

"I would like to go now to have a look at the boat. It is moored at a place called Hessle Haven, did you say?" Sidney said." And may I take the drawings?"

The man reached below his desk and picked up a cardboard tube. He rolled up the drawings, put them in the tube and passed them over to Sidney, saying as he did," Yes, Hessle Haven just outside of town down the River. It's all yours. Just bring it back in one piece." He added as an afterthought,"And yourself of course. My clerk at the desk has your account and of course a cheque would be quite in order."

Chapter Thirty Nine

Sidney left the building into October sunshine rolling up his own drawings and putting them in the tube had as he did so. It did not take him long to get a cab and to instruct the cabbie to take him to Hessle Haven. The cabbie dropped him off outside a pub that overlooked an narrow inlet from the estuary. It was crowded with craft of all types. rowing boats, pleasure craft with mast and sails and small fishing boats. The"Janus", its black funnel against the sky was one of the biggest, sitting on mud as the tide was out. As Sidney got to the gangplank a pipe-smoking old man came out of the glass fronted wheelhouse. He was the watchman.

Sidney had no identification papers to show the man so he pulled the drawings out of the tubes and said that the boat had been hired for him and he wanted to look it over. That seemed to be enough for the watchman who gave the impression that he was expecting Sidney and he told Sidney to come on board and as he had just put the kettle on invited Sidney to join him in a cup of tea. Sidney smiled but declined and simply indicated that he wanted to look around the deck. Sidney's priority was to see what place there was for the"tubes" he wanted to get fitted.

As he toured the deck Sidney saw that on the banks of the inlet there were what looked like single storey workshops behind which the business of shipbuilding and repair with its noisy hammers and grinders seemed to be going on. Sidney asked the watchman if there was a sheet metal work shop nearby where he could get some tanks made. The watchman was eager to show off his knowledge of the area and he pointed out that directly across the water there was just what Sidney was looking for. It was, he said a small factory where steel plates were cut and formed and then used to fix damaged ship's hulls. Sidney gave the man his expected tip and after asking instructions on how to get to the other side left the boat.

The workshop Sidney found himself in front of was jammed with mangle like rolling machines, vicious looking, shiny bladed hand operated guillotines and small forges their glowing red coke fires fed by the forced air of bellows worked by boys. The clatter of industry and the foreman directed dedication to task of the rolled sleeved, capped and waist-coated workers on the shop floor meant that Sidney stood unobserved and ignored for some minutes. Eventually a brawny blacksmith his eyes white in the sweat and grime of his face turned from his anvil and his hammer and cocked his head in the direction of Sidney to make the foreman aware of Sidney's presence. The foreman, a short fat man dressed in a three piece suit made dirty and greasy by his work, noticing Sidney's smartness of attire, walked over to Sidney and touching the brim of his black bowler hat, asked,"Is there anything I can do for you sir?"

"Yes", said Sidney, taking out both his drawing and the drawings of the"Janus"I would like to know if you are able to do some work for me."

The foreman suggested that Sidney should lay out the papers on what he called a marking out table. He put a hammer and file on the drawing to keep them flat on the steel surface. Before describing what he wanted Sidney told his"Fish Scientist" story.

The fore man looked at both sets of drawings and the dimensions of the tanks and he cast a glance over the haven to the"Janus"." Will you want us to weld them to the deck, bow and stern?"

"No", said Sidney."I would prefer it if you could fix them by simple brackets to the deck whereby my crew will be able to release the tanks when I have finished my research." The foreman then called over one of his workers. They both looked at the plans and the worker said that he could see no snags that occurred to him and he thought that it would be a fairly straightforward job. Sydney turned to him and said,"Do you think my drawings are accurate and plain enough? The most critical thing is that you get the diameters of the right dimensions." The worker did not address Sidney directly but simply said"Aye, I can work from them drawings." He then went back to the bench he had been working at.

The foreman then asked Sidney if he wanted to be given a price but Sidney demurred. For him it was not a question of money but only if it could be done and most importantly, when." I am sure," Sidney said,"That you will charge me a fair price. I need to have the tanks manufactured and fixed in the next few days and I am prepared to pay generously for good work performed efficiently to a time scale that I must insist on." The foreman saw the opportunity of money being paid for a relatively simple job that would not take up too much time."And anyway," he said to himself,"He's not to know that we haven't got much work in at this time."

He said out loud,"Oh yes sir, I think we can do that for you. Now let's see, today is Thursday, come back towards the beginning of next week and we'll have 'em fixed and all." He then leaned towards Sidney with something of a conspiratorial air and tapped the side of his nose."Do you think that we can make this, what we call around here"A guvvie job sir." I'd rather not put it through the books, if you don't mind. It will be cash on completion won't it sir?" Sidney nodded and took out a purse of sovereigns."Here's two sovereigns for you on account. You can charge me for the rest when the job's finished. Telephone my hotel when the job is done." Sidney wrote the number on a page of his note-book and passed it to the foreman." Now there is something else you can do. Ring for a taxi to get me back into town."

Back in town Sidney lunched once more at"The George." And then went back to his hotel room where he spent a deal of time carefully superimposing his drawings on to the technical drawings of"The Janus" and noting the arrangements he was making. He read and re-read the files he had on The Imperial Second Russian Pacific Fleet and consulted the details of its make-up. He had taken the decision to write in Russian to preserve confidentiality and in his reading of his notes he was taken back to his time at university and it felt as if he was preparing for an examination. There did not seem to be anything that he had omitted but he wanted to confirm this with Melville and also to make sure that his temporary Japanese employers knew just what he was going to do. He decided that he would visit the Wilson Line Offices the next day and make contact through their Lloyds Listening Station wireless.

Friday the eighth of October 1904 saw Sidney getting into a cab outside The Royal Hotel Hull and telling the cabbie to take him to the Wilson line Offices in Commercial Street. Once there he had no difficulty proving his bono fides once he presented his alias George Stanilaus Riley.

He spent the whole day and part of the evening involved in the technicalities, breakdowns, disconnections and delays he expected making national and international contacts by wireless. He was able in the end to get through to Makojiro who was in Brussles and to Melville in London. Their coded replies confirmed their acceptance of his intentions and effectively gave him carte blanche to carry on as he saw fit. At the same time as he was making contact with his principals he indirectly got information from the Listening Station Operators that the" Zero", Wilson's ship- board Wireless Station was still in position monitoring shipping movements well off the southern coast of Sweden and out of The Baltic. She had nothing further to report beyond the already received news that The Second Pacific Fleet would set sail on the 16th of October. As the next day Saturday was when he had arranged to meet"Big Albert" at the"Star and Garter" on Hessle Road, he took another advantage during the time he was at Wilsons and he used that to seek advice on the make-up of a trawler crew."Big Albert" had not led him the wrong way. He would need the crew that had been suggested to man the trawler, at a minimum.

For the rest of the day and into his sleep the staccato bleeps of the Morse code bothered his ears along with the crackle of static and the flash of electric sparks stayed in his eyes.

After asking the doorman of the hotel how to get to Hessle by following the river, Sidney spent the first part of Saturday walking along the River Humber towards Hessle Haven. It was a long walk for him. Hiking was not one of his hobbies. But, it did have the added compensation of being an interesting walk and it was under a clear blue sky, with an autumn chill in the air.

At St Andrews Dock he saw that there was such a community of fishing trawlers moored he could have passed over the dock as if walking over a bridge and there were many others anchored outside. It was evident that the reputation Hull had for being the base of the largest shipping line in the world also applied to its fishing fleet.

Within a mile or so he arrived at the river bank near Hessle Haven. It was a hive of industry with shipbuilding going on to the edge of the water and the ancillary industries of heavy and light engineering engaged in works to support it.

He climbed up the bank to the workshop where he hoped his order was being fulfilled and saw as he looked across the Haven to the"Janus" that the steel cylinders he had designed were already, though not fixed, on the bow and stern deck. He walked round the Haven and up the gang plank onto the boat. The watchman was either not on duty or enjoying a pint in the local bank side pub but that did not prevent Sidney examining the 'fish tanks'. They were blanked off at each end and had the hinged lids he had drawn; two running the length of the wall on the port side and starboard side of the bows and one in the stern. They were just what he wanted. At night, in the dark, at a distance the"Janus" would seem to a ship's lookout for all the world like a torpedo boat about to attack.

He made his way to Hessle the small village inland from the Haven and had a late lunch in a hotel near the railway station. He decided to catch a train for his journey back to Hull.

This was the evening of his second meeting at the"Star and Garter." So he decided to have an early dinner. He bathed and changed deciding on a mode of dress that would not make him too obvious to the clients of the public house. It was difficult, he thought maintaining at least a small impression of anonymity. In an attempt to maintain this, when he arrived at the"Star and Garter" he entered by the side door that he had left on his last visit. When inside the small ante-room he cautiously opened the door to the bar. wide enough to be able to see"Big Albert" dressed in the same suit as before standing at the bar. The public house was even more crowded than before. It was after all, Saturday night. With the action of someone who has a rendezvous, Albert took out his watch from his waistcoat pocket. He was waiting for Sidney.

Sidney attracted the attention of a barman serving towards the end of the bar and indicated to him that he wanted a message passing on to Albert. The barman passed along the bar and Albert bent towards him as he made to whisper in his ear. Albert looked up, caught a glimpse of Sidney as he closed the door and within a minute or two he came in followed by six men and a boy of around 14. They were all in shabby working clothes, two or three unshaven, the rest clean shaven and all looking pretty"down at heel", Almost the precise exemplification of the phrase"motley crew". They each removed their caps and took a chair from a stack against the wall and sat in a row in front of Sidney who had placed himself by the same table as before. Albert brought his chair up to sit next to Sidney. Albert started to introduce what was to be the crew of the"Janus".

Albert began"Well Mr.." but Sidney stopped him by saying,"I don't think it will be necessary to use anything but first names. You can call me Mr. George. I know you as Albert and as far as our friends here are concerned, at this moment I only need to know the name of the skipper. We will have a quite few days together before the trip and we can, if needs be get to know each other then. Who is the skipper?"

A tallish man of around 50 got up. He was wearing dirty flannel trousers a jacket that seemed too big for him and a waistcoat from a different suit and a grubby, once white shirt with no collar. On his feet he had clogs. He still had a shock of now graying hair and on his, hard work lined face, he had a thick moustache the ends of which were stained brown with tobacco. In a strong local accent he said,"Mr. Albert has seen me as the skipper. I have skippered fishing boats for nye on 20 years, not done it for a little while like though but give me a chance to get me hand in and I'll be as good as afore. I've worked with all these men afore, I can vouch for 'em an' say you'll 'ave no trouble wi' 'em. They're all good workers an' know their jobs if yer keep 'em at it in spite of what folks say. I've not worked with the boy though, an' Mr Albert 'll tell yer that we're two short. We 'aven't gorra bosun and we 'aven't gorr a trimmer burras we're not fishin' like we won't be short. Me name is William, Bill I mean." Sidney sensed that that there was something not quite right with this interview and getting up from the table he asked Albert, to step outside.

Once outside the street door he asked Albert what"Bill" meant by, not having skippered for a little while and what he meant when he said,"in spite of what folks say?"

Albert pursed his lips and said,"Look Mr. George you asked me to get you a fishing boat crew. It was at very short notice and at a time when everybody's either at sea or going to sea soon. Beggin' your pardon, you don't know the business. The only men around not working who could sail a boat are those, as we say are"on the cobbles". Nobody wants to take them on because they've rubbed somebody up the wrong way or they've lost their tickets, their licences for one reason or another, as you might say. To be honest with you it's usually the drink. Keep these men sober and they'll be as good a crew as you could wish for. They are the best I could do, you won't do better and they won't cost you the earth. They have not earned a wage for months, some of 'em more than that. They would sail you into Hell for a few shilling."

Sidney reflected on what Albert had said and thought that sailing him into Hell was perhaps what he was going to ask them to do. Seeing that there was little alternative he looked Albert straight in the eyes and said to him,"If you are sure you can vouch for them then, tell them to be at Hessle Haven by eight o' clock Sunday morning, tomorrow. I'll be waiting for them on a boat called the"Janus". They should be ready to start work straightaway. You can tell them that I will pay them three times the normal daily rate and give them a bonus if they bring me and the boat home safe. They will, all being equal have fourteen days work. Should I give them an advance?"

Albert managed to look the nearest he ever came to shocked,"No, no for god's sake no. They'll drink it and piss it up against the wall, if you will excuse my language. No keep them away from the drink. And as for pay well it's a different system. Usually they get a share of the catch. There isn't a daily rate and its worked out pro rata in order of seniority."

Sidney said," tell them then that I will pay half a sovereign a day with a quarter for the boy and everyone gets the same. They either accept that or they don't. I'm leaving now. I shall expect to see them all tomorrow." Sidney had thought that he would employ the crew from a day or so before the nineteenth but it was obvious now that they would need to work together for many days more if they were to be in a state whereby his exercise could be, as far as possible, guaranteed success. Sidney then said to Albert."As for your commission, shall we call it 10% of a round 50.?" Albert had not expected such generosity and he accepted the five sovereigns that Sidney counted out with alacrity. As he turned to go back into the pub, Sidney said."I don't expect we will meet again so thank you for all your help."

Chapter Forty

Sidney rose early and left the hotel before breakfast. He took some time, it being Sunday to find a cab but he was soon on his way to Hessle Haven. When his cab dropped him off outside the bank -side pub he saw that the crew were already there. They had risen early like him but walked their way to the boat. The skipper was in the wheelhouse and chief and second engineer already below. The cook was in the galley and the other two were on the deck.The tide was in and the boat was floating on it under a grey sky with the sun like a pewter trencher hardly shining through it. He was suitably impressed by their punctuality and told them so. They had started as they meant to go on.

He greeted them and asked if they had breakfasted. No one had, substantially, so the boy whose name was Louis was dispatched to shop for eggs, bacon, sausages, tea, condensed milk bread and margarine. The cook was called Horace. He was already busy lighting the galley stove. He was a short man with the appearance of a toothless greyhound on its hind legs. That was Sidney's uncharitable thought. When the boy came back with the provisions Horace soon had an enormous black frying pan spitting and sizzling with eggs, bacon and sausages. A great black "brother" of a kettle bubbled and steamed on the top of the stove. When it boiled tea was spooned into it from a cotton bag and from an opened tin of condensed milk, white sticky syrup was drooled in.

The boat's cupboards held all the crockery and cutlery required although the men had little use for knives and forks or table manners. They ate the breakfast, when it came, sitting around the galley table. They put eggs, bacon and sausages between great dripping doorsteps of fat-dipped bread and swilled it down with the milky heavily sweetened tea. It was the first time that Sidney had dined with the"peasant"class since his time in Odessa. The men however took no exception to his delicate use, by comparison of knife, fork and plate. He drank his tea however, in a somewhat unwieldy pint pot.

After breakfast pipes and cigarettes were lit and Sidney took this as the time to tell them his"Fishing Scientist" Story. Henry, who said he was The Deck Hand, he was a man in his early forties obviously at one time stocky and solid but now with a pot belly and a balding head, asked how Sidney was to obtain his samples when there was no trawl. Sidney did not know what to say. He had unaccountably not given it any thought. He was rescued by Cecil. He said he was the Third Hand."We'll long-line them won't we? That should give t'mister enough samples, isn't that right Mister?" Sidney had to admit that he was right although he didn't know what trawling was and he had the same degree of knowledge of"Long-lining."

The Deck Hand, Henry chimed in here and said that if long-lining was going to be the method then bait, hooks and line would be needed. Everybody agreed, including Sidney. The same measure of agreement was reached when Sidney raised the question of weatherproof clothing and more stores of food for fourteen days. There was general and genuine surprise over the mention of fourteen days. They had all thought the trip would be over in two or maybe three. The prospect of earning half a sovereign a day for two weeks was beyond their wildest dreams.

Sidney decided to let Horace the cook do the organizing of food purchase and Bill the Skipper said that no employer they had ever worked for had ever agreed to providing weatherproof clothing. This was going to be the trip of a lifetime, he said. Little did he know how true that was going to be, thought Sidney. Bill the skipper went on to say that he had never sailed in what was a nearly new boat. His lot he said had been to skipper rust buckets or worse floating coffins and the Chief Engineer a man in his fifties called Seth, tall but with a stoop from working under low bulkheads, wiping his hands on an oily rag had also said that he could not wait to get the boiler steamed up to try the obviously well maintained engine. His Second Engineer a wiry mop haired young man with a black beard and moustache with the name of Archie volunteered the view that they might not need to fill the bunkers up again with coal if the engine was as good as it looked. Henry and Cecil said they would see to lines, hooks and bait.

It was during this euphoria and while he was allocating monies for the various stores and items required that Sidney decided to lay the law down about drink. While they were all gathered together he put forward his conditions. Bill was the skipper he said and in all matters regarding the conduct of the boat and the men on it he was the chief but he Sidney was financing it and according to the old saying he that pays the piper, he was going to call the tune so when it came to a decision that he wanted to take he would insist on taking it. That had to be understood. The other question that he wanted to raise was that of drink. There was to be none on board. For the next fourteen days they were to be off it unless he, Sidney thought a pint or two would not go amiss. If anybody at all got drunk during the trip all bets would be off and that individual would be put ashore and would forfeit all pay. Sidney asked if that was agreed upon. Nobody disagreed. The last point he raised was that of pay. They would all be paid at the end of the trip and if all went well there would be a bonus. The atmosphere of anticipation that statement created was tangible.

The chief engineer with his 2nd who had gone below into the engine room came back up to say that they could have steam up in half an hour and as Bill the Skipper had indicated that with the tide they were on it might be a good idea to cast off to try the boat on the river for a few hours, Sidney agreed.

It was an un eventful trip and the boat seemed to behave well although because the tanks were not fixed progress was slow. True to his word Bill knew how to work the boat and it was obvious that he had experience. He also knew the River Humber with its fast moving tide and the need to follow channels in between sand banks.

They went up on the tide to Goole and a few hours later back to the Haven. The new crew of the "Janus" worked well together. As they moored up again Sidney went ashore to the metal fabricator's work shop and the fore man told him that as agreed the brackets to fix the tanks would be on the next day. Sidney told the crew that he would see them at the same time tomorrow. Bill the skipper, Horace the cook and the boy Louis volunteered to sleep on board as the watchman had left when they arrived.

Next day, by the time that Sidney got to the boat it was a hive of activity. Bill the skipper had the crew at their various jobs and the deck hand and the boy were scrubbing the decks. As smoke was coming from the galley stack it was obvious that Cecil the cook already had breakfast in hand. Shortly after he arrived the workmen came on board to fix the quick release clamps to the tanks. Sidney was pleased with the progress and was not unwilling to pay the bill when the foreman came to settle up.

All being ready Sidney discussed the possibility with Bill of a longer trip down river perhaps staying on the boat over night and returning on Tuesday's morning tide. Bill could not see why not. They had ample provisions and more than enough coal and such a trip would settle the crew down together. They might, he said even do a bit of fishing inshore up the coast towards Hornsea and Withernsea putting in perhaps to Bridlington for the night. Sidney decided that Bill would know best what to do.

The boat was made ready for sea and they went out on the tide from the Haven down river past Saltend, Hedon, Paull and towards Spurn Point and its Light Ship that marked the channel. It took longer to reach the sea than Sidney expected. Hull, he discovered is 30 miles from the mouth of the Humber. They stayed at sea as the harbor master at Bridlington said he hadn't room for a 100 footer. Bill said it was because the boat was registered in Hull. The weather was kind to them however giving them a calm night for an anchorage off Flamborough Head and they caught a lot of cod and haddock by fishing over the side with hooks baited with chunks of mackerel and long-lines. Sidney pretended to have a scientific interest in the size and type of fish caught though he had completely forgotten to bring any recording material. He made a mental note to be prepared when they went out proper.

When the catch was weighed the crew had a stone each. During the return voyage Cecil excelled himself by frying batches of haddock using beef dripping and mixing his recipe batter along with chipped potatoes. Sidney had never had fish and chips before.

They returned on the morning tide of the 12th and Sidney left them tying up the "Janus" at her mooring in the Haven telling Bill the skipper to have the crew ready to sail again on the 15th. As he promised before, they would still be on pay. Sidney was back in time for his assignation at 1.30 with his pretty little librarian; an altogether different kind of catch.

Miss Newsam had thought of little else but Sidney since she had left him to board the tram car home. She had given him her strongest cogitations when just before retiring she sat in front of the oval mirror of her dressing table, candle lit, naked under her lacy night dress brushing her long fair hair. She imagined him half-dressed, reflected, lolling nonchalantly on her bed. She thought she could see him through the bars of her iron brass-trimmed double bed perhaps smoking an exotic cigarette waiting for her. Then she would throw off her nightdress and with it her inhibitions then fold into his embrace for a night of unbridled passion. At least that's what it was suggested the heroines did in the novels she had often read.

Her mother noticed the somewhat distracted attitude she had when ministering unto her. She was slow in returning the chamber pot to the commode, the beef tea was too hot and she took an age getting up for her in the middle of the night to put bed-socks on her cold feet.

At her work in the library there was the fifty year old Chief Librarian Mr. Bickerstaff, a short, bald, portly man with pince-nez that he was always taking off and looking through over his rather bulbous nose under which he wore a toothbrush moustache. He had, unusually, cause to remonstrate with her for replacing works of fiction on the shelves reserved for historical reference.

Ordinarily Mr. Bickerstaff liked Miss Newsam and thought about her a lot. He even thought about her when he was in bed at night awake with his night shirt up to his waist next to his equally portly wife as she snored on her back pressing the paper curlers in her grey hair into the pillow. He thought about Miss Newsam when he was alone in the stack-room dutifully reading "The Romance of Lust or Early Experiences" Anonymous or Guillaume Appollinaire's "Amorous Exploits of a Young Rakehell" (Written to turn a coin when down on his luck in Paris) Both were works banned from public view by members of the library sub-committee of the Kingston Upon Hull Corporation Watch Committee and only available by making a written request to the Chief Librarian. They were cover to cover with "The Japanese Pillow Book", "The Kama Sutra" and "The illustrated Works of Aubrey Beardsley."

Then, the combination of lascivious thoughts about Miss Newsam and the stimulation of erotic literature caused the appendage on his lower abdomen to move through his flannel long-johns against the brass buttons on the fly of his trousers and he had to pause before returning to his desk to register the volumes in the Dewey Decimal Classification System.

When she got up on the day she was to meet Sidney and to take her two days leave Miss Newsam did not see the world as it was. She looked out of her bedroom window and saw, instead of the city's flat, uninterrupted skyline under October's grey dawn clouds, what she thought looked like a fairy castle silhouetted against a blue fantasy sky. She was, it would not be an exaggeration to say, so corrupted by works of literature, she almost gave herself over to the myth that a knight in shining armour might well be riding out under the castle portcullis as she stood looking through her mother's Fleur de Lys patterned lace-curtains.

Her thoughts on Sidney had so preoccupied her in the passing days since their last delightful afternoon together that now she was preparing to meet a man of such thoughtfulness, such tender kindness, a man of such culture, such delicacy of humour, such style in his dress and manner, such sophistication, education and cosmopolitan charm (he had kissed her hand), such wit and intelligence and yet a man of foreign origins who carried with him a tempting hint of dangerous sensuality. That last consideration caused her to catch her breath. She wanted to have his babies. If she had given her state of mind serious attention she would have seen that he was as much a fantasy as the fairy castle. She was as the French say seeing the world through rose-coloured spectacles;"La vie en Rose."

Sidney for his part had returned from the"Janus" to his Hotel room, promptly undressed and stepped into the shower in the bathroom. He felt unclean with alien body odour after his days on the boat enveloped in coal smoke and with people whose personal habits frankly revolted him. There was dirt under his finger nails and he needed a good shave. After his shower he could almost have said that he enjoyed the unadulterated comfort of his time at stool. The food on board had given him constipation. The ablutions on a trawler left a lot to be desired too. The men didn't even bother with the"heads" or to wash themselves afterwards. They did it in a bucket of sea water then threw the contents over the side. The narrow wooden bunks with straw palliasses called affectionately by his crew, he noticed,"Donkey's Breakfasts" were not exactly conducive to sleep for the uninitiated either and because of that Sidney took time before dressing for his rendezvous to have a little nap. He could not say that he was looking forward to what was going to be almost a week on the boat.

After what could only be called a doze, Sidney dressed simply and went down stairs to the desk to arrange the hire of a car and driver to come to the hotel entrance for around one fifteen. He also asked the kitchen that a picnic lunch be made up for two and he made a special request for a bottle of champagne with some smoked salmon. He noted the costs so that he could include all in his expenses claim.

He thought that a drive in the country in an automobile might be a good way to spend the afternoon and to impress Miss Newsam with his originality when it came to organizing an outing. He enquired of the desk clerk with regard to an interesting destination but one not too far given the time available. The Clerk suggested Beverley, the market town not far from Hull with a grand Minster and a very desirable place for tea, The Beverley Arms Hotel. That done Sidney returned to his room to dress.

He went down just before one fifteen and the motor was already there outside on the entrance drive to the hotel. It was painted red and was a Renault Type T. The luxurious leather upholstery was also in red. The driver sat in front of the brass framed windscreen at the great wooden steering wheel in his hat, goggles, gloves and driving coat. Behind the large round brass and glass headlamps the engine was running and blue smoke was issuing from a pipe at the back. A kitchen hand put the picnic hamper in and Sidney asked the driver if there were coats, hats, gloves and goggles for him and his passenger and the driver said that they were in"the boot". Sidney looked puzzled."It's at the back sir, behind, the seat under the door where you get in. I'll get the things for you."

Sidney put the heavy ankle- length weatherproof coat over his suit and replaced his hat with the more substantial motoring cap, put on the brown leather gauntlets adjusted his goggles and climbed into the back seat through the rear door and then told the driver to go around the corner into Albion Street and to stop near the library and to wait for his other passenger.

When Miss Newsam came out of the library she didn't realize that the motor was for her until Sidney approached with her car coat over his arm, doffing his cap saying,"Your carriage awaits madam"

She was amazed. She had never been driven in a an automobile before. She had once been a passenger in a char-a-banc, but a motor with a chauffeur. She could not believe it.

Sidney helped her on with her coat, hat and gloves as passersby watched with interest and once he and Miss Newsam were in their seats he asked her where she would like to go. He said he had considered Beverley but it really was up to her to choose.

Miss Newsam made up her mind immediately and she said excitedly, once more with the enthusiasm of a child that for Sidney did not have this time quite the same erotic frisson as before."Oh let's go to the sea-side, I love the sea-side, let's go to the sea-side. Let's go to Hornsea. It isn't much further than Beverley and it is such a pretty little sea-side town. My daddy use to take me there when I was a little girl. I know it is autumn but there will be shelters on the promenade where we can have the picnic you have prepared."

Sidney looked at the driver and without him having to ask the driver said,"Yes sir that will be quite in order. It is only some sixteen miles way and I have sufficient fuel and a spare can on the running board."

So Sidney agreed, although it was against his better judgment in spite of his generally held view that"You should always let them have their own way." His judgment was confirmed as they had only left the eastern suburbs of Hull when they were enveloped in a sea fret that made the journey quite uncomfortably cold even with the heavy motoring coats on.

Once in Hornsea, and Sidney had already seen it from the sea on the "Janus" the driver left them to spend the hour or so they said they would be walking on the sand and eating their picnic.

The day was not much of a success as the beach was completely deserted and the only promenade shelter they found in which to eat what was quite a luxurious picnic, was exposed to the wind. Cold spray whipped off the tops of high waves that crashed heavily against the beach breakwaters managed to reach where they were sitting, Even champagne in such circumstances does not work its magic. Miss Newsam or Chloe as she now insisted that Sidney should call her, had to admit that her enthusiasm for the sea-side might well have been too much coloured by childhood memories.

There were further disappointments to come. On the way back one of the front wheels got a puncture and there was no where they could shelter as the driver changed the tyre. But the most disconcerting one for Sidney, as he had other designs in his mind was that Chloe said she had to be home to see to her mother by seven o' clock in the evening. He had planned a visit to the theatre, a late supper and then an invitation for Chloe to come back to his hotel room for a night-cap so that he could perhaps have got his hands past the elastic of her underwear. He didn't tell her that however but simply asked the chauffeur that she be driven home with an arrangement to see her the next day, her mother permitting of course.

Chloe arrived home to her mother's usual grumblings. She had been alone all day and had suffered one of her "turns". She had not had an appetite for the cold cuts lunch that Chloe had left for her even though Chloe noticed she had cleared her plate and the sheets over the rubber mattress cover of her bed were wet because she hadn't been able to get out of bed quickly enough. Chloe tried to explain that the day was no different to a working day.

There was a difference as far as her mother was concerned. There was the possibility, although her mother knew nothing about Sidney, that Chloe might be enjoying herself. Hypochondriacs have something in common with psychopaths, extreme egocentricity.

Chloe was aware that the day had been disappointing both for her and for Sidney. She did not want the next two days of her leave to be wasted so she went to call on their next door neighbour, Mrs. Harrison. From time to time, but not often Mrs. Harrison had agreed to keep an eye on Mrs. Newsam when Chloe had found it necessary to stay late at work. Chloe did not like asking for the favour because she knew that Mrs. Harrison would gossip about her, her mother and the condition of the house, which Chloe had not always the time to keep as clean as neighbourhood standards decreed.

Notwithstanding Chloe asked her to look in from time to time over the next two days when she, Chloe was not at home. Mrs. Harrison readily agreed. Apart from other considerations she enjoyed sharing Mrs. Newsam's tonic wine. Chloe explained to her mother that Mrs. Harrison would call in and if she needed to she could always knock on the wall to summon her.

Mrs. Newsam was more interested in where Chloe would be if not with her. Chloe lied," I have to be on some library business out of town which necessitates me catching an early train to York and I may not be back until possibly the last train." Chloe had never lied to her mother before and it surprised her that she should be so facile and glib. She would, she said to herself, with such an excuse, be able to stay out quite late with Sidney.

Chapter Forty One

Sidney took his disappointment and the picnic hamper back to the hotel. He then went up and after a simple dinner, that he asked to brought to his room he sat at the desk and wrote a comprehensive report for Motojiro. He wrote it in Russian knowing that Motojiro's Russian was better than his English. He included all the activities he had involved himself in and the strategy of his plan and the tactics he was going to use to bring it about. He included a précis of the meeting he had attended at Melville's office and a carefully worked out list of expenses that took into account the monies he was likely to have to lay out for the next few days on the boat, his hotel bill and his travel to Belgium. He felt no conscience at inflating it by 50%. That was to allow for any errors he might have made in his calculations.

He then wrote a series of letters to Margaret. His attempts to make contact with her recently had been in vain and he wanted now to make the question of their divorce more formal. He wrote the same letter to her Kensington address, her bank and to her solicitors writing at the same time to his own. He then wrote to his own bank informing them to stop the amount transferred to her account from his each month that was her allowance. If nothing else did, that would elicit a response from her he wryly smiled to himself.

The next day was more of a success. It was bright sunny day and Sidney said to Chloe when they met in the morning that they return to his original suggestion and take a trip to Beverley but this time by train.

They toured the ancient town and visited the medieval Minster that Chloe said rivaled York for its magnificence. Tea at the Beverley Arms was classic with delicious sandwiches, cake and scones and cream and jam. When they caught the train home Chloe was in a euphoric mood. Her mood was such that Sidney decided to make a proposal that he wondered if she would accept. He invited her to his room in the hotel. To his mild surprise she was not shocked, her only reservation was, because she was known in this small town, how she might come to it without being seen by the hotel staff. Sidney said that it would be simple. They would enter the hotel individually by the rear entrance from the station and then he would go up first to open the door and she should follow as if she were a hotel guest. This she did.

Once she was in the room Sidney locked the door and without any further ado he took her in his arms and kissed her with a passion that was just as she had imagined he would. He took her long fair out of its pins and let it down to below her shoulders.

She hesitated at first. She felt that the situation was developing too quickly for her to control. She hardly knew him. Courtships went on for months before they reached the point where two people could actually be alone together especially for girls of her class never mind be passionately kissed. But she could not, in spite of convention conceal her desire for him. It was as if the fact of his foreignness allowed her access to his culture; after all foreigners did things so much differently, particularly when it came to sex.

That was the reason she said to herself why she did not resist when he helped her off with her jacket, then her blouse and finally the hooks of her skirt were unfastened and she stood in her corset, her underwear with lace frills at the knee, her white stockings and high boots. She almost fell into his arms and he carried her over to his bed. There he stood over her and undressed himself. She knew what was going to happen. She was about to be seduced and she could do no more than welcome it. As she prepared herself mentally she could only think of the ridiculous story of the spinster lady in India during the Mutiny who was advised, as she was about to be taken by a Sepoy,"To lie back and think of England."

Within a short time Sidney had taken off her upper garments and made her half naked and he was lavishing kisses on her breasts and caressing her belly and the mound of her sex with his left hand as he brought her fair head and mouth with his right hand to his lips for the kisses that were arousing her to distraction. No one had ever put their tongue into her mouth and she could not believe it could be so sweet. He then lay her gently on her back and moved his head between her thighs unfastening the strings of her underwear as he did and drawing her silk knickers down over her bottom, his fingernails gently touching her hips with a tenderness that overpowered her. He took her knickers over her boots leaving her nude but for them and her stockings. She closed her blue eyes and gave herself over completely to the exquisite pleasure of his tongue in the groove of her silky hair covered sex, finding, as it did with its tip, the swollen boss of her clitoris.

Miss Chloe Newsam was not a virgin. At twenty two she had donated her virginity to her first young lover. He was a boy of the same age who in a bout of beer bravado patriotism had taken the king's shilling and gone to be a soldier. For King and Country he enlisted in The East Yorkshire Regiment to fight the foreign foe in South Africa, on this occasion The Boers. During a tearful farewell, on the night of his marching away he had cajoled himself into her. Their uncomfortable lovers' bed had been a sack full of potting compost in her father's shed, at the bottom of the garden. He had quickly taken her, panting on her breast with his exertions. She waited for the gates of paradise and pleasure to open as her reading had promised. Instead all she got was a sharp pain and the sensation of something stretching until it tore and she felt what she later discovered was blood on her thighs. Within seconds he had withdrawn and ejaculated prematurely into the gusset of the white cotton of her knee length knickers and she was left wondering what all the fuss was about.

She sought consolation and hid her shame and guilt by thinking that at least she had given herself up for a dead hero, for he never came back. He never came back because he jumped ship at Dover, deserted and he had been living, since then, off the earnings of a young woman of gypsy origin in Folkestone. He only went out at night. But Chloe Newsam wasn't to know that.

Sidney's lovemaking expertise, however was born out of fornication, promiscuity and the tuition of older women, that in its priceless generosity had combined the maternal and the professionally carnal. He knew how to make the glowing skin of Chloe one tissue of delight. As they made love, he coming into her with a gentleness that caused their connection, she thought, to be like something from the world of nature. They both perspired with their exertions and their sweat oiled them both as if for a massage. They slid against each other as they began to come to the conclusion of their love-making. She reached her climax with noises emanating from her that she did not think she was capable of making.

Sidney got up from her and as she wrapped herself in one of the sheets he told her the time. It was already 8.30.

"Are you hungry?" he asked her. Her reply was that she was absolutely famished but it was perhaps time for her to go home.

"Don't worry", he said," I will order you a taxi but we must have something to eat before you go."

She got up and went into the bathroom and he followed her and quite unselfconsciously retrieved a douche from a cupboard."You must use this." He said" and I have a solution for you to add to the water that will ensure that you will be safe." He took a bottle from the same cupboard and left her to deal with it herself. She had not given the possibility of pregnancy any thought. She reflected later that perhaps she wanted it to happen. He had to return when she asked because she had not used such a device before. He helped her and it seemed the most ordinary thing in the world for him to do.

When she came back into the room to get dressed he was already in a dressing gown speaking on the hotel's internal telephone and asking that tea and sandwiches be sent up. He said,"! Will take you outside so that you can get a taxi from the station." But really all that she was concerned about was being able to leave his room and the hotel without being recognized.

"Don't worry about that, I will see that everything is alright."

And it was, she dressed and she ate the sandwiches that were brought up which he insisted on collecting at the door in spite of the waiter wanting to place them on a table and to pour the tea.

He put on street clothes and took her down the back stairs discretely to the rear entrance of the hotel and out to the station taxi-rank giving her the fare as he left her. They were to meet the next day. She was to come up to his room via again, the rear entrance to the hotel as soon as she arrived in town.

She sat in the back of the taxi, the first time she had ever been a passenger in one and felt that she had grown older in the most positive of ways. When she arrived home she dealt with the peevish mutterings of her mother with an acerbity that Mrs. Newsam was not used to but she responded to it anyway and Mrs. Harrison was ushered out of the house with a florin that she had not expected but nonetheless accepted.

When Chloe prepared herself for bed that night she felt it was a woman that she undressed. When She looked at herself naked in the mirror it was a different person who looked back at her. Her body though it hadn't changed externally was she thought, decidedly different internally. She was desired. She had been penetrated as she thought her destiny as a woman required. It made her feel confident but more significantly, complete. She had used a douche as a method of contraception. What could be more grown up? The next stage in this process was, she thought going to be even more exquisite. Love next time would also mean the possibility of the beginnings of a respectable courtship that might, and she hardly dared think about it, lead to matrimony.

The next morning she left for the first tram into town. Her mother of course grumbled but Chloe ignored her. Mrs. Harrison would come in again. In fact Mrs. Harrison, ever on the alert moved the lace curtains aside and waved from her window signaling that she could be relied on as Chloe walked down the terrace.

It was relatively early so there was no one around at the hotel. Chloe was confident that she had been unobserved as she climbed the back stairs to Sidney's room. She was excited by the subterfuge.

He was at his desk sorting out the correspondence he had prepared and waiting for her gentle knock on his door. It came and as he let her in said that he had ordered enough breakfast for two having kept a cup, saucer and plate from the day before to maintain the secrecy of their illicit and clandestine assignation. What it also maintained was the ambience of mysterious conspiracy that added to the eroticism of their rendezvous. He locked the door behind her.

As soon as she got in the door Chloe cast off her shame as speedily as she cast off her clothes. That morning she had not put on her corset. Sidney had not dressed and was still in his pyjamas covered only by his dressing gown. Her recollection of the previous day was still so fresh and she had spent the night reliving it so that she wanted her hands on his bare skin and her lips on his before any consideration of breakfast. He for his part was instantly aroused by her zealous movement towards him and she felt him rise against her belly so that she wanted to make love with him without any delay. Sidney in his career had introduced a number of demure, if not prim young women to the pleasures of the flesh but once so introduced, it never ceased to surprise him how rapidly they developed an enthusiasm for love and sexuality.

She moved Sidney towards the bed, lay on it and guided him into her and in a passion of embraces she made love to him eagerly and quickly welding herself to him with her legs around his hips as she came to climax, threshing her head and her hair from side to side in vigorous exertions.

He lay with her for a few minutes as she seemed, with her eyes closed, to be resting from the energy she had expended. They were both aroused from what promised to be slumber by a knocking at the door. Sidney told Chloe to go to the other side of the room while he unlocked and opened the door.

It was a waiter with the breakfast Sidney had commanded. Sidney took it from him, put the tray on a small table by the door, signed the bill and tipped him a six penny piece.

Sidney locked the door again and took the tray over to the bed and in dressing gowns, Chloe wearing the one provided by the hotel, they enjoyed the breakfast together. Sidney poured coffee into the cup he had put to one side for Chloe and they took it in turns to use the one set of cutlery that had come with the double helping of eggs, bacon, rolls, toast, butter and marmalade that Sidney had judiciously ordered.

After eating his fill and leaving Chloe to enjoy another cup of coffee, Sidney got up from the bed and went into the bathroom. He needed to shave.

As he stropped his razor he heard the crash of crockery and the beginning of a cry that was becoming a scream. He rushed into the room and saw to his surprise, Chloe standing by the desk her feet in the broken crockery and the remains of breakfast, her gown open showing her nakedness and she was holding his pistol and a handful of papers. She was about to scream again but as she saw him she choked the words out of her mouth, her face was white and her eyes blazing in it."You are a spy, a Russian spy." She then beat the desk and with each violent blow on the desk top with the fist grasping the papers, she screamed out hysterically. her face contorted and her teeth bared. Each scream had a second or two between it like the chiming of some gothic fantasy clock."You're married…. You're married….. You're married….. You're married.. You bastard you're married." She had heard the word pronounced by others but this was the first time her own mouth had formed it.

She had got up from the bed to finish her coffee and drifted over to put the breakfast tray on the desk. When she saw the untidy collection of papers, it had not been her intention to pry. She was simply expressing the curiosity one lover has for the other as she casually browsed through the envelopes, letters and writings strewn on its gold tooled green leather cover.

In an act of totally untypical carelessness Sidney had left the letters he had written to Margaret on the desk top intending to collect them together and to post them. One of them, the one to his banker was out of the envelope. Not only had he been careless enough to do that but the report to Motojiro was under them and the drawer where he kept his pistol was half-open.

As Chloe read the words Sidney had written to his banker……"Sirs please take this letter as instruction to cease the monthly payment to my wife Margaret Callahagn Reilly…." Her jaw dropped and her eyes widened to great black-lashed blue and white circles Her apprehension of what she read allied with her shock at seeing the Russian Cyrillic script of the report with its technical drawings of mock torpedo tubes. She put two and two together and came up with the reason why he had asked her in the library for photographs of fishing boats and torpedo boats. All this welded together with her horror and dawning comprehension and she spontaneously grasped the pistol out of the drawer. The combined effect of all that had happened in the last few minutes produced a psychological chemistry in her that was as strong in its explosive potential as carbon, saltpeter and sulphur fuse to make gunpowder blow up.

At the time all the newspapers and magazines she set out for readers in the library were alive with stories that incited Russian spy mania and what were described as Russian atrocities. Their navy had commandeered a P & O steamer and even gone to the extent of sinking a British ship.. To believe the newspapers you would have thought that there was a Russian Spy or a Russian Anarchist round every corner with a bomb under his cloak. A deal of anti-Russian feeling had been stirred up.

For her part Miss Chloe Newsam was a committed pacifist. She had personally introduced the works on International Peace by Hodgson Pratt and Countess Bertha Von Suttner onto the shelves of The City Library. Like all the thinking young women of her day she felt as many others that Women's Suffrage went hand in hand with a world without war. It was one reason why the establishment didn't want to give women the vote. It was thought they might not vote for war and war was the spring that made the bells of The British Empire chime. But for Chloe and her like there was no greater crime against humanity than war-mongering. Women and especially Chloe Newsam were pro love and pro peace and at this moment in time for Chloe love was pretty high on the agenda.

But, the accelerator that really fuelled the flames that furiously heated Chloe's brain was the discovery that Sidney was married. It set fire to her dreams of married love, of the suburban villa with rooms for her mother, (paid for by joint salaries) the pictures of two maybe three children, the reservations for the holidays in the Lake District and the photograph of the family group round the tree as Christmas, all went up in smoke.

As she rushed across the room Sidney did not get to her quickly enough to stop her banging on the locked door with one fist, the pistol in the other and shouting and screaming through it,"He's a spy, help me, let me out, he's a spy, a Russian spy." She wanted revenge for his deception and she would have it one way or another.

She was still screaming when he put his arm round her neck, knocked the pistol from her grip and then clamped his hand over her mouth. She struggled and kicked and tried to get her fingernails to his face but he held her tight. He did not try to explain. He did not offer excuses or reassurances that he was to divorce nor did he retell his story of being in fishing. He could have said that the report in Russian was for that but he didn't. He certainly wouldn't have said that he was a British Agent working for the Japanese.

He just held her tighter and tighter, his hand now over both her mouth and nose. As he held his arm round her neck he leaned back so that both her feet were off the floor. She could not breath. He was suffocating her and his arm was slowly strangling her. She could only make muffled sounds. After some minutes her struggles became weaker and weaker and the knocking of her heels against his shins stopped. Her feet began to tremble in reflex, her toes pointing down. From passionate but tender lover he had been transformed into The Angel of Death.

He held her without moving for some time, maybe 15 minutes. It was not that the horror of what he had done had transfixed him it was because of simple questions of practicality. He wanted to make sure she was dead and that no one had heard her cries. His mind then turned immediately to how he would dispose of her body. He would have to get busy. He had to arrange that his luggage go on to the ferry to Belgium and the big project would have to get underway again. It was Friday the 14th. of October, tomorrow was Saturday and they would need to go to sea on Sunday at the latest.

Chapter Forty Two

Sidney took his arm from around Chloe's neck and put it under her knees. With the other arm under her shoulders her head lolled down backwards with her long fair hair almost touching the floor. He did not find that she was very heavy as he carried her into the bathroom. Her face was already turning blue. Her eyes were glazed and fixed in her last look of fear, her tongue protruded from her mouth and she stank. She had soiled herself in her ultimate paroxysm of terror.

He laid her in the bathtub and passed his fingers over eyes to close them but he could not get her tongue back into her mouth. He fetched all her clothes, her boots and her bag, put them in the bathtub with her and went out of the bathroom locking it behind him with the key that was in the door then put the key in his pocket.

Sitting on the bed holding the pistol he had picked up from the floor he turned his mind to how he would get rid of her. In thinking this he inevitably thought of the time they had spent together. He was sad that it had come to what it had. He cursed himself for being so careless. Had he not been he would simply have left her and that would have been that. Once he had left Hull he could not, for the for seeable future, think of any reason why he might return. He did not see himself as a criminal so there would be no question of a return to the scene of the crime. There was always the possibility that Melville or the Japanese might have other work for him but it wouldn't necessarily be here in Hull.

He could not bring himself to regret what had happened. Had he let her get away the whole business would have been exposed. This was an affair of state. It was not subject to the usual scale of moral considerations. In a world of governments where conspiracy, subterfuge, clandestine agents and perfidy replaced diplomacy the death of one individual had to be counted against the possibility that whole cultures, the political union of nations, Monarchial, Imperial and economic systems might trek disastrously to their doom.

There was a war going on, The Russo-Japanese war. Albeit it was across the world but one aspect of that war, The Second Imperial Pacific Fleet would soon be sailing a very nearby sea. He, Sidney Reilly had been given the not inconsiderable responsibility of delaying the progress of that Fleet and thereby participating in and hopefully influencing the strategic outcome of that war in the favour of his paymasters, The Japanese.

Miss Chloe Newsam, Christian teetotaler, dutiful daughter, respectable librarian, law-abiding citizen and spinster of this parish had made the discovery, too late for her, that the modus operandi of even the mature democracy with its Constitutional Monarchy that she gave her most loyal support to, was government by assassination. Poor Chloe had done it all for love but she had left nothing of that behind. Mors rapit omnia, Death clears everything away.

It did not take Sidney long to work out what he should do next. First he would sort out his luggage and its destination. After he had done that he dressed and making sure the bathroom door was secure, he went out locking his room behind him putting a "Do not Disturb" notice on the door knob. On the landing below he met one of the maids and he told her that he was packing his luggage and didn't want his sheets changing until later. He went then to a ship's chandler that he had noticed on the dockside where the trawlers were moored.

Once there he asked to be supplied with the biggest tin luggage trunk they had. It had to have straps and hasps on it so that it could be locked. They would also supply the locks. And he asked to avail himself of their labeling service. They were used to requests such as"Not wanted on Voyage" and"Port Side Out Starboard Side Home" being painted on trunks. He wanted something different. He wanted his trunk which was blue, painted with words in black on both sides indicating"Department of Fisheries and Agriculture"Delicate Scientific Instruments"Fragile Handle with Care". He told them he would like it ready to be delivered to the Royal Hotel that afternoon if at all possible.

It came and was in his room by five o' clock of that evening. After it had been delivered and he had tipped the delivery man, he had a lot of difficulty getting Chloe and all her traps in it. She had already stiffened significantly: rigor mortis was quickly setting in. She was on her back and her hands and fingers had taken on the claw-like syndrome of the stiffening dead. He put the open trunk by the side of the bath and found, as he contrived to fit her in it that he had to put her on her side and to considerably exert himself to bend her at the neck, hips and knees. He contemplated momentarily cutting her into pieces but rejected the scheme as far too bloody. He did however think on the fact that had he been nearer London he could have called on someone else to clear up the mess.

At last he was able to close the lid and to lock it with the two padlocks provided. He rang to the desk and had the desk clerk call a carter. He gave his room a"Boy Scout Last Look Round" to make sure he had not left anything behind that might identify him or incriminate him and when the carters came he supervised them as they carefully took the trunk downstairs to the horse-drawn, flat-bedded cart they had come on. They did not comment on its weight. Sidney told them to wait as he would be going with them and he paid his hotel bill, checking the extras charged, such as the breakfasts and other meals he had taken in his room. He then went out to the cart and told the driver to take him to Hessle Haven. On the cart he looked for where he should sit. The only place, as the driver and his mate took up the seat, was on the trunk.

Once at Hessle Haven, they unloaded the trunk on to the deck of the"Janus". There was only Bill The skipper and Cecil on board with the boy and he was quickly sent to get the others. Sidney paid the carters and as the cart was going back along Hessle Road the boy went with it. That speeded things up. Sidney wanted to sail that evening although it was nearly a day earlier. Bill saw no reason why not. They were"coaled up" and provisioned enough for at least a week at sea. They would get steam up when the engineers arrived and be ready for sea on the tide.

After an uneventful trip down the Humber the next morning, Saturday the 15th. of October saw them moored in Grimsby's Royal Dock under the shadow of Grimsby Dock Tower, a magnificent 300 feet copy, almost, of the Torre de Mangia in The Palazzo Pubblico in Siena. Being a product of Victorian Industrial practicality it went beyond the architecturally aesthetic and had a technological function, to provide hydraulic power for opening, among other functions the dock gates.

The dock was crammed with fishing boats. They were being prepared for amalgamation in"The Gamecock Fleet" due to sail to the Dogger Bank in four days time.

Sidney had ordered Bill to sail into Grimsby to obtain a buoy and cable for the trunk full of"Scientific Instruments" that Sidney had convinced the crew he had to set down on the sea-bed. The"instruments" would gauge sea temperatures, record currents and sea-bed conditions relevant to fish habitat (In order to facilitate this holes had to be drilled in the sides). In reality Sidney's intention was to attach a rope so loosely to the trunk and the buoy that rope and buoy would drift away after a short time and so the trunk would never be recovered. He had thought of everything.

Sidney was pleased with the way things were going, particularly as they seemed to have the time he thought would be needed to get to"The Dogger Bank" by around the 20th. of October. He therefore decided that they should stay in Grimsby until the next day's tide. They would have dinner on board and Sidney consented to the purchase of bottled beer. The day developed in to quite a party. Just to be on the safe side they took on more coal."There would be plenty of space in the fish rooms,"Said Seth. For further good measure they bought more provisions. The generally held view on the part of the men of the crew was that they had never been fed so well on any trip they had ever made.

It was less of a party for Mrs. Newsam. She had slept all through the night and she wanted her breakfast. Chloe was late bringing it to her and she knew Chloe had to go to work on this Saturday morning.

She was so irritated that she got out of her bed and shouted for Chloe up the stairs. There was no reply. The house gave back only an eerie silence to Mrs. Newsam's increasingly vociferous cries, that were by now bordering on extreme crossness. She did what she had not done since she had taken to her invalid bed after donning the cloak of widowhood, she climbed the stairs up to Chloe's bedroom. It was empty and the bed had not been slept in. Chloe had stayed out all night. What was she supposed to do for her breakfast? She banged on the wall for Mrs. Harrison.

At the library Mr. Bickerstaff took his full hunter watch from his waistcoat. He was proud of his watch. It had been presented to him by the chairman of the Library Committee in recognition of his long service. He liked the click it made as he opened the lid. It was gold-filled and guaranteed for ten years and made in Prescott, Lancashire. Only the best English watches were made in Prescott. He compared the time indicated by the black fingers on the white dial with the time on the mahogany library wall clock. Miss Newsam was late. She was never late. He looked forward to the frisson of excitement he would feel as he exercised his authority over her and invited her into his office to take her to task. Miss Newsam in her self-effacing modesty had never been aware of the effect she had on Mr. Bickerstaff or people generally, men or women.

The fact of Miss Newsam's lateness at the library combined with her absence from her bed and from chapel on Sunday elicited such a degree of anxiety on the part of those concerned that by Monday morning there were serious discussions as to whether the police ought to be called. By that time Chloe was being buried at sea 30 nautical miles north, north east of Spurn point. Microscopic sea creatures were already investigating her wrinkled skin for nutrients A red painted buoy marked the spot bobbing on the waves with Bill confidently predicting that with the bearing he had taken on The Spurn Lightship, they would have no problem retrieving it on the return voyage. Sidney was privately less optimistic; with good cause, he had tied the knot of the rope.

As the trunk that now served as Chloe's coffin rocked and seesawed its way up and down in a slow descent through the 50 metres or so of murky cold waters to the bed of the North Sea off the East Coast of England, Admiral Z.F. Rozhdestvensky of The Imperial Russian Navy aboard his flag ship the modern Battleship"Prince Souvoroff" was finishing his breakfast of Kasha, bread and tea. He was almost at his wits end. He had passed a sleepless night. In fact it was one of many since he had been ordered by Czar Of All The Russias, Nicholas the Second to organize the Baltic fleet, his command, into a fighting force to take on the Japanese at Port Arthur a mere 18.000 miles away.

He had managed to form up a collection of ships that became known as the Second Pacific Fleet. It was made up of coastal defence vessels whose guns were obsolete and short range. There were warships with antiquated engines and only a handful of modern armoured cruisers and battleships.

Whatever, with enormous effort on his part and on the part of hundreds of his subordinates, many of his ratings being inexperienced and untrained, this fleet of forty two supply and maintenance vessels, warships and four modern battleships had been assembled in the Port of Libau and they were at last ready to sail. It was the 16th of October 1904 and because of rumours that ranged through Japanese sabotage, mine laying, submarines and torpedo boats Rozhdestvensky had given the order for the fleet to sail a day earlier than planned and he commanded that The Fleet was to be divided into to two squadrons sailing the same course in line astern but with an interval between the sailing of the first squadron and the second.

Eventually both squadrons put to sea for what was to become an epic voyage that was to go down in the annals of naval record. The fleet from vanguard to rearguard stretched for many miles. Old and obsolete many of the ships might have been, it was still the greatest expression of naval power in modern history and definitions such as"obsolete" have to be, in an age of industrial revolution, set against the speed of technological developments. There were ships of the"Suvorov" and" Borodino" class and battle wagons that at one time had been considered of innovatory design exampled by the"Peresviet" class and they when launched had even put the wind up the British Navy. However the world's press wrote about the armada, and the newspapers of Randolf Hearst and Lord Northcliffe gave over pages to its description, the sheer scale of it, nonetheless demonstrated that Imperial Russia was still one of the most powerful nations in the world.

The cargo ship"Zero" belonging to the Wilson Line remained on station well off the Danish coast within binocular range and it was soon sending radio signals on the Lloyd's Listening Station Wave Band indicating the size, speed, course and make- up of the Second Imperial Fleet as it took the hours it did to steam west of the sea lanes off the southern coast of Norway with the western coast of Denmark to port.

As well as sending the"Zero" was also receiving and listening and it had a lot of Morse code to listen to. From the Russian ships, at the beginning to the end of the great extended line of vessels a confusion of radio messages was being transmitted by Russian Navy telegraphists and the"Zero" was picking them up. The message content indicated a general anxiety on the part of all captains and commanders in the Russian ships. The signals transmitted…"Japanese Torpedo Boats and vessels having the appearance of torpedo boats have been sighted. outside torpedo range" continued to be transmitted for the next few days. Makojiro's matelots were obeying their orders.

The signals were passed on by Lloyds to the Admiralty Intelligence Service who then communicated them to all H.M.Ships in the relevant sea areas. A signal was sent particularly to Vice-Admiral Gerard Noel commander of the British Royal Naval Home Fleet 300 or so nautical miles to the west already manoeuvring to make a parallel course with the Russian fleet, south. No signal was sent to the"Admiral" of"The Gamecock Fleet". That fleet did not have Radio Technology and within a couple of days it would, all nearly one hundred fishing boats in it, be sailing from Hull and then Grimsby out of the Humber bound for the north eastern fishing grounds of The Dogger Bank.

Had "The Admiral" received a signal he might have considered delaying departure by perhaps a day. He would have been justified in the interests of safety at sea or just plain caution. He was to set sail through waters into which two of the largest and most powerful Navy Fleets in the world were to steam, both on War Alert. There was an International protocol recognized by navies around the globe that permitted the maintenance of an exclusion zone around fleets on War Alert. If a vessel entered such a zone by design or accident it could be regarded as belligerent and so fired upon. It was later incorporated into The International Laws of the Sea ratified in 1909.

What The"Admiral," Mr. Foot did do when the fleet set sail for"The Dogger Bank" was to stay onshore. It was unaccountable and it was unprecedented. He transferred the responsibility for this trip of "The Gamecock Fleet" to his deputy, Mr. Thomas Carr.

For Mr Foot it meant a significant economic sacrifice. As he had relinqushied his position as Admiral to his deputy he would not get his, usually substantial, share of the catch.

The"Gamecock Fleet" sailed out of the Humber on the 19th. of October. By this time the"Janus" with George Stanilaus Reilly alias Sidney George Reilly, Alias Sigmund Georgiovitch Rosenblume on board had been at sea for almost three days and had been long-lining on The Dogger bank and catching a lot of fish and storing it in the tanks on her deck A whole range of fish species had been caught that Sidney, in his wish to maintain his identity as a fish scientist was assiduously cataloguing, (he had brought stationery and writing implements this time) dissecting and even photographing.

His, by now thoroughly"shaken down" crew was assisting him and manning the"Janus" with effectiveness and efficiency. They had been helped most importantly by the weather which had as, Bill said. been"very kind". They carried on fishing. It was the easiest trip any of the fishermen on board had ever experienced. Apart from his"scientific" activities, Sidney had spent a lot of time sleeping.

On the morning of Thursday the 20th of October Sidney enquired of Bill the skipper whether they could move further east as the variety of fish being caught seemed to be diminishing. Bill's opinion was that it would diminish even more if they moved east as it was the generally held view in fishing circles that the waters to the east of"The Bank" were being over fished by the Scandinavians, the Germans and The Dutch. Sidney's motive was of course to get closer to the position of 55* 18' North and 5'East that was, in the next day or so, if all calculations coincided to be the approximate location of the first ships to pass of the Russian Fleet. However Bill's reply to Sidney's mild insistence was simply"You're the boss".

Bill set a course north by north east. rang down to Seth the chief engineer for full ahead and the"Janus" responded positively to the helm. There was hardly a sea running at all. Archie, the second engineer was also stoker and after twelve steady shovels full of coal in to the fire, he knocked the fire door shut and wiped the sweat off his brow with a dirty rag. The deck hand, the boy and the cook wound in the lines and Horace the cook went into the galley to"rustle up a pan of shackles".

Between 1.15 and 4.15 of the afternoon of the 21st. of October the Second Russian Squadron passed"The Zero". She relayed by radio all the information regarding the Squadron she could collect. The most important factor would have been that the squadron was escorting four new Battleships,"The Prince Souvorov","The Emperor Alexander 111","The Borodino,"The Orel," and the armoured transport"The Anadyi." What the lookouts on"The Zero" were also able to observe was that for some reason"The Kamchatka" had reduced speed from the twelve Knots decreed by the Admiral and so was falling well behind the other ships. She eventually stopped engines and communicated by wireless telegraphy that she had mechanical problems that had to be solved before she could continue. The squadron sailed on until they had left"The Kamchatka" 50 miles astern.

As their disabled ship with its distinctive black and yellow painted funnel wallowed in the swell the captain and crew were in a state of extreme consternation. They were alone and vulnerable in an empty sea that might, at any time according to the wireless signals intercepted reveal the presence of Japanese torpedo boats. With this threat hanging over the ship its engineers worked hard to repair the failed engines. Then what they feared might happen did. They thought they were being attacked by a torpedo boat perhaps more than one. They opened fire on the interlopers.

The interlopers were not aggressive Japanese boats but peaceful fishing boats and a Swedish steamer. Fortunately none of"The Kamchatka's" shells and machine gun bullets did any harm. Making such a mistake was not unknown in the field of naval activities. Early torpedo boats were constructed so as to have a very low profile in the water. They were difficult to see and identify. They were the scourge of modern navy ships.Even the American Navy had a reputation for firing on phenomena mistaken for torpedo boats. American Navy gunners in the past had opened fire from warships on, ocean swells, reefs, rock formations and in one case a railway train travelling across a peninsula.

The significance of the mistake"The Kamchatka's" gunners made was that it was sent as a signal to Rozdesvenky's Flagship"The Souvorov". The signal she got from"The Kamchatka" was simply,"Under attack from Japanese Torpedo boats." Calculations were then made which indicated that the Squadron should be put on an alert to possibly expect intervention at the approximate position 55* 18* North 5* east timed at 1 0' clock in the morning. The signal cancelling it as an error was received too late.

"The Janus" steamed all day and into the night. Bill continued to ask Sidney when they should heave to but by this time Sidney had only one imperative and that was to get into position to see the passing of the Second Pacific Fleet. the rest of the crew relaxed, went on watch came off watch, ate slept and didn't bother to question what was happening. They carried on enjoying a trip on which work did not seem all that important.

By the late evening they arrived at the approximate position and found only an empty sea. There was the odd almost indiscernible light far off but with the night as dark as it was along with a haze generating into low fog and a moon that only appeared now and then from behind clouds it was difficult to see anything. There was a slight wind from the south-east that pushed the sea into a long swell. They waited and let the current take them with the engine just turning over. As far as Sidney was concerned they seemed to wait a long time and Bill began to be concerned about the weather catching them out.

Then something happened that nobody on board"The Janus" could have expected. From the west there appeared a row of lights. As they came closer it became obvious that they were the lights of fishing boats; fishing boats in their dozens. They were fishing boats from"The Gamecock Fleet".

Something had happened that Sidney nor anyone else for that matter could have foreseen. That very afternoon, The 21st of October the anniversary of The Battle of Trafalgar, King Edward V11 after a consultation with his advisers had suddenly replaced the First Naval Lord, Admiral of the Fleet Walter Kerr with Sir John Arbuthnot Fisher and given him a new title First Sea Lord. Fisher was well known as a modernizer as far as The Royal Navy was concerned and he was committed to making Britain the foremost Naval Power in the World. In this he had the unremitting support of Edward V11. He believed that all competitors for the title should be dealt with, according to his motto,"Ruthlessness." And he stated this for anyone who wished to hear.

As the boats got closer, Bill confirmed where they were from, Hull and Grimsby by identifying the registration letters, H. and G. painted on their bows and sides. He left the mate at the wheel and stood at the side with the loud hailer and called across the water to a boat that was within just a few cables of"The Janus".

"What ship are you and where are you from?"

A man in a flat cap, came out on deck and through another loud hailer, and with his voice clearly carrying through the night air, shouted,"We are the"Rangoon". We were fishin' north, north east of Spurn when a bloody great Battleship 'ove into view an' told us to 'eave to. Our admiral went on board and the message went round t' fleet that we were in t'same line as t'ome Fleet steamin' down t 'east coast,on War Alert exercises wi' no lights and not answerin' to communications. We were told to shift out t'way and most of us sailed east. But what fo' ah don't know, there'll be nought doin' 'ere."

Sidney stood next to Bill with most of the crew who had left their bunks and come on deck. He heard everything the man shouted. The"bloody great Battleship" Sidney guessed was more than likely The Four Funneled Cruiser"HMS Devonshire." launched in April and so on sea trials and a fitting out cruise in The North Sea before being commissioned in The Home Fleet. What he was unable to understand was why there seemed to have been a change of orders.

Within a very short time the sea around"The Janus" was full of fishing boats and their lights. Sidney thought it looked like a festival on the Lagoon in Venice he had once been at. Without being asked Bill explained to Sidney as they stood on the deck together how the fleet fished."The way they work it is by 'aving what's called a Mark boat. When the little boats 'ave got a full catch they 'eads for t'Mark boat where there are carrier boats. They unloads their catch on t'carriers,'an t'carriers take it to market becos they can steam faster."

As he was saying this a green rocket rose high in the air and it exploded with a bang that carried far into the night. It shot out three stars."That's t'signal from t'Admiral's boat to start fishin'." Bill said.

No sooner had the rocket stars performed their high arc into the cloudy night and then dropped fizzing to be extinguished into the sea than different lights could be seen coming from the North and the North East. The lights got closer and then searchlights were switched on. The lights were from navy ships not fishing boats. They were the warships of The First Squadron of The Russian Second Pacific Fleet commanded by Admiral Folkersam.

On board the Russian ships when look outs reported the presence of the lights of other craft coming into view, Folkersam ordered his Captains to ring engine room telegraphs to slow ahead and Quartermasters were ordered to steer around what were identified as fishing boats. They were dwarfed by the great size of the warships. The Russian squadron divided into three columns and it carefully maneuvered its way through the black waters of the sea and stabbing the night with incandescent searchlights, illuminated completely the area the boats were fishing in.

Always eager to grab a legitimate opportunity to pause from the arduous work of hauling trawls and gutting fish the fishermen of"The Gamecock Fleet" stood in the fish pounds on the decks of their boats and waved,whistled and cheered as the ships passed in line. The Russian crews who were on watch, in their distinctive blue and white striped jerseys lined the rails of their ships took off their caps and returned the waves and shouts. The sounds of these shouts along with the search lights were soon lost in the night. The stern lights of the last ships faded as the Squadron carried on its Southern course. Ahead of it there were still thousands of miles of sea before it reached the Far East.

Sidney stood on the deck planks of"The Janus" and cursed. What he was convinced would happen, without his interference, had not taken place There was no confusion. There were no collisions. The incompetent, inexperienced,"hysterical" even drunken Russian crews of low morale, did not panic and mistake the fishing boats for Japanese torpedo boats. The fishing boats were directly in the path of a Naval Fleet on Full War Alert. The course of the fleet had been communicated as priority information through all available channels, to the diplomatic, naval, military and commercial agencies of every country whose coastline it would pass within miles of. It was a course decided on as one that would least interfere with busy shipping lanes. It was between 30 and 50 miles outside these. The Hull and Grimsby boats 20 or 30 miles off their usual grounds were all around and in close proximity, In spite of this the commanders of The Russian Squadron took care to avoid them. They were confirmed as fishing boats so no contact was made.

In his frustration Sidney did not allow for the fact the Fleet had been divided into two squadrons. The first squadron has passed without incident. The second squadron had still to sail by and that was the one with Rozdesvenky's Flagship"Souvorov" in the vanguard. It was around one o' clock and because of the"Kamchatka" report the look outs on board were on the alert for suspect vessels.

When the lights of the first ships in the Second Russian squadron hove into view in the distance the"Janus" was about 4000 yards away and Sidney saw through the glasses it was clear that the Russians were already taking care to navigate around the boats peacefully fishing just as the previous squadron had.Sidney saw that unless he did something and quickly the opportunity would be missed.

After the passing of the First Squadron, Bill the Skipper had gone off watch and like Seth The chief Engineer, was in his bunk. The weather was fair, although a bit misty and the sea was calm. Cecil the third hand was at the wheel and Archie the second engineer was in the engine room. Sidney told Cecil to ring down and ask for more speed and to steer towards the Russians. Cecil didn't question the order and Archie stoked the boiler so that within a minute or so the "Janus" was making about six knots. The boy who was still on deck was told to douse the lights and take down the mizzen sail of the "Janus". He did it without question.

it was not fast enough for Sidney and he ordered "Full Steam Ahead". The "Janus", with its overhaul and new boiler responded well, She picked up to 12 knots and the increase in vibrations brought Bill and Seth out of their slumber and on deck. Bill shouted, "Whose put the lights out." Sidney replied, "I told the boy to."

The Janus was making way and a bow wave and it rocked the "Gamecock" boats it passed close to. Bill took the wheel and asked Sidney what he wanted to do. Without turning to Bill, Sidney said over his shoulder, "I want to take a closer look."

On board the "Suvorov" the searchlights were switched on and that was the signal for the leading ships in the squadron to do the same. The great beams of light swept the sea to the port and starboard sides of the warships picking out in multi-million candlepower the dozens of almost stationary fishing boats scattered about the sea.

It was out of this hardly moving pack of boats that the forward lookout of the "Souvorov" spotted, through his glasses one boat moving at speed some 3000 yards off. He estimated that it was making around 10 or 15 knots. After a few seconds the boat was visible enough for him to observe what looked like torpedo sized cylinders on its foredeck. Without hesitating he shouted down the speaking tube connecting him with the bridge," Torpedo boat closing at speed off the starboard quarter." It had been expected. Gun crews were waiting at the ready. It only needed the bugle to sound action stations.

That was the sound that Sidney and his crew heard on board the"Janus" as Sidney counted off the approximate distance to 2000 yards before ordering Bill"Hard to starboard". Bill obeyed the command but the"Janus" wasn't a torpedo boat and as he didn't slacken speed before moving the helm hard over she almost keeled over and she took a lot of water over the starboard side. That's when all hell broke loose and Sidney shouted,"Don't slow her down, just get her out of here."

Initially gunfire came from only one of the Russian ships and then 3 or 4 others joined in. Light and heavy machine gun fire opened up and rattled out volleys that raked the nearest fishing boats and splashed the sea all around them. The sounds of their staccato shots were followed by the boom and flash of heavier gunfire and great plumes of water erupted as ranging shells fell short.

The fishermen on board their boats could not believe what was happening and at first some thought that they had blundered into a naval exercise. It was only when shot and shell splintered superstructure and cut down men on deck that the realization dawned that live ammunition was being used. In a panic, to escape the fusillade of shots and the whistle of artillery shells, they cut trawls and desperately worked to get steam up to get away.

The vice Admiral Thomas Carr on board his boat"Ruff" shot flare after flare up high in the air in an attempt to identify the fleet and to light the area of sea that was being fired upon so that it could be seen that they were peaceful fishing boats but the barrage of fire continued for almost half an hour. Then as suddenly as The Russian Squadron had arrived and opened up on them it ceased firing and sailed away south. The sea was quite again with the dim lights of the fishing boats on the water and the only sounds the noise of engines and the shouts from boat to boat of men seeking to know where the injured were and who they were.

As they steamed at full-speed westwards Sidney and his crew on the "Janus" saw the stars of the many flares that were shot off, the flashes of machine gun barrels and the flames from gun-ports and they heard the explosions of shell-fire that the warships of Second Russian Squadron laid down on the defence less fishing boats but they escaped unscathed.

What they left behind in their headlong flight was mayhem. Two men had their heads blown off and another so severely shocked he was to die later. And there were many men lightly wounded with injuries from shell splinters and bullets. Some seven men were seriously injured. One man had his arm amputated and another spent the rest of his life incapacitated. A number of fishing boats were badly damaged and one sank before it could be put in tow. Either by luck or judgment the Russians had fired only solid shot. Had they used explosive shells they would have annihilated those men and boats they hit. It took two days before the full story could be told and it was described variously as,"The Dogger Bank Incident" or more emphatically"The Russian Outrage."

With the head start that the"Janus" had it was only a day before she found herself in what Bill was certain was the location of the buoy that marked the spot where the trunk full of instruments had been dropped. There was nothing. Sidney thought he would continue the charade and have Bill steaming backwards and forwards for an hour or so searching for the marker and it was at this time that Sidney had the crew work the quick release cramps on the"tanks" and heave them over board. As the crew were emptied them of their fish samples Sidney replied to their questioning with the simple phrase,"they have served their purpose."

Eventually Bill was persuaded to give up his searching for the buoy and they steered a course for The Humber Estuary and home. It was on this leg of the voyage that Sidney decided to settle up with them and never were fishermen so pleased with their reward and in giving them a bonus he added that it might be better if they kept their counsel as far as"the incident" was concerned. It might look as if they had deserted their comrades in an hour of need. For a fisherman there was no greater sin.

They came into their berth in the Hessle Haven on the morning tide of Sunday 23rd of October and as she was being tied up Sidney said his goodbyes to Bill the Skipper, Horace the cook, Chief engineer Seth, 2nd engineer Archie, Third Hand Cecil, Deck hand Henry and The Boy. He then took some time searching for a cab that would take him to the ferry. He was on board as it sailed for Belgium down the river and it passed the near crippled and damaged boats involved in"The Outrage" coming up the river into Hull to land their dead and wounded and to tell their story to the world.

Sidney was in the bathroom of his cabin showering off the dirt and smell of his days on the 'Janus' as the ferry's propeller vortex gently rocked that already rusting tin trunk with Chloe's pathetic remains in it 50 feet below the surface.

The trunk would surface eventually, years hence dragged up in the trawl of an East Coast inshore fishing boat. It would be corroded and rusty to filigree with just a faint trace of paint on it and only the vestige of cloth that was once a skirt and the rotten leather of a high boot suggesting to the fishermen who hauled it in, that it was the luggage of some unfortunate passenger in a shipwreck long forgotten. It would surface as mammoth teeth, prehistoric deer antlers and Neolithic tools do from time to time, proving that The Dogger Bank was once an ancient land bridge long drowned, peopled by Neanderthals where pre-historic predatory and carnivorous beasts once roamed.

THE END

Epilogue

The Russians paid a heavy price for what was described in the world's press as an unprovoked attack on peaceful fishermen and their craft. Admiral Z.F. Rozdesvensky had not only now to face the almost impossible task of getting his fleet the 18000 mile to Japanese waters he had to do it with threat of the British Royal Navy and the British Empire declaring war on his Fleet and on his Imperial Russia.

It was not an idle threat. After the incidents of the 'Malacca' and the 'Knight Commander' 'The Russian Outrage' as British newspaper journalists described 'The Dogger Bank Incident', was the last straw. British popular opinion was hysterical in its demands to make the Russians pay. To satisfy this passion a Royal Navy fleet of some 28 capital ships was put on the alert with orders to open fire on the Russians on sight.

Something had to be done. Rozdesvensky put into a Spanish port and had the officers he considered to be at fault sent home. But this wasn't enough, so careful diplomacy was employed to find a reward from the Russian Bear that would placate, if not compensate the British Lion. The British Empire to bring us right up to date was given, compliments of Czar Nicholas the second, a free hand in Afghanistan.

There is no doubt Rozdesvenky's voyage was epic but it was dogged with problems; not least"The Dogger Bank Incident". Ships collided, crews mutinied, crews fell ill from coal dust in the lungs, ships got lost, there were difficulties in neutral ports, ships broke down and engines stalled on the cheap unsuitable coal the Germans had filled their bunkers with.

Seven months later on May the 23rd 1905 Admiral Rozdesvenky did in the end get his fleet to the Tsushima straits where he engaged the Japanese Navy and his gunners in spite of everything they had endured, gave a good account of themselves, keeping the Japanese occupied for eighteen hours. But the battle really was over before it began. It had ended effectively when the scheme to take a fleet of warships that distance was first mooted. It had resulted in worn out engines that strained to manoeuvre, demoralized crews and a tactic to protect the cream of the fleet with obsolete ships as shields, that did not work. The Japanese were not far from home and they were ready. They sank eleven Russian battleships, five heavy cruisers and eight destroyers plus many auxiliaries. 6000 Russian sailors perished. To all intents and purposes The Russian Imperial Navy ceased to exist.

It is possible to say that Old Russia did not recover from the debacle. As a direct result of the naval defeat there was a revolution in 1905 and the seeds of the 1917 revolution were no doubt sown then. But Russia managed to stave off complete collapse, by agreeing to peace negotiations set in motion by diplomats of the USA, the Russo-Japanese war ended with effectively, victory for the Japanese. There are historians of the view that had the war gone on longer the Russians would have been victorious. They could have sustained a long land war; not the Japanese.

What the Japanese did get was a confidence that was to set them up as the Great Power of the Far East. They were, after all the first non-white race to beat a strong European power. It was a boast that stood them in good stead. Even by 1910 a secret cadre of high ranking officers met frequently to discuss the implementation of a plan that eventually Japan manifest in the 1940's, the defeat of The Dutch Empire, the French Empire, the British Empire and in a final attempt to establish complete Japanese Hegemony in the Pacific, the took on the Americans.

It is perhaps worth noting that the Japanese attack on Port Arthur in 1904 was mirrored in the attack on Pearl Harbour in 1941. There was in both events the application of surprise, engineered by espionage and the use of torpedoes. At Port Arthur as at Pearl Harbour there was no formal declaration of war and there was the same strategic aim, the destruction of a grand naval fleet.

To end by returning to "The Russian Outrage", there were inquiries set up. The St Petersburg Declaration, presented to an International Inquiry in Paris absolved The Russian Navy of blame. The Russians put forward witnesses who swore that they had seen what looked like an attacking torpedo boat. The findings, in the end were that the Russians were to blame and should pay compensation. This they did, £66.000 worth. Much of it went to widows and orphans and the wounded in Hull. A great deal went to the trawler owners.

It is interesting to note, in spite of other conclusions that fishermen from both Hull and Grimsby in 'The Gamecock' Fleet testified to The Paris International Inquiry that they had seen a torpedo boat fleeing the scene after the incident but assumed that it was Russian.

Four Hull men who were congratulated for their bravery were given medals and The City of Hull got the Fishermen's Memorial which still stands at the junction of Hessle Road and Boulevard. First Sea Lord, Sir John Arbuthnot Fisher got from the Japanese for services rendered, The Order of The Rising Sun along with the stipend of £2.500 per year. Arthur Wilson and Sons got very significant concessions on Far East trade routes. The Treaty between the British and the Japanese lasted until 1922 and the Japanese Navy got a lock of Nelson's hair in a presentation box.

'The Dogger Bank Incident' made another sort of history for by the results of the Paris Enquiry it became a model within the Peace Conventions emanating from The Hague, for International Arbitrations between Nations. It was also referred to in the writings of Countess Bertha Von Suttner, the first woman to receive a Nobel Prize. The honour she was awarded in 1905 was the The Nobel Prize for Peace.

It's worth mentioning too, a ship that survived Tsuhima and the cross-fire of "The Dogger Bank Incident." She was the armoured cruiser "Aurora". She returned to the Baltic and then The River Niva in St.Petersburg Russia. She fired the shot that signaled The Storming of the Winter Palace and the beginning of the 1917 Russian Revolution.

Hull maintained its connection with the Secret Services. Susannah West Wilson, the daughter of Arthur Wilson of Tranby Croft, Hull, married John Graham Menzies and she had a son. There were unkind gossips who maintained that he was the illegitimate son of Edward V11 but Edward never acknowledged him.

Eton educated and a high ranking army officer, he became Sir Stuart Menzies Head of the Military Division in 1919 of the British Secret Intelligence Services, sometimes known as MI6. In 1924 it was alleged that Sir Stuart Menzies collaborated with Sidney George Reilly and others on"The Zinoviev Letter".The letter was said to have been written and sent by Grigory Zinoviev, Chairman of the Comintern of the Soviet Union. It's supposed purpose was to encourage Communist Party members in the British Trade Union Movement to incite insurrection. It was a forgery concocted by Reilly and others. Menzies was suspected of having leaked it to the"Daily Mail". The scandal it provoked brought down the first Labour Government.

Then in 1939 Menzies was appointed as the Director General of the S.I.S becoming the original "M" of Ian Fleming's James Bond Novels. Menzies served in that post all through the war during which one his significant activities was supervising the work of"Enigma". He remained The Director General of S.I.S. until 1952. He died in 1968.

Hull was even a destination for the German spies mentioned in our story. Gustav Steinhauer with his alias Herr Fritches tried to recruit Hull businessmen as German spies in World War One. During the war, however Steinhauer managed to get back to Germany.

Carl Frederick Mueller was less fortunate. After returning to Germany he came back to Hull from the neutral port of Rotterdam in 1915 on the North Sea Ferry The Whitby Abbey. He already knew Hull well having made a number of visits working before WW1 as a merchant seaman on English and American boats. He tried to set up a spy ring in England during World War One but failed. He was arrested, tried and was found guilty on appeal. He became the first German spy to be executed. He was shot by firing squad in the shooting range of The Tower of London.

St. Eutrope de Born, France